PARADOXES OF HAWAIIAN SOVEREIGNTY

PARADOXES OF HAWAIIAN SOVEREIGNTY

Land, Sex, and the Colonial Politics of State Nationalism

J. KĒHAULANI KAUANUI

Duke University Press Durham and London 2018

Printed and bound by CPI Group (UK) Ltd, Croydon, CR0 4YY
Designed by Courtney Leigh Baker and typeset in Arno Pro
and Avenir by BW&A Books, Inc., Oxford, North Carolina

Library of Congress Cataloging-in-Publication Data
Names: Kauanui, J. Kēhaulani, [date] author.
Title: Paradoxes of Hawaiian sovereignty : land, sex, and the
colonial politics of state nationalism / J. Kēhaulani Kauanui.
Description: Durham : Duke University Press, 2018. |
Includes bibliographical references and index.
Identifiers: LCCN 2018010545 (print)
LCCN 2018014706 (ebook)
ISBN 9780822371960 (ebook)
ISBN 9780822370499 (hardcover : alk. paper)
ISBN 9780822370758 (pbk. : alk. paper)
Subjects: LCSH: Hawaii—Politics and government—1959– |
Hawaii—History—Autonomy and independence movements.
| Sovereignty. | Nationalism—Hawaii.
Classification: LCC DU627.8 (ebook) | LCC DU627.8 .K38 2018 (print)
| DCC 996.9/04—dc23
LC record available at https://lccn.loc.gov/2018010545

He ali'i ka 'āina; he kauā ke kanaka.
The land is the chief, the people its servants.
—adapted from MARY KAWENA PUKUI,
'Ōlelo No'eau: Hawaiian Proverbs and Poetical Sayings

CONTENTS

ABBREVIATIONS

ABCFM	American Board of Commissioners for Foreign Missions
ANPRM	Advance Notice of Proposed Rule Making
DLNR	Department of Land and Natural Resources
DOI	Department of the Interior
DOMA	Defense of Marriage Act
GMO	genetically modified organism
NGO	nongovernmental organization
NHGE	Native Hawaiian governing entity
OHA	Office of Hawaiian Affairs
PLDC	Public Land Development Corporation
UN	United Nations
UNPFII	United Nations Permanent Forum on Indigenous Issues
USPACOM	United States Pacific Command
WGIP	Working Group on Indigenous Populations (later changed to Working Group on Indigenous Peoples)

PREFACE

The Hawaiian kiss is the *honi*, the nose press. In *Studies of Savages and Sex* (1929), British anthropologist Ernest Crawley devoted a chapter to "the nature and history of the kiss," claiming that "kissing is a universal expression in the social life of the higher civilizations of the feelings of affection, love (sexual, parental, and filial), and veneration." In its refined form, "kissing supplies a case, in the higher levels of physiological psychology, of the meeting and interaction of the two complementary primal impulses, hunger and love." According to Crawley, "The European kiss consists essentially in the application of the lips to some part of the face, head, or body, or to the lips of the other person. Normally, there is no conscious olfactory element, and any tactile use of the nose is absolutely unknown. It is thus a distinct species and to describe it as having evolved from the savage form is erroneous." He contrasted the "civilized kiss" with the forms of what he terms the "savage kiss." The olfactory form "occasionally includes mutual contact with the nose, as among the Maoris, Society, and Sandwich Islanders, the Tongans, the Eskimo, and most of the Malayan peoples." Sandwich Islands, of course, was the name given to the Hawaiian Islands by James Cook in the late eighteenth century in honor of John Montagu, fourth earl of Sandwich, who was then first lord of the admiralty. Crawley considered these groups to be "the lower and semi-civilized races"—a step above groups with "the typical primitive kiss," which he suggested is "made with contact of nose and cheek."[1]

This logic of civilizational hierarchies is not simply something that has long passed. *American Anthropologist*, the journal of the American Anthropological Association, published an essay as recently as 2015 questioning whether the "romantic-sexual" kiss is a "near human universal" but found that it was present in a minority of cultures sampled. As a result of their study, the researchers argue that "there is a strong correlation between the frequency of the romantic-sexual kiss and a society's relative social complexity: the more socially complex the culture, the higher frequency of romantic-sexual kissing."[2]

A NOTORIOUSLY LENGTHY and winding highway is often referred to in Hawaiian legends and songs (and now travel guides) as "the long road to Hāna"—a 52-mile highway from Kahului along the eastern shore of the Hawaiian island of Maui. Part of the route was built in the late nineteenth century for sugar-plantation workers commuting from Pāʻia to Hāna. Hence it is an undeniable part of the physical alteration of the island to accommodate capitalist expansion through a monocrop industry—a commercial thoroughfare marking the modern transformation of Hawaiʻi's economy. An earlier, lesser-known history of labor and penal law is tied to the highway: those who built it were convicted of adultery and punished by high chief Hoapili with a sentence to "work the road."[3] In 1843 the Reverend H. T. Cheever—a missionary traveling through the Pacific—admired the road to Hāna. He noted: "Yet it is a way not devoid of interest and novelty, especially that part of it which runs to Kahikinui and Kaupo; for it is a road built by the crime of adultery, some years ago, when the laws relating to that and other crimes were first enacted." He explained that it ran almost like a railroad "for fifteen or twenty miles" and was built from blackened lava "made by convicts, without sledge-hammers, crow-bars or any other instrument, but the human hands and their stone. . . . It is altogether the noblest and best Hawaiian work I have anywhere seen."[4] It is clear that one aspect of modernization in the islands was physically bound to the biopolitical discipline of Kanaka sexuality by the state (the Hawaiian Kingdom), especially as adultery itself was a relatively new concept in Hawaiʻi at the time (and the pre-Christian system allowed for multiple partners and bisexual intimacy). Western notions of marriage as a socially or ritually recognized union between two spouses bound by a legal contract establishing rights and obligations involving them, their children, and their in-laws did not exist.

IN AN 1855 SPEECH, King Kamehameha IV described the reign of his late brother, the former Hawaiian monarch. He wrote:

> The age of Kamehameha III was that of progress and of liberty—of schools and of civilization. He gave us a Constitution and fixed laws; he secured the people in the title to their lands, and removed the last chain of oppression. He gave them a voice in his councils and in the making of the laws by which they are governed. He was a great national benefactor, and has left the impress of his mild and amiable disposition on the age for which he was born.[5]

In addition to constitutional government, a series of legal changes was introduced during Kamehameha III's reign—all in the quest to secure modern recognition of Hawaiian sovereignty in the form of progress toward being a "civilized" nation. Among other actions, he privatized and commodified the communal land system, regulated and disciplined a range of Hawaiian sexual practices, imposed Christian marriage as the only legally sanctioned framework for any sexual relationships, and subordinated women through coverture, a legal doctrine whereby, upon marriage, a woman's legal rights and obligations were subsumed by those of her husband. Yet in his lifetime Kamehameha III had several sexual partners, including an *aikāne* relationship (a close friendship that may include a sexual dimension) with a man named Kaomi, a *moepiʻo* relationship (a sexually intimate union between high-ranking siblings known as a rank-preserving strategy) with his sister Nāhiʻenaʻena, and extramarital sexual affairs with select women.

ACKNOWLEDGMENTS

This book has come about as the result of many years and much support and assistance from family and friends as well as colleagues, archivists, librarians, and institutions.

This project was supported by a summer writing fellowship at the Macmillan Brown Centre for Pacific Studies at the University of Canterbury, New Zealand, which I was awarded in 2007. I also had the benefit of holding a faculty fellowship at Wesleyan University's Center for the Humanities in spring 2012 for the theme "Visceral States: Affect and Civic Life." Many thanks to Jill Morawski, Sonali Chakravarti, David Sweeney Coombs, Neetu Khanna, Patricia M. Rodríguez Mosquera, Eirene Visvardi, Leah Wright, and Angela Naimou for their intellectual support while I was in residence. That fellowship also afforded me the opportunity to teach a course linked to the project, a seminar titled "Affective Sovereignties." I also extend thanks to the students in the class, who helped me think through elements of this book as I taught materials rarely put together (affect studies, settler colonial studies, and critical indigenous studies). During that same period, I benefited enormously from lengthy and exciting engagement with Corey Capers, who influenced the conceptual and theoretical direction of this book in meaningful ways.

Mahalo nui loa—many thanks to those who read drafts of this in whole or in part, offering me invaluable critical feedback, including Dean Saranillio, Lisa Lowe, Rasha Moumneh, Marie Alohalani Brown, Mark Rifkin,

Lucian Gomoll, Judy Rohrer, Scott Morgensen, Ty P. Kāwika Tengan, Lisa Brooks, and Noenoe K. Silva. Any errors or omissions are my responsibility, not theirs.

I would like to thank all of my superb colleagues at Wesleyan University for their support, especially those who have encouraged this book project over the course of many years: Gina Athena Ulysse, Ann duCille, Demetrius Eudell, and Michael Armstrong Roche.

Other colleagues and friends also offered moral and intellectual support for this work at various times along the way: Christina Crosby, Janet Jakobsen, Neferti Tadiar, Jean O'Brien, Gale Courey Toensing, Maivân Clech Lâm, Jessica Cattelino, Robert Nichols, Lisa Duggan, and Elizabeth Povinelli. I also want to acknowledge the care and friendship of the following people who helped sustain me in different ways: Robert Warrior, Rana Barakat, Cynthia Franklin, Lisa Kahaleole Hall, Joanne Barker, Steven Salaita, Dawn Peterson, David Shorter, John M. McKinn, and K. Tsianina Lomawaima.

Mahalo to Lisa Kahaleole Hall for turning me on to writing sprints and to fellow sprinting partners along the way at different times: Sima Shakhsari, Richard T. Rodríguez, Ju Hui Judy Han, and especially Cynthia Franklin.

At Duke University Press I want to thank my editor, Ken Wissoker, for his care and steadfast support of my work; Jade Brooks (formerly at the press), who helped shepherd the manuscript into the review stage; and Olivia Polk, who assisted in getting it to the finish line.

I also want to acknowledge the librarians who have helped me numerous times along the way, including D. Keali'i MacKenzie at the University of Hawai'i at Mānoa and Kendall Hobbs and Leith Johnson at Wesleyan University.

I have been privileged to present parts of this project at various colleges and universities thanks to the labor of colleagues and support staff (too numerous to mention, but you know who you are; please know that I do as well) who made possible my visits to their home institutions, including Brown University; University of St. Joseph; State University of New York at Stony Brook; American University of Beirut; Columbia University; Tufts University; Yale University; University of Southern California; University of Connecticut; Stonehill College; University of Minnesota Duluth; Harvard University; Queensland University of Technology; Australia University of Washington; Hampshire College; University of Texas at Austin; University of Hawai'i at Mānoa; New York University; University of Michigan; University of Oregon; University of Chicago; University of Wisconsin–

Madison; University of California, Berkeley; University of California, San Diego; Williams College; Amherst College; Scripps College; University of California, Los Angeles; and City University of New York. Thank you.

My primary partner, Jason Villani, has been an enormous source of love and sustenance for me over the years. I also want to thank his family as well as my own and especially express my deep gratitude to my mother, Carol Lee Gates.

For the beautiful and visionary cover art, mahalo nui to Aaron Kawaiaea.

Thanks also go to Denisse Griselda and Fiona McLeod for their labor on my bibliography at different stages of the project.

In closing, I want to acknowledge Richard Kekuni Akana Blaisdell, esteemed elder of the Hawaiian sovereignty movement, who died on February 12, 2016. I had the privilege of working with him on and off starting in 1990, when he first embraced me as an undergraduate student and welcomed me into a rich community of struggle. His efforts on behalf of the Hawaiian people continue to compel and inspire me.

INTRODUCTION
CONTRADICTORY SOVEREIGNTY

> Our responses to the interrogatories that are posed by Interior are all no. And the reason why is because we are capable of being self-governing. But we are not capable of expressing our right to self-determination because federal policy limits this. We are not Indians. We will never be Indians and the federal Indian policy is inappropriate for our peoples.... You can braid my hair and stick feathers in it, but I will never be an Indian. I will always be a Hawaiian. Aloha.

The above testimony was delivered by Hawaiian political leader Mililani Trask on behalf of Ka Lāhui, a group known as a "Native Initiative for Sovereignty," before the U.S. Department of Interior (DOI) panel held in Hilo on July 2, 2014.[1] The session was one of fifteen public meetings held in the Hawaiian Islands that summer "to consider reestablishing a government-to-government relationship between the United States and the Native Hawaiian community."[2] Trask was responding to a set of questions on whether the DOI should facilitate a process of forming a "Native Hawaiian governing entity" that would ostensibly be similar to federally recognized tribal nations.[3] Trask answered all of these questions with a categorical "no" but did so by drawing on problematic invocations of Native Americans.

Trask's comments to the DOI are emblematic of the anti-Indigenous kingdom discourse that situates Hawaiians in opposition to "Indians" and speaks volumes about the complex political terrain that this book tackles. Her assertion "You can braid my hair and stick feathers in it, but I will never be an Indian" is an oppositional response to the federally driven proposal to recognize Hawaiians within U.S. domestic policy on tribal nations. She implies that the federal recognition scheme might attempt to "convert" her by appearance as part of a new federal policy, but that the sovereignty of the Hawaiian people stands apart—a durable political difference coded through stereotypical appearances. Trask unfortunately glosses the political status of the then 573 Native governing entities currently recognized by the U.S. government through a hairstyle and accessories, evoking braids and feathers—popular visual markers of what symbolizes an "Indian" (a socially constructed term that Europeans imposed on the Indigenous Peoples of the Western Hemisphere, who had their own respective and diverse Indigenous kinship systems and polities).[4] She also refers to a "nation to nation" relationship as something that Hawaiians would like to see, yet that is also how the U.S. government describes its arrangement with Indian tribes. But she specifies that this should happen only when both nations are given a seat at the table—indirectly pointing to the unilateral nature of the federal procedure as evinced by the Department of the Interior meetings.[5] Here she suggests that the limits imposed on self-determination for tribal nations are "inappropriate" for the Hawaiian people, but in doing so she implies that they *are* appropriate for Indians. Moreover, her argument seems to hinge on Hawaiian competency in contrast to the supposedly less competent tribal nations as the premise for her declaration "We are not Indians."

The vast majority of those who testified at the public meetings opposed the federally driven effort in light of the existence of the Hawaiian Kingdom, established by 1810 and recognized as an independent state by the major powers of the world starting in 1843 until the U.S. government backed an illegal overthrow of the monarchy in 1893. Today the project of restoring the Hawaiian Kingdom—or insisting that it still exists now—is in competition with the U.S. government's attempt to confine Native Hawaiian governance to internal Indigenous self-determination within the bounds of federal law. Although the battle over legal paths to regenerate some form of Hawaiian self-determination may seem moot given the machinations and dominance of the U.S. nation-state, this development has acutely unsettled the Kanaka Maoli (Native Hawaiian) political world, bringing to the surface deep conflict over Hawaiian national identity.

This book focuses on the effects of Christianization and the introduction of the Anglo-American legal system in relation to land, gender, and sexuality in the Hawaiian context in the early to mid-nineteenth century—and the consequences of that transformation for contemporary sovereignty politics. It explores the ways in which Hawai'i is comprehended (and alternately apprehended) within conflicting paradigms for acknowledging its status as other than simply part of the regular domestic jurisdiction of the United States, specifically as an occupied state of its own, a "tribal" entity awaiting U.S. recognition, and the territory of an Indigenous People. This book engages the ways in which Hawai'i has been situated within these various (and often incommensurate) frameworks and traces the limited passages available to Kanaka Maoli in order to try to realize prior history and contemporary assertions of self-determination. *Paradoxes of Hawaiian Sovereignty* specifically seeks to demonstrate how white American notions of property title, state sovereignty, and normative gender relations and sexuality become intimately imbricated in aspirations for Hawaiian liberation and in mobilizing available categories for acknowledging Kanaka distinctiveness—hence the word "paradoxes" in the title of this book.

Trask's rhetorical attempt to contrast Kanaka Maoli with Indian tribes is reminiscent of similar attitudes a decade earlier that revealed a stance of political superiority. For example, I was struck by an exchange in 2004 among several prominent Kanaka Maoli men who self-identify as Hawaiian Kingdom nationals (rather than U.S. citizens). The discussion took place on an online Hawaiian sovereignty forum. One man rhetorically asked a series of questions: "Which of the Native Americans have had treaties worldwide and consuls throughout the world? How many were involved with blanket international affairs or recognized any country's independence? How many were recognized as peers with other recognized nations throughout the world, including the United States? How many of them had treaties of friendship and commerce with the rest of the world nations?"[6]

In response, another chimed in: "We had a King that was accepted in world courts and entertained by Heads of State throughout the world. . . . We were a worldwide recognized nation, were any of the Native Americans in the same league?" Here the reference point is a male monarch, although the last ruler of the Hawaiian Kingdom was Queen Lili'uokalani. As though Hawaiians were the first nonwhite people to have international relationships with Europeans, yet another boasted that "Hawai'i was not a tribe of people when it joined up with world nations. We were a most favored, friendly, neutral Independent nation." This thread conveys a political perspective that is now commonplace among those who support de-occupation and fully renewed recognition of the kingdom.

In follow-up emails, these same individuals problematically generalized the hundreds of different U.S. federally recognized Native governing entities by citing their limited political status as domestic dependent nations as evidence of American "brainwashing" and "colonized mentalities" among tribal nations. These remarks revealed a dire lack of knowledge about the historical significance of federal recognition for tribes, the context of the Indian Reorganization Act of 1934 (and Indigenous resistance to it), and the fact that tribal nations that held treaties with numerous European governments were recognized as independent. The doctrine of "domestic dependent sovereignty" to subordinate tribal sovereignty within the confines of U.S. rule was not crafted until the U.S. Supreme Court ruled in *Cherokee Nation v. Georgia* (1831). Attitudes such as those found in the online forum imply that Hawaiians were historically "more civilized" than other Indigenous Peoples and therefore "more advanced" historically and today. These political sentiments naturalize Native Americans' limited political status based on chauvinistic (mis)understandings of what constitutes a "tribe" as somehow inherently domestic and dependent.

David Chang traces Kanaka (dis)identification with American Indians to the early nineteenth through the early twentieth centuries. He demonstrates that what Hawaiians read about and wrote about American Indian peoples in nineteenth-century newspapers reveals a series of overlapping shifts in the representation of Indians that can be considered three distinct phases. In a first phase, American Christian missionaries taught Kanaka that "the Indian" was a model of all things that Hawaiians must not be, portraying Indians as a negative model (ignorant and savage). He documents a shift in Hawaiian-language newspapers by the 1850s that reflects direct social contact between Kanaka Maoli and American Indians because of Hawaiians' work in the fur trade, the gold rush, and other areas of labor. These representations were increasingly sympathetic and coincided with Kanaka control of an independent press by the 1860s. Still, Indians remained a negative model for Kanaka, but in a new way. For Hawaiians, "American Indians represented an outcome that Kanaka who were engaged in the defense of their national sovereignty hoped to avoid." The third phase followed the U.S.-backed overthrow of the Hawaiian Kingdom and 1898 annexation. As Chang shows, the next shift "moved Indians from being 'what we must not become' to 'what we have now become like.'" In other words, Kanaka increasingly saw a *likeness* between their situation and that of American Indian peoples.

> Because dispossession was the undesirable shared experience behind this identification of Kānaka with Indians, naming Kānaka as being like Indians was both politically potent and inherently unstable. . . . American Indians had functioned as a negative referent for Kānaka through the nineteenth century—from the 1820s when missionaries held Indians up as a model of how not to live, to later in the century when aloha ʻāina (patriots) declared that Kānaka were like Indians when they were dispossessed. Kānaka could, therefore, identify with Indians, but the connotations of this identification were frequently negative. It could spur Kānaka to resist colonization, but it could also encourage them to declare themselves to be different from Indians, who were the very sign of the colonized.[7]

This form of signification is precisely what I want to examine in the context of Hawaiian political battles regarding independence versus federal recognition.

In *The Transit of Empire: Indigenous Critiques of Colonialism*, Jodi Byrd tracks how "Indianness" has propagated U.S. conceptions of empire, where the figure of the Indian functions as transit—a trajectory of movement. She argues that the contemporary U.S. empire expands itself through a transferable "Indianness" that facilitates acquisitions of lands, territories, and resources. Byrd makes the losses of Native Americans visible—and therefore grievable (rather than merely lamentable)—while insisting that the colonization of Indigenous nations is the necessary starting point from which to reimagine a decolonial future that centers Indigenous agency.

Byrd also challenges Hawaiians' dominant perceptions (or articulations in these cases) for their resonance with pervasive white settler disavowals by critically examining how this transit of empire has played out in the Hawaiian sovereignty context: "Many Hawaiian activists, especially kingdom sovereignty nationalists, focus on understanding the Hawaiian archipelago as the site of exceptionalism within the trajectory of US empire-building. Hawaiʻi is in this view a militarily occupied territory logically outside the bounds of American control, while American Indian nations are naturalized as wholly belonging to and within the colonizing logics of the United States."[8] Byrd's analysis of "paradigmatic 'Indianness'" helps to situate Hawaiian Kingdom nationalists' disavowals of indigeneity in a deeper genealogy of "civilized"/modern nation-making that has required Hawaiian elites to fight the "savagery" within. Additionally, I would add, many are politically invested in tracing just how *well* Hawaiians adapted to Westernization as evidence of the capability for self-governance and are fixated on this particular narration of Hawaiian history and a state-centered legacy.

The political contest made visible by the DOI meetings emerged from a federal drive lasting more than a decade to contain the Hawaiian sovereignty claim via proposed congressional legislation, the Native Hawaiian Government Reorganization Act. The bill was arguably one of the most controversial U.S. legislative proposals regarding Native Hawaiians since the 1959 Hawaii State Admissions Act, popularly known as "the Akaka bill" because U.S. senator Daniel Akaka (D-HI) introduced it. Beginning in the 106th U.S. Congress in 2000 and continuing through early 2012, the senator purportedly sponsored this bill to secure the recognition of Native Hawaiians as an Indigenous People who have a "special relationship" with the United States and thus a right to internal self-determination.[9] Although promoted as legislation that would offer parity for Native Hawaiians in relation to federally recognized tribal nations, the bill proposed something quite different given the provisions spelled out for the state government vis-à-vis the federal government and a Native Hawaiian governing entity (NHGE). This is because the state would maintain civic and criminal jurisdiction over citizen-members of the proposed NHGE—meaning less self-governance than for most federally recognized tribes.[10] Although Akaka's proposed legislation was widely supported across Hawai'i and the continental United States among Native Hawaiians and liberal allies, kingdom nationalists and other independence advocates opposed this legislation in any form—and now continue to resist federal recognition by other means (including the proposed Department of Interior process) while asserting that the Hawaiian Kingdom still exists under international law.

As many contemporary kingdom nationalists view anything less than independent statehood as "backward," I address this political sentiment in relation to the limited status that states impose on Indigenous Peoples worldwide regarding their self-determination within the bounds of the existing states that encompass them. In the Hawaiian context, the focus of some of these nationalists has been misdirected at tribal nations rather than at the federal government. I suggest that this distancing and logic entails the feminization of indigeneity, which is relegated to what is seen as characteristically "female" by Western norms. Here some nationalists tend to render Indigenous Peoples feminine in relation to masculinist states. In this configuration, Western nations are seen and treated as rational, strong, worldly, independent, and active, while Indigenous Peoples occupy the supposedly female role as savage, weak, domestic, dependent, and passive—and are treated as such. Ironically, these notions of what is considered female are Western: women were not viewed or treated as fragile, helpless, or submissive in precolonial Hawaiian society.

As my previous work documents, the current state-driven push for federal recognition is problematic for outstanding Hawaiian sovereignty claims because the kingdom, previously recognized as an independent state, provides Kanaka Maoli and others with a rare legal genealogy.[11] As a result, many of those affiliated with kingdom restoration initiatives have by and large disregarded the bill, seeing its potential effect on the kingdom as irrelevant because it emanates from the United States, understood simply as an illegal foreign occupying force. This position is clearly articulated by Keanu Sai, chair of the Council of Regency, who currently serves as (self-designated) acting minister of the interior. Sai's welcome letter on the website hawaiiankingdom.org asserts that the Hawaiian Kingdom government is "presently operating within the occupied State of the Hawaiian Islands" and further notes: "Since the Spanish-American War, 1898, our Nation has been under prolonged occupation by the United States of America." Other kingdom nationalist political entities include the Reinstated Hawaiian Government, led by Henry Noa, who identifies himself as the prime minister; Ke Aupuni O Hawaiʻi Nei, which claims to be the revived Kingdom of Hawaiʻi, with Leon Siu serving as foreign minister and Kealoha Aiu serving as minister of the interior; Mahealani Asing Kahau, queen of Aupuni o ko Hawaiʻi Pae ʻĀina; and Akahi Nui, with James Akahi as king of the Kingdom of Hawaiʻi on Maui, to name some of them.[12] While it is unclear how great the political following of each one is in terms of constituents, it is clear that their combined stance constitutes a marked shift within the independence movement.[13]

Kingdom nationalists tend to reject the United Nations (UN) protocols for decolonization as well as Indigenous rights as remedies for the Hawaiian case, instead focusing on the Law of Occupation. A special committee guides the UN decolonization process with regard to the implementation of the Declaration on the Granting of Independence to Colonial Countries and Peoples. This entity was established in 1961 by the General Assembly with the purpose of monitoring the implementation of that declaration.[14] With regard to Indigenous rights, the UN General Assembly passed the Declaration on the Rights of Indigenous Peoples in 2007 after decades of activism and the drafting process.[15] Rather than taking up either of these two approaches for the Hawaiian case, kingdom nationalists tend to rely on the Hague Regulations of 1899 and 1907, international treaties negotiated at the First and Second Peace Conferences at the Hague. These were among the first formal statements of the laws of war and war crimes in the nascent body of secular international law. Given that the United States purportedly annexed Hawaiʻi in 1898, before these statements were negotiated, those who cite them apply them retroactively. In this logic Hawaiʻi is merely occupied by the United States; kingdom nationalists argue that Hawaiʻi was never colonized: therefore decolonization is an inappropriate political strategy.[16] Because the Hawaiian nation afforded citizenship to people who were not Kanaka Maoli—and because of its status as an independent state—kingdom nationalists tend to distance themselves from Indigenous rights discourse as well.

Despite the disavowal of colonialism by kingdom nationalists, it is precisely Western European and U.S. settler colonialism that creates both the conditions for kingdom nationalism to articulate itself in the modern Western terms of nation, manhood, law, developmental temporality, and historicism and the settings within which that form of nationalism may inadvertently obscure its own reproduction of settler colonial logics in relation to its representation of indigeneity. In other words, the organization of the kingdom nationalist discourse is evidence of the very settler coloniality that it denies. This mythology ignores a range of historical and social conditions, including Hawaiians' historical loss of language and everyday cultural practices as white American culture became hegemonic. This history of dispossession has dealt a severe blow to the collective sense of Indigenous well-being that continues into the present. Settler colonialism is an oppressive structure that Kanaka Maoli still endure today. This form of subjugation includes ongoing institutional racism, military expansion, Indigenous criminalization, homelessness, disproportionately high incarceration rates, low life expectancy, high mortality, high suicide rates, and other forms of structural violence. It leads to the constant unearthing of burials, the desecration of sacred sites, economically compelled outmigration, and many more outrages, not least of which is the ongoing process of illegal land expropriation from which these issues arguably stem.[17]

Patrick Wolfe's concept and theory of settler colonialism is apt here. He contrasts settler colonialism with franchise colonialism and—through comparative work focused on Australia, Israel-Palestine, and the United States—shows how settler colonialism is premised on the logic of elimination of Indigenous Peoples. As Wolfe notes, because settler colonialism "destroys to replace," it is "inherently eliminatory but not invariably genocidal." He is careful to point out that settler colonialism is not simply a form of genocide because there are cases of genocide without settler colonialism and because "elimination refers to more than the summary liquidation of peoples, though it includes that." Hence he suggests that "structural genocide" avoids the question of degree and enables an understanding of the relationships among spatial removal, mass killings, and biocultural assimilation. In other words, the logic of elimination of the Native is also about the elimination of the Native *as Native.* Because settler colonialism is a land-centered project entailing permanent settlement, as Wolfe puts it, "invasion is a structure not an event."[18]

Wolfe also argues that as a land-centered project the operations of settler colonialism "are not dependent on the presence or absence of formal state institutions or functionaries."[19] Hawai'i offers numerous examples of social transformation that were settler colonial in nature, long before the U.S.-backed overthrow in 1893 or purported U.S. annexation in 1898, which took root under the authority of the Hawaiian Kingdom. As the Hawaiian case shows, the structural condition of settler colonialism cannot simply be remedied by deoccupation.[20] Setting legal definitions aside momentarily, settler colonialism is itself a form of occupation.[21]

The state-centered Hawaiian nationalist challenges to U.S. domination entail a problematic and profound disavowal of indigeneity that goes hand in hand with an exceptionalist argument that Kanaka Maoli never endured colonialism prior to the 1893 overthrow due to the legacy of an independent nation. Furthermore, some claim that the Hawaiian people are not Indigenous simply because of that history, because they assert the ongoing existence of the kingdom.[22] They maintain that the category is by definition complicit with legal notions of political dependency vis-à-vis both federal laws (U.S. policy on federally recognized tribes) and the limited rights of Indigenous Peoples as delineated on the United Nations Declaration on the Rights of Indigenous Peoples adopted by the General Assembly in 2007. The Hawaiian case is particularly instructive in showing both the possibilities and limitations of Indigenous practices within and against the U.S. empire. I strive to make sense of Hawai'i as a unique legal case, but without exceptionalizing it. Legally it may be extraordinary, but this is true only if we exclude the structures and formations of settler colonialism from the picture. Unlike occupation and franchise colonialism, settler colonialism is still not regarded as unlawful.

This book problematizes the ways in which the positing of the Hawaiian Kingdom as simply needing to be restored (through deoccupation) works to demean and diminish Hawaiian indigeneity. I also demonstrate how dominant articulations of kingdom nationalism rely on treating Hawaiian history in the nineteenth century before the "Bayonet Constitution" of 1887 (or sometimes everything before the 1893 U.S.-backed overthrow) as strictly emerging from the history of the kingdom as an independent state, ignoring the increasing pressure on the Hawaiian government to remake itself (and the desire of Hawaiian elites to remake themselves) in ways conducive to being acknowledged as civilized within the Family of Nations. The rejection of indigeneity as a frame in the present, then, continues this implicit civilizational imperative, replaying the legacy of seeking to disown aspects of Hawaiian history, culture, and identity deemed "savage" and to assert a properly heteropatriarchal nation-statehood that will allow Hawai'i and Hawaiians to be seen as rightful rulers of themselves. That project also works through the various conceptual, political, and ethical implications of articulating these various forms of national identity and Indigenous Peoplehood.

While the main intervention of this work is in respect to rethinking the status of the Hawaiian Kingdom and indigeneity for envisioning Hawaiian decolonization, liberation, and self-determination, I engage with feminist and queer studies analytics to interrogate heteropatriarchy and heteronormativity within the broader projects of normalization and civilization because of my focus on colonial modernity in relation to land, gender, and sexuality. For example, the consequence of private property is related to questions of gender and sexual propriety. The sovereignty and recognition of the Hawaiian Kingdom were predicated on the logic of capitalism that intersected with a colonial sovereignty—the necessary condition for the modern state. Christian conversion was central to this process as, among other things, it imposed a framework regarding gender and patriarchy with particular consequences for anything outside of a Western form of heterosexual monogamy. These Christian mores fit within the global forces of capitalist imperialism.

IN THE REMAINDER of this introductory chapter, I offer several sections to ground the broader project. The first gives an overview of the Hawaiian Kingdom as it emerged as an independent state in the early nineteenth century. The second section examines the ways in which some kingdom nationalists disavow a colonial past when it comes to affirming the sovereignty of the kingdom as independent. The third section explains what I mean by "paradoxes" of the contemporary Hawaiian political claims with regard to the many contradictions that arise while asserting statist claims that often seem in tension with Indigenous ones. The fourth section sets forth my argument regarding the ways in which Hawaiian elites advanced a forms of colonial biopolitics in the early to mid-nineteenth century as a way to regulate the population vis-à-vis new state power geared toward protecting its sovereignty in the face of constant Western imperialist threats. The fifth section is a critical look at how the politics of the concept of sovereignty is taken up in Native studies—including pre-European modes glossed as such, Westphalian origins of European sovereignty imposed globally, and the domestic dependent form structured by the U.S. government. The sixth section details my varied methodological approaches, guiding paradigms, and epistemological interventions. I end with an overview of the chapters that follow.

The Emergence of the Hawaiian Kingdom

Precolonial Hawaiian society was a hierarchical class society based on both ascribed and achieved status. The main classes that constituted the Hawaiian social order were the chiefly class, the *ali'i,* and the common people, known as *maka'āinana,* with *kaukauali'i* (lesser chiefs) serving as a buffer in this successive hierarchy.[23] Samuel Kamakau lists eleven different gradations of chiefs within Hawaiian society.[24] He also mentions in-between classes such as the *ali'i maka'āinana* chiefs in the countryside living as ordinary people, without the attendant restrictions of the chiefly class. The social order was and continues to be based on principles of bilateral descent, in which descent groups are formed by people who claim each other by connections made through both their maternal and paternal lines. According to Jocelyn Linnekin, "since rank was bilaterally determined, descent could be traced upward in a myriad of ways, the details varying contextually depending on what was advantageous in a given situation."[25]

As Lilikalā Kame'eleihiwa explains, the role of the ali'i was to serve as mediators between the divine and the human, as Kanaka Maoli worshipped thousands of gods and demigods.[26] They also determined the correct uses of the *'āina.* The ali'i were a floating class, tenuously related to the people on the land and dependent on them for support.[27] Today many Hawaiians refer to the *maka'āinana* as the people who were the "eyes of the land," as in *maka* (eye) *'āina* (land), while E. S. Craighill Handy and Mary Kawena Pukui gloss the term as people "belonging to the land" (*ma-ka-'āina-na*).[28]

The Hawaiian concept of *pono*—the balance of forces that brings together spiritual and material realities—was central to this hierarchical yet still reciprocal relationship. As Jonathan Kay Kamakawiwoʻole Osorio explains:

> For Makaʻāinana the concept of pono linked them as well as the Aliʻi into a relationship with the powerful gods whose mana made the miracle of life possible. This means that they were to be productive as planters of taro and as fishermen; but also as crafters of the beautiful kapa cloth and moena (woven mats) that achieved such high quality in Hawaiʻi. It was the produce and art work of the Makaʻāinana that nourished and adorned the body of the Aliʻi and graced their residences. At the same time it was the Aliʻi whose presence and disciplined behavior also guaranteed that the akua would continue to bless the endeavors of the people as a whole.[29]

This was the social world that Captain James Cook found when he arrived in the Hawaiian Islands in 1778. Although scholars debate whether he was the first European to do so, his voyages to Hawaiʻi ushered in multiple waves of foreigners, leading to rapid changes caused by mass death among Kanaka Maoli due to disease and competing interests among European forces.

Beginning in 1795, Kamehameha I violently transformed a Hawaiian society of multiple paramount island chiefs—starting with Hawaiʻi, Oʻahu, Maui, Molokaʻi, and Lānaʻi—into one monarchical government, with the islands of Niʻihau and Kauaʻi voluntarily joining the kingdom by 1810. With the aid of Western gun power and other technologies, through a prolonged process of conquest, he assumed the throne as the first king. Kamanamaikalani Beamer's challenging book *No Mākou Ka Mana: Liberating the Nation* argues that the Hawaiian Kingdom is a Hawaiian creation based on ancient statecraft and that Hawaiian society had the makings for the foundation of the monarchy prior to contact with foreigners:[30]

> I trace the rise of the mōʻī (supreme chief who rules an island), the development of the ʻaha aliʻi (council of chiefs), and the establishment of palena (place boundaries), and the redistribution of lands through a kalaiʻāina (land carving). The institutions of the aha aliʻi, mōʻī, palena, and kalaiʻāina order both lands and society by creating a centralized government, establishing a system of place boundaries that protected and regulated resources, and redistributing lands and their resources among aliʻi (chiefs) and makaʻāinana (commoners). These structures constitute pre-European Indigenous Hawaiian "state-

> craft," a system of bounding lands and resources under chiefly authority. Furthermore, the existence of the aupuni (government) in ancient Hawaiian society enabled the Hawaiian Kingdom to create a nation-state by modifying existing structures rather than replacing or erasing the ancient forms of governance, chiefly rule, and land management.[31]

Hence Beamer argues that the Hawaiian Kingdom was not a European imposition but instead was a modification of preexisting ancient Kanaka Maoli structures. He acknowledges that "the Hawaiian Kingdom 'modernized' to gain respect in the international community" but emphasizes the chiefs' agency in mastering European and American law to direct the nation's destiny. Beamer suggests that they "implemented certain structures as a method for controlling Europeans within the kingdom and, to a lesser extent, for restricting foreign interference in the islands."[32]

Debates as to whether the kingdom was "Western" are tied to the different ways in which people understand the formation of the monarchy and its legacy in relation to Hawaiian agency vis-à-vis various forms of Western encroachment as well as Christianization by white American missionaries. In 1819, after Kamehameha I's death, the mother of his children, Keōpūolani (the highest-ranking chief in the archipelago), moved to end the *ʻaikapu* (the eating taboos that were part of the traditional religious system) with her son Liholiho, who was named as successor to the throne.

In 1820 Calvinist missionaries from New England arrived. They were sent by the American Board of Commissioners for Foreign Missions (ABCFM) —the first American Christian foreign mission agency, founded just a decade earlier. One of their immediate undertakings was fundamentally to transform traditional Indigenous kinship practices in a way that imposed patriarchal norms.[33] This process included the ascendancy of patrilineal naming, patriarchal citizenship, and patriarchal marriage. Notably, Keōpūolani, along with Kaʻahumanu (one of Kamehameha I's favorite women), who served as regent with executive power to Liholiho (now Kamehameha II), enacted many of the major changes that would make their way into the kingdom's laws.[34]

Kamehameha I might be said to have exercised royal absolutism during his reign, but it was hardly unqualified, given the kingdom's status as a nominal British Protectorate for the first several years of the monarchy. That form of rule rapidly changed. Kaʻahumanu took up the position of *kuhina nui* (co-ruler)—a political role that she arguably created for herself once Kamehameha I died. Together Kaʻahumanu and Liholiho quickly overturned the most fundamental laws governing the society, including the *kapu* system (religious codes protecting all deemed sacred), prior to the missionaries' arrival. When Liholiho died while visiting England, his brother Kauikeaouli was successor to the throne as Kamehameha III but was too young to rule. So Kaʻahumanu maintained almost sole power until he took up the office a decade later.

By the 1840s the kingdom had become increasingly Westernized under the leadership of Kamehameha III, which was further intensified thereafter with the consolidation of both Kanaka Maoli chiefly sovereignty and male leadership. In 1840 the king promulgated the nation's first constitution, which asserted a Christian nation to protect the common people from power abuses of the chiefs under one law for both. It was then that the king voluntarily relinquished his absolute powers and attributes by recognizing three grand divisions of the government: the king as the chief executive, the legislature, and the judiciary. The constitution drew on the earlier bill of rights in 1839, which was "published for the purpose of protecting alike, both the people and the chiefs of all these islands, while they maintain a correct deportment; that no chief may be able to oppress any subject, but that chiefs and people may enjoy the same protection, under one and the same law."[36] King Kamehameha III dispatched a delegation in 1842 to the United States and later to Europe, endowed with the ability to secure the recognition of Hawaiian independence by the major world powers of the time. On December 19, 1842, the Hawaiian Kingdom obtained the assurance that U.S. president John Tyler recognized the kingdom's independence and subsequently received formal recognition by Great Britain and France in 1843.[37] This legacy of state recognition is key to the contemporary assertions of national claims.

Sally Merry argues: "To a large extent the new system was managed by foreigners who already understood the maintenance of its practices. Unlike many of the colonized states of Africa, Hawaii did not adopt a dual legal system for foreigners and natives but created a unitary system modeled on the West."[35] In *Colonizing Hawaiʻi: The Cultural Power of Law* Merry argues that the Hawaiian appropriation of Western law entailed a two-part transition. The first part was the shift "from a Hawaiian legal order premised on divine authority to a Protestant Christian one premised on the authority of Jehovah," with the second being "the rapid transformation of the legal system to an Anglo American one that replaced Jehovah with a sovereign populace." She asserts that the first shift (religious law) allowed for more Indigenous forms, whereas the second (secular law) did not. Accounting for the context for the second transition, Merry calls attention to the increasing number of foreigners employed by the kingdom in powerful positions.

> This is the sovereignty paradox of the late 1840s: in order to produce a government able to deal with the foreign residents and to gain respectability in the eyes of the imperialist foreign community, the leaders adopted the forms of government and rule of law, but these forms required foreigners skilled in their practices to run them. And as foreigners developed and ran these new bureaucratic systems of law and government, they redefined the Hawaiian people as incapable, naturalizing this incapacity in racialized terms.[38]

This is just one of the many paradoxes of Hawaiian sovereignty that this book seeks to examine, especially as they impinge on contemporary nationalist struggle.

Disavowing Colonialism

Curiously, the same Hawaiian political activism that does not acknowledge colonialism as a social formation has influenced the scholarly world, with some writers refuting past studies by Kanaka authors who critically analyze colonialism in Hawai'i.[39] Some fixate on legal proof as to whether or not Americans or other Westerners "legitimately" colonized Hawai'i (as though colonial domination can be justified by the law) in order to assert that there was no de jure colonialism in Hawai'i vis-à-vis international law while ignoring the de facto colonial processes that unfolded prior to 1893.[40] This line of thinking resists understanding colonialism as a social force that was part of the "civilizing" projects brought by missionaries and others. What is to be gained by such a rigid argument? One benefit has been the centering of Indigenous agency and the problematization of Western encroachment as overdetermined. But to suggest that Hawaiian history in the nineteenth century can be told outside of the history of colonialism (in all its forms) is problematic at best and folly at worst. It is crucial to avoid the binary of agency versus resistance—along with the refusal to place the discussion of Indigenous agency in the context of structural limitations that necessitated Indigenous resistance.

For example, Beamer highlights the agency of the founders of the Hawaiian Kingdom and how ruling ali'i selectively appropriated tools and ideas from the West, including laws, religion, educational models, protocols, weapons, printing and mapmaking technologies, seafaring vessels, clothing, names, and international alliances. He argues that they created a hybrid system based on an enduring tradition of Hawaiian governance, which was intended to preserve, strengthen, and maintain *lāhui* (the nation). Beamer contends that only after the U.S. occupation beginning in 1893, which transferred the power of the monarch to a *haole* (foreign or white) oligarchy, did "faux-colonial" or "quasicolonial" events begin.[41] One can see the strong affective appeal of this rereading of Hawaiian history, especially when the authority of "legal fact" bolsters it by arguing that the Hawaiian Kingdom continues to exist as a sovereign and independent state and is merely occupied. This form of legal positivism could also perhaps be read as a way to refute the logics of elimination endemic to settler colonialism, which constructs the Native as someone to be eliminated.[42] It may also be seen as a serious effort to reclaim a sense of dignity and pride in past accomplishments, a historical adaptation that is enabling a reframing of Hawaiian history as more than a story of dispossession and promoting a collective sense of wholeness. But Beamer makes a false distinction between colonialism and the civilizing mission as though they are unrelated. Hawaiian modernity is of course something to be reckoned with as a specific cultural formation, but I argue here that it cannot be separated from imperial forces that culminated as forms of settler colonialism.

As Osorio has suggested in another context also related to Hawaiian sovereignty, "One crucial aspect of law is that it enables contending and competing groups within a society to coexist, compensating for the lack of faith between them by requiring that they place their faith in the law instead."[43] His insight gets at the theological component of sovereignty examined by Wendy Brown, who notes that in Western contexts the Judeo-Christian conception of God has been replaced with the state.[44] Nonetheless, in challenging the religious aspects of how law is often regarded as the greatest authority, challenging legal positivism—the notion that the law is objective and value-free—should also be a priority.

This history of modern transformation (presented as a progressive teleology) ought to be viewed in relation to the uneven trajectory of settler colonialism and its "tipping point" (where a series of small changes becomes significant enough to cause a larger, more important change) that led to haole encroachment within the Hawaiian government, as Osorio so convincingly argues in *Dismembering Lāhui*.[45]

Examining international political economy and conditions of national sovereignty, Mark Rifkin points out the structural pressures that Hawaiian leaders were under as early as the 1820s. Besides missionary dominance, there was the economic debt. He documents how U.S. naval ships were already in Honolulu by 1826. Captain Thomas ap Catesby Jones had arrived there on the *Peacock* to negotiate two agreements—one guaranteeing Americans the right to trade in Hawai'i and securing favored nation status for the United States and the other allowing Hawaiians to gather sandalwood and other materials for "taxes" as part of raising income for chiefly debts due to U.S. citizens. Theorizing transnationalization, Rifkin examines "how and why private transactions outside of national borders were made the subject of foreign policy and action by the U.S. military" and how debt served as a way for the United States to leverage a free trade agreement. In looking at the status of the Hawaiian Kingdom's national subjectivity "produced in this dialectic of formal independence and foreign economic control," Rifkin advances a concept of "debt sovereignty." He suggests we understand this as a case "in which the terms of domestic governance are slotted into a prefabricated mold and defined by the dictates and interests of another country to whom the exploited nation's people have no political appeal in a process narrated as the free choice to participate in the capitalist world market." As such, he argues that American influence at the time was imperial in the way that it reshaped the political economy of the kingdom through militarized diplomacy in order to ensure Hawaiian participation in international trade to promote the expansion of U.S. capitalism.[46] Hence we have the issue of Hawaiian leaders under duress, which undoubtedly shaped the entire range of their policy choices.

Setting aside for the moment the argument that the process of Hawaiian adaptation to Western modalities led by the ali'i was not colonization, settler colonialism, or even "faux-colonial" or "quasicolonial," let us consider the concept of coloniality as theorized by Walter Mignolo in *The Darker Side of Western Modernity: Global Futures, Decolonial Options*. He defines coloniality as "the underlying logic of the foundation and unfolding of Western civilization from the Renaissance to today," the "colonial matrix of power," which he argues was foundationally interconnected to historical colonialisms.[47] As Mignolo explains, coloniality is the substance of the historical period of colonization: its social constructions, imaginaries, practices, hierarchies, and violence. Vast differences exist in the histories, socioeconomics, and geographies of colonization in its various global manifestations. For example, French colonization in Tahiti differs from British colonization in Aotearoa and Te Waipounamu (aka New Zealand), which both differ from Chilean colonization in Rapa Nui (aka Easter Island). However, as Mignolo argues, coloniality—the establishment of racialized and gendered socioeconomic and political hierarchies according to an invented Eurocentric standard—is part of all forms of colonization. That would include both Britain in North America (a settler colonial case) and Britain in India (a franchise colonial case), despite their differences.

Whether one believes that Hawai'i or Kanaka Maoli underwent colonization prior to 1893 in the form of settler colonialism or not, this case study demands a reckoning with the dominance of coloniality, which entails an understanding of decolonization beyond its limited scope within international law or the easily available historical and political case studies of former colonies. Moreover, as Mignolo argues, coloniality manifested throughout the world and determined the socioeconomic, racial, and epistemological value systems of contemporary society, commonly called "modern" society. This is precisely why coloniality does not just disappear with political and historical decolonization, the end of the period of territorial domination of lands when countries gain independence. Given this distinction, coloniality is clearly part of the logic of Western civilization.[48]

Kingdom nationalist framings of sovereignty typically neglect the imperialist origins of international law and the Westphalian concept of sovereignty. As Antony Anghie's work argues, international law is born of colonial encounter and emerges as the institutional means to manage that encounter through the regulation of colonial difference.[49] The kingdom's quest for international recognition entailed an adaptation to nineteenth-century European conventions of statehood in which "civilized manhood" was crucial to the representation of the nation.[50] Acceptance by world powers necessitated an independent nation that displayed a Christian masculine face, which served as a sign of its modernity.[51] This shift had profound implications for Hawaiian land tenure, gender, and sexuality. Throughout the nineteenth century states recognized Hawaiian Kingdom sovereignty precisely because Indigenous elites reformed the monarchy to meet their criteria. Kanaka Maoli elites appropriated this model of government in response to Western encroachment in order to protect Hawaiian sovereignty.

It seems crucial to recognize the aspects of Hawaiian cultural practices that missionaries deemed savage and in need of eradication, which the monarch and ruling chiefs then set out to change. In *Aloha Betrayed: Native Hawaiian Resistance to American Colonialism* Noenoe K. Silva also offers a compelling history of Kanaka Maoli resistance to these forms of degradation, the political, economic, and linguistic oppression that can be understood as colonialism.[52] As she argues: "It was in response to foreign aggression, and also to missionary claims that the Kanaka ʻŌiwi were savage and uncivilized, that the mōʻī and the aliʻi nui changed their ways of government by adopting a constitution on which European and American types of laws could be based and by adhering to international norms of nation-statehood. These moves were made with the goal of preserving sovereignty—that is, to avoid being taken over by one imperial power or another."[53] It is this strategy that my book examines; I suggest that Indigenous chiefs enacted forms of colonial biopolitics—paradoxically keeping imperialism at bay by introducing Christian edicts that likely matched what European powers would have introduced themselves if any of them had formally colonized Hawaiʻi.

The Paradoxes

I explore several contradictions of Hawaiian sovereignty by bringing my analyses together through a look at the connections among indigeneity, race, gender, and sexuality in considering the strategy that chiefly elites used to secure recognition as it was already within a field of coloniality, including Western racism. This process effectively necessitated social war on pre-European Kanaka ontologies, which served a form of colonial biopolitics. I examine this legacy in relation to contemporary Hawaiian nationalism. For example, Leon Siu, a visible and ardent kingdom nationalist, is also a staunch Christian evangelical minister who was on the front lines of organizing against civil union and same-sex marriage in Hawaiʻi in the name of "preserving traditional marriage in Hawaiʻi."[54] How can we understand this position when the missionaries introduced matrimony under the authority of the Hawaiian monarchy?

The pattern that we see time and time again within national liberation struggles is the rejection of same-sex practices and women's power and authority by invoking tradition to say that they are Western colonial imports. But something distinctly different seems to be at play in the Hawaiian case: an acknowledgment to some extent that both are Indigenous but that the people have moved beyond these traditions in becoming modern, civilized. In other words, for many Hawaiians (especially those who identify as Christian, including those who are nationalists) same-sex sexuality and other sexual practices (such as polyandry and polygyny) that were seemingly once commonplace are relegated to the "savage" past, while elements of patriarchal dominance are excused in the recitation of the lineage of "great kings." Hence the establishment of the monarchy is seen as defensive, while also moving Kanaka Maoli past the primitive toward what gets cast as progress. Also, some seem to think that making the argument in and of itself will revive the kingdom, which will "arrive" without any political organizing or mass effort because of the promise of international law.

The title *Paradoxes of Hawaiian Sovereignty* speaks to the conflicts and contradictions that arise with regard to contemporary Hawaiian political claims in light of a complicated history of modernity for Hawaiians, which developed in the context of keeping imperial nations at bay. A paradox is a statement or tenet contrary to received opinion or belief, especially one that is difficult to believe. It sometimes has a negative connotation, as being in conflict with what is held to be established truth and hence absurd or fantastic—such as the unextinguished claim to restore an independent Hawaiian state—despite investigations, analyses, and explanations that may nevertheless prove it to be well founded or true.[55] What tropes and governmental practices are taken up and for what ends? What gets mobilized in the name of or with the aim of protecting Hawaiian sovereignty? What is the trade-off? The restoration of an independent state in a world where that claim is subordinated to U.S. global domination poses several political and legal problems. But it also remains unclear whether that claim is beneficial to the primary claimants—the Kanaka Maoli people—given the enduring structure of settler colonialism.

David Scott addresses the concept of paradox in his book *Conscripts of Modernity: The Colonial Tragedy of Enlightenment,* suggesting a defensible view of Enlightenment that does not oblige a simple choice for or against. Addressing the legacy of slavery, he develops an "argument that modernity was not a choice New World slaves could exercise but was itself one of the fundamental *conditions* of choice." As Scott puts it, "The tragedy of colonial enlightenment . . . is not to be perceived in terms of a flaw to be erased or overcome, but rather in terms of a permanent legacy that has set the conditions in which we make of ourselves what we make and which therefore demands constant renegotiation and readjustment."[56] This enduring inheritance, then, shapes the possibilities that necessarily mean ongoing forms of reckoning. Nonetheless, for Indigenous Peoples in settler colonial contexts, the political prospects vis-à-vis the question of the "precolonial" may also be central to these determinations. Indigenous resurgence is a liberatory framework grounded in distinct precolonial epistemes.[57]

It is not that people in the kingdom nationalist milieu are suggesting a return to an originary Indigenous position; the effort is geared toward revitalizing a monarchy that predates the U.S. occupation. Meanwhile, my interest here is in exploring kingdom nationalist investment in apocatastasis, restoration in the religious sense, wherein I offer a critique of the romantic politics of redemption that are implied. Hawaiian leaders today, like elites back then, are engaged in a political war over what form sovereignty should take. Yet there are myriad paradoxes: while the historical recognition of the kingdom is what enables the enduring claim to restore independent statehood, that legal genealogy is riddled with a history of Indigenous denigration and criminalization. What complex predicaments arise when contemporary kingdom nationalists assert state sovereignty at the expense of indigeneity, given that the world recognized that sovereignty precisely because the kingdom became Christian and male-dominated in its official leadership? The relationship between Western sovereignty, which is hegemonic around the globe, as an "Obligatory Passage Point" to independence is also a paradox.[58] Furthermore, the move to independence for the nation requires the subordination of women and the oppressive revision of sexual customs—at least in its current juridical straitjacket, which enabled Hawaiians to be seen as modern subjects in the first place. Thus this book revisits Michel Foucault's call to find alternatives to the juridical model of sovereignty as a prerequisite for decolonial imaginings of the future—Indigenous resurgence to promote the specific forms of action and the spiritual and ethical bases for a transformative movement.

I argue that it is imperative to reconsider Hawaiian indigeneity as an epistemological resource for rethinking land, gender, sexuality, and the very concept of sovereignty toward selectively revitalizing Indigenous ontologies for the twenty-first century. In other words, I look to Indigenous values that are not premised on capitalist exploitation, destructive land tenure practices, male domination, or sexual subordination in order to suggest a new ethics of relationality that is life sustaining.

Colonial Biopolitics

Engaging Foucault's invaluable work on the problem of sovereignty to investigate the technologies of biopower, I suggest that the Hawaiian case also requires an engagement with theories that enable a reconfiguration of sovereignty outside of its dominant Western meaning. I examine how the Hawaiian Kingdom exercised colonial biopower in the name of projecting its state sovereignty. In *Society Must Be Defended* Foucault argues that "politics is the continuation of war by other means."[59] Some philosophers have suggested that underneath the "politics is war" thesis is Foucault's valorization of premodern barbarism, interpreting him as advocating a return to the (presocial contract) state of nature understood as primitive and lawless.[60] However, as he suggests, it is not a return so much as a rethinking of how to characterize the world with its multiplicity of the ways in which power operates.

Foucault traces both the historical and political discourse that makes war the basis of social relations to the end of the civil and religious wars of the sixteenth century. He argues that from the seventeenth century onward, "the idea that war is the uninterrupted frame of history takes a specific form: the war that is going on beneath order and peace, the war that undermines society and divides it in a binary mode, basically is a race war." That is, it is a war of division or bifurcation within European social orders. His analysis of racism and the modern state focuses on internal conquests to maintain exclusions within in order to ensure the well-being and survival of the social body by a "protective state." As Foucault puts it, "This is the internal racism of permanent purification, and it will become one of the most basic dimensions of social normalization."[61]

Foucault critically examines how the right of war undergoes a major transformation in the early nineteenth century.[62] He traces the emergence of state racism to this period through the regulatory power of biopolitics, the practice of modern states and their regulation of their subjects through "the subjugations of bodies and the control of populations," such as the regulation of customs, habits, health, and reproductive practices—techniques that constitute biopower. As such, politics is the continuation of war by other means and, as he argues, rights are also an extension of war. Biopower contrasts with traditional modes of power based on the sovereign's right to kill and marks the shift in governance with an emphasis on the protection of life rather than the threat of death. Therefore Foucault insists that we need a way to analyze this regulatory power in terms other than the juridical model of sovereignty—to go beyond looking for the single point from which all forms of power derive. As Foucault argues in *The History of Sexuality, Vol. 1*, despite the modicum of democracy throughout the Western world, "the representation of power has remained under the spell of the monarch. In political thought and analysis, we still have not cut off the head of the king."[63]

Ann Laura Stoler's careful work *Race and the Education of Desire* asks why colonial context is absent from Foucault's history of a European sexual discourse, which for him was central to the making of the bourgeois subject. Stoler challenges what she terms his "tunnel vision of the West" and his marginalization of empire by turning to his treatment of race in what were then (in the early 1990s) his little-known 1976 Collège de France lectures in which he theorized the relationship of biopower, bourgeois sexuality, and what he identified as "racisms of the state." In turn, she argues that a history of nineteenth-century European sexuality must also be a history of race: "State racism has never been gender-neutral in the management of sexuality; gender prescriptions for motherhood and manliness, as well as gendered assessments of perversion and subversion, are part of the scaffolding on which the intimate technologies of racist policies rest."[64]

Whereas Stoler puts select empires back in the frame to show how colonialism was part and parcel of the sexual discourse that was central to the making of the European bourgeois subject, this book looks at imperialism from the other direction by exploring the colonial biopolitics of governmentality by an Indigenous independent state. The concept of colonial biopolitics illuminates the governing of Indigenous life, death, reproduction, gender, sexuality, relation to land and property, and other sites of state power over both the physical and political bodies of the Hawaiian population, while providing a means to demonstrate that settler colonialism is a historical and ongoing form of governmentality in which Indigenous life is simultaneously eliminated and assimilated, affirmed and negated. The colonial biopolitics of the Hawaiian Kingdom includes both the targeting and administration of the biological by Western colonization, occupation, and assimilation of the islands and the particular ways in which Hawaiian Kingdom nationalism adopts and remythologizes certain biopolitical forms of descent, custom, privatization, gender, and sexuality.

In the Hawaiian context of the 1820s–1840s through the late nineteenth century, Kanaka elites—with the assistance of missionaries—fighting to stop Western imperialism worked to reorganize Indigenous social forms to ensure the well-being and very survival of the social body by a protective state. Focusing specifically on the privatization of land along with the imposition of degraded gender status for women across genealogical rank and new confining sexual norms for Kanaka Maoli, I argue that this radical restructuring of Hawaiian society as a protective measure against Western imperialism became a form of colonial biopolitics linked to the regulatory power of Hawaiian state racism in the early nineteenth century. This reorganization of social forms was a strategy to fight Western racism, yet it necessitated a transformation of the Indigenous polity to secure some racial respectability. In the Hawaiian case, what distinguishes biopolitics from the monarchical "right to kill" is that the chiefs' constitutional developments and property initiatives were justified in terms of protecting Hawaiian sovereignty and promoting the welfare of the people.

By the time Kamehameha III was functioning as the monarch in practice and not just in name, the changes that he implemented in Hawaiian governance and land tenure through the 1830s and 1840s were narrated and rationalized at the time as beneficial for the common Hawaiians. Also during this period, the modern Hawaiian state intervened in sexual relations for "the good of the state." It was the chiefs in tandem with the missionaries who drew those lines of distinction organized around racializing notions of savagery, not an emergent Hawaiian bourgeoisie asserting authority over the emergent state apparatus. Nonetheless, these elites implemented a system of liberal governance that to some degree undermined the social hierarchies based on lines of descent (e.g., undercutting the ties between the chiefs and their obligations to the common people) and called for new ways of naturalizing the inequities on which an emergent bourgeois order would be based.

By 1840, through its first constitution, the Hawaiian Kingdom was defined as an egalitarian society. As mentioned earlier, this governing document stipulated that "no chief may be able to oppress any subject, but that chiefs and people may enjoy the same protection, under one and the same law."[65] This was power defined by the right of the state to protect the life of the social body and thus the right to make live those deemed a threat to the social body—the "deviant" but potentially recuperable bodies and the "abject" bodies. This newly calculated "management of life" brought together the discipline of the individual body and regulatory controls over the life of the people institutionally in order to produce a normalizing society. Here I use Foucault's formulation as a way of addressing the cleavages that emerged within nineteenth-century Hawaiian society and the ways in which those lines of distinction were organized around racializing notions of savagery. But the Hawaiian elites' institution of norms of private property, as well as heteropatriarchal understandings of home and family in the 1830s and 1840s, does not resemble Foucault's concept of the "race war" because there was no newly created, horizontally integrated bourgeois that turned its own mode of self-authorization against other Kanaka. In other words, characterizing these external imperialist developments as an "internal conquest" does not capture the pressures already being exerted on Hawaiian governance by the 1840s and the ways in which elites sought to navigate those pressures.

These decisions were already taking place within a field of imperialism, as evidenced by the force of white American imperial power prior to the mid-nineteenth century. Although this work focuses on events of the 1820s to 1840s onward in relation to contemporary nationalist politics, the U.S. government exerted direct military and political influence in Hawai'i starting in 1826, decades before formal diplomatic recognition and the treaties that were ratified by Congress. The United States, Great Britain, and France engaged in an ever-escalating struggle for more extensive spheres of license in Hawaiian law and social life (via claims to its "most favored nation" status). This increasing pressure on Hawai'i arguably played a large role, as efforts to create legal sources for Hawaiian authority intensified while developing what amounted to an order in which the status of the average Kanaka was profoundly different from that of foreigners.

The Politics of Sovereignty

Scholars within Native studies robustly debate the concept of sovereignty. Some suggest that it be abandoned altogether due to its Western roots, while others suggest that the term has gone from describing that singular supreme power over a body politic to a more porous term given its changing meanings and deployments within Indigenous contexts. Still others suggest that, rather than discarding the term, we need to theorize Indigenous sovereignties and how they distinctly differ from the Western concept of sovereignty.[66]

Taiaiake Alfred has argued that "sovereignty" is a problematic political objective for Indigenous Peoples. He critiques Indigenous leaders who claim to want to restore it as a form of collective empowerment: "Because shallow-minded politicians do not take the concept of sovereignty seriously, they are unable to grasp that asserting a right to sovereignty has significant implications. In making a claim to sovereignty—even if they don't really mean it—they are making a choice to accept the state as their model and to allow Indigenous political goals to be framed and evaluated according to a 'statist' pattern. Thus the common criteria of statehood—coercive force, control of territory, population numbers, international recognition—come to dominate discussion of indigenous peoples' political goals as well."[67]

In later work Alfred reiterates his argument and adds that "the word, so commonly used, refers to supreme political authority, independent and unlimited by any other power." He further suggests that the term "sovereignty" must be framed within an "intellectual framework of internal colonization," which he defines as "the historical process and political reality defined in the structures and techniques of government that consolidate the domination of indigenous peoples by a foreign yet sovereign settler state." Alfred suggests that the concept of sovereignty is fundamentally at odds with Indigenous political modalities and that the conceptual imposition pervades notions of governance in problematic and practical ways: "inter/counterplay of state sovereignty doctrines—rooted in notions of dominion—with and against indigenous concepts of political relations—rooted in notions of freedom, respect, and autonomy—frames the discourse on indigenous 'sovereignty' at its broadest level." Here "the actual history of our plural existence has been erased by the narrow fictions of a single sovereignty" that are controlling, universalizing, and assimilating.[68]

Therefore Alfred urges us to link the intellectual and structural forms of colonialism because sovereignty is always already Western—based on absolutist notions of power emerging from the monotheism that undergirds the formation of monarchies and their modern offspring: "'Aboriginal rights' and 'tribal sovereignty' are in fact the benefits accrued by indigenous peoples who have agreed to abandon autonomy to enter the state's legal and political framework. Yet indigenous peoples have successfully engaged Western society in the first stages of a movement to restore their autonomous power and cultural integrity in the area of governance. The movement—referred to in terms of 'aboriginal self-government,' 'indigenous self-determination,' or 'Native sovereignty'—is founded on an ideology of indigenous nationalism and a rejection of the models of government rooted in European cultural values."[69] Refusing the concept of sovereignty altogether, as a decolonizing alternative, Alfred suggests that Indigenous Peoples look to their respective traditions as a resource for building better societies.

Joanne Barker, in contrast, suggests that the term "sovereignty" has gone from describing that singular supreme power over a body politic to being a more porous term, given its changing meanings and deployments within Indigenous contexts. She acknowledges: "Of course, translating indigenous epistemologies about law, governance, and culture through the discursive rubric of sovereignty was and is problematic. Sovereignty as a discourse is unable to capture fully the indigenous meanings, perspectives, and identities about law, governance, and culture, and thus over time it impacts how those epistemologies are represented and understood." However, Barker also notes that sovereignty took on renewed currency after World War II in the context of international law as a legal category tied to the right of self-determination and that "the discursive proliferation of sovereignty must be understood in its historical context."

> What is important when encountering these myriad discursive practices is that sovereignty is historically contingent. There is no fixed meaning for what *sovereignty* is—what it means by definition, what it implies in public debate, or how it has been conceptualized in international, national, or indigenous law. Sovereignty—and its related histories, perspectives, and identities—is embedded within the specific social relations in which it is invoked and given meaning. . . . It is no more possible to stabilize what *sovereignty* means and how it matters to those who invoke it than it is to forget the historical and cultural embeddedness of indigenous peoples' multiple and contradictory political perspectives and agendas for empowerment, decolonization, and social justice. The challenge then, to understand how and for whom sovereignty matters is to understand the historical circumstances under which it is given meaning. There is nothing inherent about its significance.[70]

This embedded notion of sovereignty opens up a space to trace how the term has proliferated with many definitions and is currently evoked to mean different things at different times.

Scholars have also been more specific about what sort of sovereignty is meant to draw the contrast between Western sovereignty and Indigenous sovereignties. As Aileen Moreton-Robinson argues in an Indigenous Australian context: "Our sovereignty is embodied, it is ontological (our being) and epistemological (our way of knowing), and it is grounded within complex relations derived from the intersubstantiation of ancestral beings, humans and land. In this sense, our sovereignty is carried by the body and differs from Western constructions of sovereignty, which are predicated on the social contract model, the idea of a unified supreme authority, territorial integrity and individual rights."[71] Moreton-Robinson's theory of Indigenous sovereignty is relevant to Hawai'i since Indigenous Kanaka sovereignty (premonarchical) also happens to be widely understood as embodied—grounded within complex relations among and between myriad deities, humans, ancestral beings, the land, and all of the natural world ties.

Any examination of colonial domination necessarily entails a focus on sovereignty—the contrast between Western constructions of sovereignty and Indigenous sovereignty. In the Kanaka context, Indigenous sovereignty has yet to be properly documented let alone theorized because the legacy of the kingdom overwhelms Hawaiian political genealogies. Various Hawaiian terms are used as a gloss for sovereignty, including *ea* (life, air, breath, and also to rise, go up, raise, become erect; sovereignty, rule, independence) and *kūʻokoʻa* (independence, liberty, freedom; independent, free). Indigenous law consisted of the *kānāwai* (law, code, rule, statute, act, regulation, ordinance, decree, edict; legal; to obey a law; to be prohibited; to learn from experience) and *kapu*—the system of laws setting what was taboo (sacred or restricted) versus *noa* (common, free).

It is important to note that in 1843 King Kamehameha III declared the independent state's motto to be *Ua mau ke ea or ka ʻāina i ka pono,* commonly translated as "The life of the land is perpetuated in righteousness."[72] In the 2009 film *Hawaiʻi: A Voice for Sovereignty,* which documents his speech at an annual community event called Kūʻokoʻa, scholar Kaleikoa Kaʻeo commented on this motto: "What's important here in the Hawaiian concept: ua mau ke ea o ka ʻāina. Ke ea o ka ʻāina, the life of the land, the sovereignty of the land is that very place. Hawaiians don't see that their sovereignty comes from a particular king. Our sovereignty does not come from a constitution. The sovereignty doesn't come from the gun. The sovereignty doesn't come from arms. But in fact the sovereignty comes from the land. So even according to our own cultural understandings, the land itself is our sovereignty." Here we see the potential of Kanaka Maoli indigeneity to undermine notions of Western state power with a nonproprietary relationship to the land as the foundation.[73]

In *A Nation Rising,* Noelani Goodyear-Kaʻōpua explains that *ea* refers to "the mutual interdependence of all life forms and forces." Ea roots Kanaka in land, *ke ea o ka ʻāina,* in a way that contrasts with the 1648 Westphalian system of states and instead articulates sovereignty according to a land-based system rather than a state-centered system. She also notes that the term *ea* "also carries the meanings of 'life' and 'breath,' among other things. A shared characteristic in each of these translations is that ea is an active state of being. Like breathing, ea cannot be achieved or possessed; it requires constant actions, day after day, generaton after generation. . . . Unlike Euro-American philosophical notions of sovereignty, ea is based on the experiences of people on the land, relationships forged through the process of remembering and caring for wahi pana, storied places."[74] A look at Hawaiian indigeneity in relation to ea, then, also allows for the more general consideration of non-Western models of sovereignty and how they may inform our politics and social practices.

On the one hand, my use of the term "sovereignty" as a gloss for the term *ea* is consistent with its use in the Hawaiian nationalist movement. Yet we can also make a conceptual distinction: this project aims to add to the conceptual network to use an alternative meaning as Hawai'i offers a particular conceptual and theoretical framework. On the other hand, we can acknowledge the juggernaut of Western civilization and what is coming through Western constructions while still making other worlds legible. In this respect, the project traces a different lifeworld without disavowing the colonial Enlightenment.

In Western modalities, land and people are objectified as property, which has implications for gender and sexual roles and relations. Decolonization requires an examination of how the establishment of the Hawaiian Kingdom transformed Indigenous ontologies and how a consideration of prestate Kanaka sovereignty may inform our politics and social practices. For example, in the traditional Hawaiian context Indigenous sovereignty arguably allowed for multiplicity in terms of authority even as precolonial (and premonarchical) society was highly stratified with ali'i (chiefs), kahuna (priests), konohiki (land stewards), and the maka'āinana (common people). It is this multiplicity in relation to Indigenous sovereignty, gender, and sexuality that my intervention seeks to foreground, in order to identify the paradox of Hawaiian sovereignty and move toward decolonial possibilities in spite of vast structural constraints.

I aim to show the ways in which nineteenth-century sociopolitical formations are both reproduced and transformed in contemporary discourses and practices of Indigenous sovereignty. My treatment of Hawaiian sovereignty calls for a reconsideration of claims made possible under (or in opposition to) the sign of indigeneity. I use the term "indigeneity" as an analytic and "Indigenous" to mark a subject position—a sociospatial formation that references the people who preceded settlement. While I am critical, I do not intend to position the Hawaiians who use of Western state power and techniques as less "Indigenous" or inauthentic as Kanaka than those who do not make use of Western elements, whose power is rooted in prestate or antistate orientations. However, I do suggest that the latter may be more conducive to Hawaiian flourishing and substantive self-determination on the grounds of Indigenous resurgence of forms of relationality to land and all living entities. While I do not want to propose that formations of governance, land tenure, and social life that can be understood as similar to modes of Western state power—supporting capitalistic forms of private property or fundamentally disjunctive from pre-European patterns—are less "Indigenous," I do assert that modes grounded in Hawaiian epistemes and spaces (both social and geographical), especially those not routed through the post-Kamehameha monarchy, may be preferable. Thus the critique of kingdom nationalists might be understood less on the grounds of "indigeneity" per se than on the grounds of the "Indigenous" as a sign associated with a particular set of life ways that explicitly or implicitly are deemed uncivilized. My defense of those philosophies and lifeways rejected by some kingdom advocates (and by some Hawaiian elites in the nineteenth century), then, lies in explaining their political and ethical significance to Hawaiian pasts and futures, rather than in claiming them as more truly authentic than forms deemed "Western."[75]

Methodological Approaches

I must first acknowledge the limits of this work because of my lack of command of the Hawaiian language, which means that I have largely relied on English-language sources. Although this book's emphasis is on contemporary cultural politics and legal quandaries, it certainly would have benefited from the use of nineteenth-century primary sources in the Hawaiian language, which could illustrate more directly and precisely how changes in Hawaiian governance and land tenure were narrated and justified by the monarch and chiefs at the time. Still, it is my hope that by laying out some political and legal history that will perhaps be new to most readers, this book will contribute to the critical study of the problems and limits of Hawaiian statist nationalism.

In terms of social positioning, this work is informed by my participation in the Hawaiian sovereignty movement, with which I have been actively affiliated since 1990 in select ways appropriate to my social and geographical location as a diasporic subject. The work is guided by the cultural mandate and principles of *kuleana* (responsibility, which in turn affords privileges) and *nānā i ke kumu* (look to the source). My dialogic approach to this writing about contemporary political development draws on a genealogical way of knowing. Kanaka Maoli genealogies order the Hawaiian world not only in terms of lineage and kinship ties to ʻāina; they also structure the relation to time, space, and history. The Hawaiian terms for past and future are *ka wa ma mua* and *ka wa ma hope*, respectively. *Ma mua* (the past) is that which is in front of us; *ma hope* (the future) is that which is behind us. As Osorio puts it, "We face the past, confidently interpreting the present, cautiously backing into the future, guided by what our ancestors knew and did."[76]

As I delineate in *Hawaiian Blood: Colonialism and the Politics of Sovereignty and Indigeneity*, Kanaka Maoli typically refer to both the lineage and the kinship systems as "genealogy" and use the term interchangeably with the Hawaiian term *moʻokūʻauhau*. One of the many meanings of *moʻo* is a succession or series, while *kūʻauhau* is defined as pedigree, lineage, old traditions, genealogies, historian, and to recite genealogy. *Moʻo* can mean lineage as well as succession, while *kūʻauhau* can be used to describe someone who is skilled in genealogy and traditional history.[77] *Moʻokūʻauhau* is embedded in meaningful practices and historical circumstances, which are reflected in its persistence throughout the culture and language today. In Hawaiian terms genealogy socially locates all Kanaka Maoli in relation to different collectivities and relationships and provides the grounds for indigeneity because it is the basis of the fundamental connection to the ʻāina. But genealogies are always partial and contextual. This Hawaiian conception resonates with Foucault's theory of genealogy, which also seeks to show the plural and sometimes contradictory past without the construction of a linear development or a subject that is transcendental in relation to the field of events.[78] Foucault's concept of genealogy is the history of the position of the subject, which traces the development of people and society through history. His genealogy of the subject accounts for the constitution of knowledges and discourses, not of origins.

Drawing on approaches in Native and Indigenous studies, settler colonial studies, American studies, cultural studies, and cultural anthropology, this interdisciplinary project engages in critical discourse analysis and archival research with a close examination of contemporary and historical documents of Hawaiian nationalist statements and position papers. I read the contemporary materials for representations and proposals having to do with land claims, status issues regarding men and women of different genealogical ranks, and sexual practices and intimate relationship arrangements. I am concerned with Christianization and the privatization of land and the transformation of relationships between and among people and land, especially with regard to property and propriety—including the primacy put on heterosexual monogamy and gendered coverture that came along with these developments. My archive includes the three different kingdom constitutions (1840, 1852, 1864), along with select Hawaiian Kingdom Civil and Penal Codes from that period. These historical legal records document the ascendancy of patrilineal naming practices, the construction of patriarchal citizenship, and the imposition of marriage. They also show how the kingdom government criminalized a range of domestic and sexual arrangements and practices, including adultery, multiple partners, children born out of wedlock, questionable paternity, and close familial matings once held in esteem for procreating high-ranking chiefly offspring. I examine the implications of these changes and the regulation of property as well as land tenure and inheritance. In each chapter I trace some of the paradoxes of contemporary Hawaiian sovereignty, given the legacy of the anti-imperialist strategy turned on the Indigenous polity, and examine the implications for negotiating the structural conditions of settler colonialism while protecting the relevant legal claims.

Scholarship in American studies and cultural studies has offered nuanced critiques of power from the political and historical experiences of failed (or ongoing) revolutions in the First World (various critiques of race, ethnicity, class, gender, sexuality, and science), and postcolonial and subaltern studies have offered sustained criticism on the unfinished nationalist liberation movements in the Third World. But the still colonized "Fourth World" remains.[79] "Fourth World," a term coined in 1974 by George Manuel, names the "indigenous peoples descended from a country's aboriginal population and who today are completely or partly deprived of the right to their own territories and its riches." While the fields of cultural anthropology and cultural studies have advanced important work to show the constructed as well as the contested nature of identities, insisting that culture and identity are neither innocent nor pure, assertions of Indigenous identity have too often been quickly dismissed on grounds of hybridity and essentialism.[80] Within American studies, the question of engaging indigeneity as a meaningful category of analysis (in relation to race, ethnicity, class, gender, and others) has historically been relegated to the field of Native American studies. Arguably, this is not only because of the history of the subfields of ethnic studies as distinct from American studies but also because few scholars have taken up the question of indigeneity as something that implicates most aspects of American culture, politics, policy, and society, as the United States is a settler colonial state. Settler colonial analyses have sometimes been fruitful interventions in the field of American studies. As I have written elsewhere, however, "Settler Colonial Studies does not, should not, and cannot replace Native and Indigenous Studies."[81]

Indigeneity is a counterpart analytic to settler colonialism; any meaningful engagement with theories of settler colonialism needs to tend to the question of the Indigenous People(s) of any given settler colonial context. In asserting indigeneity as a category of analysis, the question of its substance always arises. Just as critical race studies scholars insist that race is a useful category that is a distinct social formation rather than a derivative category emerging from class and/or ethnicity, indigeneity is a category of analysis that is distinct from race, ethnicity, and nationality—even as it entails elements of all three of these. However, Indigenous Peoples' assertions of distinction and cultural differences are often heard as merely essentialist and therefore resembling static identities based on fixed inherent qualities. As such, what remains for some scholars as well as national and international governmental actors is the question as to whether indigeneity has any substance that can be used as a foundation to make a claim. In terms of both cultural and political struggles, one of the tenets of any claim to indigeneity is that Indigenous sovereignty—framed as a responsibility more often than as a right—is derived from original occupancy or at least prior occupancy. Like race, indigeneity is a socially constructed category rather than one based on the notion of immutable biological characteristics. Moreover, global political movements tending to the legacy of colonial dispossession have shaped how scholars comprehend (and apprehend) the Indigenous as a subject of study (and indigeneity as an analytic).

Importantly, the growing field of Native and Indigenous studies is not merely about the study of Indigenous Peoples but also about privileging Indigenous methodologies as a way of decolonizing knowledge production. For example, besides being rooted as an offshoot of ethnic studies, the field of Native American studies is in many ways a corrective to an earlier version of the discipline of anthropology that emerged as an extension of colonial rule. As Linda Tuhiwai Smith's important intervention suggests, for the colonized, the term "research" has historically been shaped and conflated with European colonialism in ways that continue to entrench academic research in problematic ways, in which imperialism is embedded in disciplines of knowledge and tradition as "regimes of truth." As she argues, the decolonization of research methods is essential for reclaiming control over Indigenous ways of knowing and being.[82]

In the Hawaiian context the significance of precolonial history for what might be termed "Indigenous sovereignty projects" needs careful attention. Here it is important to point out that precolonial history in Hawai'i includes only the late eighteenth century if we trace back to Captain Cook's arrival in 1778 as the watershed event that ushered in European and white American imperialism and settler colonialism. Within Native studies, the questions of the "precolonial" and "tradition" have particular salience for studies in gender and sexuality; here feminist and queer studies methodologies in particular inform my project. In *Native Acts: Law, Recognition and Cultural Authenticity* Joanne Barker focuses on the politics of recognition, membership, and disenrollment as well as marriage and sexuality. She examines gender and colonialism in relation to legal rights and notions of cultural authenticity within Native communities that potentially reproduce the injustices of sexism and homophobia (as well as ethnocentrism and racism) and that define U.S. nationalism as well as Native oppression.[83] In grappling with the questions of sexual and gender expression, Mark Rifkin addresses the use of the discourse of tradition to explore the complex relationship between contested U.S. notions of normality and shifting forms of Native Peoples' governance and self-representation in *When Did Indians Become Straight?* He shows both how white American discourses of sexuality have included Native Peoples in ways that degrade Indigenous social formations and how Native intellectuals have written back to reaffirm their peoples' sovereignty and self-determination. In grappling with the questions of sexual and gender expression as he addresses the use of the discourse of tradition, Rifkin identifies and theorizes how Native Peoples reckoned with what he theorizes as "the bribe of straightness," a dynamic that "includes arguing for the validity of Indigenous kinship systems (Native family formations, homemaking, and land tenure) in ways that make them more acceptable/respectable to whites."[84] Notably, Scott L. Morgensen has theorized biopolitics in relation to settler colonialism in various contexts. In *Spaces between Us* Morgensen demonstrates how white settler colonialism is a primary condition for the development of modern queer politics in the United States. He traces the relational distinctions of "Native" and "settler" that define the status of being "queer" and theorizes a biopolitics of settler colonialism, in which the imagined disappearance of indigeneity ensures a progressive future for white settlers.[85] Elsewhere Morgensen also examines how settler colonialism remains naturalized within understandings of biopower as theorized by Giorgio Agamben and Michel Foucault and its relation to coloniality more broadly.[86] Moreover, he demonstrates how biopolitical processes structure the ways in which white settler societies actively universalize Western law in ways that sustain settler states and bolster their regimes of global governance.

Other select studies on gender and sexuality in relation to colonial modernity and empire particularly influence this work, as does the literature on women and nationalism, race and sexuality, and decolonization.[87] Antoinette Burton discusses "the unfinished business of colonial modernities" with a focus on "the limited capacity of the state and other instruments of political and cultural power to fully contain or successfully control the domain of sexuality."[88] She engages Tani Barlow's definition of colonial modernity, as a concept that "can be grasped as a speculative frame for investigating the infinitely pervasive discursive powers that increasingly connect at key points to the globalizing impulses of capitalism." As an analytic it can "suggest that historical context is not a matter of positively defined, elemental, or discrete units—nation states, states of development, or civilizations, for instance—but rather a complex field of relationships or threads of material that connect multiply in space-time and can be surveyed from specific sites."[89]

Instead of using the word "traditions," which raises notions of (in)authenticity, I refer to "practices" here when assessing documentable customs. The distinction also serves as a broader intervention in Hawaiian studies and Hawaiian nationalist projects, where "tradition" and "culture" continue to be discussed and deployed as though they were/are bounded objects. Mari Matsuda defines custom as a "body of traditional practices and beliefs that were part of the Hawaiian understanding of human life and social organization before western contact and the imposition of state created law." For example, she explains that in Hawaiian society "using and giving, rather than possessing, characterized attitudes towards land."[90] What I want to emphasize is that tradition is a set of cultural practices that are continuously reshaped and transformed.

To be clear, this is not a bid for cultural purity; I am not suggesting that we fixate on the possibility of restoring Hawaiians to any "original" condition. However, precolonial (not merely prekingdom) practices—even if they can never be fully "known"—can serve as epistemological and ontological resources for rethinking our current conditions and can provide insight into developing potential contemporary models for an alternative to dominant, colonial, hetero, and gender normativity. As Ella Shohat asserts: "The question, in other words, is not whether there is such a thing as an originary homogenous past, and, if there is, whether it would be possible to return to it, or even whether the past is unjustifiably idealized. Rather, the question is who is mobilizing what in the articulation of the past, deploying what identities, identifications, and representations, and in the name of what political vision and goals."[91]

Many scholars have pressed charges of romanticization or, worse, essentialism in response to works that engage, let alone attempt to reconstruct, anything constituted as precolonial. My aim here is not to take part in advancing exotic primitivism or glorifying pre-European Hawaiian society but to insist that the relationship to land is part and parcel for Indigenous subjectivity committed to decoloniality. Although postcolonial theory references culture, nation, state, and often territory (especially in relation to examinations of diaspora), the "in-betweenness" that is privileged is too often not rooted enough to reckon with Indigenous subject formation as inextricably bound to concepts of land as kin and therefore relational in a particular way. It also tends to presume that indigeneity is not already hybrid and complex, through evoking genealogy. In its full potential postcolonialism is an engagement with and contestation of colonial discourses, power structures, and social hierarchies. Land, gender, and sexuality are prime sites by which to critically examine the justification of colonial domination via representations of the colonized as a perpetually inferior people, society, and culture due to their supposedly backward relationship to land, gender relations, and savage sexualities.

Paradoxes of Hawaiian Sovereignty contrasts Indigenous sovereignty (ea) with both Hawaiian Kingdom sovereignty and the state-based liberal sovereignty of the United States that affords Native nations only "domestic dependent sovereignty." Notions of democracy tie them together, as do particular kinds of self-determination. Each has its own model of governmentality embedded in radically different notions of sovereignty and, as such, dissimilar notions of virtue. While this is not a call to return to the past, it is a critical draw *from* the past—or at least from contemporary understandings of that past.

Overview of the Chapters

Chapter 1, "Contested Indigeneity: Between Kingdom and 'Tribe,'" examines the dissonance over Indigenous status in both the controversy over federal recognition, focused on the Akaka bill that was introduced and debated repeatedly from 2000 to 2012, and the sector of the independence movement that aims to reinstate the Hawaiian Kingdom. I explore the complications involved in privileging Kanaka Maoli as an Indigenous People in the midst of what is right now a full-fledged nationalist movement currently threatened by the federal effort to contain the independence claim. I delineate the politics of the state-driven proposals for federal recognition of Native Hawaiians as a tribal nation. Then I focus on the ways in which kingdom nationalists who are opposed to this form of federal recognition (an NHGE based on the U.S. government's limitations on "Native sovereignty") have also demeaned the standing of Kanaka Maoli indigeneity in their articulations of the independence claim. The debate over the status of the Indigenous in relation to these two models of nationhood—both of which are based on Western rights models—reveals several paradoxes. The specific legal status of Native governing entities is structured by U.S. federal limitations that contain them as "domestic dependent sovereigns," although the U.S. government acknowledges that their respective sovereignty is inherent. While the historical recognition of the kingdom as an independent state is what enables the enduring legal claim that exceeds the U.S. domestic model, that legal genealogy is riddled with a history of Indigenous deprecation actively reformed through biopolitical measures, legal and otherwise.

In the remainder of chapter 1, I trace the emergence of the term "Indigenous" as a political and legal category within U.S. and international law. Focusing on the specifics of the Hawaiian case, I attempt to account for the political incentives that may explain why independence activists advocate that Kanaka Maoli disidentify as Indigenous in order to reclaim the kingdom. I suggest that some Kanaka Maoli reject Indigenous identity as a means of relief from the political condition of indigeneity.

Chapter 2, "Properties of Land: That Which Feeds," focuses on Indigenous kinship to land and revisits the two competing sovereignty models of contemporary Hawaiian nationalist projects—the assertion of kingdom existence (and/or monarchy restoration) and the push for a federally recognized Native Hawaiian governing entity—in relation to the legacy of commodifying land as property. Here again, each involves deep paradoxes: the claim to "national lands" in the kingdom restoration model is based on "perfect title" to the Crown and Government Lands, while the Native Hawaiian governing model features "Native lands" limited by the legal concept of "Aboriginal title." Both of these responses to U.S. empire are lodged in normative legal frameworks and their respective property regimes. I argue that they both are problematic in terms of decolonizing Indigenous self-determination, even while it is crucial to challenge the U.S. government and its subsidiary's claims to having "perfect title" to stolen lands. I examine the legalities that undergird both, as well as the cultural logics at work, in order to challenge their presuppositions that Hawaiian sovereignty relies on a proprietary relation to land.

I offer a brief summary of the 1848 Māhele land division and related legislation in its political context and consequences. In this case, "land rights" are a form of biopower, a technology of power that relates to the kingdom government's concern with fostering the life of the population and centers on the poles of discipline and regulatory controls. Individual land holdings through fee-simple title became a basic dimension of social normalization. With Westphalian sovereignty as the basis for governance that served to underwrite Western imperialism and its international political domination, the regime of private property was and remains central for the "achievement" of statehood. Here a paradox of Hawaiian sovereignty is that the Māhele is what enables a national claim to the stolen Kingdom Crown and Government Lands in the contemporary period. The irony is that they have yet to be privatized (as of the time of writing) because they have been held by the 50th state as "public lands." Yet it is through their original privatization by the kingdom that they were constituted as Crown and Government Lands in the first place.

The remaining part of this chapter outlines some of the claims to "perfect title" with regard to Hawaiian lands to show the limits of the political project of deoccupation in the form of kingdom restoration that does not get at the root issue of land expropriation, which is the fundamental condition of settler colonialism. I then examine how the U.S. government contains Native governing entities and challenge the federal recognition model. In conclusion, to advance a decolonial model, I offer an example of how some Kanaka Maoli are challenging U.S. and Hawai'i state claims over these same lands but privileging Indigenous knowledge as the basis for revitalizing Hawaiian ontologies and epistemes in nonproprietary relation to the land, which is genealogical and based upon kinship relations to land over time.

Chapter 3, "Gender, Marriage, and Coverture: A New Proprietary Relationship," examines the impact of Western laws and culture in Hawai'i, which entailed a radical restructuring of the status of women starting from 1820, when New England missionaries introduced Christianity. Calvinism and the common law of coverture were two primary determinants of Hawaiian women's shifting status. The missionaries introduced Western ideas to Hawaiian society that dictated the domestic subjugation of women in social, political, and economic realms. Male prominence manifested itself in the Western political structure of the kingdom, which eventually degraded women's status. I first lay out the historical background to document the restructuring of the status of women through Christianization and coverture. I then trace the ways in which the Hawaiian Kingdom became more Westernized as it subordinated chiefly women's status in the realm of state governance, arguing that the privatization of land as property and coverture as a marker of "propriety" both signaled a shift to proprietary relationships between Kanaka and land and between men and women. Marriage itself was a conduit to this exclusivity and as such was a restrictive imposition to subordinate Hawaiian women. Moreover, the marriage codes became not only a way to regulate Hawaiian women's sexual activities, especially with foreign men, but also to protect them once sailors violently insisted that they were entitled to sexual access to Hawaiian women. As regent of the kingdom, Ka'ahumanu declared the 1825 verbal edict of heteromonogamous Christian marriage, making the Seventh Commandment kingdom law.

To examine the legacy of coverture for the contemporary question of Hawaiian women's political rights within the politics of deoccupation nationalism, I feature a case study of a document produced by David Keanu Sai, a contemporary scholar and political leader who identifies himself as temporary regent of the Hawaiian Kingdom. In 1998 he issued a memorandum addressed to "Subjects of the Kingdom" from "Office of the Regent" regarding "suffrage of female subjects." In it he delineates his research on nineteenth-century kingdom election laws in the civil codes, case law, and other legal documents in order to ascertain the intent of a particular statute as it relates to the representative body, to ascertain whether women's participation in the electoral process is a political right in today's kingdom. As the political subordination of women was central to the Hawaiian bid for status as modern civilized subjects, I examine the regulatory power of biopolitics in the context of the modern Hawaiian state (the constitutional monarchy) and its modes of exclusion. Paradoxically, although the kingdom had been further democratized by the 1840s, the internal push for normalization with regard to Indigenous gender (and sexual) norms through the imposition of marriage and its attendant legal coverture was taken up in order to adopt European masculinist conventions of statehood. The legacy of this colonial biopolitics has repercussions for the contemporary sovereignty movement that I examine through a critical analysis of Sai's memo and its gesture of gender equality.

Chapter 4, "'Savage' Sexualities," opens with a look at a Christian evangelical and kingdom nationalist Leon Siu and his public statement link-ing the contemporary forms of recognition regarding same-sex sexuality and gender identity with the prolonged U.S. occupation of the kingdom. Siu argues that only by following Christian moral edicts does the Hawaiian Kingdom have a chance to be restored. He selectively valorizes Kamehameha III's role as monarch, highlighting the way that he enshrined Christian laws in the early nineteenth century. In 1827 and 1829 the king issued an edict referred to as "No Ka Moe Kolohe" ("of mischievous sleeping," translated in official government documents as "concerning illicit intercourse"), a law that he himself did not abide by. King Kamehameha III himself had both a male lover and a sexually intimate relationship with his sister as well as other known "affairs" with women while unmarried and after he married. Yet he implemented the laws against "mischievous sleeping," and the policing of sexuality was an essential part of the nineteenth-century transformation of the Hawaiian state. Kanaka elites fighting to stop Western imperialism with the assistance of former missionaries worked to reorganize Indigenous sexual models, as precolonial sexual practices were regularly cited as evidence of Hawaiian "savagery." Prior to Christianization, Indigenous practices were diverse and allowed for multiple sexual possibilities. Sibling and other close consanguineous matings in the service of producing genealogically high-ranking offspring among the chiefly class, same-sex sexual practices within both common and chiefly classes, and women's sexual agency within both common and chiefly classes—what I term "savage sexualities"—were besieged with surveillance, reform campaigns, and penalty regimes for those caught "backsliding" into so-called heathendom. Hence Western settler sovereignty manifested through a discourse of superiority in the realm of both governance and sexuality, in contrast to the supposed lawlessness of Indigenous Peoples seen as sexual degenerates. These new standards foisted on Hawaiian society—and claimed by elites as a form of social normalization—served to undercut Indigenous ontologies and their basis for (embodied Indigenous) sovereignty.

The second part of the chapter deals with this legacy for contemporary Hawaiian nationalist politics. Turning to activism related to same-sex sexual legacies, as well as third gender and transgender identities, I examine debates about what constitutes Indigenous tradition. Battles over same-sex marriage have created deep divisions within Hawaiian communities, especially among those who identify as Christians. I then turn to claims that same-sex marriage serves as a form of decolonization. With a critical analysis turned back to interrogate state regulation of sexuality and intimate partnerships, I challenge that assertion. The chapter concludes with a look at how these debates are taken up in Indian Country (Native America) in light of the earlier passage of the Defense of Marriage Act, which was later struck down by the Supreme Court of the United States.

The conclusion, "Decolonial Challenges to the Legacies of Occupation and Settler Colonialism," offers some modest suggestions for negotiating the paradoxes of Hawaiian sovereignty. Given the multifaceted juridical straitjacket that enabled Kanaka Maoli to be seen as modern subjects in the first place, kingdom nationalists have brought these contradictions into sharp relief. Some continue to emulate Western monarchical power. My closing chapter aims to size up the implications of their attempts to secure rule. Many are still captive to this move that was effective for Hawaiian elites in the mid-nineteenth century. This strategy may still be politically productive for the legal claims, but it flattens the contours of indigeneity in violent ways. Nationalists are still subjects of colonization as they mount their claims in the terms of the imperial forces.

The Hawaiian situation demands an approach that is not state-centered in order to explore recuperating a decolonial Indigenous modality. But this involves a serious predicament, as the U.S. government would be happy to see the independence movement relinquish its claims. In other words, while Hawaiians may "still have not cut off the head of the king,"[92] it is clear that the United States is trying to behead the Hawaiian Kingdom. Hence I am not suggesting that Kanaka Maoli simply abandon the claim to independent statehood. The claim itself may not be viable or even desirable, but it is an important one with which to wage battle against U.S. empire. The U.S. government—if ever pressed by the world community—cannot substantiate its claim to the Hawaiian Islands because the archipelago was never ceded through treaty or conquest. But those active in the kingdom movement draw on histories of kingdom sovereignty, which are gendered in complicated ways that also have deep ramifications for sexual politics. This book is not an "alternative" approach so much as an attempt to reclaim or (re)appropriate traditional modalities in principled ways that are enabling and potentially freeing. While kingdom nationalists tend to conceive of indigeneity as a state of dependency and domesticity, my work suggests that it is actually a fluid source of dynamic power—molten, the very source of Kanaka sovereignty.

ONE. CONTESTED INDIGENEITY
Between Kingdom and "Tribe"

That is what we are talking about here in this context—what's called Native sovereignty in the United States. . . . This is a very special little semi-autonomous sovereignty that was devised by the Founding Fathers of the United States of America. They treat the Natives that they found on the Eastern seaboard of the United States in a special way and as we've mentioned already over 560 organizations have taken advantage and it is an advantage of this special kind of sovereignty. Well, you know, the way I see it is it is an American thing. It's their ballgame, it's their ballpark, they own the gloves, they own the bats, they own the balls, they own the uniforms! And if we wanna play in this ballpark, we have to follow these rules and they're not onerous. Read the bill. They're not onerous. But we need to follow their rules.

This loaded quotation is an excerpt from a TV segment featuring Bruss Keppeler (1937–2014), a Native Hawaiian attorney who served as a leader within the Association of Hawaiian Civic Clubs.[1] The show aired on major network television in Hawai'i on January 14, 2009, and was produced by the Office of Hawaiian Affairs, a state agency. The purpose of the show was to "inform the public on legal implications of the Native Hawaiian Government Reorganization Act."[2] The legislative proposal called the "Akaka bill"—named for its sponsor, Senator Daniel Akaka (D-HI)—was then before the House and the Senate and had been reintroduced multiple times since its defeat. Throughout its lifespan, from this federal legislation's emergence in 2000 until 2012, Akaka had asserted that he introduced it in order to secure the recognition of Native Hawaiians as an Indigenous People who have a "special relationship" with the United States and thus a right to self-determination. Passage of the bill would have laid the foundation for a nation-within-a-nation model of self-governance defined by U.S. federal law as "domestic dependent nations" to exercise limited self-governance.

Notice that Keppeler qualifies the term "sovereignty" with "Native." This "Native sovereignty" is nonthreatening to the U.S. government—"a very special little semi-autonomous sovereignty" that provides no ground to challenge the power of settler colonialism or occupation. Keppeler credits "the Founding Fathers of the United States of America" with creating it and does not acknowledge that the sovereignty of tribal nations is inherent and preexisted the formation of the United States. Yet in a sense he is right in that the U.S. Supreme Court crafted the concept of "domestic dependent nationhood" that subordinates tribal nations to U.S. governmental power, even though that same government acknowledges tribal sovereignty as inherent (and not delegated). Keppeler's suggestion that "they treat the Natives that they found on the Eastern seaboard of the United States in a special way" denies and erases the settler colonial violence used to found the U.S. settler state and subsequently incorporate tribal nations within the bounds of it. While he is correct in admitting that Native sovereignty is "an American thing" (a domestic dependent sovereignty) and that the U.S. government owns the playing field, he suggests that the rules are not onerous, without admitting that the United States asserts plenary power over Native nations and thus switches the rules whenever it suits the federal government's interests.

This is not to demean tribal sovereignty. As David E. Wilkins and Heidi Kiiwetinepinesiik Stark define it, tribal sovereignty is "the intangible and dynamic cultural force inherent in a given Indigenous community, empowering that body toward the sustenance and enhancement of political, economic, and cultural integrity. It undergirds the way tribal governments relate to their own citizens, to non-Indian residents, to local government, to the state government, to the federal government, to the corporate world, and to the global community."[3]

Still, these same scholars have carefully documented and theorized about the limits to the exercise of tribal sovereignty, especially given how the U.S. Supreme Court has ruled in ways that have downgraded its power. The court has moved away from the concept of intrinsic tribal sovereignty that predated the arrival of Europeans and has adopted the view that tribal

FIGURE 1.1. Editorial cartoon in 2015 by Marty Two Bulls (Oglala Lakota). Reprinted with permission of Marty Two Bulls.

sovereignty, and the attendant freedom of the tribes from encroachments by the states, exists because Congress has chosen to confer select protections on Native nations. As such, some Native Americans have warned Kanaka Maoli against buying into this model of governance.

The state-driven push for federal recognition is problematic for outstanding Hawaiian sovereignty claims. Hence the legislation deeply divided Native Hawaiian communities throughout the archipelago and the continental United States. Although there was widespread support for the legislation among Kanaka Maoli, many opposed it in favor of the restoration of the independent state of Hawaiʻi under international law. In any case, state officials seem driven to go another route to try to contain the independence claim.

As noted in the introduction, the U.S. Department of the Interior held public meetings in July 2014 on the question of Procedures for Reestablishing a Formal Government-to-Government Relationship with the Native Hawaiian Community. The DOI explained that "the purpose of such a relationship would be to more effectively implement the special political and trust relationship that currently exists between the Federal government and the Native Hawaiian community." This suggests that the department considered the shift for administrative convenience, not for political purposes. Yet the subject of the hearings suggests otherwise: how is it possible to have a government-to-government relationship with a "community"? Dictated and confined by the structures of U.S. federal law, the concept of "reorganization" itself is a misnomer. It was unclear what prompted the DOI meetings, especially with so little warning (the press release announcing them gave just a few days' notice).[4] To many, this seemed to be a last-ditch effort driven by the trustees of the Office of Hawaiian Affairs (OHA) and the Council for Native Hawaiian Advancement to take the executive route to securing the federal recognition of a Native Hawaiian governing entity (NHGE) because the legislative path had long failed. With the subsequent retirement of Senator Daniel Akaka, along with the death of Senator Daniel K. Inouye (who held seniority in the Senate), it seemed that officials of the 50th state along with their affiliates were to take this alternative route through the DOI. Given the federal criteria used from 1978 to 2015 to recognize Indian tribes, however, which the Hawaiian people would not meet, this alternative route acknowledgment could be facilitated only by changes to the federal regulations at the time.[5]

In August 2015 the press secretary for the DOI confirmed that the department would "propose a rule that establishes an administrative procedure that the secretary would use if the Native Hawaiian community forms a unified government that seeks a formal government-to-government relationship with the United States."[6] The formation of that governing entity has been developing in a concerted way will—with the Native Hawaiian Roll Commission (created by state legislation) working with the Office of Hawaiian Affairs and a vendor called Naʻi Aupuni (created in 2014 specifically to oversee the elections process of some estimated 95,690 Kanaka Maoli, as of 2015). Naʻi Aupuni had been certified to participate in the formation of a Native Hawaiian government as of 2015.[7] But as many Kanaka Maoli noted during the public hearings, political relations between the U.S. government and the Hawaiian people should be a matter for the U.S. Department of State, not the Department of the Interior.

Indeed, even then Office of Hawaiian Affairs chief executive officer (CEO) Kamanaʻopono M. Crabbe, who was said to be more responsive to kingdom nationalists than the OHA trustees were, made an effort to confer with the U.S. secretary of state. On May 5, 2014, Crabbe submitted a letter of formal request to John F. Kerry "Re: Inquiry into the Legal Status of the Hawaiian Kingdom as an Independent Sovereign State." The memo specifically asked the U.S. Department of State for a legal opinion on the current status of Hawaiʻi under international law, outlining four specific questions:

> First, does the Hawaiian Kingdom, as a sovereign independent State, continue to exist as a subject of international law?
>
> Second, if the Hawaiian Kingdom continues to exist, do the sole-executive agreements bind the United States today?
>
> Third, if the Hawaiian Kingdom continues to exist and the sole-executive agreements are binding on the United States, what effect would such a conclusion have on United States domestic legislation, such as the Hawaiʻi Statehood Act, 73 Stat. 4, and Act 195?
>
> Fourth, if the Hawaiian Kingdom continues to exist and the sole-executive agreements are binding on the United States, have the members of the Native Hawaiian Roll Commission, Trustees and staff of the Office of Hawaiian Affairs incurred criminal liability under international law?[8]

No response to Crabbe's letter was ever reported. However, many kingdom nationalists and other independence advocates applauded his effort and witnessed the backlash by some of the OHA trustees, who called for his resignation. These events provided immediate context for the DOI's visit to the islands in the summer of 2014.

The public record (revealed by the video of each of the fifteen meetings held in Hawaiʻi) reveals that over 95 percent of all the people who spoke at these public consultations opposed the procedures being considered by the DOI.[9] The vast majority who spoke out are Kanaka Maoli. The Council for Native Hawaiian Advancement and the Office of Hawaiian Affairs together attempted to advance the narrative that opponents were merely a loud minority of independence supporters who showed up at these meetings and that the vast majority of Hawaiians really support federal recognition. In a brief report on the proposed DOI procedures, OHA trustees also asserted: "The proposed administrative rule should not prospectively attempt to limit the inherent sovereign rights of the reorganized Native Hawaiian government that insure it under U.S. domestic law. Likewise, the rule should open a path for reestablishment of a domestic government to government relationship that will not, as a legal matter, affect paths for international redress."[10] On the face of it, this may seem to be a caveat in the service of the national claims under international law; but the ill-defined concept of "international redress" certainly is different for states than it is for Indigenous Peoples and colonies. Here we see the OHA representatives attempting to graft the U.S. government's recognition of an independent state to a people's Indigenous status. Nonetheless, many Native Hawaiians support this effort because they have been told that it is the only politically realistic thing that they can expect to achieve to restore some form of self-governance.

This chapter examines the contestation over indigeneity in both the controversy over the federal recognition legislation (which was debated off and on at the congressional level from 2000 to 2012) and the sector of the independence movement that insists that the kingdom already exists (or aims to reinstate the monarchy). I explore the complications involved in privileging Hawaiian indigeneity, given the fraught situation of Kanaka Maoli and Hawai'i's current political status—as a people and a place—in the midst of what is right now a full-fledged nationalist movement currently threatened by the federal attempt to sidestep the independence claim. I then delineate the politics of the Akaka Bill legislative proposal in order to account for the debates surrounding the U.S. recognition of delegated versus inherent "Native sovereignty," which reveal the state's interest in containing the Hawaiian claim.

Next I focus on the ways in which kingdom nationalists who are opposed to this form of federal recognition of a Native Hawaiian governing entity based in the concept of "Native sovereignty" have also demeaned the standing of Kanaka Maoli indigeneity in their articulations of the Hawaiian independence claim. I trace the emergence of the term "Indigenous" as a political and legal category. The United Nations Declaration on the Rights of Indigenous Peoples, adopted by the UN General Assembly in 2007, is a key site for examining the limits put upon Indigenous Peoples with regard to self-determination. Focusing on the specifics of the Hawaiian case, the chapter attempts to account for the political incentives that may explain why independence activists advocate that Kanaka Maoli disidentify as Indigenous in order to reclaim the kingdom. I suggest that some Kanaka Maoli reject Indigenous identity as a means of relief from the political condition of Indigenous status, where they also read claims to Hawaiian indigeneity as a simultaneous admission of U.S. colonial subjugation of Hawai'i and a yielding to that subordination.

In this case, the power of Indigenous (premonarchical) sovereignty is obscured precisely because it was the distancing from the prior form of governance that enabled the Kanaka Maoli people to assert sovereignty to secure recognition in the form of an independent state. In the 1840s Kamehameha III advanced the kingdom in ways that protected Hawaiian sovereignty by countering the imperial forces of the U.S. and European governments that claimed racial and religious supremacy. Considering the ways in which colonialism shaped the internal bifurcations within European societies, the race war that Foucault theorized emerged from modern European states as these states created the law of nations to justify their own imperialism. As a response, Hawaiian elites adopted this paradigm of self-governance to assert their own sovereignty and resist Western encroachment, but it was in effect colonialism by proxy (or a preemptive form). Western norms of sovereignty that emerged from the European Peace Treaty of Westphalia of 1648 which created a new system in central Europe based upon the concept of coexisting sovereign states, became central to international law—and continue to dominate international politics, theory, and practice. Moreover, these norms are still regarded as the legitimate basis for international political domination of independent states over peoples. Yet the state system is arguably obsolete—at least for the survival of Indigenous Peoples and customary lifeways.

Today the project of asserting (or restoring) the kingdom is in competition with the U.S. attempt to subordinate Native Hawaiians by confining governance to internal self-determination within the bounds of federal law. Yet the state-centered Hawaiian nationalist challenges to U.S. domination entail a problematic and profound disavowal of indigeneity. There are dual models of sovereignty in place here: on the one hand, the kingdom; on the other, a Hawaiian "U.S. domestic dependent nation." These are the two dominant responses to U.S. colonial occupation, yet both are problematic. Thus I argue for the need to reconceptualize Indigenous status—but not the sort demeaned by the kingdom project or subordinated by the U.S. government in its domestic dependent framework. Assertion/restoration of the kingdom and the bid for federal recognition (whether through the Akaka bill or the DOI process) are two responses to U.S. empire that are lodged in normative frameworks—even though controversial for different reasons. But each also entails a paradox for Hawaiian sovereignty: the contemporary kingdom as anti-Indigenous monarchy on the one hand and the

Indigenous-specific Native Hawaiian governing entity limited by federal policy on the other. Although one is Hawaiian and one is American, both are Western state models. What are the cultural logics that undergird them? Here the structure of settler colonialism complicates the terrain—both the kingdom and the United States want to respond to this political question internally and through their own respective legalities. Herein I challenge both their presuppositions.

Whose Indigeneity?

Although the Hawaiian Kingdom (1810–1893) cannot be characterized as a settler state, Kanaka Maoli (and allies) who assert independent Hawaiian state sovereignty in order to counter the U.S. settler state still manage to elide (prestate) Indigenous sovereignty. Under the U.S. settler state, most Kanaka Maoli have been subordinated by the Hawai'i state government since it became the "50th state" (1959). The U.S. colonial government ruled Hawai'i as an organized territory from 1900 to 1959. Before that Hawai'i was an unorganized territory from 1898 to 1900. Prior to the 1898 annexation by the United States, the Republic of Hawai'i governed the islands from 1894, after reconstituting the "provisional government" largely composed of American business leaders involved in the 1893 overthrow of Queen Lili'uokalani.

As laid out in the introductory chapter, from 1795 to 1810 Kamehameha I violently transformed a Hawaiian society of multiple paramount island chiefs into a singular monarchy. His eldest son, Kamehameha II (born Liholiho) was (in)famous for breaking the *kapu* system of religious laws that governed the entire society soon after he succeeded to the throne. This occurred in by 1819, just before the first Christian mission to the islands in 1820, when Calvinists from New England arrived. Kamehameha III (born Kauikeaouli) officially succeeded to the throne in 1825 (after Liholiho died in 1824) but was too young to rule at the age of twelve. Ka'ahumanu (who had served as regent to Liholiho) carried on as kuhina nui and exercised de facto and de jure power until Kauikeaouli was old enough. He then ruled as Kamehameha III until 1854.

In 1840 the monarch promulgated the kingdom's first constitution, which asserted that the kingdom was transforming itself into a Christian nation in order to protect the common people from power abuses by the chiefs under one law for all. Thus by then the kingdom was already a liberal government, despite having a head of state selected through the logic of divine right.

By 1843 Britain, France, and the United States recognized the Hawaiian Kingdom as an independent state. In 1848 King Kamehameha III began to privatize the traditional land-tenure system, a key phase of Westernization for the monarchy. Subsequently the kingdom was recognized around the globe as part of the "Family of Nations," by then recognizable as both a Christian and a male-led nation. The official diplomatic relations between the kingdom and the United States developed over several decades. The treaties negotiated between the two were made after the U.S. government and other nations had already recognized the kingdom as an independent state. It is important to note that the treaties with the United States were not concerned with land or governance (they were not treaties of cession); instead the treaties specified relations of peace and friendship, commerce, and navigation. The kingdom negotiated diplomatic relations and international treaties not only with the United States (1849, 1870, 1875, 1883, and 1884) but also with Austria-Hungary (1875), Belgium (1862), Denmark (1846), France (1846 and 1857), Germany (1879), Great Britain (1836, 1846, and 1851), Italy (1863), Japan (1871 and 1886), the Netherlands (1862), Portugal (1882), Russia (1869), Samoa (1887), Spain (1863), the Swiss Confederation (1864), and Sweden and Norway (1852).[11]

Hawaiian assertions of the continuing existence of the kingdom today typically stop short of reclaiming Kanaka Maoli Indigenous status. Indeed very few Hawaiians look to premonarchical forms of Hawaiian sovereignty, because indigeneity is too often viewed as a source of disempowerment and fundamentally something beyond which Kanaka have "progressed." I suggest that this is in part because the U.S. proposals for federal recognition tie Hawaiian indigeneity to political subordination vis-à-vis U.S. state power in the form of congressional plenary power. This rejection also extends to nomenclature. For example, many spheres of the kingdom restorationist projects are hostile to the term "Native Hawaiian." For reasons that are unclear, the preferred terms seem to be "Aboriginal" or "Hawaiian Native," but not "Indigenous." Yet today the term "Indigenous" is the privileged term globally over and above the others—perhaps as a result of worldwide political struggle to press for the right of self-determination for Indigenous Peoples.

The adjective "Indigenous" has its origins in the mid-seventeenth century. The *Oxford English Dictionary* traces its etymology back to late Latin:

indigenus (born in a country, native; from *indigena,* a native) and defines it as "born or produced naturally in a land or region; native or belonging naturally *to* (the soil, region, etc.)," as well as "inborn, innate, native," and "of, relating to, or intended for the native inhabitants."[12] This definition takes the geography of a country for granted. Yet it can be reductive to use the term to refer to anyone born in a particular place. For example, white Americans in the United States have historically seized the concept for themselves in pressing nativist claims to place and belonging without regard for Indigenous Peoples who are present. Jean M. O'Brien traces the genealogy of this myth of the "vanishing Indian" to white settler assertions of nativism that claim the Indians had vanished despite their continued presence. She argues that this mythmaking became a primary means by which white Americans asserted their own modernity while denying it to Indian peoples. This erasure and subsequent memorialization of Indigenous Peoples served the settler colonial goal of refuting Indian claims to land and rights.[13]

The term "Aboriginal" has also been in use for hundreds of years (as early as the seventeenth century) as an adjective to describe the Native inhabitants of areas that were explored and colonized by Europeans. The *Oxford English Dictionary* defines "Aboriginal" as "pertaining to things or land or persons or members of a race, which are Indigenous *to,* or first occupied, a specified territory" (emphasis in the original). The noun "Aborigine" was in widespread use in areas colonized by Europeans during the mid-nineteenth century. It derives from the sixteenth-century plural "Aborigines" (original inhabitants), who in Western classical times referred to the people of Italy and Greece. It comes from the Latin phrase *ab origine* (from the beginning).

This political struggle over terminology is steeped in history and deep visceral convictions regarding these legacies. Within conventional Western epistemological frames, indigeneity itself has historically been viewed as incommensurate with civic life because it is already defined as premodern and uncivilized. Westerners historically viewed Indigenous Peoples as lawless, with no (advanced) civilization, no religion or government, so they largely considered Indigenous Peoples to be living in a state of nature—the "natural condition" of humankind before the rule of human-made law and established government. The concept of the state of nature undergirds the social contract theory that is the basis of (Western) sovereignty and civil society. The notion of the social contract implies that the people give up some rights to a government or other authority in order to maintain social order; it is the centerpiece of the idea that legitimate state authority must be derived from the consent of the governed. In most versions of social contract theory, there are no rights in the state of nature, only freedoms. It is the contract that creates rights and restrictions relating to the individual's "natural rights" based on the Enlightenment principles of citizenship and inalienable rights. From this common starting point, the various philosophers of social contract theory attempt to explain, in different ways, why it is in an individual's rational self-interest voluntarily to give up freedom in the state of nature in order to obtain the benefits of political order. Thus social contract theorists have argued that the formation of the democratic state within modernity was enabled by a contract among humans to decide to live together, govern, and make laws for such living.

Drawing on Carole Pateman's work on the "gender contract," Charles Mills engages in a deep criticism of classic Western social contract theory and argues that the "social contract" has shaped a system of global European domination and is indeed a "racial contract" because it originally stipulated who counted as full moral and political persons. The "universal" liberal individuals—the agents of social contract theory—were European men who collectively identified as white and fully human. Mills traces this view from the time of the New World conquest and subsequent colonialism to theorize the expropriation contract appropriate to the white settler state.[14] Building on his work, Robert Nichols argues that social contract theory operates in terms of a "settler contract" and functions to deny the claims of Indigenous Peoples.[15] He shows how "social contract theory has served as a primary justificatory device for the establishment of another axis of oppression and domination: an expropriation and usurpation contract whereby the constitution of the ideal civil society is premised upon the extermination of Indigenous peoples or the displacement of them from their lands."[16]

In the U.S. context, as Kevin Bruyneel argues, one of the defining elements of American colonial rule is the fastening of Indigenous Peoples to the concept of "colonial time" by locating them "out of time," where they are not allowed modernity. This "shackling indigenous identity to an archaic form" upholds the concept of authentic Indigenous Peoples always being already primitive/static (positioned to continuously struggle for recognition of their humanity), while the colonizer is always characterized as civilized/advanced, thereby rationalizing domination of Indigenous Peoples as a form of "progress."[17] It is this enduring notion of the "savage" that continues to be used by states in their attempt to justify political subordination, such as the "domestic dependent nation" status subject to U.S. plenary power in the case of federally recognized tribal nations.

Federal Recognition of Native Hawaiians

Proponents of the U.S. federal recognition have continuously advanced three key legal developments for their argument: the ruling in *Rice v. Cayetano* by the Supreme Court of the United States (SCOTUS), which was repeatedly misconstrued regarding how the opinion discussed the political status of the Hawaiian people; the lawsuits that followed in the aftermath of the ruling; and a long line of legislation passed by the U.S. Congress that already recognizes Native Hawaiians as an Indigenous People, such as the 1993 Apology Resolution (Public Law 103-150) regarding the 1893 overthrow, which calls for "reconciliation." The first bill originated in March 2000 when Senator Akaka and the rest of the Hawaiʻi congressional delegation formed the Task Force on Native Hawaiian Issues. This was just one month after the ruling in *Rice* that struck down Native Hawaiian–only voting for Office of Hawaiian Affairs trustee elections as unconstitutional. The ruling in this case set off a flurry of additional lawsuits attacking the constitutionality of federal and state funds earmarked for the Native Hawaiian people for health, education, housing, and elderly care.[18] The immediate stated goal of the task force was to clarify the political relationship between Hawaiians and the United States through the U.S. Congress.

The bill did not survive committee when Akaka first introduced it and has been defeated by Republican opposition in each subsequent Congress.[19] The legislation also spanned the terms of three Hawaiʻi governors, Ben Cayetano (Democrat), Linda Lingle (Republican), and Neil Abercrombie (Democrat). In the early period when the legislation was first conceived, the Council for Native Hawaiian Advancement became a key driving force in support of the federal bill along with the two primary Hawaiʻi state agencies, the Office of Hawaiian Affairs and the Department of Hawaiian Home Lands. Hawaiʻi's congressional delegates attempted to push through the bill despite massive opposition to it among the Kanaka Maoli people, who are affected by it first and foremost. In 2000 the delegation held a five-day hearing on the bill—the only one since its inception. Despite overwhelming opposition to the bill from two distinct camps (pro-independence nationals and pro-American conservatives), the delegation reported quite the opposite to Congress.

Conservatives' refusal to support the measure became more pronounced when the administration of George W. Bush took a position against the legislation.[20] Although the legislation gained committee approval in both the House and Senate throughout that period, it remained stalled when it came to a floor debate. Despite multiple revisions and reintroductions of new drafts aimed at satisfying Department of Interior concerns and appeasing Republican critics who called the proposal a plan for "race-based government," the legislation never progressed to a Senate vote. The new administration of President Barack Obama in 2008 firmly supported the bill, but it was ultimately rejected due to opposition from the Hawai'i state government under the Lingle administration after it had been revised to acknowledge that the sovereignty of the NHGE would be recognized as "inherent" rather than delegated by the 50th state.

Conservatives were not the only ones who opposed the legislation. Many Kanaka Maoli committed to the broader national claim also actively opposed it. From the oppositional testimony at the hearings in 2000 throughout the decade that followed there were numerous protests, petitions, and online organizing to stop the legislation. Many opposed to the Akaka bill also cited the U.S. Apology Resolution, but they did so to affirm the case for Hawaiian independence, not federal recognition of a domestic dependent sovereignty. This stance was bolstered by the Apology Resolution itself, which maintains that "the Indigenous Hawaiian people never directly relinquished their claims to their inherent sovereignty as a people or over their national lands to the United States, either through their monarchy or through a plebiscite or referendum."[21] Organizations opposed to federal recognition include those that form the Hawaiian Independence Action Alliance: the Pro-Kanaka Maoli Independence Working Group, Ka Pakaukau, Komike Tribunal, Hui o Na Ike, Ka Lei Maile Ali'i Hawaiian Civic Club, Koani Foundation, 'Ohana Koa, Nuclear Free and Independent Pacific (Hawai'i), Spiritual Nation of Kū-Hui Ea Council of Sovereigns, Living Nation, Settlers for Hawaiian Independence, and Movement for Aloha No Ka 'Āina. The activist group Hui Pū was formed in July 2005 specifically to defeat the bill. Although the founders of Hui Pū have noted that it is not an independence group, the work of the prominent activists who drove the multiple forms of resistance certainly had the effect of keeping the claim of independent statehood on the table within the broader Hawai'i community.[22]

Kingdom nationalists have been bolstered by this activism. For independence activists and other supporters who advocate for the restoration

FIGURE 1.2. Signs from a 2009 antistatehood march protesting the Akaka bill and calling attention to the U.S. Apology Resolution. Photo courtesy of Kyle Kajihiro.

of a Hawaiian nation under international law, the entire bill is seen as a farce. The historical harm that the United States first did in Hawaiʻi in the 1893 overthrow brought down not a Native Hawaiian governing entity but the Hawaiian Kingdom government, an independent state including both Kanaka Maoli and non-Indigenous subjects. Consequently, the Kanaka Maoli people and others have accumulated fundamental political and other claims against the United States under international law since that time. Those who support Hawaiʻi's independence have pointed out problems with the proposal because of the limitations on recognizing Hawaiian sovereignty as delineated by the model imposed on Indian tribes.

A brief overview of the distinct status of tribal nations bounded by the United States seems in order here. As recognized sovereigns, tribal nations are subject to the U.S. Trust Doctrine, which is a "unique legal relationship" with the U.S. federal government.[23] The U.S. Constitution acknowledges the separation of tribal governments and their citizens from other U.S. citizens, mentioning "Indian tribes" in two places: article 1, section 2, clause 3, and article 1, section 8.[24] The first constitutional phrase specifically makes a distinction between Indian tribes with no relationship to the states and individual Indians considered to be regular citizens over whom the states might extend tax liabilities.[25] The second phrase states that "Congress shall have the power to regulate commerce with foreign nations and among the several states, and with the Indian tribes," which acknowledges them as distinct but not the same as foreign nations.[26] The U.S. Supreme Court has interpreted the commerce clause to assert that the U.S. government has plenary power over tribal nations, which is exclusive and preemptive (see the discussion below). With regard to what the U.S. government outlines as the "inherent powers of tribal self-government," federal policy stipulates:

> Tribes possess all powers of self-government except those relinquished under treaty with the United States, those that Congress has expressly extinguished, and those that federal courts have ruled are subject to existing federal law or are inconsistent with overriding national policies. Tribes, therefore, possess the right to form their own governments; to make and enforce laws, both civil and criminal; to tax; to establish and determine membership . . . ; to license and regulate activities *within their jurisdiction*. . . . Limitations on inherent tribal powers of self-government are few, but do include the same limitations applicable to states, e.g., neither tribes nor states have the power to make war, engage in foreign relations, or print and issue currency.[27]

Although tribal powers are extensive, a U.S. domestic legal framework restricts this form of self-determination.

Until late 2012 the last major attention to the Akaka legislation consisted of two substantially different versions of the bill in 2009: S. 1011 and H.R. 2314.[28] There was little activity on either until December 17, 2009, when the Senate Committee on Indian Affairs passed a newly amended proposal with changes developed by the Department of Justice in conjunction with the state Office of Hawaiian Affairs, the Council for Native Hawaiian Advancement, and the Native Hawaiian Bar Association. These revisions were meant to improve the bill, which had been whittled down to appease conservative opposition. U.S. congressman Neil Abercrombie had tried to pass the same heavily amended version of H.R. 2314 in the House Committee on Natural Resources the day before, but last-minute letters of opposition from Hawai'i's Republican governor, Linda Lingle, prompted him to set aside the proposed revisions. So the committee passed the unamended version.

A crucial difference was that the House version suggested that the NHGE would derive its powers solely from federal delegation, whereas the Senate version specifically acknowledged that a Native Hawaiian governing entity's powers would derive from the inherent sovereignty of the Indigenous Hawaiian people. This conflict exposed the entire proposal for what it was—a way to undercut the more robust sovereignty claim. Written into the bill was a stipulation that the future NHGE would be excluded from certain laws pertaining to federally recognized Indian tribes, which happen to be the same laws that greatly benefit tribal nations. The "Applicability of Certain Federal Laws" section noted that any future Hawaiian nation within the framework of federal law would not be allowed to have the secretary of the interior take land into trust. This is important because under U.S. law only land held in trust by the federal government on behalf of tribal nations may be used as part of their sovereign land base where they can assert jurisdiction. Most notably, this section of the House bill also states: "Nothing in this Act alters the civil or criminal jurisdiction of the United States or the State of Hawaii over lands and persons within the State of Hawaii." The Senate version (S. 1011) did initially not make the same stipulation but still stated that the NHGE, the federal government, and the state "may enter into negotiations" that are "designed to lead to an agreement" addressing land, governmental authority, and the exercise of criminal and civil jurisdiction.

The two bills had other differences, but both bills allowed the Hawai'i state government a seat at the negotiating table with both the federal government and the NHGE from the start, which sets this legislation apart from the dominant model of federal recognition legislation and processes.[29] It also is important to note that in both versions the negotiations that would follow passage of the bill concern land, governmental authority, and the exercise of criminal and civil jurisdiction. None of these—not land, not jurisdiction, not assets, and not governmental power—were guaranteed in the bill. They would be negotiated by representatives of the future NHGE in a sit-down with federal and state representatives, who would not have anything resembling an equal footing, given U.S. congressional plenary power. This also sets the legislation apart from federal recognition of tribal nations in general, as state administrations are typically excluded from the nation-to-nation negotiations. Although the weaker of the two versions passed in both the House and Senate committees, the legislation was stalled and state officials tried a new approach—seeking Hawai'i state recognition once Abercrombie took office as governor.

On July 6, 2011, Abercrombie signed S.B. 1520 into law, known as Act 195—the "First Nation Government Bill"—to provide state authorization of a process for the creation of an NHGE.[30] The legislation empowered the governor to appoint a five-member Native Hawaiian Roll Commission to lay the foundation for participation in a new governing body. Abercrombie declared: "This is an important step for the future of Native Hawaiian self-determination and the ability for Native Hawaiians to decide their own future. . . . This Commission will put together the roll of qualified and interested Native Hawaiians who want to help determine the course of Hawai'i's indigenous people."[31] Activists at the event where Abercrombie signed the bill into law protested the supposed surrender of the Hawaiian Nation to the U.S. government, as the trustees of the Office of Hawaiian Affairs and other state agents poised for transition to the new "First Nation."[32]

Among those who attended the signing ceremony for the bill were groups representing the ali'i (chiefly) societies and trusts, OHA trustees, Native Hawaiian civic clubs, and state lawmakers. Kanaka Maoli and other Hawaiian nationals protested the event, holding signs with declarations such as "Hawaiian Independence," "'A'ole Pono, 'A'ole Pau" (Not Just, Not Finished), "Our Nation, Not Your State," and "Hell no, we won't enroll"—followed by "and neither would the Queen." In many ways that historical moment marked the depressed culmination of a decade of resistance to the Akaka bill and state cooptation of the Hawaiian sovereignty struggle.

Abercrombie appointed former governor John Waihe'e to lead the new commission to prepare and maintain a roll of qualified Native Hawaiians who would work toward the "reorganization."[33] On July 20, 2012, the effort was named Kana'iolowalu, which entails an online registry to create a base roll of Native Hawaiians who will then be eligible to participate in the formation of a governing entity.[34] This process is arguably the first documented evidence of collective acquiescence to the U.S. government or its subsidiaries. Hence the question of whether there will be sustained opposition to this state-driven initiative in order to protect the outstanding Hawaiian sovereignty claim is pressing.

On March 30, 2011, just three months before passage of the "First Nation Government Bill," Senator Akaka introduced S. 675 to the Senate Committee on Indian Affairs.[35] On April 7, 2011, the Senate Committee favorably reported the bill without amendment but on September 13, 2012, ordered it to be reported favorably with an amendment in the nature of a substitute. The amendments were substantial and reflect the passage of Act 195 in the Hawai'i state legislature. The structural framework of the proposal subordinates Hawai'i's rightful status as an independent nation by admitting only the right of limited self-determination: "Congress possesses and exercises the constitutional authority to address Native Hawaiian conditions; the

Native Hawaiian people have the right to autonomy in internal affairs."[36] These amendments finally looked as if the proposal would allow for parity with federally recognized tribal nations. The fallout in 2009, however, indicates that the very question of acknowledging that the Native Hawaiian governing entity has inherent sovereignty was a severe sticking point that ruptured the bipartisan support from the Hawaiʻi state executive branch and congressional delegation during Governor Lingle's term.

On December 17, 2012, an amended version (S. 675) was placed on the Senate Legislative Calendar under General Orders. This last version of the federal legislation, titled "The Native Hawaiian Government Reorganization Act of 2012," was "a bill to express the policy of the United States regarding the United States relationship with Native Hawaiians and to provide a process for the recognition by the United States of the Native Hawaiian governing entity." As the 113th Congress opened, Democrats controlled the Senate and Republicans controlled the House. The House Committee on Natural Resources never moved the proposal further, and it seemed to stop entirely.

Meanwhile the Kanaʻiolowalu initiative at the local level moved along full steam to develop a base roll of Native Hawaiians, a registry of individuals to sign on to take part in the formation of the "First Nation" within the state process. According to the Office of Hawaiian Affairs, registrants would "then be eligible to participate in the formation of a sovereign government, and also gather signatures from Hawaiians and non-Hawaiians on petitions declaring support for the reunification of Native Hawaiians and recognition of Native Hawaiians' un-relinquished sovereignty." The initial goal of those driving the initiative was to register 200,000 Native Hawaiians. Kanaʻiolowalu was originally set to run through July 19, 2013, but on March 17, 2014, the deadline was extended to May 1, 2014, in order to gather more names. Once the roll was finished, the commission published the registry to start the process of holding a convention to organize a Hawaiian governing entity.[37] Many defenders of the Kanaʻiolowalu process insist that the creation of a "Native Hawaiian Roll" would not preclude a bid for restoring independence and that they are committed to an "inclusive process." But they do not take into account that the Hawaiʻi state (the "50th state") is not in the business of passing laws that enable anything outside of the U.S. federal framework. Act 195 was not about crafting a process that allows for anything other than a state-recognized "First Nation" that will form in anticipation of passage of the Akaka bill. This is a structural problem; it is a state process in the service of federal recognition.

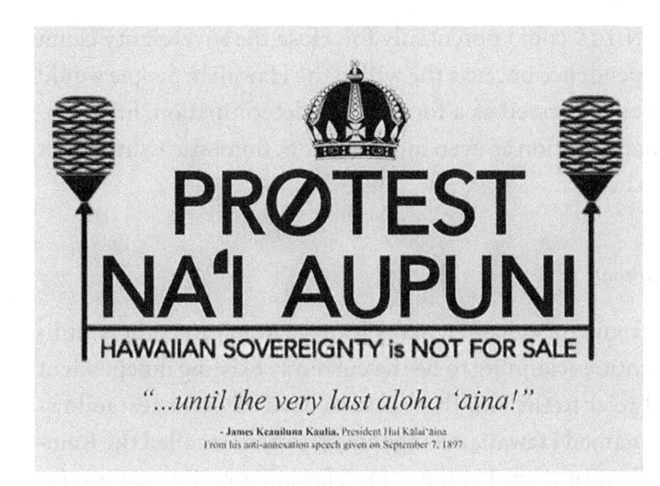

FIGURE 1.3. A graphic protest sign opposing Naʻi Aupuni that circulated on social media.

Naʻi Aupuni was established simultaneously with the DOI announcement of the new administrative procedure and criteria for Native Hawaiians in September 2015. The Office of Hawaiian Affairs created this entity in 2015 to assist in the process of establishing a Native Hawaiian governing entity utilizing the roll created by Kanaʻiolowalu. Naʻi Aupuni attempted to hold an election in December 2015 but suspended it due to legal challenges and a slim list of participants. The group subsequently held a constitutional convention in February 2016 but the following month announced that it would not be conducting a ratification vote, deciding that it was best to defer until there was a "broad-based group" to ratify a constitution for any future Native Hawaiian governing entity.[38]

Still, on September 23, 2016, the DOI announced the final rule "to create a pathway for reestablishing a formal government-to-government relationship with the Native Hawaiian community," which sets out "an administrative procedure and criteria that the U.S. Secretary of the Interior would use if the Native Hawaiian community forms a unified government that then seeks a formal government-to-government relationship with the United States."[39]

This process, like the earlier legislation, limits Hawaiian self-determination due to the fundamental legal distinction between "Indian tribes" and "foreign nations" under the U.S. Constitution and federal law with specific regard to the unextinguished sovereignty of the Hawaiian Kingdom. These state-driven efforts appear to be preemptive attempts to squash outstanding sovereignty claims that were not legally extinguished when Hawaiʻi was admitted as the 50th state of the American "union." Moreover, federal recognition of an NHGE could potentially foreclose the sovereignty claim for Hawaiian independence because the will of the Hawaiian people would appear to have been expressed as a form of self-determination, firmly locating the Hawaiian question as even more of a U.S. domestic issue than it currently seems to be.

Asserting Kingdomhood

As noted in the introductory chapter, many Kanaka Maoli and others affiliate with political entities claiming to be the currently existing independent state itself. Here I refer to the two that seem to have the strongest following. One is simply named Hawaiian Kingdom; the other is called the Reinstated Hawaiian Government. Unlike some Hawaiian nationalist groups who are actually resisting the federal legislation, those affiliated with these kingdom initiatives tend simply to disregard the bill without any direct action. They see its potential effect on the kingdom as farcical because it stems from a foreign government—the United States. They also reject UN laws as a remedy for restoring Hawaiian nationhood. Thus they refuse to engage both the protocols for decolonization (because they make a distinction between a colonial territory and an occupied state) and any form of Indigenous rights (because Indigenous Peoples' rights under international law are distinct from the rights of states). Instead they rely on the Hague Regulations' laws of occupation (1899 and 1907), international treaties negotiated at the First and Second Peace Conferences at the Hague, which were among the first formal statements of the laws of war and war crimes in the nascent body of secular international law.

Perhaps surprisingly, much like neoconservatives who opposed the Akaka bill, many kingdom restoration proponents have also dismissed Indigenous self-government as "race-based" government by casting the Hawaiian Kingdom as a "color-blind" (and therefore more modern) government.[40] This is because non–Kanaka Maoli were also included as kingdom subjects. Here too kingdom proponents engaging in this problematic critique rarely acknowledge that Indigenous governing systems by and large have always managed to incorporate outsiders too, even if they do not do it under the auspices of a state government. Moreover, they seem to have little understanding that contemporary tribes with U.S. federal recognition may limit their citizenry to those who are of their particular Indigenous ancestry because the U.S. government maintains that its trust obligation is limited to those who have ancestors from any given Native nation and not non-

Natives.[41] But this discourse is also problematic in the way it naturalizes U.S. domination over tribal governments. Speaking to the debates about the Akaka bill among Hawaiians, Jodi Byrd considers "how a paradigmatic 'Indianness' has functioned within resistances, Indigenous and haole, radical and conservative, to that legislation." It "serves to erase the transnational distinctions of all the peoples who collapse under its sign and as it is reified, the sign itself—which now bears indigeneity, sovereignty, and racial minority—becomes the site of contention as Indigenous and occupied peoples throughout the empire struggle to resist U.S. hegemony. In the process, and precisely because 'Indianness' serves as the ontological scaffolding for colonialist domination, anticolonial resistances . . . risk reflecting and reinscribing the very colonialist discourses used to possess and contain American Indian nations back onto the abjected 'Indian' yet again."[42] Here we see that the normalization of U.S. subordination of Indian tribes positions them as having resigned their political aspirations.

Kingdom nationalists also tend to avoid an analysis of colonialism (let alone settler colonialism as a structural condition), because they presume that to talk about colonialism in Hawai'i is to legitimate Hawai'i as a former U.S. colony rather than an occupied state and thus see the two in binary form. Since the U.S. Congress unilaterally annexed Hawai'i through its own domestic law, supporters of deoccupation argue that the kingdom was never really annexed and its territory continues to be merely occupied by the United States. They do not acknowledge that forms of American colonialism arguably began long before the formal takeover of Hawai'i by the United States, let alone that the assimilationist policies imposed on Kanaka Maoli throughout the twentieth century are colonial in nature. Because the kingdom had already secured recognition of its independence in 1842, deoccupation supporters declare their status as kingdom nationals of a nation that has already "achieved" self-determination. Unfortunately, this political discourse of achievement has been framed in a way that is demeaning to Indigenous Peoples who have not formed states (for a variety of reasons both historical and political) and includes a reluctance to emphasize oppression specific to Kanaka Maoli living under U.S. domination.

Yet the United States held Hawai'i as a colony after annexation in 1898. In a list of non-self-governing territories compiled by the United Nations in 1946, the U.S. government reported Hawai'i. Although Hawai'i was on that list and therefore entitled to a process of self-determination to decolonize, the U.S. government predetermined statehood as its status by treating its political status as an internal domestic issue. The 1959 ballot in which the

FIGURE 1.4. The Hawaiian flag (used by both the Hawaiian Kingdom and Hawai'i as the 50th state) demanding the end of U.S. occupation, from a 2009 antistatehood march. Photo courtesy of Kyle Kajihiro.

people of Hawai'i voted to become a state of the union included only two options: integration and remaining a U.S. colonial territory.[43] Among those allowed to take part in the vote, settlers as well as military personnel outnumbered Hawaiians. By citing the internal territorial vote, the U.S. State Department then misinformed the UN, which in turn considered the people of Hawai'i to have freely exercised their self-determination and chosen to incorporate with the United States.[44]

Although international law provides no single decisive definition of colonialism, the UN Declaration on Colonialism "indicates that a situation may be classified as colonial when the acts of a State have the cumulative outcome that it annexes or otherwise unlawfully retains control over territory and thus aims permanently to deny its Indigenous population the exercise of its right to self-determination."[45] This historical lineage of the world standard on colonialism is worth revisiting, even though the UN process of decolonization has historically excluded Indigenous Peoples who were enduring settler colonial situations. Part of this is due to the "saltwater thesis": to avoid having to deal with the Native American question in relation to self-determination, the U.S. government pushed to codify eligibility for decolonization based the presence of "blue water" between the colony and the colonizing country.[46]

By UN criteria established the following year, the ballot would have included independence and free association as choices.[47] On December 14, 1960, the UN General Assembly issued a Declaration on the Granting of Independence to Colonial Countries and Peoples, Resolution 1514 (XV).[48] In 1960 the General Assembly also approved Resolution 1541 (XV), which defined free association with an independent state, integration into an independent state, or independence as the three legitimate options of full self-government.[49] Resolution 1541 refers to territories that are "geographically separate and distinct ethnically and/or culturally" without specifying what "geographically separate" must entail.[50] Nonetheless, this chapter of the resolution has been accepted as applicable mainly to overseas colonization. At stake is the prohibition of the Indigenous claims to the same self-determination granted to "blue water" colonies by Resolution 1514, "which can logically lead to independence." Hence the phrase "all peoples have the right of self-determination" has been mainly applied to inhabitants of *territories* destined for decolonization, rather than Indigenous Peoples.[51] For example, in 1999 the people of East Timor finally had the opportunity to vote on their political status through a UN-sponsored plebiscite and voted for full decolonization from Indonesia. Although the East Timorese are an Indigenous People, it was the status of East Timor as a colony of Indonesia since 1975 (and before that of Portugal since the mid-sixteenth century) that qualified them for the right to full self-determination, not their status as an Indigenous People per se.

The United Nations recognized Hawai'i as a non-self-governing territory from 1946 to 1959, during which Kanaka Maoli and others were eligible for full decolonization. Some argue, therefore, that the most straightforward legal argument in support of independence is the decolonization model. Under the leadership of the late Kekuni Blaisdell, the Pro–Kanaka Maoli Independence Working Group, Ka Pakaukau, and the Komike Tribunal have consistently worked to educate the Hawaiian community about the aborted option under the decolonization model and have advocated that contemporary Kanaka Maoli should be entitled to a plebiscite to exercise their right to self-determination and determine what model of governance they would prefer. Many sovereignty activists who advocate for kingdom restoration, however, reject this strategy of reinscription on the list of non-self-governing territories. They make a distinction between a colonial territory (e.g., Guam, a U.S. territory) and an occupied state (the Hawaiian Kingdom).

As an alternative, those organized to restore the Hawaiian Kingdom Government advocate for deoccupation rather than decolonization and rely on the international laws of occupation by retroactively drawing on regulations created during Hague Convention IV in 1907, specifically article 43.[52] Accordingly, those who identify as kingdom subjects demand that the Hague Regulations, and not the UN Charter providing for self-determination, guide the recovery process. Because the kingdom had already secured recognition of its independence in 1842, deoccupation supporters declare their status as kingdom nationals of a nation that has already "achieved" self-determination. The U.S. Congress unilaterally annexed Hawai'i through its own domestic law, so supporters of deoccupation argue that the kingdom was never really annexed and its territory is merely occupied by the United States.

Importantly, Sai argues that the United States never acquired Hawai'i (which is an attribute of its status as a sovereign state) and that the laws of occupation (Hague Conventions) contain a presumption of continuity of independence and not extinguishment. Colonization presumes that independence is in the colonizing state until transferred to the decolonized territory according to the principle of self-determination, which is the basis of article 73 of the UN Charter and the Committee on Decolonization. In theory, both decolonization and deoccupation allow for independence, while the current UN Declaration on the Rights of Indigenous Peoples falls short of allowing that option (even as it can advance and support the world's Indigenous Peoples in the struggle for recognition of distinct rights), including Kanaka Maoli in Hawai'i. But Sai works from the (legal) assumption that the Hawaiian Kingdom continues to exist as a sovereign and independent state, so the question is how nationals exercise that sovereignty, not how to reestablish what has already been founded.[53]

Any discussions of decolonization are too quickly dismissed in legal terms. The problem then becomes a battle over international law, rather than one focused on the white supremacist practices and policies that are part and parcel of the colonial subordination of Kanaka Maoli, whether Hawai'i is considered to be a former U.S. colony or not. Certainly, the myriad oppressions faced by the vast majority of Kanaka Maoli are linked to Indigenous land dispossession and colonial-induced poverty.[54]

The formation of Hawai'i as the 50th state of the union, of course, has been used to silence the possibility of decolonization from the United States. Here it seems that the blue-water doctrine holds no effective meaning even though Hawai'i is over 2,000 miles from California and nearly 5,000 miles from Washington, D.C. Therein lies the paradox. While Hawai'i was a "distant" U.S. colony during the first half of the twentieth century, it was an independent state before the U.S. takeover, which complicates conventional and legal notions of "self-determination" in discussions of most Indigenous Peoples. Yet it is clear that Kanaka Maoli are also an Indigenous People.

Indigenous Peoples and International Law

As a culturally contested category, "Indigenous" has weighty political and legal questions and implications—and no one definition. Although the UN system has not adopted any official definition of the term,[55] the most frequently cited definition appeared in the 1986 report of UN special rapporteur José Martínez Cobo titled "Study of the Problem of Discrimination against Indigenous Populations." He defines Indigenous Peoples as "those which, having a historical continuity with pre-invasion and pre-colonial societies that have developed on their territories, consider themselves distinct from other sectors of the societies now prevailing in those territories, or parts of them." Cobo explains that "they form at present non-dominant sectors of society and are determined to preserve, develop and transmit to future generations their ancestral territories, and their ethnic traditional medicines and health practices, including the right to protection of vital medicinal plants, animals and minerals."[56] Indigenous Peoples are immensely diverse in terms of language, political structure, gender ideologies/practices, beliefs, and culture. For example, some are matrilineal, while others are patrilineal, and still others are bilateral in the way they trace kinship. Indigenous Peoples generally tend to be egalitarian in terms of gender relations in governance, though some privilege men over women and vice versa—and among many communities there are more than two genders. Besides cultural specificity, they have a wide range of different relations to the regions and nations within which (or in relation to which) they live.

In considering "Who Is Indigenous?" the UN Permanent Forum on Indigenous Issues (UNPFII) produced a fact sheet in 2005, which answered the question in this way:

> It is estimated that there are more than 370 million indigenous people spread across 70 countries worldwide. Practicing unique traditions, they retain social, cultural, economic and political characteristics that are distinct from those of the dominant societies in which they live. Spread across the world from the Arctic to the South Pacific, they are the descendants—according to a common definition—of those who inhabited a country or a geographical region at the time when people of different cultures or ethnic origins arrived. The new arrivals later became dominant through conquest, occupation, settlement or other means.[57]

In identifying (rather than classifying) those who are Indigenous, the UNPFII considers several factors, including: (1) self identification as Indigenous Peoples at the individual level and being accepted by the community as a member; (2) historical continuity with precolonial and/or presettler societies; (3) a strong link to territories and surrounding natural resources; (4) distinct social, economic, or political systems; (5) distinct language, culture, and beliefs; (6) forming nondominant groups of society; (7) resolving to maintain and reproduce their ancestral environments and systems as distinctive peoples and communities.

In terms of inclusivity and identity, the UNPFII suggests that "the most fruitful approach is to identify, rather than define indigenous peoples" based on the fundamental criterion of self-identification.[58] The principle of self-identification has been a hard fought battle, because one of the most common forms of racism against Indigenous Peoples in modern times is the pernicious falsehood that they are entirely extinct or diluted due to racial and/or cultural mixing. Indigenous Peoples are subject to a standard of authenticity based on a colonial logic of biological and cultural purity—notions undergirded by the fields of physical anthropology (throughout the nineteenth and early twentieth centuries), and cultural anthropology (during the late nineteenth and early to mid-twentieth centuries) and eugenics (in the early twentieth century).[59]

In the twenty-first century Western states continue to impose this notion of the "premodern" savage as a mechanism of control in their negotiation involving the legal status and land rights of Indigenous Peoples. Within the world community there is no consensus that Indigenous Peoples have the right to full self-determination under international law—an option that would allow for the development of nation-states independent from their former colonizers like the postcolonial Third World. This limitation reflects the long-term battle over whether Indigenous Peoples should be considered "peoples" in the context of the UN Charter of 1945, the UN Declaration Regarding Non-Self-Governing Peoples in article 73, and UN Resolution 1514: "all peoples have the right to self-determination; by virtue of that right, they freely determine their political status and freely pursue their economic, social, and cultural development."[60]

On September 13, 2007, the UN General Assembly adopted the Declaration on the Rights of Indigenous Peoples, which is the result of nearly three decades of activism. It is the most comprehensive international human rights document addressing the rights of the Indigenous Peoples all over the world. They have worked for decades to ensure that their *preexisting* human rights are recognized and upheld by global nation-states, especially since the domestic laws in most settler states have not protected their ability to assert their self-determination. Key issues of struggle include the right of ownership and control of territory and resources, protection of sacred sites and lands, self-governance, and decision-making authority vis-à-vis the dominant population. Central to all of these is the question of Indigenous Peoples' right to self-determination under international law. Because the basic criteria defining colonies under international law include foreign domination and geographical separation from the colonizer, Indigenous Peoples until now have been at a disadvantage in terms of the application of decolonization protocols, an issue heatedly debated throughout the world community.

Regarding the question of self-determination for Indigenous Peoples, the frequently cited report by Cobo states: "Self-determination constitutes the exercise of free choice by indigenous peoples, who must, to a large extent, create the specific content of this principle, in both its internal and external expressions, which does not necessarily include the right to secede from the State in which they may live and to set themselves up as sovereign entities. *This right may in fact be expressed in various forms of autonomy within the State.*"[61]

The right to full self-determination would include an option to allow for the development of nation-states independent from their former colonizers, as has been available to the postcolonial Third World. But for Indigenous Peoples, that right is limited only to internal self-determination within the existing nation-states in which they are included. The use of the term "peoples" (plural), which signifies legal rights under international law over and above the term "people" (singular), has been the most contentious part of this debate. This form of discrimination can be traced to the Law of Nations, which institutionalized the international legal discrimination against Indigenous Peoples.[62]

The establishment of the Working Group on Indigenous Populations (WGIIP) in 1982, under the UN Economic and Social Council, led the effort to draft a specific instrument under international law that would protect Indigenous Peoples worldwide.[63] Initially the WGIIP submitted a first draft declaration on the rights of Indigenous Peoples to the Sub-Commission on Prevention of Discrimination and Protection of Minorities, which was eventually approved in 1994.[64] The draft was then sent to the UN Commission on Human Rights for further discussion. The declaration was stalled for many years due to states' concerns about some of its core statements—namely, the right to self-determination of Indigenous Peoples and the control over natural resources existing on their traditional lands. In 1995 an open-ended intersessional working group was formed with the understanding that some version of the declaration would be adopted by the General Assembly within the International Decade of the World's Indigenous Peoples (1995–2004). The UN Commission on Human Rights extended the mandate of the working group into the Second International Decade of the World's Indigenous Peoples (2005–2015) and also urged the working group to present a final draft declaration on the rights of Indigenous People for UN adoption.

The Human Rights Council of the United Nations was the first to adopt the declaration in June 2006 and offered a recommendation that it be adopted by the General Assembly.[65] The vote of the General Assembly was 143 in favor of the declaration, 4 against, and 11 abstentions. Notably, the 4 votes against the adoption came from white settler states, all with a strong Indigenous presence in terms of political resistance to First World domination: Australia, Canada, New Zealand, and the United States. Many attribute the opposition of these states to governmental fears of secession and independence by Indigenous Peoples, which potentially threaten to disrupt the contiguous land mass of the settler nation-states that encompass them.

Regarding the issue of self-determination, however, the newly adopted declaration is ambiguous. On the one hand, article 3 states: "Indigenous peoples have the right of self-determination. By virtue of that right they freely determine their political status and freely pursue their economic, social, and cultural development." On the other hand, article 46 (the last) states: "Nothing in this Declaration may be . . . construed as authorizing or encouraging any action which would dismember or impair, totally or in part, the territorial integrity or political unity of sovereign and independent States." For example, the U.S. government would surely be threatened if the Navajo Nation were to seek independence, given that the asserted boundaries of the states of New Mexico, Colorado, Utah, and Arizona fall within the traditional Diné territory. Given these two seemingly contradictory articles, how are we to understand what the right to self-determination means and to what extent it can be realized by Indigenous Peoples?

Since Kanaka Maoli constitute the vast majority of those able to claim status as kingdom subjects, activists supporting an independent Hawaiian state could invoke the question of territorial integrity.[66] The principle of territorial integrity is usually operative vis-à-vis other states (one state is prohibited from invading and accessing another state's territory, although this certainly happens nonetheless). Thus article 46 can be used as a political leverage point to advocate for the territorial integrity of the Hawaiian Kingdom as a state. The U.S. government violated the Hawaiian state's territorial integrity when it supported an illegal overthrow and unilaterally annexed Hawaiʻi in contravention to U.S. federal law, its treaties with the Hawaiian Kingdom, and international law operative at the time. Hence de-occupation supporters demand that the U.S. government withdraw from Hawaiʻi. Still, the U.S. government casts independence claims as attempts at "secession"—a complete misnomer.

Before the passage of the declaration, many governmental officials assumed that the right of Indigenous groups to self-determination would lead to secession. This assumption was used to deny Indigenous Peoples this right. Even members of the working group and the UN special rapporteurs have shared this assumption. Maivân Clech Lâm suggests that it is possible for Indigenous Peoples to exercise self-determination without threatening the territorial integrity and sovereignty of the surrounding state, especially since most have visions of becoming autonomous without becoming nation-states.[67] Instead, most seek mutually negotiated free association, a relationship in which newly recognized sovereignty states may associate with the nation that previously held them in order to access economic and military provisions.[68] Situations differ, depending on the state in question and its location.[69] These debates involve continuous contestation over the concepts of sovereignty, self-determination, self-government, and autonomy, which differ in meaning and intention within different contexts.[70] Today international lawyers who favor nation-states argue that Indigenous Peoples do not have the unqualified right to self-determination under international law, while those who favor Indigenous Peoples argue that they do.[71]

Conclusion

The complex history of Hawai'i and its multiple transitions—from governance by multiple island chiefs to sovereign kingdom to occupied colonial territory to the so-called 50th U.S. state—presents a unique challenge for thinking through the options for decolonization that are available to Kanaka Maoli and others who may identify as kingdom subjects. Given the layers of history and foreign intervention, there is no clear or easy way to resolve this problem, especially so long as the U.S. government continues to dominate nations across the globe with its political and military power. The history of both settler colonialism and occupation has generated a variety of options, but none seem sufficient in their current scope. Each has serious limitations.

The status of domestic dependent nation that would be granted Native Hawaiians through a process of federal recognition does not recognize the kingdom's history of sovereign existence or take into account the unjust occupation or overthrow of the monarch inflicted by the U.S. government. At the same time, relying on presently existing international law regarding Indigenous Peoples also has the limitation that in its present state such law still gives priority to existing nation-states and puts the preexisting rights of Indigenous Peoples as nations on a back burner. While this may change, for the moment neither of these options provides Kanaka Maoli or other kingdom heirs with the satisfaction of recognizing their previously independent status. Yet the deoccupation model, while taking account of this independent status, also denies settler colonialism in terms of the culture, language, and territory to which the Kanaka Maoli have been specifically subjected. Of course, the militaristic analysis of occupation seems easier than dealing with the complicated legacy of the United States treating Hawai'i as a colony after the 1898 annexation, along with the structural conditions of settler colonialism that continue through the present.[72]

In the end, therefore, no alternative seems to both recognize the kingdom's previous history of sovereignty and provide Kanaka Maoli with both cultural and territorial restitution. Furthermore, although Kanaka Maoli constituted the majority of kingdom subjects prior to the 1893 overthrow, both Kanaka Maoli and others claiming to be kingdom subjects are together in the demographic minority when it comes to Hawai'i's current population. This raises the (demographic) question of how the kingdom government would be restored if pursuing independence opened up as a feasible political goal, since minority-led governments are viewed as unacceptable within the contemporary world community.[73] In response to this problematic, the normative solution under international law that would have all citizens equally enfranchised without any differential status for Kanaka Maoli and other kingdom heirs raises the possibility that Kanaka Maoli would once again be a vulnerable Indigenous minority under an independent Hawaiian government and thus have to rely on invoking and mobilizing Indigenous rights, as is now the case.

This situation demands an approach that is not state-centered in order to explore fully what prestate Kanaka Maoli indigeneity has to offer in the way of rethinking the confines of state sovereignty as well as Indigenous sovereignty overdetermined by state formation. But doing so would create a serious predicament, as the U.S. government would be happy to see the independence movement relinquish its claims. The fact that the Akaka bill is a federal proposal that did not spring from Hawaiian communities themselves is very telling. Hence I am not advocating that Kanaka Maoli simply abandon the claim to independent statehood. The claim itself may not be viable or even desirable, but it is an important one with which to wage battle against U.S. empire. This is particularly true because the U.S. government—if ever pressed by the world community—cannot substantiate its claim to the Hawaiian Islands, as the archipelago was never ceded through treaty or conquest. This claim is meaningless, however, if there is nothing left to reclaim.

The ongoing work of demilitarization and environmental restoration (at the very least) is essential—not only to life in the islands but also indeed to the entire world. This is no exaggeration, because Hawai'i is home to the U.S. Pacific Command (USPACOM), whose "Area of Responsibility... encompasses about half the earth's surface, stretching from the waters off the west coast of the U.S. to the western border of India, and from Antarctica to the North Pole." This area also includes thirty-six nations that are collectively home to more than 50 percent of the world's population and three thousand different languages.[74] Needless to say, the destiny of Indigenous sovereignty in the Hawaiian case is inextricably tied to the fate of U.S. domination. In the epigraph to this chapter, Keppeler asserted (referring to the U.S. government): "It's their ballgame, it's their ballpark, they own the gloves, they own the bats, they own the balls, they own the uniforms! And if we wanna play in this ballpark, we have to follow these rules." There are multiple ballparks; it seems that in the Hawaiian case several games are going on at once.

The gain of federal recognition is touted as affording the Hawaiian people "special opportunities," but the reality suggests that this would amount to little more than securing eligibility to apply for certain grants. There is much to lose with the shift in political status for Kanaka Maoli, however, since participation in an NHGE—such as signing up for a Native Hawaiian roll to vote in its creation—would be the first documented acquiescence to U.S. authority in collective terms. As many have suggested, it is unwise to surrender the political claim simply because it looks unfeasible at this time, especially because the central reason it seems impossible is because of U.S. political domination over the globe.

I suggest that the emphasis should be on protecting the existing claims by opposing all U.S. governmental attempts to change Hawaiian legal status to further domesticate the question of sovereignty. The political project of restoring independent Hawaiian nationhood does not, in and of itself, solve the problem of decolonial resurgence of Indigenous practices. Part but not all of this predicament is demographic, as it raises the question of Kanaka Maoli distinction: if Kanaka Maoli are no longer asserting self-determination as a distinct people, then why bother? If there is no meaningful cultural and political differentiation, then all that is left is just another oppressive multiracial liberal state project that has a Hawaiian name on it, given that neither the deoccupation model nor the NHGE model accounts for this complicated history of settler colonialism or global U.S. political domination.

The contestation over indigeneity in relation to the two models of nationhood delineated above reveals several paradoxes. For one, the specific legal status of Native governing entities is structured by U.S. federal limitations that contain them as "domestic dependent sovereigns," even though the U.S. government acknowledges that their respective sovereignties are inherent. Nothing in that model challenges the U.S. settler state, which authorizes its political authority through the doctrine of discovery. While the historical recognition of the kingdom as an independent state is what enables the enduring legal claim that exceeds the U.S. domestic model, that legal genealogy is riddled with a history of (premonarchical) Indigenous deprecation. This major reorganization of social forms as a strategy to fight Western racism through independent nationhood necessitated a racist transformation of the Indigenous polity.

As chapter 2 shows, this shift entailed the privatization of land through fee-simple title as a basic dimension of social normalization. With Westphalian sovereignty as the basis for governance that served to underwrite Western imperialism and its international political domination, the regime of private property was and remains central for the "achievement" of statehood.

TWO. PROPERTIES OF LAND
That Which Feeds

Whether you're for a nation within-a-nation model or for the independence model, we need those lands! That's all we've got. And the land is not real estate. Is our ʻāina [land] real estate? No, ʻAʻole! Our ʻāina is Papahānaumoku [Earth Mother], and all the other akua [deities]. It's Kānehoalani, it's Konahuanui. That's our land . . . our ancestors. . . . Be very, very careful about this reconciliation and settlement business. If we don't have land, then we cannot be a people, we cannot be a nation. We cannot preserve our spiritual and family relationship to our ʻāina without our ʻāina. . . . Kūʻē [resist] that settlement! Kūʻē that settlement because we need all that land. It is ours; we *are* the Hawaiian nation! It's not theirs. . . . Keep saying that. We got claims on the land? No, it's *ours*; they're the ones trying to claim *our* land. . . . Whose land is that? It's Hawaiian national land! It's land that belongs to Lāhui Hawaiʻi, it's land that belonged to the Hawaiian Kingdom. It's our land and they are trying to steal it, they're trying to make a claim on it. We don't make claims, we make demands! Kūʻē!

Renowned Kanaka Maoli scholar and activist Noenoe K. Silva delivered this compelling rally speech on November 25, 2008, during a protest held at the Hawaiʻi State Capitol.[1] The purpose was to demand that then governor Linda Lingle withdraw her appeal of the "ceded lands" case to the U.S. Supreme Court. The Kupuʻāina Coalition organized the gathering, which also included a march beforehand. According to its guiding statement of purpose, "Kupu'āina believes, in accordance with the Hawai'i Supreme Court's January 31, 2008, landmark ruling, that the state of Hawai'i should not sell 'ceded' lands before resolving the unrelinquished claims of Native Hawaiians."[2] While the state views land as its property to be bought and sold as real estate, Silva reminds the crowd that the 'āina (land: literally, "that which feeds") is the Earth Mother, Papahānaumoku (literally, "she who births the islands"); Kānehoalani, the father of Pele, the fire deity; and Konahuanui, whose being is manifest in the Ko'olau mountains.[3] Here the reverence for the 'āina is front and center; the mountains, streams, winds, animals, and trees are living entities with names. Some of them are the *kino lau* (embodied manifestation) of deities, while others are *'aumākua* (ancestral family gods).

The case that prompted the protest was the culmination of many years of the attempt by the executive branch of the state of Hawai'i to sell the 1.2 million acres of land known as the Hawaiian Kingdom Crown and Government Lands. These national lands were first portioned as such through the Māhele land division of 1848 under the authority of King Kamehameha III. They constitute approximately 29 percent of the total land area of what is now known as the state of Hawai'i and almost all the land claimed by the state as "public lands." According to section 5(f) of the 1959 Hawaii State Admissions Act, these lands, whether retained or sold (and the proceeds from their sale or income), are to be used for five specific purposes, including "support of the public schools and other public educational institutions, for the betterment of the conditions of native Hawaiians, as defined in the Hawaiian Homes Commission Act, 1920, as amended, for the development of farm and home ownership on as widespread a basis as possible for the making of public improvements, and for the provision of lands for public use."[4] The U.S. federal government claimed these lands when it unilaterally annexed the Hawaiian Islands through a Joint Resolution by the U.S. Congress in 1898 after they had been "ceded" by the Republic of Hawaii, which had established itself a year after the armed and unlawful overthrow of the monarchy in 1893.[5]

When the U.S. Congress issued an apology to the Hawaiian people for the overthrow in 1993, one of the preambulary ("whereas") clauses of the resolution included an admission that the U.S. government does not have title to these lands: "the indigenous Hawaiian people never directly relinquished their claims to their inherent sovereignty as a people or over their national lands to the United States, either through their monarchy or through a plebiscite or referendum."[6] One year later, however, the state attempted to sell some of these same lands. In response, Kanaka Maoli scholar and activist Jonathan Kay Kamakawiwoʻole Osorio launched a lawsuit to prevent the sale based on the fact that the U.S. government had already acknowledged that the lands had been stolen. Eventually three other Kanaka Maoli individuals—Pia Thomas Aluli, Charles Kaaiai, and Keoki Maka Kamaka Kiili—joined the suit as co-plaintiffs, as did the state Office of Hawaiian Affairs, to challenge the executive branch of the state. By the time the case made its way to the Hawaiʻi Supreme Court in 2008, the unanimous ruling stipulated that the state could not sell these lands in light of the Apology Resolution and that the question before the court was ultimately a political one to be determined via settlement between the state and the Hawaiian people.[7] The state appealed the ruling to the U.S. Supreme Court in *State of Hawaii v. Office of Hawaiian Affairs et al.*, in which the executive branch asked the high court whether or not the state has the authority to sell, exchange, or transfer these lands.

On March 31, 2009, the Supreme Court issued its ruling in the case. It reversed the judgment of the Hawaiʻi Supreme Court and remanded the case for further proceedings with the stipulation that the outcome be consistent with the Supreme Court's opinion on the apology, insisting that the Apology Resolution does not change the legal landscape or restructure the rights and obligations of the state. In essence, the Supreme Court deemed the apology merely symbolic when it comes to the question of land title. As the ruling states, the apology would "raise grave constitutional concerns if it purported to 'cloud' Hawaii's title to its sovereign lands more than three decades after the State's admission to the union."[8] According to the high court, the 50th state has "perfect title," meaning free of liens and legal questions as to ownership of the property, which is a requirement for the sale of real estate to ensure the land is free and clear for purchase.[9] The court could not dismiss the Apology Resolution on the grounds that it was merely a joint resolution of Congress, because it presumably would clarify that the U.S. government annexed Hawaiʻi through a resolution of Congress rather than an international treaty—hence the possibility of exposing a double standard. Instead the judges focused on six verbs in the thirty-seven preambulary "whereas" clauses ("acknowledges," "recognizes," "commends," "expresses," "urges," and even "apologizes"),[10] finding that they have no legal bite: according to the court, these verbs used by Congress do not have the force of a demand under the law to be obeyed. They are "not the kind that Congress uses to create substantive rights."[11]

Once the case was remanded back to the state, the Hawai'i Supreme Court dismissed it out after some of the original plaintiffs brokered a deal with the governor and attorney general to have the case dismissed due to new legislation that had passed in the state legislature to provide for the sale of these lands through resolutions in piecemeal fashion. Although Osorio, one of the four individual plaintiffs, refused to take part in the sellout, the Hawai'i Supreme Court dismissed the case by saying it was no longer "ripe for adjudication."[12] As such, the case reveals just how enduring U.S. imperial rule and settler colonial land expropriation is into the twenty-first century.[13]

Prior to this ruling, during the prime years of contestation over the Akaka bill for federal recognition (2000–2012, detailed in chapter 1), the obliteration of the Hawaiian Nation's title to these lands was arguably at stake. In other words, the legislation looked like a sure way for the state to settle outstanding claims in the Apology Resolution to lands that the U.S. government had already acknowledged as unrelinquished. It seemed that federal recognition would immediately set up a process for extinguishing most claims to land title, except for whatever the state of Hawai'i and the federal government might have been willing to exchange for that recognition. Even then the U.S. federal government would probably not hold it in trust. Therefore it could not be considered the sovereign territory of any Native Hawaiian governing entity (NHGE) within the U.S. federal system. The 2009 U.S. Supreme Court ruling demonstrates that the federal government affirms the state's claim to these lands, however, so it seems highly unlikely that any future NHGE would be able to reclaim them to assert jurisdiction. Even if an NHGE was successful in winning some of them through adjudication, these lands are not contiguous, which further complicates question of territorial jurisdiction for any self-governing domestic dependent "Hawaiian nation." Under U.S. domestic law, federally recognized Native governing entities are allowed limited self-determination, but only over their own land base as sovereign territory. This is a contradiction in terms, given that the land must be held in trust by the U.S. federal government through the Department of the Interior (DOI) in order for it to be used as a base for jurisdiction.

Chapter 1 argues that the current state-driven push for federal recognition is problematic for outstanding Indigenous sovereignty claims and discusses the contestation over Indigenous status in both the controversy over the legislation (along with the DOI's alternative process) and the segment of the independence movement that asserts the enduring existence (or reinstatement) of the Hawaiian Kingdom and U.S. deoccupation. In the case of federal recognition, even if the U.S. government would recognize an NHGE as having delegated or inherent sovereignty, that entity would still be subordinate to federal powers as a "domestic dependent nation" because of the political domination of the U.S. government vis-à-vis Native sovereigns. As we saw in chapter 1 with the UN Declaration on the Rights of Indigenous Peoples (2007), member states have delineated the limits of self-determination in the rights of Indigenous Peoples that they purportedly affirm to be domestic rights within existing states. As kingdom nationalists rightly assert, Indigenous political status connotes subjugation under both U.S. domestic law and international law. As Indigenous Peoples themselves the world over have insisted, however, their status is about something much deeper—original or prior occupancy that entails a distinct relationship to land, humans, and nonhuman animals and all elements of the natural world as related entities with whom they share kinship obligations. These relationships are radically different ontologically from Western modes.

Since nonstatist Indigenous claims are often about stewardship in relation to land, this chapter revisits the two competing sovereignty models of contemporary Hawaiian nationalist projects: Hawaiian Kingdom existence/restoration through deoccupation and seeking U.S. federal recognition for an NHGE. In relation to the legacy of commodifying land as property, I examine the implications of both projects. Here again, each involves deep paradoxes. The construction of "national lands" in the kingdom model is based on "perfect title" to the Crown and Government Lands, whereas the designation of "Native lands" is limited by the legal concept of "Aboriginal title" that structures the NHGE model. Both of these approaches are lodged in normative legal frameworks and their respective property regimes. As such, I argue that they are problematic for decolonial Indigenous resurgence and self-determination, even though it may be politically crucial to challenge the U.S. government and its subsidiary's claims to having "perfect title" to Hawaiian lands (since it acquired these lands from those who stole them in the overthrow with the assistance of U.S. Marines). I examine the legalities that undergird both approaches in order to challenge their presuppositions, as they rely on a proprietary relation to land rather than a decolonial relation to the ʻāina outside of Western legal frameworks.

First, I offer a brief summary of the 1848 Māhele land division and subsequent related legislation including the Kuleana Act of 1850 to establish their political context and consequences. Part of Kamehameha III's undertaking to advance the kingdom in an effort to protect Hawaiian sovereignty from European encroachment was to privatize communal lands. I argue that this enclosure and propertization of land established by the monarch and other elites—both Hawaiian and foreign—within the model of independent statehood that met Western standards was part of a colonial biopolitical governmentality. This transformation of communal land holdings is a prime example of Foucault's "politics is war" thesis, in which politics is the continuation of war by other means and, as he argues, rights are also an extension of war. In this case, "land rights" are a form of biopower, a technology of power that relates to the concern of a government (in this case the Hawaiian Kingdom) with fostering the life of the population and centers on the poles of discipline and regulatory controls. The Māhele and related laws arguably created a bifurcation within the social order that produced racism through the modern state as protector by maintaining exclusions in the name of ensuring the well-being and survival of the social body. Here individual landholdings through fee-simple title became a basic dimension of social normalization by the Hawaiian Kingdom through its regulation of subjects' customary practices that were commoditized. As the privatization measure severed ties between the makaʻāinana (the common people) and the *konohiki* (land stewards) vis-à-vis the ʻāina, it also remade the relationships between and among Kanaka Maoli (of various ranks) in relation to the state.

With Westphalian sovereignty as the basis for governance that served to underwrite expanded Western imperialism and global European political domination, the regime of private property was and remains central for the "achievement" of statehood. A paradox of Hawaiian sovereignty here is that the Māhele and related legislation enable a contemporary national claim to the stolen Kingdom Crown and Government Lands. The historical irony is that because they have been held by the 50th state as "public lands," they have yet to be further privatized (as of the time of this writing), although they are constantly under threat. Yet they were constituted as Crown and Government Lands in the first place through their original privatization by the kingdom.

Second, I outline some of the claims to "perfect title" with regard to Hawaiian lands to show the limits of the political project of deoccupation in the form of kingdom existence/restoration that does not get at the root issue of land expropriation, which is the fundamental condition of settler colonialism. I do this by offering two cases of haole elites in Hawaiʻi who have amassed vast tracts of Hawaiian land—in one case nearly an entire island. The first case is Harold Freddy Rice, who holds an immense segment of the island of Maui, and the second is Larry Ellison, who recently purchased 98 percent of the island of Lānaʻi.

In the third section, I detail the restrictions that the U.S. government places on Native governing entities and challenge the federal recognition model. Both the kingdom nationalist position and the position supporting an NHGE rely on competing notions of land title, but both have their limits. In the kingdom model even assertions of "perfect title" accommodate for colonial land expropriation like the vast tracts of land that chiefs and foreigners were able to obtain for themselves as individuals, while the federal recognition model is bound to a legal framework in which the U.S. government concedes Native nations' self-determination only based on "Aboriginal title." Meanwhile it asserts absolute title over all lands, including those on which tribes assert (limited) civic and criminal jurisdiction—their reservation homelands.

In conclusion, to advance a decolonial model, I offer an example of how some Kanaka Maoli are challenging the United States' and Hawaiʻi's claims over these same lands by privileging Indigenous knowledge as the basis for revitalizing Hawaiian ontologies and epistemes in nonproprietary relation to the ʻāina that are genealogical and custodial.

Land Tenure, Genealogy, and the Privatization of Hawaiian Land

Examining the history of the Hawaiian Kingdom's 1848 privatization of communal land—and its accompanying processes and legislation that first created what came to be the Crown and Government Lands—is crucial to any understanding of the continuing struggles over the ʻāina in the twenty-first century. What is commonly referred to as the 1848 Māhele land division was a process that unfolded over the course of five years with three main instruments: the creation of the Board of Commissioners to Quiet Land Titles (referred to herein as the Land Commission) enacted by statute on December 10, 1845; the 1848 Māhele division itself, which defined the separation of previously undivided land interests of King Kamehameha III and the high-ranking chiefs and lesser chiefs known as konokihi; and the Kuleana Act of 1850, which enabled common people to acquire fee-simple title to land for the first time in Hawaiian history.

Lilikalā Kameʻeleihiwa documents (white) American participation in the push for the land division process, which took place less than three decades after the missionaries arrived in 1820 to convert Kanaka Maoli to Christianity. She notes that many of those who immediately profited from the land tenure transformation were the Calvinist missionaries-turned-businessmen whose recommendations were crucial in promoting the change.[14] In the capitalist venture, white American and European merchants, who constituted the bulk of the foreign population in Hawai'i at that time, saw in the Māhele the opportunity to acquire land of their own. Also, foreign business owners who were not citizens of the kingdom also pushed for investment incentives. Though there were several rationales, the publicly stated purpose of the land division was to create a body of landed commoners who would then prosper by means of their small farms.[15] This rationale involved an inverted logic, however, because everyone had access to land under the communal system.

Some missionaries saw the land division as a way to improve the lot of the maka'āinana. In the midst of massive depopulation, which played a dire part in this historical period, many believed that the privatization of land could help save Hawaiians from extinction: that the acquisition of land in fee simple (also known as freehold land) would help them in reestablishing a life of farming.[16] As Osorio points out, "As far as the missionaries were concerned, the strange and, for them, uncertain land tenure was the cardinal reason for the unabated depopulation and despair within the Hawaiian community." Private property was required to make the common people both industrious and prudent—"a key element of a society's recognition of individual interests." The death of Kanaka Maoli reached crisis proportions: mounting epidemics caused the decline of the population by one-half from 1803 to 1831.[17] This decline, which continued unabated through the next several decades, had many effects on society as a whole.[18] Also, as Osorio explains:

> One result of the great dying off of Hawaiians was the weakening of the traditional land tenure system that had sustained the pre-Contact chiefdoms. The labor-intensive subsistence economy and extensive cultivation of mauka (upland) areas had been the basis for, and also a sign of, a healthy and prosperous civilization. The system was especially vulnerable to rapid depopulation, which inexorably led to the abandonment of thriving lo'i (taro patches) and homesteads as the labor needed to maintain them continued to diminish. Nevertheless, this weakened system might have well survived in some kind of altered form if it had not been for the Māhele.[19]

In terms of tradition, all of the land was the responsibility of the Mōʻī (previously the paramount chief of each island but now the monarch), who was required by ancient custom to place the chiefs in jurisdiction over the land and the people on it. Kamehameha III had to contend with the "depopulation of areas that had once been thriving agricultural communities, important to the collective food and revenue base of the entire society."[20] Hence we can see the shift to privatization by the state as a form of colonial biopolitics related to protecting and renewing the declining Indigenous population. But urbanization was also a factor. As Jocelyn Linnekin notes, as "emigration came to be perceived as a problem in the 1840s, foreign residents and missionaries pressed for the establishment of individual land titles, arguing that private property would result in pride of ownership and would motivate commoners to remain on the land."[21] Yet it seems to have had the opposite effect. In any case, here was the remaking of a people, whether the Māhele is understood as a process that protected the common people's customary access or as one that privileged a version of the yeoman farmer model of individualization in relation to land title and created a new form of inheritable property.

Osorio has described the Māhele as "the single most critical dismemberment of Hawaiian society."[22] Prior to the 1848 division, land tenure patterns were characterized by values and practices of reciprocity rather than private ownership. Hawaiian land tenure was managed through a hierarchy of distribution rights that was contingent on chiefly politics with a succession of caretakers. Kanaka Maoli can still evoke myriad genealogical connections today because there were no exclusive boundaries between defined sets of relatives or bounded descent groups associated with land.[23] Linked to this flexibility and mobility is the fact that the proportion of chiefs was greater than the number of ancestral lines to which they can trace their ancestry. Given that Kanaka Maoli are all related to each other somehow, the multitude of genealogical possibilities also made for the structural variability of the Hawaiian chieftainship, as social arrangements were in constant flux.[24] Distribution itself is always in flux (like the land itself), as exemplified by the traditional process of redistribution of lands through *kalaiʻāina* (land carving).

Each island (*mokupuni*) was ruled by a paramount chief (mōʻī) and "divided into large sections, or moku-o-loko ('islands within,' often known simply as moku)." These *moku* were further divided into *ʻokana* or *kalana* (districts) composed of many *ahupuaʻa* (traditional wedge-shaped sections of land). A mōʻī allocated ahupuaʻa to lesser chiefs, who entrusted the land's administration to their respective konohiki, who in turn administered land access for maka'āinana, who labored for the chiefs and fulfilled tributary obligations.

> The ahupua'a were usually wedge-shaped sections of land that followed natural geographical boundaries, such as ridge lines and rivers, and ran from mountain to sea. A valley bounded by ridges on two or three sides, and by the sea on the fourth, would be a natural ahupua'a. The word ahupua'a means "pig altar" and was named for the stone altars with pig head carvings that marked the boundaries of each ahupua'a. Ideally, an ahupua'a would include within its borders all the materials required for sustenance—timber, thatching, and rope, from the mountains, various crops from the uplands, kalo from the lowlands, and fish from the sea. All members of the society shared access to these life-giving necessities.[25]

Here land and ea were together linked to sustainability. As Osorio put it, "Untroubled by the Judeo-Christian theology that placed human beings in a position of dominance over the earth and its other creatures, Hawaiian political systems favored not one political class over another, but the land—'āina—over the others."[26] Yet, despite this reverence for land in the Indigenous social world, Hawaiian rank and status are reckoned in hierarchical terms.

Jon Chinen explains that when "King Kamehameha I brought all of the islands under his control at the beginning of the nineteenth century, he simply utilized the land system in existence. After setting aside the lands he desired for his personal use and enjoyment, Kamehameha I divided the rest among his principal warrior chiefs for distribution to the lesser chiefs and, down the scale, to the tenant-commoners." After he died on May 8, 1819, in accordance with his will, his son Liholiho was recognized as the new sovereign, Kamehameha II. He made only a few changes in the distribution of lands, leaving the great majority of the lands with the chiefs who had been rewarded by his father. "These sovereign powers descended with the crown to Kauikeaouli, who became King Kamehameha III upon the death of his brother in England on July 14, 1824." Foreigners pressured the king and his chiefs to enact a bill of rights in 1839, which, Chinen argues, was "the beginning of a complete change in the government and in the land system in Hawaii."[27] According to the bill of rights: "Protection is hereby secured to the persons of all the people, together with their lands, their building lots, and all their property, while they conform to the laws of the kingdom, and nothing whatever shall be taken from any individual except by express provision of the laws." It also states that a "landlord cannot causelessly dispossess his tenant,"[28] These rights and laws of 1839 were published in Hawaiian as *He Kumu Kanawai a me Hooponopono Waiwai.* They "made startling changes in the authority of the chiefs and the Mōʻī by pronouncing 'God had bestowed certain rights alike on all men and all chiefs, and all people of all lands.' This declaration—codifying Christian monotheism as the state religion dictating governance—positioned everyone, chiefs and people, kanaka and haole, into one definition of people, all entitled to the rights granted by God."[29]

Kamehameha III promulgated the first constitution on October 8, 1840, which was an amended form of the bill of rights. "This constitution changed the Hawaiian government from an absolute monarchy to a constitutional monarchy. Among other things, the constitution established a bicameral legislature consisting of a house of nobles and a representative body chosen by the common people. This representative body permitted the commoners to participate for the first time in their government. Another important feature was the creation of a supreme court, consisting of the king, the king's advisor known as the kuhina nui, and four judges appointed by the representative body."[30] Also, under the section on "exposition of the principles on which the present dynasty is founded," it is clear that there was no absolute ownership of land:

> The origin of the present government, and system of polity, is as follows: Kamehameha I was the founder of the kingdom, and to him belonged all the land from one end of the Islands to the other, though it was not his own private property. It belonged to the chiefs and people in common, of whom Kamehameha I was the head, and had the management of the landed property. Wherefore, there was not formerly, and is not now any person who could or can convey away the smallest portion of land without the consent of the one who had, or has the direction of the kingdom.[31]

But, as Chinen notes, this was the first formal acknowledgment by the king that the common people had some form of protected interest in the land, aside from "the products of the soil."[32] This protected interest arguably stands today, despite the Māhele division and its accompanying legislation.[33]

As Kamanamaikalani Beamer explains: "There had been private ownership of land prior to the Māhele, but only in a few select cases where an individual had acquired title through deed, oral or written, granted by either the mōʻī or kuhina nui. The constitution of 1840 affirmed that only these two offices could convey allodial title." This type of title refers to absolute ownership of real property that is free of any superior landlord.[34] The constitution allowed for the people's "vested rights" to land and therefore provided a legal foundation for the mōʻī, aliʻi, and makaʻāinana to acquire allodial title to land. Prior to the Western concept of rights in the Hawaiian context, vested rights could be understood as *kuleana* (to have responsibility or interest). Beamer points out that this segment of the constitution dealt in part with the ownership of land and served to codify ancient land rights held by the mōʻī, aliʻi, and makaʻāinana within the structure of the *kālaiʻāina* (carving the land). In that old system, "the mōʻī awarded lands, but they were not the mōʻī's sole property; the makaʻāinana also had rights to their ʻili, moʻoʻāina, puakūʻāina, kīhāpai, and to other resources within their ahupuaʻa."[35]

In 1848 King Kamehameha III first divided the lands of the kingdom between himself and the chiefs and konohiki. Before the division of lands with the high chiefs and lesser chiefs was completed, the king had planned to subdivide his reserved lands between the government and himself—Government Lands were distinct from the Crown Lands, which were reserved for the monarch and his descendants. He was deeply concerned over the hostile activities of the foreigners in the Hawaiian Islands and "did not want his lands to be considered public domain and be subject to confiscation by a foreign power in the event of a conquest."[36] Hence part of his decision was shaped by an effort to fend off Western encroachment and protect these lands as an element of Hawaiian sovereignty. The king surrendered part of his original share in the lands that became the Government Lands and reserved the smaller portion for his own use.[37]

> The King, wishing to keep his private domain intact in the event foreigners conquered the islands, executed the day after the completion of the Mahele, two documents to stave off foreign appropriation. In the first, he gave to the government, for the benefit of the chiefs and the people, approximately 1.5 million acres out of the nearly 2.5 million acres that he claimed in the Mahele. In a second document, the King registered the remaining royal lands for himself, his heirs, and successors. The lands so registered became known as Crown lands, in contradistinction to government lands. The Legislature later confirmed these instruments executed by Kamehameha III.[38]

Until a later law prevented alienation of these lands by the Crown, Kamehameha III administered these lands through his agents as might any citizen under the system of private property ownership. They were sold, mortgaged, or leased at will, and the resulting revenues were diverted to his personal use.

Next was the Kuleana Act of 1850, which enabled commoners to acquire fee-simple title to land for the first time in Hawaiian history. The awards made by the Land Commission to maka'āinana were called kuleana awards. As several scholars have noted, only 8,421 claims were awarded out of 14,195 applications made for kuleana awards in 1848 (among approximately 80,000 Hawaiians at the time). Most scholars explain this small number by suggesting that few Hawaiian commoners registered their land claims, especially since they were required to pay for the survey of the lands that they set out to secure, and those who did found that their lands were frequently lost to fraud, adverse possession, tax sales, and undervalued sales to speculators.[39] Others have speculated that many were uninterested in small plots of rural land, especially when they required wide-ranging gathering rights to maintain a traditional subsistence lifestyle.[40]

Maivân Clech Lâm offers six reasons for the low number of people who participated in this institutionalized private land ownership: the timeline for registering and processing the land claims was unrealistic; the maka'āinana were new to the written word and distrustful of the written law; most could not afford the survey fees; taking an award might limit their task of sustaining themselves on awarded lots only (because formerly traditional subsistence required the utilization of the whole ahupua'a); the common people preferred the old system: some tenants assumed that the previous land tenure arrangement would simply continue if they did not act to change anything; and some probably feared that any attempt to file for kuleana lots within the ahupua'a or *'ili* (subsection) of the konohiki would invite reprisal. By traditional precedent, carried over into the Māhele guidelines, abandoned or uncultivated lands would revert to the konohiki of the ahupua'a. Hence kuleana lands were allowed to slip back by default into the hands of either the government or the chiefs of the surrounding land.[41]

Maka'āinana who applied for kuleana lands were named *hoa'āina* (literally friends of the land), which the law translated into English as "tenants" in relation to "landlords." But as Osorio argues, these new designations were problematic and incommensurable with the customary definitions of Hawaiian cultural practice, in which "Ali'i were not landlords who owned the land and its produce. They were konohiki who had responsibilities that extended above and below them. The maka'āinana were not tenants, entitled to live on and work the land as long as they paid for it in produce or labor; their entitlements were fundamentally different."[42] The roles of the makaʻāinana, the konokiki, and the aliʻi were all related to the ethic of *malama'āina*—proper care for the land.[43] This was a hierarchical system to be sure, but it was based on reciprocity. Kapāʻanaokalākeola Nākoa Oliveira offers an account explaining how land was central to Hawaiians across rank differences.

> From the highest ranking chiefs to the general population, ancestral Kanaka had an undeniable connection to the ʻāina. The social norms that prevented physical interaction between the aliʻi and the makaʻāinana led to distinct behavioral patterns characteristic of each segment of the population. Aliʻi had kapu that created barriers between themselves and lower-ranking people in society, and had the kuleana of ensuring that the makaʻāinana and ʻāina were productive so that the needs of the people and the ʻāina were in balance. While aliʻi had the advantage of being able to acquire some more ʻāina through warfare, thus extending their domain and rewarding supporters with interests in their newly attained ʻāina, it was equally possible for aliʻi to be forced to forfeit lands should they be defeated in battle. As a result, aliʻi were a highly mobile societal unit and were often forced to (re)construct ties to the places that they ruled. . . . Makaʻāinana, on the other hand, generally enjoyed long-standing ancestral ties to the lands they lived on. In spite of wars and changes in government, the makaʻāinana rarely feared being displaced from their kulāiwi. Their presence on the landscape was more permanent than the temporal rule of the aliʻi. Makaʻāinana had the kuleana of working the ʻāina, fishing the sea, and honoring the aliʻi. For these islanders, living in accord with nature and one another was key to their survival. . . . Makaʻāinana enjoyed close interaction with other makaʻāinana. Extending over many generations, these relationships between families residing in the same ahupuaʻa were strong. Interdependence and reliance on one another created a societal bond that ensured that people of all ranks worked together for the common good of all.[44]

Oliveira's description conveys the principles of reciprocity across social hierarchies that speak to relationality with land at the center.

Osorio suggests that from the makaʻāinana point of view the Kuleana Act worked to try to sever all traditional ties to the chief. "If the konohiki has no right to their labor and could not deny them access that only the law guaranteed, then what was left to obligate the chiefs to the people?" He asserts:

> There can be no question that the Māhele, which allowed private ownership of land, also established the indigenous occupants, both Ali'i and Maka'āinana, as competitors rather than as caretakers of the 'āina. After 1850, Native people were forced to appeal to the courts to allow them to fish, to gain access to irrigation water, and even to farm and graze lands that were unoccupied. For the most part, these decisions, even when they resulted in favor of the hoa'āina, only conferred rights that they had once universally enjoyed. Thus law became the arbiter between a family that the law itself estranged.[45]

Here we see a new form of governmentality in relation to the rise of capitalism in the islands, which relates to gender and sexuality (as the following chapters show), in light of how "law became the arbiter between a family that the law itself estranged." Through the enclosure of the ahupua'a (like the enclosure of extended family through the regulation of sex and gender) rights were constituted as a form of war through colonial biopolitics by state mediation. Not only had the relationships between the chiefs and the common people become disaffected through this process, but the haole were treated with favoritism over the maka'āinana by the chiefs. Nearly a month before the maka'āinana rights to land were made explicit in the Kuleana Act, in July 1850, the legislature decided to allow haole who were not naturalized to own and sell lands.[46] The Resident Alien Act of 1850 gave foreigners the right to buy land in fee simple.[47] As Osorio notes, the debate was not over whether haole should own land, since some already did. Before 1850, however, ownership had been linked to citizenship. In other words "every haole resident was to be allowed what had once been reserved exclusively to the chiefs and the people: control and use of land."[48] These transformations continue to implicate the politics of land in Hawai'i, including haole ownership (discussed further below).

To clarify, the Māhele did not in itself alter the rights of the maka'āinana to the land because it did not convey any actual title to land.[49] Chinen explains: "The *Mahele* itself did not convey any title to land. The high chiefs and the lesser konohikis who participated in the Mahele and who were named in the Mahele Book were required to present their claims before the Land Commission and to receive awards for the lands quitclaimed to them by Kamehameha III. Until an award for these lands was issued by the Land Commission, title to such lands remained with the government."[50]

Still, scholars debate whether the enclosure of the ahupua'a and the transition to royal patents ultimately had the effect of dispossession and whether the commodificaton of land hastened the dislocation of the common people.[51] Previous treatments of the Māhele suggest that less than 1 percent of the total land acreage passed in fee simple to the common people under the Kuleana Act.[52] David Keanu Sai was one of the first to contest the prevailing assessments and offer a radically different analysis.[53] Drawing on a report submitted as part of the minister of interior's report to the 1882 Kingdom Legislature by W. D. Alexander (later published as "Brief History of Land Titles" in the *Hawaiian Almanac* in 1891), Sai argues that Kanaka Maoli tenants received in excess of 180,000 acres.[54] He asserts that the figure of 30,000 acres for the maka'āinana lands is accurate only when calculated from the number of Land Commission Awards. Purchasers of portions of the Government Lands, sold as a means of obtaining revenue for the monarchy, were issued Royal Patent Grants, which differed from the Royal Patents issued upon Land Commission Awards in that recipients of these grants were not required to obtain their award from the commission. In other words, the figures would be higher with accounting of land acquisition by other means.

In addition to Sai's finding that the maka'āinana were able to purchase more land than previously understood, there is a new wave of scholarly work by kingdom nationalists who have reassessed the Māhele. Kamanamaikalani Beamer suggests that the process protected more rights for the maka'āinana by securing them in perpetuity. Donovan Preza argues that the Māhele was a *condition* but not a sole determinative factor in land dispossession of the common people.[55] And 'Umi Perkins has engaged the question of the alienation of Kanaka Maoli from land by making the case that social erasure and the notion of a time expiration on claims to kuleana lands allowed for the "radical forgetting of place" that pervades the contemporary claim of broad-based dispossession as presumably irreversible. One of the factors at play in these different interpretations of the Māhele is the variation of readings on the main purpose of the division itself. Beamer asserts: "The Māhele was an instrument that began to settle the constitutionally granted vested rights of the three groups in the dominium of the kingdom—the mō'ī, ali'i, and maka'āinana. To privatize the land system, these rights needed to be settled because the declaration of Rights and Laws of 1839 and the Constitution of 1840 both codified the concept that the lands of the kingdom were jointly owned by these three groups."[56]

Beamer further explains that the establishment of "distinct land bases for the mō'ī, the government, and the chiefs—which ultimately made large-scale private ownership possible—was nevertheless still subject to the rights of maka'āinana to make their claims for land." He notes that the 1 percent statistic frequently offered for maka'āinana awards seems to draw only on kuleana awards, not including government grants acquired as a result of section 4 of the Kuleana Act of 1850, and that it also does not take into account that "the native tenants continued to possess the right to divide out their interest in the dominium." While he acknowledges that it may be impossible to have a final accounting for the exact acreage of Government Lands acquired by maka'āinana, new research by Preza shows that approximately 167,290 acres were purchased by the maka'āinana between the years of 1850 and 1893. Combined with the 28,658 acres acquired as a result of the Kuleana Act, this would make 185,948 acres acquired as a result of the Māhele process overall.[57] Furthermore, Beamer questions the previous assertions that the Māhele dispossessed the common people at all, given that the vested rights of the maka'āinana were meant to exist in perpetuity: "In fact, the Māhele process may have secured 'Ōiwi rights as well as title to lands rather than being a means of severing traditional relationships to 'āina."[58]

Beamer also challenges the notion that the land division was a Western imposition. He asserts that the Māhele and the Kuleana Act were both "hybrid initiatives," similar to the previous custom of *nā kālai'āina* (land distributions by ruling chiefs). He explains that the main difference was that the Māhele was the final kālai'āina.

> 'Āina conveyed through the Māhele allows a chief to take the award to the Land Commission, where the title would be validated. These awards enabled chiefs to gain allodial or fee simple title upon payment of a commutation, which extinguished the government's interest in those lands. Once the government's interest in 'āina was removed, chiefs could then receive a Royal Patent that confirmed fee-simple ownership of the 'āina, which continued to be "subject to the rights of native tenants." This process meant that even fee-simple allodial title to 'āina was a hybrid kind of private property, one that continued to have a condition on title that was to provide for maka'āinana, as was consistent with early Hawaiian custom.[59]

Beamer also indirectly speaks to the biopolitical aims of the land division and distribution. He asserts that Kauikeaouli and the ali'i of his time authorized these "hybrid laws" for the betterment of the people at large. "In response to the depopulation of 'Ōiwi and the increasing pull of urban areas as a place to live and work, these laws attempted to get maka'āinana back on the land by granting them title to lands, so that cultivation might again thrive. Kamehameha IV commented on these ideas in a speech on January 5, 1856." In addition to attempts "to empower the maka'āinana to return to being cultivators of the land," the creation of private property by the ali'i "also allowed for large government tax revenues and safeguarded national interests, since private property was respected by the European and American nations."[60]

For Beamer, the Māhele and its accompanying legislation was the result of chiefly agency, "not because of imposed colonial prowess, but through the selected appropriation of aspects of European governance, politics and law."[61] Yet neither factor is mutually exclusive of the other; Hawaiian elites seem to have selectively appropriated aspects of European modes as a way to negotiate colonial encroachment. Thus I suggest that they enacted their own form of colonial biopolitical governmentality in the face of foreign advancements at the local level and Western imperialism more broadly.

As noted above, Preza has reexamined the question of dispossession resulting from the Māhele. His study of the transition of land tenure in Hawai'i to a system of private property argues that the Māhele was a necessary yet insufficient condition for dispossession.[62] Through the identification of previously unexamined data (the records of the fee-simple sale of Government Land), he offers an alternate explanation for dispossession in Hawai'i: the loss of governance.[63] Preza also questions the current understanding that the maka'āinana received only 28,658 acres of land, less than 1 percent of Hawai'i's total lands. As he explains, under that view, the maka'āinana's access to land was thought to be limited to the Kuleana Act of 1850, lands received in fee simple by the maka'āinana. Thus this view does not account for the other ways in which Hawaiians could acquire land. Preza focuses on the purchase of Government Lands by the maka'āinana: "These lands are not accounted for in the *Kuleana* statistic because they are a different species of original title. The Land Commission was authorized by statute to handle *Kuleana Awards* while the Minister of the Interior was in charge of the fee-simple sale of Government Land. These sales were accounted for by different government agencies." Preza further argues: "Accounting for the sale and trends of Government Land reveals a better explanation for dispossession: the loss of governance resulting from the overthrow of the Hawaiian government in 1893." Hence, the author makes a distinction between the loss of governance and the loss of land.[64]

Like Beamer, Preza suggests that the shift to the privatization of Hawaiian land was a hybrid formulation. "From this approach, one can understand the Māhele in a broader context as a transition of existing Hawaiian rights, usages, and custom rather than as an imposition of American rights, usages, and custom." Here he is also suggesting more continuity between customary practice and the new system of privatization. "There is a critical distinction to be made here between the Māhele providing the opportunity for foreigners to buy land and foreigners actually acting upon that opportunity immediately following the Māhele. To support an argument for an initial dispossession, one would expect land acquisition immediately following the Māhele to be dominated by foreigners." Preza agrees with Osorio's framing of dispossession in the broader context of laws and legal structure but differs on his interpretation of Hawaiian Kingdom law as a "Western" institution, suggesting that it operates within an either/or binary of assimilation/resistance. "The issue of control versus ownership of land is a significant one as it gets at the distinction between a loss of governance (control) and the loss of real property (ownership). Non-recognition of sovereignty through colonization preceded most, if not all, transitions to systems of private property by aboriginal people. Such was not the case in Hawai'i and this fact is not reconciled by any of these aforementioned works." Preza also asserts that the common people's calls for help were in fact answered.[65]

According to Beamer, "The maka'āinana protested the konohiki taking more than their share of resources from ahupua'a, the right of foreigners to become Kingdom subjects, and other matters directly affecting their own position and well-being." He cites this as evidence that they had "accepted some of the benefits of constitutional government since the practice of petitioning the government contrasts to a time when the maka'āinana had no say in ali'i governmental decisions."[66]

Osorio offers quite a different interpretation of the agency exhibited by the common people in their appeals: "Petitioning was the Maka'āinana's opportunity to reinforce the traditional relationship that existed between them and the Ali'i as well as to define them both together as a people united against the incursions of foreigners." According to Osorio, "petitioning is based on a relationship that quite explicitly places the petitioner in a position of subordinance, the very position that defined the Maka'āinana and their successors, the hoa'āina. The petitions used before 1850 stated that the undersigned requested that their nominees 'serve with the Nobles' in the legislature, something that was consistent with their cultural norms. Their representatives would convey their concerns to the Mō'ī and the Ali'i while actually depending on the Aliʻi to make the decisions, as the ruling chiefs have always done."[67]

Perkins also addresses this period of the privatization of land in Hawaiʻi. "Kuleana—'native tenant rights' were embedded in this system, then concealed, and misconstrued as gathering rights. This entire system was built upon the foundation of traditional Hawaiian land tenure." Perkins understands the 1850 Kuleana Act as having provided a means for makaʻāinana to divide out their "native tenant rights" and gain a fee-simple title to the lands under their cultivation. He argues that those rights were ignored, concealed, and later misconstrued as "gathering rights" and that courts have been able to appear liberal by debating the *extent* of gathering rights, while obscuring the expanded rights of makaʻāinana rooted in Hawaiʻi's land tenure system. Like Sai, Beamer, and Preza, Perkins also contends that twentieth-century scholars have misconstrued the 1850 Kuleana Act (along with the 1848 Māhele itself), which has contributed to the confusion over Native tenant rights. He examines both the foundations of the introduced system of land law and late–nineteenth-century legal responses to kuleana rights. Perkins also explores the simultaneous existence of multiple legal regimes. In examining the question of the alienation of Kanaka Maoli from the land, he finds that social erasure and the notion of a time expiration on claims to kuleana lands allowed for the "radical forgetting of place" that permeates the contemporary hegemonic claim of broad-based dispossession as a fait accompli: "once the aliʻi committed to the capitalist paradigm, no alternate path existed in the nineteenth century to ameliorate the alienation of Hawaiians from land, other than the usage rights represented in the *Oni v. Meek* case of 1858, which defined and limited native gathering rights."[68]

Perkins examines the emergent scholarship of Sai, Beamer, and Preza that reframes the Māhele as an effort to account for a transition in the land tenure system in the kingdom that would allow for capitalist development. These works challenge critiques of the Māhele as capitalist exploitation and replace it with a positivist and legalist description of the Māhele as merely an institution of an emerging and modernizing nation-state. These rereadings of the division and follow-up legislation claim that they served to empower Kanaka, because the "undivided shares" existed in the *dominium* of the kingdom—the government's ownership of all Hawaiian land based on sovereignty. Whereas earlier scholarly literature stressed the detrimental effects of land privatization, Perkins's view is that the economics of the common people's situation and the processes of erasure and forgetting led to alienation, rather than the design of the Māhele process itself. As he explains: "The system of vested interests was an attempt to prevent this from becoming a generational problem, as the rights were perpetually renewed to those born after 1848." Like the other scholars whose works reframe this period of change, Perkins asserts that the "entire system was built upon the foundation of traditional Hawaiian land tenure."[69]

Again we see another case for continuity:

> This revised conception leads to a different understanding of the Māhele/Kuleana Act process. The mōʻī held vested rights as the head of the government. The King also held land as a konohiki in fee simple. The chiefs, in their capacity as konohiki, held land as vested rights in the dominium and, after dividing out their interests, in fee simple. Makaʻāinana held vested rights in the dominium and could divide out their interests and gain fee-simple title, but could not divide out *as a class*. . . . Thus, all land held in the system of proprietary rights was subject to the rights of native tenants. Foreigners held land only as proprietary interests, and did not hold vested rights in the dominion of the Kingdom. In addition to these layers were gathering rights, which were usage rights rather than ownership. Thus, a layered system emerged consisting of the dominium (divided between the king, aliʻi and makaʻāinana), proprietary interests (fee simple, leasehold and life estates), and gathering rights (usage rights).

Here Perkins suggests that Māhele merely divided the interests in land of the king and the konohiki, converting their right in the dominium of the kingdom to a basic proprietary interest through fee-simple title, and that the Kuleana Act was the same process for the makaʻāinana. He argues that it was the ruling oligarchy after the 1893 overthrow that abridged the makaʻāinana rights in land.[70]

In addition to the debates about the adverse affects of the Māhele, the contemporary status of these lands and the endurance of the makaʻāinana position in relation to them is still unresolved to this day.[71] As Lâm argues (and the scholars above would agree), the Kuleana Act of 1850 enabled the makaʻāinana to acquire fee-simple title to land for the first time but did not terminate their traditional rights to land, which were quite extensive. Lâm makes the case that the act introduced a system of rights parallel to customary use practices and prerogatives, rather than one that supplanted them.[72] After the illegal overthrow of the monarchy in 1893, Government and Crown Lands were joined together; after annexation in 1898, they were managed as a public trust by the United States. As Jon Van Dyke notes, at statehood in 1959 all but 373,720 acres of Government and Crown Lands were transferred to the state of Hawaiʻi, so "these lands must be examined as a separate entity and their unique status recognized. Government Lands were created to provide for the needs of the general population; Crown Lands were part of the personal domain of Kamehameha III and evolved into a resource designed to support the mōʻī, who in turn supported the Native Hawaiian people."[73]

The ways in which land enclosure and new private property regimes disrupted the Hawaiian social order worked as forms of colonial biopolitics. They exemplified a form of racism institutionalized by the Hawaiian Kingdom as a modern state—in the quest to protect its sovereignty from Western imperialism—even as they were enacted to ensure the survival of the social body. The Māhele of 1848 together with the Kuleana Act of 1850 formed a basic dimension of social normalization—those who were marked as "civilized" landowners in contrast to those who were not.[74] Although the plan was a strategy by the monarch to put Hawaiians on the same playing field as the otherwise would-be colonizer, paradoxically it submitted to colonial logics. This is not to disregard the agency of the mōʻī and other aliʻi but to account for the structural forces that shaped their adaptation and to assess the costs. This site of mid-nineteenth-century biopolitics—imposed by a constitutional monarchy providing equal rights for all—entailed the regulation of its subjects as part and parcel of the commodification of land customs and social practices: holding of fee-simple titles became a way to transcend supposed savagery. While individual land ownership was central to the making of the bourgeois subject, land rights became a venue to dispossess the common Kanaka. Those who fared best under the new system were Hawaiian aliʻi, missionaries, and their descendants. While the vast lands that they secured are rooted in "perfect title," in the contemporary period we now see the relationship between settler colonialism and the amassing of great wealth by a few, the core tenet of capitalist accumulation.

Perfect Title and Its Imperfect Problems

The deoccupation model of Hawaiian sovereignty has focused on the kingdom's "perfect title" to the Crown and Government Lands, in contrast to the federal recognition model of self-governance, highlighting the U.S. government's theft of lands of another nation. This approach is lodged in the normative (Anglo-American) legal framework and its property regime

—with title to land being the centerpiece. A paradox of Hawaiian sovereignty here is that the Māhele land division and attendant land awards and follow-up legislation are what enables a national claim to the stolen Kingdom Crown and Government Lands in the contemporary period, yet the original privatization of those same lands by the kingdom constituted them as such in the first place. While the illegality of the U.S. overthrow and annexation is central to any claim of Hawaiian national sovereignty, and rightly so, the deoccupation model does not account for settler colonial domination because of its limited juridical fixation. Hence stopping short of asserting or proving perfect title with regard to Hawaiian lands does not get at the root issue of land expropriation central to the structure of settler colonialism. My examination of the limits of this approach focuses on the illegality of land acquisition by offering two cases of haole (white) elites in Hawai'i who have amassed vast tracts of Hawaiian land—an entire ahupua'a and nearly an entire island. I suggest that both cases are important in understanding how massive land acquisitions within private property regimes—literally part and parcel of contemporary settler colonialism—were made possible only through the Māhele land division in the first place. Although the chain of title looks clear enough from the two accounts that follow, both would be illegitimate according to Sai's contention regarding land title, because the last transaction took place under the territorial government and/or 50th state governments—not the Hawaiian Kingdom government.

Sai argues that all titles in Hawai'i originate from the Hawaiian Kingdom government, whether by Royal Patents or Land Commission Awards. All subsequent conveyances between individuals are registered at the Bureau of Conveyances.[75] He contends that a recorded deed of sale or other form of transfer is required to establish a chain of title. Sai points out that the provisional government (formed after the overthrow) seized control of the kingdom's Government and Crown lands without conveyance and further claimed them when the actors involved in the 1893 overthrow established the Republic of Hawai'i in 1894. Furthermore, there is no record of conveyance from the so-called Republic of Hawai'i to the United States from the purported 1898 annexation. In other words, the kingdom never ceded territory to the United States or any other government.

My intention here is not to counter Sai's claims. As mentioned above, they are backed by normative legal frameworks and as such are noncontroversial except that they call into question U.S. legitimacy in relation to Hawaiian land, given the legacy of settler colonial theft. My aim is to expose how the privatization of land under King Kamehameha III enabled massive accumulation for the minority in a way that has arguably left a legacy that continues to produce an ongoing dispossession. I offer two "headline" stories of elite white men who have amassed vast acreage of Hawaiian land for themselves based on earlier transactions made during the reign of the Hawaiian Kingdom.

On January 22, 2010, the *Wall Street Journal* featured an article about Harold Freddy Rice, "Living in Old Hawaii: Henry Rice's 10,000-Acre Ranch Dates Back to the Monarchy." It starts: "Hundreds of years ago, Hawaiian kings would hand out to subordinate rulers thin slivers of land that stretched from volcano to sea. The system of rule via these plots, *ahupua'a,* was abolished in the 19th century, and much of the land was split up and sold as the value of Hawaiian real estate skyrocketed." Notice here the colonial framing, in which the author naturalizes the commodification of Hawaiian land and its market value. The article also asserts that "kings" controlled the "slivers" of land "hundreds of years ago," although the first king in Hawai'i was Kamehameha I, who united the island just over two hundred years ago (by 1810). As explained earlier, paramount chiefs on each island included both men and women, so the author mischaracterizes Hawaiian culture in patriarchal terms. The piece goes on to describe Rice as a "fifth-generation Hawaii native"—a depiction that itself effaces Kanaka Maoli indigeneity by positioning anyone born on the islands as "native." The article notes that he lives within "one of the few nearly intact *ahupua'a* left in the islands: 10,000 acres of ranchland stretching continuously from the top of Mount Haleakala down towards the sunny beaches of Maui's south shore." It also notes that appraisers say the ranch is likely worth close to $50 million. In terms of title, Rice says the ahupua'a "was first handed to a Hawaiian, who sold it to a Chinese potato farmer, who sold it to a sugar magnate, who sold it to his grandfather, Maui senator Harold W. Rice, in 1916." We learn that the five-bedroom, four-bathroom Cape Cod–style home built by Rice's grandfather in 1917 is "immaculately preserved" with many of the original furnishings, including a buzzer that the "grandfather used to ring for the servants."[76]

The Rice who owns the home, ranch, and entire ahupua'a today became renowned as party to a controversial case decided by the U.S. Supreme Court in 2000, *Rice v. Cayetano.* The lawsuit was about the restricted state elections for trustees to the Office of Hawaiian Affairs, along with the very existence of the office. Prior to the court ruling, participation in state elections was restricted to Native Hawaiians, of any Hawaiian ancestry, who resided in Hawai'i. Rice was denied the right to vote because he is not Hawaiian by any statutory definition.[77] As plaintiff in the case, Rice claimed that both the trust managed by the office and the OHA voting provisions were racially discriminatory and violated the Fourteenth and Fifteenth Amendments to the U.S. Constitution, which are meant to provide equal protection and to guarantee the right of citizens to vote, respectively. According to the state, the trust is for the benefit of "Native Hawaiians" (defined by a 50 percent blood quantum rule), but the court decreed that the state's electoral restriction enacted race-based voting qualifications and thereby violated the Fifteenth Amendment.[78]

One of the issues highlighted in *Rice v. Cayetano* was that Rice is a fourth-generation resident of Hawai'i. Harold Freddy Rice's great-great grandfather, William Harrison Rice (1813–1862), was a missionary teacher from New York who traveled to Hawai'i in the ninth company of missionaries from the American Board of Commissioners for Foreign Missions (ABCFM) on the ship *Gloucester*, leaving from Boston on November 14, 1840, and arriving in Honolulu on May 21, 1841. He eventually managed an early sugar plantation and completed the first irrigation system for sugar for the Līhu'e Plantation on the island of Kaua'i. His son, William Hyde Rice (1846–1924), was a businessman and politician who served in the Hawaiian House of Representatives from 1870 to 1890 and helped to draw up the 1887 Constitution of the Kingdom of Hawaii (known as the "Bayonet Constitution"). He eventually served as the last governor of Kaua'i, appointed in 1891 by Queen Lili'uokalani, whom he later helped to overthrow and place under house arrest. Under the Republic of Hawaii, he served in the senate from 1895 to 1898. His son, Harold Waterhouse Rice (1883–1962), was the Maui senator (1919–1947) who bequeathed the Maui ahupua'a to the Rices of today.[79] Needless to say, this cursory genealogy of Harold Freddy Rice reveals a deep colonial legacy, as his forebears affected Hawaiian governance and political autonomy in destructive ways.

Harold Freddy Rice's property chain can be traced through a broader context of settler colonialism, which—in Patrick Wolfe's terms—always entails the logic of the elimination of the Native. Recalling that settler colonialism "destroys to replace,"[80] Rice exemplifies a case of land acquisition dependent on expropriating lands from the Indigenous People. Here Rice becomes the "Native" while actual Kanaka are relegated to the past as he pushes for "equal rights" and a "color-blind" yet multicultural American liberal state.

In the second case, a *Los Angeles Times* headline on June 22, 2012, announced: "Oracle Founder Larry Ellison Buying Hawaiian Island of Lanai." Ellison, then Oracle Corporation chief executive officer, purchased 97 percent of Lāna'i, an approximately 140-square-mile island in the Hawaiian chain that includes two resorts and more than three thousand residents. Ellison, said to be the third richest American, purchased the property from Castle & Cooke.[81] The island was known for the production of pineapple until David Murdock (CEO of Castle & Cooke) turned to tourism and the development of high-priced residential projects. After much speculation as to the cost, it has been confirmed that Ellison paid $300 million for the island.[82] The sale also included the island's two luxury hotels (the Four Seasons Resort Lanai at Manele Bay and Four Seasons Resort Lanai Lodge at Koele), two championship golf courses, and other assets. Since the purchase, among other property upgrades, Ellison has added a 50-acre tennis academy to the island.[83] As early as eight months after Ellison purchased the tiny island, his representatives are reported to have said that the island might need to double in population for a labor force,[84] presumably non-Kanaka because settler colonialism depends on the logics of the elimination of the Native.[85]

Merchant partners Samuel Northrup Castle and Amos Starr Cooke founded Castle & Cooke, the company that sold the land to Ellison, in Honolulu in 1851. In 1995 the business became successor to the real estate and resort business of Dole Food Company.[86] It boasts that its corporation's diversified businesses "include residential and commercial real estate, visitor attractions, resorts, aviation and renewable energy" and also claims: "By fostering the development of new business divisions, the company adapts its operations to reflect the needs of our diverse communities. These strategic efforts have planted the seeds for future innovations that will continue to honor Hawai'i's people and its way of life. We are proud to be a part of Hawai'i's history and responsibly embrace its future."[87]

Ellison's "Private Eden" is open for business after the complete renovation of two Four Seasons hotels, with one of them (Four Seasons Resort Lanai) offering an executive suite for $21,000 a night called "Ali'i." Besides selling visitors the promise that they too can be hosted like a Hawaiian chief for the right price, his Eden project is referred to as "a sustainable society-building experiment steered by luxury tourism."[88]

But building this environmentally sustainable society has had dire consequences for the island's ecology. As Laura E. Lyons documents, Ellison's plans entail the implementation of at least one hundred wind turbines 400 feet tall that threaten to disturb Hawaiian burials and otherwise destroy sacred land: each requires a concrete base 10 to 20 feet deep. The project will also entail massive underwater cables to connect the wind farms to the island of O'ahu. In her work about the Ellison purchase and projects on the island, Lyons theorizes how the "hyper-capitalism . . . that the sale of Lāna'i represents lays bare a set of social relations much more akin to feudalism." This is because the people living on Lāna'i "are repeatedly told that they have very little choice but to participate in whatever projects their billionaire landowner wants to pursue, since whoever that person is owns the land and most of the businesses and so controls the majority of jobs on the island." Meanwhile "many residents feel that the influx of capitalism over the last ninety years . . . has not created enough stability or prosperity for those who live on the island year around that they can afford to be silent and just accept whatever plans develop." As a result, several groups are active in monitoring the developments and resisting them—including Lāna'ians for Sensible Growth, Friends of Lāna'i, who demand transparency in the planning process, and the protest group Kupa'a no Lana'i, formed in 2012 for the purpose of preserving and protecting ancient and historically significant sites on the island, including the boundary lines of the various 'ahupua'a.[89]

Importantly, as Lyons explains, groups like Kupa'a no Lana'i refuse "to buy into the logic that would have capitalism as the inevitable and only conceivable way to organize their communities economically and politically, and as refusing to buy into a rhetoric based on the fear of, indebtedness to, and dependency on landowners like Murdock and Ellison." Moreover, she notes that their effort, "like many other organizations in Hawai'i, particularly Native Hawaiian groups involved in fighting aspects of the new feudalism, revolves around the preservation and protection of the land and cultivates alternative logics, if not also economies, by insisting that the land, not capitalism, will provide for their needs."[90]

The colonial roots of the Castle & Cooke collaboration run deep in Hawai'i. Samuel Northrup Castle was also an early missionary to Hawai'i, arriving in 1836—a layman who managed the financial affairs of the mission. Amos Starr Cooke (1810–1871) and Juliette Montague Cooke (1812–1896) were appointed by Kamehameha III to run the Chief's Children's School (later renamed the Royal School in 1846) in Honolulu, founded in 1839.[91] They were also from the American Board of Commissioners for Foreign Missions, part of the eighth company to Hawai'i, which sailed from Boston on December 14, 1836, on the *Mary Frazier*, arriving in Honolulu on April 9, 1837. The purpose of the Royal School was to educate the children of ali'i to become the next generation of Hawaiian rulers, including Lydia Kamakaeha, who later succeeded to the throne as Queen Liliu'okalani.[92] By 1849 Amos Cooke worked for Samuel Northrop Castle, who served as a secular supply agent for the mission. They co-founded Castle & Cooke as a private business (a general store), when the ABCFM reduced funding for the Hawai'i stations. Castle & Cooke became one of Hawai'i's "Big Five" corporations that wielded great political power during the early twentieth century in the islands.[93] The others were C. Brewer & Co., Theo H. Davies & Co., Amfac, and Alexander & Baldwin.

Castle & Cooke eventually secured Dole's pineapple plantations throughout the archipelago, including the large one on the island of Lāna'i, where the company claimed ownership of about 95 percent of the island through purchase. By buying up properties and consolidating his holdings toward single ownership of the island, by 1922 James Dole, the president of Hawaiian Pineapple Company (later renamed Dole Food Company), had bought Lāna'i for $1.1 million and transformed it into a pineapple plantation, turning the island into the world's top supplier.[94] In 1985 David H. Murdock purchased Lāna'i as CEO of Castle & Cooke (then owner of Dole). Prior to the Dole purchase, Walter M. Gibson had acquired most of the land by the 1870s for ranching. Gibson was another white American in the line of owners. He had close ties to the monarchy, previously serving as prime minister of the kingdom after holding office as minister of foreign affairs as well as minister of the interior during King Kalākaua's reign in the 1880s.

A timeline of these land transactions shows how foreigners managed to amass large holdings on the one island.[95] As the Lāna'i Culture & Heritage Center (a nonprofit charitable organization dedicated to documenting Lāna'i's history) documents, through the Māhele in 1848 Kamehameha III apportioned land on the island among the government, the chiefs, and the people, despite broad protest from the common people.[96] Five of the thirteen ahupua'a were granted to chiefly awardees, while the eight remaining ahupua'a were retained by the king and the government. The king granted several small house lots and planting fields to approximately fifty-five Native tenants.

In 1863 Chief Ha'alelea sold the ahupua'a of Pālāwai to Walter Murray Gibson for $3,000, to use as a Mormon settlement. Between 1866 and 1887 Gibson secured several government leases and eventually purchased multiple ahupua'a on the island, including an 1886 purchase of the ahupua'a of Maunalei from the estate of Emma Kaleleonālani (daughter of Pane Kekelaokalani). When Gibson died in 1888, his daughter and son-in-law inherited his land, "which at the time of his death included fee-simple ownership of five ahupua'a, and leasehold rights on all remaining lands, except for small parcels granted to native tenants not previously purchased by Gibson." His estate was settled after the U.S.-backed overthrow, during the rule of the Republic of Hawaii in 1896. The lease of Kingdom Government Lands in Keālia Aupuni, Pāwili, Kama'o, Mahana, and Kaunolū was confirmed for the full term of their respective periods by the new government. Gibson's heirs then formed the Lanai Land Development Company and eventually partnered with Honolulu businessmen to organize the Maunalei Sugar Company, Ltd.[97]

After the U.S. government claimed Hawai'i as a colonial territory, Charles and Louisa Gay purchased a portion of the estate from Gibson's heirs in 1902 and in a few years possessed most of the land on Lāna'i with fee-simple title. In 1906–1907 Charles Gay was granted fee-simple ownership of all Hawaiian Kingdom government land (eight ahupua'a) on Lāna'i, erroneously deemed "ceded." In 1909 the Gay family mortgaged its land holdings on Lāna'i to William G. Irwin and Company. And in 1910 William G. Irwin (and his wife), Robert W. Shingle, and Cecil Brown formed the Lanai Ranch Company, which later became the Lanai Company, which conveyed four lots to Charles Gay for agricultural purposes in 1911. In 1917 the Lanai Company conveyed its Lāna'i holdings to Frank and Harry Baldwin of Maui, who operated under the name Lanai Ranch. In 1921 the Gay family begin to plant pineapple on the island and agreed to sell harvested fruit to the Haiku Fruit & Packing Company on Maui.

James D. Dole "bought out the Baldwin interests on Lāna'i for $1.1 million in 1922 and set in motion plans that ultimately made Lāna'i the world's largest pineapple plantation."[98] In 1960 Hawaiian Pineapple Company Ltd. changed its name to Dole Corporation. Castle & Cooke bought out Dole Corporation in 1961. David H. Murdock purchased Castle & Cooke (including much of the island of Lāna'i) in 1985.

The cases of both Rice and Ellison highlight the imperfections of "perfect title." They illustrate how settler colonialism structurally enables land expropriation through regimes of private property even while having no liens attached. Each man's holdings seem based on unbroken chains of ownership, despite later transactions taking place after the overthrow of the kingdom. The origins of each acquisition are rooted in Indigenous deprivation for corporate accumulation.

Meanwhile these proprietary forms are naturalized in each case and reproduced in media accounts. For example, the article about Rice ends with the following: "Mr. Rice still talks fondly of his banking days, when he was active in all kinds of community organizations from schools and tourism boards to the YMCA. But the transition back to the early mornings and manual labor on the ranch, he said, was natural. 'Just like riding a bicycle,' he said."[99] Like muscle memory, life on the Maui ranch for the settler is a skill that, once learned, is never forgotten. Ellison normalizes the extraordinary as well: "It's surreal to think that I own this beautiful island. It doesn't feel like anyone can own Lanai. What it feels like to me is this really cool 21st-century engineering project, where I get to work with the people of Lanai to create a prosperous and sustainable Eden in the Pacific."[100] Ellison, "playing chief," positions himself as a leader of the future, while the island gets positioned as part of reviving the most palatable part of the Hawaiian "past,"conjured by the fantasy of Eden.

These questions of land and title and governance demonstrate the limits of the deoccupation model of kingdom nationalists. An entire archipelago is occupied, yet, given the structural conditions of settler colonialism, the call for the United States to "deoccupy" Hawai'i is surely inadequate when it comes to the question of land. The question of territorial contiguity is a pressing one, as is the enduring ecological devastation wrought by foreign investment since 1848. The privatization of communal lands through the enclosure of the ahupua'a, the U.S. government's seizure of these lands as part of its expanding territory, and the push for Hawaiian "land rights" are all based on a proprietary relationship to land that undergirds its objectification and commodification. If property is a bundle of rights, and rights (in Foucault's formulation) are a form of war in the name of politics, then property is a form of war, colonial biopolitics. In this case, the shift in governance with an emphasis on the protection of life (access to land) still works to justify state power rationally. Hence "the head of the king" remains intact in the reliance on juridical regimes of power: "perfect title" then and today.

Native Lands in Trust: U.S. Policy on Tribal Jurisdiction

The federal recognition model with its proposed NHGE relies on a very different concept of land title than deoccupation, but also allows for private land expropriation. It is bound to a legal framework in which the U.S. government only concedes Native nations' self-determination based on "Aboriginal title." Meanwhile the federal government claims absolute title over all lands, including those on which tribes continue to assert (limited) civic and criminal jurisdiction—their reservations. Under U.S. law, federally recognized Native governing entities are allowed limited self-determination, but only over their own land base as sovereign territory. This is a contradiction in terms, given that "Native lands" must be held in trust by DOI to be used as a base for jurisdiction. In other words, if a tribal nation buys back some of its original territory in fee simple, it cannot be added to a reservation land base unless the U.S. government approves. Moreover, as stated, the U.S. government claims ultimate ownership over all Native lands, including reservations. The assertion is based on the 1823 ruling in *Johnson v. McIntosh*, 21 U.S. (8 Wheat.) 543, by the U.S. Supreme Court.

The landmark decision in *Johnson* held that private citizens could not purchase lands from Native Americans. The case is the first in what has come to be known as the Marshall Trilogy, named after Chief Justice John Marshall, which also includes *Cherokee Nation v. Georgia* and *Worcester v. Georgia*. The trio is a staple in nearly every case relating to the question of tribal nations' exercise of self-determination. The court laid out the foundations of the "doctrine of discovery" and created the concept of "Aboriginal title" to land—an American invention—to deny Indian tribes the same rights to land as the European colonizers, holding that Indians are "an inferior race of savages." As Native legal scholars have pointed out, the court perpetuated a racist judicial language of Indian savagery to define and subordinate Indian rights.[101] *Johnson* remains the authoritative precedent in contemporary case law, so the language of racial inferiority still undergirds the U.S. federal Indian policy that undermines Native sovereignty. As Steven Newcomb demonstrates, the U.S. government continues to rely on the religious concepts of Christendom, exemplified by the papal bull in 1492 enshrined in the Supreme Court's ruling, in order to justify the taking of Indigenous lands and to deny the original independence of tribal nations. He demonstrates that the case is premised in part on the Old Testament narrative of the "chosen people" with a divine right to the "promised land" and that the U.S. government continues to rely on the religious distinction between "Christians" and "heathens."[102] Indeed, this distinction continues to undergird U.S. law and therefore the limitations imposed on tribal self-governance, as discussed in chapter 1.

While it is essential to critique and challenge *Johnson* and its use of "occupancy" and "tenancy" rights that demean Indigenous relations to land practices and lifeways as "heathen" and serve as a racist rationale for the United States to claim absolute ownership to Indigenous lands, the paradoxical task is to counter U.S. claims to ownership without asserting that Indigenous peoples owned the land in a Lockean sense. Tribal nations may make claims to their traditional territories, but decolonial modes acknowledge that the land does not belong to the people(s): the people(s) belong to the land.

With regard to what the U.S. government outlines as the "inherent powers of tribal self-government," federal policy stipulates that tribes have the right to license and regulate activities *within their jurisdiction*; to zone; and to exclude persons from tribal lands. Limitations on inherent tribal powers of self-government are few but do include the same limitations applicable to states. Neither tribes nor states have the power to make war, engage in foreign relations, or print and issue currency. American Indian and Alaska Native tribal governments, businesses, and individuals may also own land as private property, but they are subject to state and local laws, regulations, codes, and taxation.[103]

The U.S. government claims Indian reservations as reserved *federal* lands, like military and public lands. Federal policy defines a federal Indian reservation as "an area of land reserved for a tribe or tribes under treaty or other agreement with the United States, executive order, or federal statute or administrative action as permanent tribal homelands, and where *the federal government holds title to the land* in trust on behalf of the tribe." Not every federally recognized tribe has a reservation (and there is just one federal Indian reservation in Alaska, the Metlakatla Indian Community of the Annette Island Reserve in southeastern Alaska). Other types of "Indian lands" are allotted lands (remnants of reservations broken up during the federal allotment period of the late nineteenth and early twentieth centuries issued to individual Indians through fee simple and in trust under various treaties and laws); restricted status lands ("also known as restricted fee, where title to the land is held by an individual Indian person or a tribe and which can only be alienated or encumbered by the owner with the approval of the Secretary of the Interior because of limitations contained in the conveyance instrument pursuant to federal law"); and state Indian reservations (lands held in trust by a state for an Indian tribe, not subject to state property tax but subject to state law). American Indian and Alaska Native tribes, businesses, and individuals may also own land as private property, but they are subject to state and local laws, regulations, codes, and taxation.[104]

The Oneida land case is most telling in this regard. In the landmark decision *City of Sherrill v. Oneida Indian Nation of New York* (2005), the U.S. Supreme Court rejected the tribe's attempt to reassert tribal sovereignty over parcels of land reacquired by the tribe in fee simple.[105] In 1997 and 1998 the tribe purchased land parcels amounting to approximately 17,000 acres on the open market that had been part of its original reservation. This was an attempt to recuperate traditional territory after a long history of dispossession by the state of New York. The Oneida Indian Nation originally lived on about 6,000,000 acres but by 1920 had only 32 acres. After the repurchase the City of Sherrill sought to impose property taxes on the land, while the tribe maintained that the property was tax-exempt as tribal lands. In the majority opinion of the court, Justice Ruth Bader Ginsburg held that the tribe's purchase of the land did not restore tribal sovereignty over the land. The court's rationale in its decision was centered on judgments about temporality—too much time had passed. The tribe had not sought to regain title to the repurchased lands during the two hundred years since they were last "possessed" by the Oneidas as a tribal entity in 1805. The court described this as an effort to rekindle "embers of sovereignty that long ago grew cold" and referred to the tribe's sovereignty as "ancient," too old to pursue in the ways the tribe wanted.[106] This logic is exemplary of what Kevin Bruyneel theorizes as "colonial time"—locating Indigenous Peoples out of time. As Jean O'Brien's work shows, the "authentic Indian" is not allowed modernity.[107] In the majority opinion the court also suggested that the unification of tribal lands was a problematic and "disruptive remedy," given that the town "and the surrounding area are today overwhelmingly populated by non-Indians, and a checkerboard of state and tribal jurisdiction" would seriously burden the administration of state and local governments. Furthermore, the court asserted that it would "adversely affect landowners neighboring the tribal patches."[108]

In another case, the U.S. Supreme Court also dealt with related questions of the rights of a "Native governing entity" to assert its sovereignty over fee-simple land. In *Alaska v. Native Village of Venetie Tribal Government* (522 U.S. 520, 1998), the court ruled that Venetie's land base did not count as Indian Country in the legal sense—as sovereign territory defined to include all dependent Indian communities in the United States. The court paradoxically ruled that Venetie did not qualify because its lands are not held in trust by the U.S. federal government. Thus the village's tribal government cannot assess taxes, enforce its own laws, or assert jurisdiction over these lands as American Indian governments do on reservations.

Both of these cases, among others, are instructive for the question of territory and jurisdiction in the case of the federal government recognizing a Native Hawaiian governing entity. The court ruled in the state of Hawaii land case that the 50th state has "perfect title," even though the court had affirmed the unadjudicated land claims of the Hawaiian people (perhaps recognizing an Indigenous claim to them as "Native lands" rather than conceding that they are the *national lands* of the Hawaiian Kingdom). But those lands are not contiguous, which complicates matters of jurisdiction for any future Native government. Even if the lands were adjoining, any domestic dependent NHGE would be required to have them put in trust by the U.S. government, which would mean surrendering title to them.

Conclusion

The ongoing threat to Hawaiian sovereignty is the 50th state's attempt to sell the Kingdom Crown and Government Lands. When met with protest, the state government has concocted ways to further alienate the lands in other ways. For example, the state of Hawai'i legislature passed legislation in 2011 that resulted in Act 55 and created a Public Land Development Corporation (PLDC) within the Department of Land and Natural Resources (DLNR). The PLDC was to be governed by a five-member board of directors as a state entity to develop 1.6 million acres of state lands and generate revenues for the DLNR through "public-private partnerships."[109] The act was later repealed due to mass protest across the islands, expressed during public hearings.[110] Clearly the state is poised to do the next best thing to alienating them in fee-simple title: enable the highest bidder to develop them without regard for state laws on the environment, zoning, and burial desecration. The state considers these lands "public" yet leases them in the service of various private industries, increasingly biotech, like the lease to Syngenta to conduct genetically modified organism (GMO) experiments, research, and development of corn and soybeans on the island of Kaua'i.[111] As possession is regarded as nine-tenths of the law in the U.S. system, developers investing in these lands for their own commercial purposes may well be considered land "owners" by the state. In any case Act 176 of 2009 (brokered in exchange for dropping the lawsuit, as noted above) still stands, allowing for sale of these lands by requiring a supermajority legislative approval for the sale or gift of trust lands.

As Silva put it in her rally speech cited at the beginning of this chapter, whether Kanaka Maoli are in favor of the domestic dependent model or independence, preserving the spiritual and familial relationship with the 'āina is crucial to Hawaiian peoplehood. Therefore resisting state-driven settlements is an urgent necessity. In the face of massive structural confines of U.S. domination, asserting Indigenous agency to advance decolonial futures is crucial for sustainability on multiple levels.

Some Kanaka Maoli are challenging U.S. and Hawai'i (50th) state claims over these same lands, while privileging Indigenous knowledge as the basis for revitalizing Hawaiian ontologies and epistemes in nonproprietary relation to the 'āina. One such renewal project—among numerous others—that emerged from an organization called Kamakakūoka'āina (Ancestral Vision of the Land) was called AVA Konohiki. The focus was on food sustainability, especially for the island of O'ahu, which is so heavily urbanized. Those involved digitized handwritten documents that were written and produced in the 1840s and 1850s, when lands in Hawai'i were first privatized. These land records, written by Kanaka Maoli ancestors, include detailed descriptions of land management practices. The work is complemented by courses in Hawaiian culture, language, history, land studies, geographic maps, and current practices, to enhance Native Hawaiian student knowledge of ancestral wisdom. The project also included cultural retreats to study ancient chants and rituals having to do with the elements of nature and land. The stated goal was "to train young Native Hawaiians to be Konohiki, or traditional Hawaiian Land Stewards, who manage the water, land, agricultural and fishing resources of 1,300 ahupua'a, in order to provide food for a population of 1 million people. In 1848, we had 252 Konohiki; in 2012 we have 12."[112] The AVA project acknowledges and works from the historical legacy of the Māhele, but in a restorative way that is based on Indigenous knowledge and island sustainability rather than a proprietary relationship to land.

Yet AVA Konohiki was funded by a federal grant from the Administration for Native Americans and employs at least one kingdom nationalist, Donovan Preza (whose work on the Māhele land division is discussed above). While this may seem to be a contradictory political stance, it speaks to Indigenous agency in relation to settler colonial domination in the context of the U.S. occupation. The project drew on Indigenous knowledge and genealogical relations to land, as these same groups who are offering a decolonial model around land use have also been squeezed out of using the land by the priorities of the settler state to prioritize public-private partnerships as it replaces industrial agriculture with biotech.

Another example of land-based Indigenous resurgence is the case of Mālama 'Āina Koholālele (Caring for the 'Āina of Koholālele). No'eau Peralto offers a history of how the group that he is part of, Hui Mālama i ke Ala 'Ūlili (Group for the Care of the 'Ūlili Pathway), convened in November 2013 at Koholālele, popularly referred to today as Pa'auilo Landing, to plot a community garden project envisioned years earlier. Hui Mālama i ke Ala 'Ūlili sought to reestablish "an 'ohana centered space to return our hands

FIGURE 2.1. A few months after the members of Hui Mālama i ke Ala ʻŪlili began their garden at Koholālele (kalo in the foreground and guinea grass in the background). Photo courtesy of Leon Noʻeau Peralto.

to the land, and to share the food and stories of this ʻāina with others in our community." The group worked together to clear the land of invasive grass, remove truckloads of garbage, and plant indigenous food plants. Importantly, as Peralto points out, no one in the group had claim to the land: "We are not the owners or the lessees of this ʻāina. We have no codified ʻrights' to it other than the kuleana [responsibility] embodied in our bones. We are simply the ʻŌiwi descendants of this ʻāina, following the instructions of those who came before us: if you mālama [care for and tend to] this ʻāina, it will mālama you." The intergenerational group worked with a Hawaiian elder who gave the garden a name to imbue it with mana (spiritual power), which is how it came to be named Mālama ʻĀina Koholālele. On land that had been "exploited as ʻproperty' for over a century and called by the name of the sugar plantation mill it serviced for just as long, an act as ʻeveryday' as consciously calling a place by its proper ancestral name is profound." Peralto names this an "everyday act of resurgence" that "not only counters the erasure of the name, histories, and genealogies of Koholālele, [but] it further reasserts our responsibilities as the descendants of this place to mālama ʻāina—to care for and protect the long-term well-being of that which sustains us physically and spiritually as a people."[113]

The group further delved into the history of Koholālele to learn about the deities that frequent the place and the songs and chants associated with it. Drawing on the spiritual foundations of aloha ʻāina (love of the land) and mālama ʻāina rooted in place, the Hui is further cultivating ritual practices and ceremonies aimed at ensuring the abundance of food resources in the sea and on the land: "We have not forgotten the names of our ancestors. We have not forgotten our responsibilities to care for them. The ʻŌiwi caretakers of this ʻāina are here to stay. We are pulling the weeds of our dependence, recalling the roots of our resurgence, and replanting the seeds of our reemergence as the thriving descendants that our ancestors prayed for. And it all began with some seemingly 'everyday' actions. Gather with your family. Clear a space. Make a garden. Gift it a name. And commit to it." In little over a year, Peralto explains, the garden quadrupled in size, with over 1,500 people working the land since 2013, when they had just 30. But, as he is careful to point out, the group has not merely grown in size and number: "The cultivation of this garden and the fulfillment of our shared kuleana together has grown our relationships with this land and with each other." Here we can see how this life-sustaining project is deeply rooted community building—to feed and care for each person—while committed to regularly tending to the land, the cherished elder.[114]

If we revisit Foucault's call that we "execute the king," I want to suggest that we must shift away from proprietary relationships to land as a prerequisite for decolonial imaginings of the future. A paradox of Hawaiian sovereignty is that we have a legacy of land privatization as a form of colonial biopolitical governmentality. But a decolonial turn entails taking seriously the meaning of ʻāina—that which feeds, a living entity, our relative—and demands restoring an ethical relationship with the land that is not premised on capitalist extraction, exploitation, and exhaustion. To feed the people while not destroying the ecosystem necessitates restorative measures exemplified by those working to renew the *loʻi kalo* (taro beds), those laboring to eradicate foreign plants and clean soil from the toxic legacy of monocrop plantations such as those that fed the sugar industry, and those fighting against GMO experimentation (to name only a few). It is imperative to reconsider Hawaiian indigeneity as an epistemological resource for rethinking land along with the very concept of sovereignty toward selectively revitalizing indigenous ontologies for the twenty-first century.

THREE. GENDER, MARRIAGE, AND COVERTURE

A New Proprietary Relationship

On August 12, 1998, the 100th anniversary of the formal ceremony marking the unilateral U.S. annexation of the Hawaiian Islands,[1] I attended a mass gathering at ʻIolani Palace. This site served as the governmental center of the Hawaiian Kingdom until the 1893 overthrow of Queen Liliʻuokalani as constitutional monarch. Dozens of Hawaiian sovereignty groups occupied the grounds of the palace at the 1998 event, which included speechmaking, hula, traditional chanting, a nationalist hip-hop performance, and a ceremony that entailed lowering the U.S. flag and replacing it with the Hawaiian flag.[2] I stood watching a few dozen Kanaka Maoli men stand on the steps of the Palace with Hawaiian leader Henry Noa, who claims the title of prime minister of the self-declared Restored Hawaiian Kingdom (now called the Lawful Hawaiian Government). Noa publicly discussed his political goal of returning to the 1864 constitution of the monarchy and suggested that it was the last legitimate governing document of the nation.

As I stood there, I considered the fact that the 1864 kingdom constitution did not allow Hawaiian women independent civil status. I was next to a new acquaintance, a Kanaka man who had been pressuring me to affiliate with Noa's particular political initiative. When I asked him why only Hawaiian men stood on the steps, he explained to me that women did not have a say in the kingdom yet because in that constitution only men had the right to vote. So I asked again why he thought I should support them. He assured me that "we need to get our kingdom restored first, *then* we men can vote to change the constitution to include you women, *after* the kingdom." He expected me to support something that disenfranchised Kanaka women and hold out for the fulfillment of the promise that the men would grant us our political rights at a later time (assuming that the kingdom would indeed be restored). His explanation sounded to me like another problematic version of "after the revolution" faced by women in Third World liberation struggles the world over from their male counterparts in response to "the woman question" throughout the mid- to late twentieth century.[3] But what I witnessed on the steps of the palace in 1998 felt somewhat new to me in the Hawaiian political context. In terms of what I had previously researched about the sovereignty movement in the 1970s and 1980s and what I witnessed myself throughout most of the 1990s, Kanaka women held top leadership positions.

Referring to that period through the late 1980s, Jocelyn Linnekin notes: "Certainly the historical encounter between gender constructions continues to play itself out in Hawaii today, as the state government, dominated numerically by non-Hawaiian men, confronts many strong and vocal Hawaiian women in political leadership roles."[4] In the 1990s Haunani-Kay Trask identified Hawaiian women's prominence within the islands' Indigenous nationalist movement. She argued that Hawaiian women were on the front lines of the Hawaiian sovereignty struggle: "a great coming together of women's *mana* [that] has given birth to a new form of power based on a traditional Hawaiian belief: women asserting their leadership for the sake of the nation." Trask further asserted that Hawaiian women were the most visible, the most articulate, and the most creative leaders. As she put it: "By any standard—public, personal, political—our sovereignty movement is led by women."[5]

Since the late 1990s or so, however, male leadership has become much more pronounced. This especially seems to be the case in the independence segment among kingdom nationalists, where a military analysis of occupation has swept the movement—perhaps giving some Kanaka men an easier point of access in light of women's visible leadership in earlier decades, which some have resented. As Ty P. Kāwika Tengan has shown, many Hawaiian men have felt profoundly disempowered by the legacies of colonization and by the tourist industry, which promotes a feminized image of Native Hawaiians in addition to occupying a great deal of land. As a response, a group of Native men on the island of Maui in the 1990s decided to refashion and reassert their masculine identities in a group called the Hale Mua (Men's House), which promoted warrior masculinity through practices including martial arts, woodcarving, and cultural ceremonies. Tengan documents how Hale Mua rituals and practices connect to broader projects of cultural revitalization and Hawaiian nationalism and addresses the tensions that mark the group's efforts to reclaim Indigenous masculinity in debates over nineteenth-century historical source materials and during political and cultural gatherings held in spaces designated as tourist sites. He also highlights the militarization of Hawaiian masculinity. Many of the men involved come from military or para-defense backgrounds, which he suggests may be possible influences on this leadership style and political project. Although Noa's group is not affiliated with the Hale Mua, the Mua had a prominent physical presence at the palace that day holding guard. Assertions of Hawaiian Kingdom nationalism seem imbricated in this period's wave of militaristic analysis within sovereignty politics.[6]

Noa and his male supporters at the 1998 political gathering at ʻIolani seemed to have an unspoken expectation that a governing document that excluded Kanaka women at large would get broad-based support across gender lines. What can we make of this political approach, given that the last reigning monarch was a woman? And what about the new constitution that Queen Liliʻuokalani was set to promulgate in 1893, which was the catalyst for the U.S.-backed overthrow? The kingdom had several constitutions: 1840, 1852, 1864, and 1887. But people privileged the 1864 constitution under Kamehameha IV's reign over the 1887 constitution because a white militia group—the Honolulu Rifles—forced the 1887 constitution on King Kalākaua to strip him of executive powers.[7] What events prior to 1864 might account for that particular constitution disenfranchising Hawaiian women, given the ample evidence that principal chiefs prior to the formation of the monarchy included numerous women? How had the formal legal status of Hawaiian women—both common and chiefly—shifted from the first constitution in 1840 and the second constitution of 1852 prior to the version promulgated in 1864?

Examining the introduction of marriage and coverture illuminates the precise ways in which the interlinked processes of cultural colonization and development of a constitutional state disempowered Kanaka women in the nineteenth century. This chapter examines that historical legacy for the contemporary question of Hawaiian women's political rights within the politics of deoccupation nationalism. I first lay out some historical background to offer a sketch of precolonial norms regarding gender, especially with regard to Hawaiian women. The most dramatic change in sexual philosophies and conceptions of women came with the introduction of

Christianity after 1820.[8] Hence I focus on the restructuring of the status of women through missionary Christianization and legal coverture brought about by the newly introduced form of marriage. Laying out some of the distinct notions of sexual unions and partnering from the precolonial period and how they differ from Christian heterosexual marriage, I argue that marriage itself was a conduit to the transformation of Hawaiian women's legal status and as such was a colonial imposition in order to subordinate. Yet it also emerged as a biopolitical tool to protect the people at large. What were the motivations for Kanaka Maoli—especially the chiefs—to implement Christian moralities and laws? Were these different for men and women across social class? Considering the changes, influences, and relationships that brought about conversion and the interrelated transformation of economies, systems of gender and sexuality, and politics, this is a complex history and system of relationships, which show a rapidly transforming and shifting response to colonialism.

The emergence of the (Western) state form and its project of specifying individuals and their reproductive capacity for biopolitical governance illustrate Foucault's "rights as war" argument: both Christianization *and* the constitutional monarchy recognized by European states took place through adaptation of Western law as heteropatriarchal law. I examine the regulatory power of biopolitics—the control of the entire population—in the context of the modern Hawaiian state and its limitations on common Kanaka women subjects. As Foucault argues in *History of Sexuality, Volume 1*, sex has historically been the most intense site at which discipline and biopolitics intersected, because any intervention in population through the control of individual bodies fundamentally had to be about reproduction and also because sex is one of the major vectors of disease transmission. Hence sex had to be controlled, regulated, and monitored if the population was to be brought under control. The missionaries were extremely concerned with this sexual activity, continually haunted by the specter of prostitution. The regulation of Kanaka sexuality through the banning of adultery as an effort to contain prostitution led to a new form of governmentality in the mid-nineteenth century—a missionary logic by which the Hawaiian polity would be governed. When Ka'ahumanu declared the 1825 verbal edict of heteromonogamous Christian marriage, the Seventh Commandment became national law.

This chapter reveals another paradox of Hawaiian sovereignty: although the kingdom had been further democratized by the 1840s, the internal push for normalization with regard to Indigenous gender and sexual norms constituted a form of colonial biopolitics. The adoption of European masculinist conventions of statehood was in the service of protecting Hawai'i from Western takeover. As the new laws imposed marriage as the only model to contain sexual activity, they also subsumed women's subjecthood under their husbands', producing the disenfranchisement of women through state regulation of sexuality. Tracing the ways in which the Hawaiian Kingdom became more Westernized as it subordinated chiefly women's status in the realm of state governance, I argue that the privatization of land as property and coverture as a marker of male propriety both signaled a shift to proprietary relationships between Kanaka and land and between men and women—all new forms of enclosure.

This legacy has repercussions for the contemporary sovereignty movement, which I explore in a case study that speaks to the way this legacy plays out in the contemporary independence movement. Here I offer a close reading of a document produced by David Keanu Sai in 1998 in the recent nationalist context. Sai—a contemporary scholar and political leader who identifies himself as chairman of the Council of Regency and acting minister of the interior of the Hawaiian Kingdom—issued a memorandum from the "Office of the Regent" addressed to "Subjects of the Kingdom" regarding "the suffrage of female subjects." His memo grapples with the question of women's political rights in the present, given his own reading of mid- to late nineteenth-century Hawaiian Kingdom constitutions and civil codes, which I examine through a critical analysis of the memo and its liberal gesture of "equality."

Transforming Indigenous Gender and Sexual Practices

The scholarly literature on precolonial Hawaiian society suggests that relations between women and men were egalitarian within their respective genealogical rankings. The social order was hierarchically sustained through chiefly strata determined by lineage rather than gender.[9] It had two main classes: *ali'i nui* (high chiefs) and the *maka'āinana* (common people), with *kaukau ali'i* (chiefs of lesser rank) serving as a buffer in this hierarchy.[10] The pathbreaking works of Lilikalā Kame'eleihiwa and Noenoe K. Silva, who draw from Hawaiian-language sources from the mid-nineteenth century documenting precolonial chants and histories, provide abundant evidence of women within cosmological traditions as deities and within society as chiefs.[11] Both high-ranking Hawaiian women and men held governing positions as paramount chiefs and lesser chiefs before the formation of the monarchy in the early nineteenth century.[12] Jocelyn Linnekin argues that "the ideology of male interpersonal dominance and superiority was weakly developed" in Hawai'i prior to white American influences. She also documents how Kanaka women of all genealogical ranks were considered strong, active agents, autonomous within the context of an interdependent polity. Historically, they were symbolically associated with land, were valued as producers of high cultural goods, held a separate domain of female ritual and social power, were seen as powerful autonomous beings, and were points of access to rank, land, and political power.[13]

In terms of structural power and significance within chiefly society, Hawaiian women figured crucially in the strategies by which men effectively raised their own status and ensured higher rank for their children.[14] "This symbology not only concerned the chiefs; a similar complex of meanings surrounded women among maka'āinana, for whom access to land was the analogue to chiefly status ambitions." Because Hawaiian women were key to rank differentiation, they were in a sense "a pivot point between chiefs and commoners—the means by which the social rank of one's descendants can either rise or fall."[15] As Kame'eleihiwa explains:

> Those at the top were *kapu,* or sacred, and possessed *mana.* Those at the bottom were *noa,* common or free from *kapu* and, by extension, without the necessary *mana,* or power, to invoke a *kapu*—although even a common fisherman, if successful, had some *mana.* Those in between were on a sliding scale, having less *mana* the farther down the triangle they slipped and the farther they fell from high lineage. These differentiations in status were designated by birth. There tended to be, however, a constant shift away from *kapu* because [male] *Ali'i Nui* found it difficult to mate only with high female *Ali'i Nui.* Those intermarrying with *Ali'i* of lesser rank produced *kaukau ali'i* who, in turn, could descend with the same facility to *maka'āinana* rank.[16]

Both symbolically and politically, "Hawaiian women historically served as points of access to power and were associated with achieving and demonstrating *mana.*"[17] Moreover, through their association with high kapu (that which is sacred) and inherent rights in the land, high-ranking Hawaiian women signified access to status and political authority while also using position and mana for their own ends. E. S. Craighill Handy and Mary Kawena Pukui explain that genealogy was a carefully guarded "historical science" within the ali'i class, handled by 'Aha Ali'i (Council of Chiefs, precursor to the kingdom's Privy Council), where order and right in the matter of succession, formal unions of those who were high ranking, and claims to relationship with the high-born had to be proven genealogically.[18]

In terms of female sexuality, chastity was safeguarded for successional considerations with regard for genealogically high-ranking women.[19] Virginity was a requirement only in terms of primogeniture so that chiefs could have their first chief born of the highest possible rank.[20] The ʻAha Aliʻi preserved these genealogies by monitoring physical paternity, but contested fatherhood could be accommodated even when the patrilineage was unclear. The child could also claim lineage from both probable fathers—recognition of *poʻolua* (two heads). The term *punalua* describes the relationship between first and secondary mates who are not family relations in cases where one man had two female partners or one woman had two male partners. The purpose of the punalua was to safeguard children born from such triangles, as all three adults would be responsible for caring for them. Also, punalua typically received each other as siblings and treated each other as relatives.[21]

The intimate relationships between *kāne* (men) and *wāhine* (women) are sometimes referred to in the literature as "marriages," but that term does not correspond to Kanaka relationships. Unions were sometimes called *awaiāulu* (to bind securely, fasten). Leilani Basham has noted that the "binding" of the awaiāulu, different from binding in a legal sense, referred to the connection of *aloha* (love, compassion, care).[22] *Hoʻāo* (to stay until daylight) is a traditional way of registering interest in an enduring intimate relationship.[23] *Hoʻopalau* is said to express a formal intention to become partners similar to an "engagement."[24]

In terms of anything akin to monogamy in traditional Hawaiian society, Kamakau provides one history suggesting that the development of social acceptance of multiple partners became something specific to elites. He identifies Hulihonua and Keakahulilani, first woman and man, as the earliest ancestors of Kanaka. For twenty-eight generations from Hulihonua to Wākea "no man was chief over another." The first ruling chief, Kapawa, ruled over the island of O'ahu twenty-five generations later. After that chiefs ruled "kingdoms" on each island. According to Kamakau: "It was Wakea (son of Luamea) who introduced the hewa [wrong] of mating with many women (moe lehulehu)." He explains that unions were divided into two kinds in succeeding generations: "those in which men took many wives and women many husbands, and those in which there was but one wife or husband." He adds: "Formerly, the latter were in the majority. It was the chiefs and wealthy people who took more than one wife or husband." From here Kamakau delves into moralizing examples of women taking too many husbands. He describes a marriage called *hoʻāo paʻa*, which he defines as "an ancient custom by which a man and a woman were bound in a lasting union (ua paʻa loa ka noho ana), a man not to desert his wife nor a woman her husband." He explains that "this form of marriage, in which each took a single mate, originated as a command from *the god* to Hulihonua and his wife Keakahulilani, and lasted from their time down to that of Kahiko Luamea, 27 generations later."[25]

Curiously, Kamakau identifies one god here, seemingly invoking a Judeo-Christian conception of God even though traditional Hawaiian society was polytheistic. In any case, the prevailing literature on ancient Hawaiian society (perhaps after the period Kamakau describes above) suggests that marriage was a "flexible arrangement" even for the nonchiefly class. "Girls and boys past puberty engaged in social activity with a number of partners. Around the age of eighteen they settled into marriages which were sometimes enduring but could be dissolved easily if alternative relationships were desired."[26] Lifelong partnerships were not expected.[27]

Notably, Hawaiian kinship was (and still is) reckoned bilaterally, through both the maternal and the paternal lines. Kanaka Maoli family units—known as *ʻohana*—are traditionally intergenerational and include the *mākua* (parents and relatives of the parent generation), the *kūpuna* (grandparents and relatives of the grandparent generation), and *keiki* (children). A form of fostering, *hānai* (to feed), typically entailed cases of blood kin in which a child was given to another relative besides the birth parents, such as grandparents, aunts, or uncles.[28] Nonbiological children could also be incorporated into the ʻohana through "adoption," known as *hoʻokama* (to make a child).[29] Kanaka Maoli traditionally practiced matrilocal (uxorilocal) residence patterns in which women drew in extra manpower in the form of "husbands," so that offspring were likely to be closely affiliated with the mother's kin.[30] Childcare was not seen as specifically the mother's responsibility or even as a generally female concern.[31]

Needless to say, this world was quite different from the New England world of the first Christian missionaries from the then dominant Congregationalist tradition. Their arrival took place in the midst of the Second Great Awakening (a Protestant revival movement during the early nineteenth century in the United States). In 1819 the American Board of Commissioners for Foreign Missions dispatched a mission to the "Sandwich Islands." The timing of the missionaries' arrival was key. The same leaders who orchestrated the dismantling of the kapu (sacred or restricted) system—the ancient Hawaiian code of conduct of laws and regulations relating to the sacred power of the chiefs and deities and the religious world at large—authorized the missionaries to land in the islands to do their work. By the time they arrived in Hawaiʻi in 1820, the *ʻaikapu* (gender segregated eating) had been overturned for one year. That was the first formal act of taking down the kapu system overall, which had already been breaking down with increased foreigner presence. Its regulatory force became unsustainable.[32] Kamehameha II abolished the kapu system under the direction of his mother Keōpūolani and his late father's other wahine, Kaʻahumanu, who had now become co-regent by occupying a new role called *kuhina nui*.

According to Kameʻeleihiwa, Kamehameha I established the political office of kuhina nui for his consort Kaʻahumanu just before his death, but she inherited the position "from her father Keʻeaumoku, who had been instrumental in bringing Kamehameha to power."[33] Kaʻahumanu became de facto ruler when Kamehameha died in 1819, declaring to his son Liholiho that Kamehameha had commanded that they rule together. She was said to have told Kamehameha II, "O heavenly one! I speak to you the commands of your father. Here are the chiefs, here are the people of your ancestors; here are your guns; here are your lands. But we two shall share the rule over the land."[34] Kaʻahumanu dominated the governance of the kingdom for thirteen years, first with Kamehameha II until his departure for England and death there in 1823 and then in relation to his brother Kauikeaouli (Kamehameha III).[35] Under her, "the office of kuhina nui was strengthened so that it shared equal rights with the Mōʻī in making decisions over matters of land disposition and politics."[36] The first constitution (1840) included the role of kuhina nui written into the foundation of the government structure: "In the executive powers under the constitution the *kuhina nui* was given control of all the business of the king, handling all land and all documents in his name and was the 'King's special counselor in the great business of the kingdom.' In the judicial powers under the constitution, the *kuhina nui* sat with the king in presiding over the Supreme Court."[37]

Central to their pedagogy of piety, the missionaries had to find a way to convert Hawaiians. They deemed Kanaka to be heathens due to their non-Christian status, which included polytheistic spiritual worship and cultural customs and practices seen as morally repugnant, so this would entail an entire new way of behaving. One of the key problems that they identified was Hawaiian sexuality, which for missionaries was "a source of shame, anxiety and frustration," while for Kanaka it was "a source of great pleasure, aesthetic beauty and religious affirmation of life."[38] In Hawaiian society the missionaries encountered homosexuality, polyandry, polygyny, and chiefly procreation among those within close degrees of consanguinity.

The missionaries were also compelled to reckon with the political reality of the overriding power of the ruling elites. When Liholiho (Kamehameha II) "declared that only the chiefly group, and wives and children of foreigners, could receive mission instruction, there was no alternative but to obey."[39] "Early missionary journals indicate that one of the initial goals of the company was to convert the important ali'i and convince them that the customs and regulations which ordered the lives of the Hawaiians should be brought in line with Christian theology."[40] They relied on their power to enforce the initial conversion of the archipelago and then to impose the legal codes that the missionaries considered essential.[41]

Gender roles in society seemed to be defined by dualities, yet not in mutually exclusive binaries. For example, women could take "men's roles" and vice versa. As Pukui et al. explain, "Two types of 'professional' women filled occupational roles in the masculine world. There were nā kāula, women priest-prophets, and the koa wāhine, or wāhine kaua. The koa wāhine (brave, bold, women) or wāhine kaua (battle women) were Hawai'i's Amazons." They add: "These were women trained in warfare. They went with their men, and when the men were fighting, the women prepared their food, though cooking was usually man's work. They nursed their wounded. And if they had to fight, they fought. They asked to become nā wāhine koa and the men trained them."[42] David Malo notes that nonelite women also worked alongside men.[43]

Hawaiian women were differentiated by chiefly and nonchiefly status. Hence, as Caroline Ralston has noted, they cannot be analyzed as a single homogenous group, given genealogical rank differences and the highly stratified indigenous social context. In terms of power, high-ranking women had better standards of living due to the advantages of access to resources, including the fruits of other people's labor.[44] Patricia Grimshaw notes: "To begin with, the Americans soon realized the enormity of the gulf that existed between high-born Hawaiian women and women of nonchiefly rank. Women as well as men of the chiefly class wielded enormous power: rank superseded gender in terms of power, status, and authority despite the fact that certain symbolic representations of gender referred to all women."[45] As missionary Hiram Bingham admitted: "The females of rank at the islands, and even those without rank, have, by some means, secured to themselves a high degree of attention and respect from their husbands and others."[46]

His comment suggests that Hawaiian women were not subordinate to men within comparable genealogical rank.

Christianized Chiefs

The first company of missionaries who arrived in 1820 included the Reverend Hiram Bingham and his wife, Sybil Mosley; the Reverend Asa Thurston and his wife, Lucy Goodale; Samuel Whitney and his wife, Mercy Poridge; Dr. Thomas Holman and his wife, Lucia Ruggles; Daniel Chamberlain and his wife, Mary Wells; and the printer Elisha Loomis and his wife, Maria Theresa Sartwell.[47] Liholiho (Kamehameha II) initially gave them permission to stay for one year.[48] By the time he became monarch as Kamehameha II in 1825, only two Kanaka in Hawai'i had been baptized: Pua'aiki (aka Bartimeus), who was accepted into the church on July 10, 1823, and the ali'i wahine Keōpūolani, who was baptized in her dying hour by missionaries William Ellis and Samuel B. Ruggles two months later on September 16.[49] As noted earlier, it was Keōpūolani who ended the 'aikapu along with her son Liholiho (Kamehameha II) and Ka'ahumanu. She greatly influenced the other ali'i, as she was the highest-ranking person in the archipelago and birth mother to the ruling monarch. In 1823 Keōpūolani helped missionary William Richards establish a church in Lāhainā. According to Osorio: "Here she was behaving as a traditional Ali'i Nui, appealing to the power of the akua (deities) to bring life to the land, but it also seems that she feared for the destiny of her own soul, begging the mission to baptize her as she lay dying."[50] She previously had partnered with two other men besides Kamehameha I. After the king died and she backed the mission, she eventually gave up one of these two men. As Grimshaw explains: "The question of polygamous marriages caused the mission particular difficulty, because this issue applied mainly to the chiefs. Missionaries urged the chiefs to choose the spouse nearest in age to themselves and to separate from the rest."[51]

At least one other chief's conversion was of paramount importance at this time: Kapi'olani, of the island of Hawai'i. Grimshaw explains that Kapi'olani had at first declared herself "too wicked" to be baptized and was ambivalent about the missionaries in general but eventually came around to supporting them. She dismissed all of her intimates except Nāihe as her husband and threw herself energetically behind the mission. In June 1825 the 'Aha Ali'i, Ka'ahumanu herself, William Pitt Kalanimoku, Kapi'olani, and Kapule announced that they were candidates for church membership and began a six-month probation that ended in December.[52] Other Christian women chiefs included Kīnaʻu and Kekāuluohi (both of whom were Kaʻahumanu's nieces and later served as kuhina nui).

Jane Silverman asserts that Kaʻahumanu's part in abolishing the old laws (the kapu system) is a crucial context for her eventually declaring the new Christian laws. Kaʻahumanu already held considerable command as kuhina nui of the monarchy since Kamehameha II died of measles in London when his brother Kauikeaouli, heir to the throne, was just twelve years old. She would reign until Kamehameha III was old enough to exercise his position and thus had a long period in which to introduce and strengthen reforms.[53] It was "Kaahumanu herself who arbitrated the presence and influence in Hawaii of the American Board of Commissioners for Foreign Missions (ABCFM) until her death in 1832." Her conversion to Christianity and backing of the missionaries was a way for her to consolidate influence: she is credited with inaugurating a "religious, legal, and social revolution."[54] She used literacy and the Christian religion to enhance her authority and power.[55] As Marie Alohalani Brown notes: "Kaʻahumanu's conversion led to greatly increased support of the missionaries' proselytizing efforts, which includes the promotion of literacy as an important evangelizing force."[56] Kameʻeleihiwa suggests that Kaʻahumanu wanted Hawaiʻi to be governed by Christian law not only because she found out that Western governments were Christian but also to enable a way to rule foreigners in Hawaiʻi while also providing a new structure from which to care for her own people. "From this standpoint, Christianity seemed the only path to *mana* that incorporated control of Hawaiʻi with control over the ever-present and ever-intrusive outside world; this was the official government position until her death."[57] Here we see the colonial biopolitical element in terms of the role of the early Hawaiian state in implementing policies regulating sexuality both as a protective measure and in the quest to secure sovereignty recognition of the kingdom.

But Kaʻahumanu's entry into Christian life was not without its issues and negotiations. On October 8, 1821, she and Kaumualiʻi (paramount chief of the island of Kauaʻi) married after he left Kapule (who preferred to stay with Kaumualiʻi's son, Kealiʻiahonui). After Kaumualiʻi died of illness in 1824, Kaʻahumanu began a relationship with Kealiʻiahonui.[58] Missionary Elisha Loomis recorded his concern about the question of Kaʻahumanu's relationships as well as what he considered an incestuous relationship:

June 2—A delicate and somewhat difficult subject was brought up in our meeting last evening. Kaahumanu and Keluahonui [Keali'iahonui] wish to know what is duty in regard to themselves, whether to marry or separate. Keluahonui [*sic*] is the son of Taumuarii [Kaumuali'i], who was the husband of Kaahumanu. Keluahonui has lived with Kaahumanu as a husband even before his father's death, and has continued with her till some months since, when, understanding that for one to have his father's wife was an abomination not known among the heathen, in the time of St. Paul, they separated; and they now desire expressly the opinion of the Mission as to their duty. It appears to be their desire to be married. But after considerable discussion it was the unanimous opinion of the mission that they ought not to be united. For one to have his father's wife is an abomination (much) known among the heathen here, as is almost every species of incest. At the time of our arrival here Rihoriho [Liholiho] had 5 wives, one of whom had been the wife of his father, and 2 that were his half sisters. At present many of the people begin to be enlightened, on this subject and desire to regulate their conduct by the word of God.[59]

Loomis expresses his disapproval of Ka'ahumanu's choice of Keali'iahonui because she was the wife of his father. Even though he and Ka'ahumanu were willing to commit to each other through Christian marriage, Loomis explains that it would still be an abomination. He also condemns Kamehameha II's (Liholiho's) having had multiple women (including some siblings) when the missionaries first arrived, wishing to eradicate "incest" and multiple partnering.

Ka'ahumanu had asked to be baptized, but the missionaries were unconvinced that she was ready. Before she was finally able to be accepted as a member of the church, she had to relinquish her intimate relationship with the son of her late husband. "Hiram Bingham was not willing to baptize her while she remained the wife of the son of her late husband." They each complied, seeing it as their duty because the missionaries viewed their connection as an abomination. When Ka'ahumanu was ill after Kaumuali'i's death and she was in Lāhainā to bury him, she proclaimed a code of laws for the island of Maui based on Christian teachings. She thought that she herself was on the brink of death and vowed to do all that she could to exert her influence.[60]

As Silverman explains: "During the time when the chiefs were being groomed for baptism, Ka'ahumanu moved to suppress prostitution and adultery. In August 1825 she sent out a crier for three nights calling out a prohibition against 'loose and lewd practices.' Her edict also forbade wives to leave their husbands or husbands to leave their wives. The moral code of the missionary women and the exclusiveness in which Kaahumanu had been brought up were similar in that both served the purposes of their societies in protecting bloodlines, family power, and inheritance of family property."[61] Some ali'i followed Ka'ahumanu's verbal edict of heteromonogamous Christian marriage declared in 1825, while others resisted.

Eventually Ka'ahumanu was baptized as Elizabeta (Elizabeth) on December 4, 1825 (along with several other chiefs: the first group baptism).[62] The mixed gender group also included Kapule, Keali'iahonui, Nāmahana, La'anui, Ka'iu, Kala'aiāulu, and Kalanimoku's young son Leleiōhoku, each of whom took a Christian name. A second group of Kanaka became fellows of the Kawaiaha'o church after they were baptized on December 9, 1827: Lazarus Kamakahiki, Abraham Naoa Ieki, John Papa 'Ī'ī, Ana Waiakea Kamakahiki, and Abel Wahineali'i.[63] These members of the Kawaiaha'o church stood firm as a line of defense.

Sally Merry discusses the conditions and structural constraints that accompanied these changes and also points to the biopolitical elements of the redefinition of relationships, including intimate and familial ones.

> The Christian ali'i sought salvation for themselves and their people through the promised eternal life and benefits of civilization. At the same time, the twin problems of extensive foreign debts and catastrophic population decline required both more labor from the maka'āinana and better rates of childbirth and child survival. Prosecuting adultery might check population decline and strengthen the nation through more stable families and improved parental care. Yet defining the family failed to ameliorate the basic causes of population decline: introduced diseases, rampaging cattle populations destroying gardens and grass for thatching houses, and increasing tax burdens on the farming population.[64]

That same month, soon after the chiefs were baptized, they gathered to adopt the Ten Commandments as the basis for the law of the nation. Governor Boki of O'ahu, influenced by the traders, went toe-to-toe with missionary Bingham, especially regarding the Seventh Commandment.

> As translated by the missionaries the Commandment read, *Mai moe kolohe oe* (Thou shalt not sleep mischievously), a prohibition the mis-

sionaries hoped was general enough to include all possibilities. For the missionaries it was part of their campaign to bring the behavior of the Hawaiians into conformity with the teachings of the Bible. Marriage was to be established to develop stable monogamous families as the basis for Christian society. Bingham also thought marriage would prevent prostitution. Kaahumanu expressed her social approval by hosting wedding suppers patterned after New England customs. Her support of the institution of marriage means she had to put a good face on it and assent even when she thought the wrong couples got together.[65]

Besides the influence of missionary men like Bingham, many of these social changes were undertaken with the guidance of the missionary women. They worked with and on Kanaka women in an attempt to institutionalize their own norms in their principal campaign in the battle to reform the Hawaiian family over the maintenance of monogamous marriage. As Patricia Grimshaw suggests, the conjunction of the female chiefs and forceful missionary women was critical: "The Hawaiian women were receptive in particular ways to the wives' influence. The interaction of the two groups of women was of incalculable importance in the complex intercultural negotiations and in the resulting balance of power by the end of 1825." Their relationships were complicated by the fact that the missionary women found the Hawaiian women's habits (especially bodily practices) revolting. The Hawaiian women reached out to missionary women, who were clearly lonely at times but not always responsive, seeing the Hawaiians as "half naked natives." They seldom wanted physical contact with Hawaiian women: "They did not want them at births; they did not want their ministrations in illnesses; they did not respond to kisses and embraces."[66]

Nonetheless, Jennifer Thigpen documents the effectiveness of the relationships between high-ranking Hawaiian women and missionary women, arguing that these relationships became vital to building and maintaining the diplomatic and political alliances that ultimately shaped the islands' political future. Male missionaries rarely comprehended the authority of Hawaiian chiefly women in a range of matters because their early attempts to Christianize the Hawaiian people were based on racial and gender ideologies brought with them from New England. But the missionary wives gained understanding through the relationships that they developed with these powerful Hawaiian women—interactions shaped by Hawaiian values and practices that situated the Americans as guests in relation to the chiefs as their beneficent hosts. Missionaries eventually introduced Christian religious and cultural tenets through this mode. Thigpen argues that they ultimately provided a foundation for American power in the Pacific and accelerated the colonization of the Hawaiian nation. These early relationships were structured by the ali'i desire for Western clothing.[67]

Although the missionary women necessarily worked with chiefly women, "it was the lives of the ordinary women that became the focus of mission concern and active interference."[68] Missionary women expected to find that common Hawaiian women were abject drudges for the rest of society but found that overall none were overburdened with work, because material wants were easily met. Some even complained that Hawaiian women slept too much.[69] The missionaries considered their "idleness" to be the core of their supposed immorality. The notion of laziness was linked to the charges of promiscuity and lack of concern with promoting "domestic comfort and harmony."[70] The missionaries saw their central goal as helping Kanaka to achieve genuine piety, which they saw as the bedrock for the construction of the good man and the good woman. The missionary wives focused on women and girls in the 1820s and 1830s, to instill lessons of proper femininity and appropriate female behavior. They sought to educate women as a way to bring them closer to grace. Formal instruction became a keystone of their proselytizing endeavor through these links between piety and literacy.[71]

The missionaries were extremely concerned with this sexual activity and continually haunted by the specter of prostitution.[72] "The missionary women deprecated such sexual indulgence even more vehemently when the sexual relationship involved American and European sailors, who rewarded sexual favors with Western material goods (and with Western venereal disease, the nasty part of the bargain)." White male sailors were said to prey on young Hawaiian women and girls as resources for their sexual demands.[73] Writing about the androcentric and Eurocentric nature of the documentation and scholarly analyses of women in the Pacific at large and Hawaiian women in particular, Caroline Ralston notes that Hawaiian women's sexuality is a common topic in ethnohistorical sources, especially the highlighting of the "promiscuity" and "licentiousness" of ordinary women who willingly established sexual liaisons with foreign males (many of whom were sailors). These encounters have been ill defined as "prostitution" simply because women expected items in exchange for sexual acts and encounters. Ralston suggests that "prostitution" is a loaded term: use of it in the Hawaiian context for the early contact period (post-1778 to the early nineteenth century) is untenable and misses the importance of the Indigenous agency of common women accessing Western resources. Ralston argues that these sexual exchanges, and the material goods accrued through them, enabled ordinary Hawaiian women to exercise greater influence than before in terms of their local kin group. As the number of foreign vessels increased, chiefs used the power of the kapu to try to establish monopolies on articles suitable for foreign exchange from the 1790s onward.[74] "As was the case in the first years of the mission, it was the conjunction of the Western male's sexual predacity and the Hawaiian's ease with sexuality which most affronted missionaries' sense of propriety and drove a strong wedge between the mission and the rest of the foreign community." The nonmissionary haole (foreigners) outnumbered the missionary haole, so the aim was to convert Hawaiians who could resist seduction by the rest. As Grimshaw explains, "If the mission women rejected the Hawaiians as strange heathens, they similarly rejected the rest of the foreign community as heathen strangers. Hawaiians were a source of anxiety and tension rather than a pool of friendship because their way of living constituted the evil which Americans had sacrificed themselves to eradicate."[75]

The Seventh Commandment Becomes National Law

The disputes regarding the Seventh Commandment were related to how it came to be law in the Hawaiian context in the first place and the complicated implications for kingdom sovereignty. Sally Merry notes that the Hawaiian Kingdom prohibitions against adultery and fornication in 1827 and 1829 "stem directly from ideas about adultery held in New England" and were especially informed by a Massachusetts statute of 1784 that imposed penalties and public humiliation. She documents the 1830–1860 campaign against adultery in Hawai'i, which included redefining marriage and adultery in the law as well as prosecuting adultery and fornication.[76] The threat of foreign men's violence as they demanded unlimited access to Hawaiian women commoners catalyzed the earliest legal edicts regulating their sexuality.

The path to enshrining the Seventh Commandment as Hawaiian Kingdom law was bound up with the chiefs' assertion of the monarchy as a distinct polity. This new national authority would be forged through the regulation of Hawaiian female commoners' sexuality. Yet this occurred in the context of duress, as a response to the violence of foreign men irate that their access to these women was being obstructed. Prior to the formalized laws against adultery, Ka'ahumanu had issued a verbal edict against any form of traffic in women, what the sailors understood as prostitution.

As Silverman notes: "As a Christian ruler, Elisabeta Kaahumanu became enmeshed in controversy over regulating the sexual behavior of women. Repeated confrontations with foreigners over the casualness of their intimate relations with Hawaiian women hastened Kaahumanu's formulation of a code of laws for the nation. In imposing restrictions, in requiring Christian standards of behavior, Kaahumanu emerged as a leader of a moral movement that had limited success." In August 1825 twenty sailors at Lāhainā, Maui, directly confronted Ka'ahumanu about her first restriction on prostitution. They had first gone to Bingham to protest, but he told them to go to the kuhina nui, who had made the law. The consultants, traders, and seamen all challenged his position: they saw Ka'ahumanu as the visible authority but insisted that the change came from Bingham. According to Silverman, "Kaahumanu told the sailors that the word of God had enlightened her. Now she knew what was right, and she intended her people to follow the word of God."[77] High chief Kalanimoku, who functioned as prime minister at this time, sent a message to try to diffuse the situation, warning that his soldiers would detain the men in a fort if they persisted in their aggressive behavior.

As Silverman explains, another incident referred to as the "Buckle crisis" reified the kapu. Captain William Buckle of London had reportedly paid the guardian of a Hawaiian mission schoolgirl named Leoiki to take her. The girl appealed to missionary William Richards to save her from being forced to go, but he was unable to. Richards then went to the chiefs to ask that they consider a ban on women going to the ships. Buckle had returned eight months later with Leoiki, who was then pregnant. Ka'ahumanu placed a restriction on any traffic in women in the port of Lāhainā. In response, Buckle's furious crew on the *Daniel IV* of London went ashore as a gang to attack Richards at his home, because he was the one who had informed the kuhina nui of the sale of Leoiki. The sailors tried to force him to lift the restrictions, since they still assumed it had to be a missionary who issued the ban rather than Ka'ahumanu. In response, Kanaka protected Richards from the attack, and the kapu remained.[78]

Ka'ahumanu responded to the attack at Lāhainā by enforcing the same kapu at the port of Honolulu. There she punished two women who were sexually engaging sailors by ordering their heads shaved. Governor Boki sided with the seamen but had his own motivations: he had been taxing each woman who went to the ships. However, he did not yet oppose Ka'ahumanu openly. "Instead he commanded that the women of his household and those dependent on him no longer go to women's meetings [of the church]."[79]

At the same time, violent attacks by foreigners increased. Ka'ahumanu temporarily lifted the ban because she was unable to sustain it when the USS *Dolphin*, commanded by Lt. Jack Percival, arrived at Honolulu in January 1826. Percival went to a meeting of the chiefs' council and threatened them with physical force if they did not give in.[80] He asked Ka'ahumanu who had put the law in place, assuming that it could not have been her. Even when she said that she had done so, he insisted that it had to have been Bingham. Percival noted that the English ship belonging to George Gordon, Lord Byron, had been allowed women (even though it had not) and demanded that an American ship be given the same privilege.[81] This is a vivid example of European assertions of white male entitlement to Hawaiian women's bodies for sexual pillage.

Missionary Bingham includes Ka'ahumanu's account of her exchange with Percival and how he pushed to find out who exactly set the tabu. She asserted that she herself had issued the edict, but Percival kept insisting that it was Bingham. She countered by saying that the edict was by the authority of God, that Bingham had merely brought them the Word of God. Bingham was livid that sailors on Lord Byron's ship supposedly had access to women and talked about this as a form of discrimination, as though "the embargo on lewd women, of the islands, was an insult to the U.S. flag!" Ka'ahumanu questioned Percival: "But why are you angry with us for laying a tabu on the women of our own country. If you brought American women with you, and we had tabued them, you might then justly be displeased with us." Percival even went to talk with Boki to try to push him to lift the tabu, even though Ka'ahumanu said clearly that he was below her in terms of rank and that she was ruling the kingdom as Kauikeaouli's guardian. Percival threatened her: "Send and liberate the women. If you still hold them, I will myself liberate them. Why do you do evil to the women?" She replied: "It is for us to give directions respecting our women—it is for *us* to establish tabus—it is for *us* to bind, liberate, to impose fines." Percival's retort was to put down the missionaries as a "company of liars" by suggesting that women were not subject to tabus in America. According to Bingham's description of Ka'ahumanu's account, "He snapped his fingers in rage, and clenched his fists, and said, 'To-morrow I will give my men rum . . . look out . . . they will come for women; and if they do not get them, they will fight. My vessel is just like fire. Declare to me the man that told you the women must be tabu, and my people will pull down his house. If the women are not released from the tabu to-morrow, my people will come and pull down the houses of the missionaries."[82]

Ka'ahumanu had punished two women living with haole men (one of whom was an officer of the American warship that Percival cited), sentencing them to work carrying stones for a new church. While Ka'ahumanu and several chiefs were assembled in the house of Kalanimoku to worship, along with Boki and Namahana and others, several seamen who belonged to the *Dolphin* rushed in and asked, "Where are the women?" When Percival demanded that the women be let go, Ka'ahumanu refused. He threatened that he and 150 of his men would tear down the missionaries' house if the women were not released by the next day.[83] The crew came on shore the next day carrying sticks and knives. They rioted at Kalanimoku's house and attacked Bingham in his yard. Governor Boki feared that they would set fire to the town and convinced the chiefs to let the women go to the ship. The sailors won out and stayed for three months, earning the name "mischief making man-of-war." As Bingham put it, "Never did the advocacy of licentiousness or opposition to the tabu appear more odious." In the end, Ka'ahumanu did not enforce the ban while Percival's ship remained in port but imposed it again when it left.[84]

After that lengthy and violent imposition by the foreign men and Ka'ahumanu's concession, she traveled to O'ahu in the summer of 1826 with Bingham and a large retinue, to prepare the people for adoption of the laws. During the same period American and British consuls along with some ships' captains put together their own proposals for a code of laws. "The recurring turmoil, divisions, name-calling and anger growing from differing attitudes on controlling the sexual behavior of women needed to be brought to an end. One way to determine the standard would be for chiefs to adopt a law for the whole nation which would clearly prohibit prostitution and set the punishment for breaking it. Kaahumanu was adamant that while they were assembled the council should finally decide upon a national code of laws."[85]

Meanwhile, other trouble was looming in Hawai'i's waters. Bingham recounts another episode, noting that Captain J. Elisha Clark's whaling ship *John Palmer* took off from Lāhainā with two women who had ignored the kapu and gone aboard. Clark was said to have received women and concealed them, knowingly violating the kapu.[86] After Governor Hoapili demanded that the captain return the women who were held on the ship, the crew members fired their cannon toward the mission house, just barely missing it. When that ship reached Honolulu, an American newspaper arrived that quoted missionary Richards on the Buckle affair mentioned earlier. It noted that a Captain Buckle of London had paid $160 to a chief for Leoiki. Any charges related to buying someone as a slave were punishable in England at the time, so Richards was called to answer. Governor Boki and John Young sided with Buckle, who denied the charges, while Kaʻahumanu called a meeting with the chiefs, select missionaries, and Richards to discuss the case.[87]

Besides the persistent disbelief among the sailors and captains as to who held the power in the assertion of these new laws, another question arose: sovereign authority.

> The council agreed to six laws, but Boki balked at putting them into effect until they could be sent to England for approval. He had been urged to that view by the British consul. Kaahumanu suggested that her brother Kuakini take their proposed laws to King George and let him cross out what he didn't like. Boki urged that they have the British consul send the laws to England. . . . She questioned Boki whether when he met King George, the king had left it for them to do. . . . Boki had replied that the king had left it for them to do.

Governor John Adams Kiʻiapalaoku Kuakini intervened by asking everyone to consider carefully the problem that he identified. If the chiefs asked England to make laws for them, they would subsequently move to enforce them by sending warships to Hawaiian waters and control what ships would come and go. "We shall forever be their servants, we shall no more be able to do as we please." This was a clear threat of foreign encroachment if the Hawaiian leaders did not promulgate their own laws, which had implications for the future of the kingdom's sovereignty. When Kaʻahumanu agreed, the "chiefs decided to publish the laws they had agreed on. After the laws were printed but before they were orally proclaimed, passionate opposition by the British and American consul and the traders forced the chiefs to compromise." They decided to adopt only the first three proposals as law. Kaʻahumanu then called on the chiefs, the common people, and the foreigners to abide by the new laws. As she warned, "murder would be punished by hanging, and a thief or an adulterer would be put in irons."[88]

In the end the high chiefs issued just three of the Ten Commandments as law: the prohibitions against murder, theft, and adultery. The law to prohibit prostitution had been dropped under pressure from the foreigners and opposition by Boki. His success had called Kaʻahumanu's leadership into question by invoking Kalanimoku. He served in a capacity akin to prime minister during the reigns of Kamehameha I and Kamehameha II and the beginning of Kamehameha III's reign. Some speculated that "Kaahumanu might not have tolerated being blocked by Boki and the traders who backed him." The traders even insinuated that Kalanimoku's power was superior to Ka'ahumanu's. Bingham, however, thought that "the confrontations over the moe kolohe kapu reinforced Ka'ahumanu's position of power among the chiefs." Governor Boki and Kalanimoku explained that they held their office by authority of Ka'ahumanu, and Hoapili cited her authority as the source of his position as well. Missionary Thurston also weighed in, calling Kalanimoku "unquestionably the great man, the greatest if you please, in the nation at the time. But then there was a woman above him & she could have called him to order at any time."[89] Kalanimoku commanded the military forces and could have imposed his wishes by force, but his loyalty toward Kamehameha I endured.

As was her prerogative, Ka'ahumanu moved in an unparalleled way by enforcing the law against adultery on some of the most important chiefs, especially those who happened to be her political opponents. As Silverman explains:

> She punished Governor Boki and his friend the chief Kekuanoa, fining them eighty piculs of sandalwood for adultery and drunkenness, and fined the women chiefs involved forty piculs. It was astonishing for chiefs to be called to account before the law as though they were commoners. Kaahumanu did not have the chiefs put in irons as the law prescribed. Neither did her punishment reflect Western cultural values, where the stigma and punishment of the women in adultery was graver than that of the man. Her precedent of fining men twice as much as the women in adultery cases continued in the courts through the Monarchy period.

Yet word spread among the traders that Ka'ahumanu had taken a young Captain Lewis as her lover, which greatly distressed Bingham.[90] As Silverman notes, it seems she did not fully embrace the ideal of sexual chastity for women.

Osorio notes that the institution of sumptuary laws signaled a commitment to the new deity by Ka'ahumanu and her Council of Chiefs. "These laws . . . created drastic revisions in Kanaka ways of life. In particular, laws prohibiting fornication (virtually any sex outside of marriage), although reinforcing monogamy and church-ritualized marriage, may have had much to do with encouraging a society-wide infiltration of the church's influence." They affected traditional morality and custom and also resulted in the Hawaiians' repudiation of their own culture and values as well as in their trust in foreigners to tell them what was acceptable.[91]

Here we see colonial biopolitics and governmentality playing out, where the regulatory power of normalization ushers in modernity in vividly material ways. In any case, it is clear that the incidents that led to the battle over "prostitution" and the law against adultery were based on Hawaiʻi's status at the time as an imperial contact zone, a site of racialization and territorialization loaded with contested agency and battles over defining space and relationality. This is a prime example of what Ann Laura Stoler has theorized as the "intimacies of empire."[92] Here the Hawaiian state emerged globally, becoming legible to the Western world through regulatory forms of the sexed bodies of common Kanaka women being identified, specified, and managed, arguably with multiple sovereigns at play.

Marital Imposition

In 1827 and 1829 Kamehameha III issued the laws against "mischievous sleeping," which criminalized, among other things, prostitution and illicit intercourse (fornication and adultery). As noted earlier, Christian marriage was written into the laws of the kingdom as the only legal sexual relationship. Bigamy was outlawed, and common law marriage (cohabitating sexually) was not permitted without formal marriage. Hence the law made a man and a woman "man and wife" if they lived together. Therefore any sexual activity outside of (heteromonogamous) marriage was banned; everything else constituted "adultery" or worse. These new norms were in line with Anglo-American society, in which "adultery and fornication, along with sodomy, rape, statutory rape, and prostitution were all illegal in New England in the early 1800s." Now the major elements of Christian law were set in Hawaiian law and the method of solemnizing unions was established.[93] "Christian rules on consanguinity or affinity were to apply; thus, intermarriage of siblings in upper-strata marriages was outlawed immediately, along with polygamy and polyandry. Marriages which had already been entered into 'heathen' style, if not repugnant to scriptural rules, were to be considered permanent (lest everyone rush to change partners); but from that date onward, future marriages should be formalized, in the presence of witnesses, by a missionary or chief."[94]

The missionaries "ardently believed that the absence of true marriage in Hawaiian culture was responsible for desertion and the absence of any 'real' family."[95] Yet it was precisely family that they faulted for fueling Hawaiian women's lack of subservient behavior. The 'ohana model of family (intergenerational and extended) was perplexing to the missionaries, who could not tell which adults were parents to which children, which men were with which women, and so forth. This flexibility of the intergenerational and extended family in terms of interpersonal care and socialization was challenging to their focus on "personal responsibility" and attempts to inculcate proper motherhood in tandem with subservient wifehood and authoritative husbandry. "Pressure to reform the family continued with an effort to induct Hawaiians into the responsibilities of parenthood. The persuasion of Hawaiian women to devote more time to child care, however, was yet another frustrating task." As missionaries complained, boys and girls would "roam from morning to night. Both sexes together, under no parental control, almost naked." Missionaries even attributed high infant mortality "to the laziness and lack of affection of mothers." The missionaries also identified Hawaiian mothers' mobility as a problem, such as a woman leaving her husband and children to travel. They were also alarmed at the practice of hānai: they saw the giving away of children to be unnatural and an affront to what was supposed to be maternal instinct.[96]

Sally Merry argues that by the mid- to late nineteenth century "the Kingdom had placed a new emphasis on the nuclear family and the enclosure of women within it." As she notes: "These processes of refashioning the family and sexual subjectivity paralleled other efforts to constitute a nation according to European understandings of that entity."[97] These laws were central to the nineteenth-century Western civilizing process, where the bourgeois family was the model to be emulated.

> Rather than in state, church, or school, the main thrust of the reform endeavor should be shaped around the family life of Hawaiians. The Hawaiian wife and mother would be targeted as the agent for regeneration; the main reliance, then, would be upon instilling "moral and religious culture" in the females. The meaning of marriage and chaste sexuality would be made plain; the role of housewife and mother would be elucidated; then the influence of the Hawaiian woman, at the center of her well-regulated family, would ripple outward, redeeming wayward children, errant husbands, and, finally, the whole kingdom, for godly living.[98]

Anglo-American laws redefined Hawaiian masculinity to encompass ownership and control over property, including land and eventually women and children. The family group consisting of a pair of adults tied by marital partnership and their children was a structure common to the New England missionaries, which they assumed to be the most proper and universally civilized form of social organization.

With the emergence of protoindustrialization and early capitalism, this form of family was understood as a financially viable social unit. "While missionaries dreamed of ways to introduce a cash crop which would offer Hawaiian men a place in the market place economy, wives pressed for an avenue to household production for women." This included laundering, sewing, knitting, mending, and ironing. Missionary women faced the reluctance of Hawaiian women to demonstrate "the proper submission that a wife owed to husbandly authority." Missionary women complained about Hawaiian women in their diary accounts and letters, frustrated with their resistance to lessons on how to be subservient to their husbands, and identified the "problem of marital deference" as widespread among the general population. "It was the kinship network, the 'relations,' that many missionaries realized were the stumbling block to submissive wifely behavior."[99] Hawaiian women's bonds of reciprocity with their kin superseded their ties with their respective husbands.

This proved to be a very particular factor in relation to high-ranking Hawaiian women. Missionaries disapproved of older chiefly women's marriages to younger men where there was a great disparity in rank, age, or influence. As the logic went, "If the older partner were a male chief, the tension would not be so severe." With regard to ordinary Hawaiian women, they tried to discourage them from what they viewed as coarse and inappropriate pastimes such as boxing, surfing, horse riding, dancing, card playing, gambling, and smoking and to redirect them to other pursuits.[100]

With the government's new laws against adultery came imprisonment or hard labor as the penalty. As one missionary reported: "Adultery built the road system in Hawaii." The missionaries became obsessed with the abidance of the Seventh. They found that "adultery" was prevalent and that there was little disapproval of "sexual irregularity" (probably homosexual activity) and consequently little fear of loss of character if discovered.[101] One factor apparently was the problem of translation. An account in 1836 by Lorrin Andrews, an early American missionary to Hawai'i who later became a judge, complained that Kanaka Maoli had so many terms for what he considered illicit intercourse that it became a problem in terms of forbidding them. In a letter published in the *Missionary Herald*, Andrews wrote about the "unthinking character of the people" who "have no idea of generalizing, or of deducing a general rule from particular cases, or of drawing a conclusion from premises made ever so clear: hence they need the same instruction to teach them how to use their knowledge as they did in giving them original ideas." He noted: "Everything is specific and of particular application. So in moral subjects. In translating the seventh commandment, it was found they had about twenty ways of committing adultery, and of course as many specific names; and to select any one of them would be to forbid the crime in that one form and tacitly permit it in all the other cases. It was necessary, therefore, to express the idea in another way, viz, 'Thou shalt not sleep mischievously.'"[102]

An unnamed missionary wife also complained about the language barrier preventing the missionaries from conveying the *intent* of those who wrote the law: "No sooner did ground appear to be gained than evidence of ignorance or sin reappeared. One wife realized that though she could speak Hawaiian, she had not sufficient fluency to understand how Hawaiians really thought, how to analyze their character. One needed to name every trifling particular about conduct, for Hawaiians believed they had acted morally when they observed a rule but in fact did not have sufficient judgment to sense the *spirit* of the law."[103] This passage is perhaps ironic: it seems as if Kanaka Maoli were already taking a "juridical" approach to the new rules, conceivably as a form of resistance—not necessarily due to lack of discernment, as some missionaries assumed.

Grimshaw explains that efforts to "introduce Hawaiians to the proprieties of the wedding ceremony paled in comparison with the task of persuading them to the meaning of the union itself."[104] Beyond understanding the significance of marriage, and altering Kanaka behavior and practice to achieve it, the missionary pursuit had an emotional element to it. As Ralston explains, "Once initial conversion had been effected the missionaries were determined through legal and religious means to erase the Hawaiians' positive sexual concepts and replace them with 'proper' feelings of guilt, shame and the need for modesty in speech, dress and behavior."[105] This was certainly an issue tied to emotion. Grimshaw explained: "If marriage was concerned with the regulation of sexual accessibility, it was also, however, concerned vitally with proper authority and proper feeling between husbands and wives. These were difficult concepts to impart, not readily conducive to civil or legal codes, but essential nevertheless. The delicate balance involved in the definition of submissiveness of wife to husband almost defied explanation in terms of chiefly Hawaiians. Missionaries had no choice but to accept the enormous power of chiefly women, despite continuing uneasiness."[106] Here we see the tensions in notions of authority vis-à-vis chiefly Hawaiian women's power and those in the lessons promoted by the missionaries that were grounded in women's deference to men.

Judith Gething traces the radical restructuring of Hawaiian women's status from 1820 to 1920, arguing that the two primary determinants were the Christian religion and the common-law theory of coverture. The Congregational Christianity of these missionaries derives from John Calvin and John Winthrop, who delineated a subservient role for women. They believed that women were important and worthy of salvation but that their sphere was to be separate from men's. In the New Testament the letters of Paul to various second-century Christian congregations detailed the role that women were to have in the church and family.[107] Here the husband is the head of the wife, who submits to him. Coverture (a covering) is a legal doctrine whereby, upon marriage, a woman's legal rights and obligations were subsumed by those of her husband. Coverture was an English common-law tradition brought by settlers to North America, whose descendants later brought it to Hawai'i through the Christian mission. The principle is grounded in Christian belief in the unity of spouses and undergirds a legal fiction in which "man and wife" were considered a single entity, where the woman's new self after marriage is that of her "superior": her husband.[108] In this tradition, unmarried women had the right to own property and make contracts in their own names, such as freely execute a will, sue, or be sued directly and sell or give away their own property. Coverture rendered a woman unable to engage in these acts without her husband's consent; by law she is civilly dead. Common-law coverture was established in the law as early as 1841 in Hawai'i. In general, this rule implicated a range of legal restrictions on women and narrowly circumscribed their activities; women could not vote, run for political office, or serve on juries.[109]

But in the Hawai'i case, in the context of monarchical government, Hawaiian women in general could not vote but did serve on juries. Those who were high ranking were able to rule as island-wide governors and hold appointed positions in the House of Nobles. As one missionary, Lorenzo Lyons, complained in 1836, "Paul's injunctions are not observed on the Sandwich Islands. Women often usurp authority over the men & hold the reins of government over large districts."[110] Moreover, it was primarily high-status women with great political power who held the position of kuhina nui. This position was unique in the administration of the Hawaiian Kingdom and had no equivalent in Western governments of the day. The kuhina nui held co-authority with the monarch in all matters of government and was empowered to veto any decision.[111]

Some missionaries were pleased when a married woman at least tacked "wahine" (woman) onto her husband's name rather than retaining her own after marriage. One example was chief Kalakua, who started going by the name "Hoapili Wahine" (Hoapili's woman) once she married Hoapili.[112] Here we see that "woman" became a gloss for "wife."[113] As Gething notes: "The final major coverture-related disability appeared in 1860, when a married woman was required to adopt her husband's name. Legitimate children were to adopt their father's name and illegitimate children their mother's name." The issue of surnames itself in Hawai'i came about as a result of conversion, in which converts would take a Christian name and often would use their Kanaka names as last names. In cases where female chiefs, for example, resisted taking on their husband's names, a patrilineal naming practice was already in place. Gething cites the example of Fanny Kekelaokalani Young to discuss ali'i women who "always used their maiden names." She notes that Young was the wife of George Naea and mother of Queen Emma, married to Kamehameha IV, the king who signed the name-change law. Importantly, though, she was daughter of a chiefly woman named Ka'ō'ana'eha and John Young, a British subject who became an important advisor to Kamehameha I during the formation of the kingdom and later became governor of the island of Hawai'i. Hence Fanny Kekelaokalani already carried a patrilineal surname: Young.[114]

As Gething explains, "In the period between 1840 and 1845 numerous laws were passed attempting to regulate the morality of the populace and to deal with problems deriving from the imposition of Christian marriage restrictions on a population accustomed to other ways for men and women to relate to each other."[115] The principles were fully adopted in the laws of Hawaiian Kingdom, as noted in the preface to the *Translation of the Constitution and Laws of the Hawaiian Islands,* written in 1842. In 1845 a new law titled "The Marriage Contract" outlined the basic parameters of the common-law responsibilities and disabilities.[116] As Osorio notes, the sumptuary laws forbidding "fornication" prompted thousands of marriage ceremonies among Kanaka Maoli over the years but did not suffice for "the problem of dealing with property difficulties between Hawaiians and foreigners." As he explains, the marriage laws themselves "clearly indicated the difficulties of long-term international contact for foreigners and Hawaiians.[117] Merry points out that debates in the Hawaiian Kingdom legislature in the mid- to late nineteenth century were concerned with "rich foreigners enticing [Hawaiian women] . . . way from their husbands."[118] As Linnekin suggests, the position of Hawaiian women on the whole seemed to shift such that non-Hawaiian men had become points of economic access and status for Hawaiian women by the mid-1840s through processes of U.S. colonization.[119] But it is also the case that nonmissionary white men liked to marry ali'i wahine who held lots of land—they got rich on their wives' landholdings. For example, James Campbell was a carpenter when he got to the islands. He married Abigail Kuaihelani Maipinepine, who was a high-ranking woman, and subsequently became a wealthy businessman and one of the largest landowners in the islands.[120]

The rights of foreigners to marry Native women were also debated. An article in one law provided that an alien wishing to marry a Kanaka woman must place a bond of $4,000 and promise to make the Islands "his home for life." If the man ever left Hawai'i, the money would be forfeited: three-fourths of the amount would be transferred to his deserted family for their care and support. In 1848 O'ahu governor Mataio Kekūanāo'a (who later served as kuhina nui during the reigns of Kamehameha IV and V) addressed the legislature about several problems relating to the marriage laws in regard to foreign men, "including men deserting women to return home and how the law prevented the woman from marrying another man until after the death of her first husband," women left destitute, foreigners who married Kanaka women returning home with their children, foreign men inheriting land and property after a wife's death rather than the lands reverting back to the Mō'ī, and foreign husbands beating the women they were married to. Kekūanāo'a was concerned about the disposition of children and assets as well as desertion and mistreatment. His concerns suggest that the formality of marriage may have been a pretense for haole men who had no intention of spending their lives in the Islands yet were determined to make their stay as comfortable as possible so long as it lasted (with Kanaka women). Still, "the monetary bond was seen as separating the fortune hunters from men of means among the foreigners, and the smaller bond coupled with the oath of allegiance was, so far as the kingdom was concerned, more than ample to test the individual's seriousness about remaining in Hawai'i." Speaking to the other advantages of haole men securing a place with high-ranking Hawaiian women, Kekūanāo'a noted the importance of the oath: if marriage to a high-ranking female chief had taken place during the time when no oath was required, "a part of this country would have been lost to us."[121]

In 1845 the kingdom government became more exclusively male when kingdom law merged married women's civic status with that of their respective husbands, whereby they lost the legal right to alienate or dispose of property. This coincided with missionary descendants' pressure on King Kamehameha III to privatize communal landholdings, which led to the 1848 Māhele land division that increased the wealth of these same foreigners, who managed to secure vast extensions of land. Hence land enclosure and the new proprietary regime resembled the enclosure of Hawaiian women's sexuality vis-à-vis the law and the imposition of marriage as a form of propertization.

Even in the context of commodification of land for the first time, however, of the small proportion of lands that common Kanaka were able to secure, Linnekin found a number of women holding land (divided and granted as freehold title) after the Māhele and subsequent Kuleana Act of 1850. She draws from the evidence of statements made by claimants in the Māhele land records in an attempt to discern why there was "a statistical shift in the inheritance pattern such that land increasingly came into the hands of women." In the case of the making of the Hawaiian bourgeois subject, the issue of gender in relation to privatized landholdings did not play out in the ways that might be expected: women in particular gained central significance as stable landholders in local communities during the decade of the Māhele. Linnekin argues that the statistical increase in women's landholding was a practical and traditional response under the circumstances and was compatible with Hawaiian cultural logics. In the absence of male kin and on behalf of their extended families, women claimed land as guardians or "place-holders." While acknowledging that although both male and female commoners (Hawaiians at large) suffered alienation of land exacerbated by the division, she persuasively argues that they "retained a certain cultural and community integrity" while challenging the notion that women are inevitably "devalued" in colonial situations.[122]

Once women were married, the law worked to strip them of their personhood. But while the missionaries, with the support of the aliʻi, worked to instill legal and social transformations of Hawaiian gender norms and roles, issues of genealogical rank determined Hawaiian women's status in ways where gender subordination was not clear-cut. Even as the ideology of male dominance came to characterize the laws and face of the monarchy, women's local status and authority in relation to men's did not change substantially. As Linnekin importantly notes, there was a distinction "between the formal legal status of Hawaiian women during this period and their position in local-level social organization." She argues that while the legal status reflects what she calls Euro-American ideology, "this did not immediately supplant the indigenous cultural valuation that, minimally, recognized women as powerful beings." Linnekin suggests a dissonance "between women's legal disability and their active role and valuation within the rural, commoner Hawaiian community, as well as between women's legal standing and the actual political power of high-ranking chiefesses through the nineteenth century."[123] This suggests some consistency of customary practice outside formal law.

This discrepancy concerning formal legal status and recognition of women's mana and significance—to different degrees depending on genealogical rank—is important and may account for the persistence of Hawaiian women's standing in the contemporary period, including their leadership roles in the nationalist struggle. With regard to the question of political rights in light of this legacy of uneven legal recognition, I now turn to a discussion about Hawaiian women's suffrage from the mid- to late nineteenth century. Like the story at the beginning of this chapter, it pertains to a political event in 1998, a hundred years after the unilateral and illegal U.S. "annexation" of the Hawaiian Islands—but this time with a different leader and governing entity.

Memo on the Suffrage of Female Subjects (1998)

On March 12, 1998, David Keanu Sai issued a memorandum addressed to "Subjects of the Kingdom" about the "suffrage of female subjects." The memo was in response to the question of gender-specific terminology in legal statutes for voter eligibility in elections for representatives of the kingdom. Sai explains:

> On March 12, 1997, at a public meeting held at the Queen Liliʻuokalani Children Center at Halona, it was brought to the attention of this office by a female subject of the Kingdom that there is no provision in the law that bars female subjects from voting in the election for Representatives of the Kingdom. She asserted that although the "voter qualification" statute specifically relates to the male gender, ß15, chapter III, title I, provides, in part, that ". . . every word importing the masculine gender only, may extend to and include females as well as males." Based upon the dubious nature of this statute in its relation to-

ward both genders, I have diligently researched the election laws and have arrived at the following conclusion.[124]

As further documented in the memo, Sai examined the 1839 Bill of Rights, the first Kingdom Constitution of 1840, and an 1840 statute providing the means of electing the representative body in accordance with the requirements of that constitution, which was enacted by the House of Nobles and signed into law by the king.

Sai notes that Kamehameha III's 1839 bill of rights declared "protection for the persons and private rights of all his people from the highest to the lowest." In the first constitution of the kingdom, promulgated in 1840, Kamehameha III declared and established legal equality among all his subjects: "Chiefs and people alike." Sai suggests that the king thereby voluntarily deprived himself of some of his powers and attributes as an absolute sovereign while granting certain political rights to his subjects. The Constitution of 1840 specifically "provides a provision respecting the Representative Body, that there '. . . shall be annually chosen certain persons to sit in council with the Nobles and establish laws for the nation. They shall be chosen by the people.'" Sai notes that these political rights were conferred upon all subjects of the kingdom and not limited to a specific gender or genealogical class. Moreover, he suggests that the 1840 constitution prevents the exclusion of women from participating in the legislative body because it "provides for certain women to serve in the government as members of the House of Nobles."[125] Indeed, fourteen individuals served in the first House of Nobles as it was newly constituted at the time in addition to Kamehameha III and the kuhina nui (Kekāuluohi), four of whom were high-ranking Hawaiian women. Each was referred to by name in the constitution: Hoapili Wahine, Kekauʻōnohi, Konia, and Keohokālole.

Sai explains that he consulted twenty-eight more legal statutes spanning 1845 to 1886 that pertain to election laws in order to discern the intent of the laws with regard to gender specificity and their mention of males and females. He specifically set out to determine whether they reveal any provision precluding women from participating in the electoral process and found that all of those laws and codes fail "to disclose any provision precluding the female gender from participating in the electoral process." Sai summarizes that "the intent of the election statute was to have a Representative Body chosen by the people in order to help establish laws for the nation together with the King and Chiefs, and not a Representative Body to be chosen exclusively by men." He asserts that an inclusive definition is "in line with the intention of the Declaration of Rights of 1839, and the granting of the first Constitution, 1840, that . . . conferred certain political rights upon his (King Kamehameha III's) subjects, admitting them to a share with himself in legislation and government." Citing *Black's Law Dictionary,* Sai further notes "*political rights* are defined as the '. . . power to participate, directly or indirectly, in the establishment or administration of government, such as the right of citizenship, that of *suffrage,* the right to hold public office, and the right of petition.'"[126]

Curiously, though, even after asserting that the bill of rights, constitution, and civil codes that he consulted all fail "to disclose any provision precluding the female gender from participating in the electoral process," Sai ends the memo with this proviso:

> The issue here is not a question of whether Hawaiian women can or cannot participate in the election of Representatives or serve as a candidate for the House of Representatives, but whether there is any provision in the election laws that precludes Hawaiian women from participating. If no such provision exists, as the case may be, then Hawaiian women do have a right to participate in the electoral process under their *political right,* and . . . the male gender referred to in the "qualifications of electors" does not preclude the female gender, *provided* the female is a subject of the Kingdom, of the age of 20 and is neither an idiot, an insane person, or a convicted felon.[127]

The reframing of what the actual question is seems perplexing: it is "not a question of whether Hawaiian women can or cannot participate in the election of Representatives or serve as a candidate for the House of Representatives, but whether there is any provision in the election laws that precludes Hawaiian women from participating." While it is true that the memo states that the female subject of the kingdom merely asserted that there is no "provision in the law that bars female subjects from voting in the election for Representatives of the Kingdom" and did not ask whether or not Hawaiian women can or cannot participate in the election of representatives or serve as candidates for the House of Representatives, it is the case that Kanaka women in fact *did not* hold suffrage during at least most of the nineteenth century in elections to the House of Representatives.

The legislature of the kingdom was bicameral, as provided by the 1840 constitution until 1864. The monarch, with the advice of the Privy Council, appointed the members of the House of Nobles, while the members of the House of Representatives were elected by popular vote. It is unclear from the language of the first constitution, granted by Kamehameha III on October 8, 1840, how the "Representative Body" of the kingdom was selected. The 1840 constitution states: "There shall be annually chosen certain persons to sit in council with the Nobles and establish laws for the nation. They shall be chosen by the people, according to their wish. From Hawaii, Maui, Oahu, and Kauai. The law shall decide the form of choosing them, and also the number to be chosen. This representative body shall have a voice in the business of the kingdom. No law shall be passed without the approbation of a majority of them."[128]

It is unclear which, if any, of the individuals from these four island districts chosen to sit in council with the House of Nobles were women and whether women selected any of them, but there is nothing to suggest female exclusion. With regard to Kanaka women, the 1840 constitution spells out the role of the kuhina nui (Kekāuluohi at the time) and mentions the legacy of Kaʻahumanu (although Kekāuluohi followed Kīnaʻu as kuhina nui). As noted above, the four aliʻi women members of the House of Nobles are named.[129] The king appointed the members of the House of Nobles with the counsel of the members of the Privy Council (which was made up of the kuhina nui and select advisors).

The 1852 constitution was drafted by William Little Lee (an American attorney and also a member of the kingdom's House of Representatives) and was the first to subject the monarch (Kamehameha III) to a separation of powers.[130] Whereas past kings were under the Council of Chiefs, this constitution created and clarified the executive, legislative, and judicial branches of government. The legislative body consisted of a lower House of Representatives and the House of Nobles. Article 75 specifies that the House of Representatives "shall be composed of not less than twenty-four nor more than forty members, who shall be elected annually." Article 76 states in part: "The representation of the people shall be based on the principle of equality, and shall be forever regulated and apportioned according to the population, to be ascertained by the official census." The two following articles mention male subjects specifically:

> Art. 77. No person shall be eligible for a Representative of the people, who is insane, or an idiot, or who shall at any time have been convicted of any infamous crime, nor unless he be a male subject or denizen of the kingdom, who shall have arrived at the full age of twenty-five years, who shall know how to read and write, who shall understand

accounts, and who shall have resided in the kingdom for at least one year immediately preceding his election.

Art. 78. Every male subject of His Majesty, whether native or naturalized, and every denizen of the kingdom, who shall have paid his taxes, who shall have attained the full age of twenty years, and who shall have resided in the kingdom for one year immediately preceding the time of election, shall be entitled to one vote for the Representative or Representatives, of the district in which he may have resided three months next preceding the day of election; provided that no insane person, nor any person who shall at any time have been convicted of any infamous crime, within this kingdom, unless he shall have been pardoned by the King, and by the terms of such pardon been restored to all the rights of a subject, shall be allowed to vote.

Here it would seem clear enough: "a male subject" and "every male subject." But, as crucially noted by the Ka Hoʻoilina project (launched in 2002, which includes online Hawaiian-language resources with contemporary translations): "Although translated as 'every male subject,' the original Hawaiian—'O kēlā mea kēia mea o nā kānaka maoli'—means 'all Hawaiian people,' without reference to gender."[131] So here it seems that Lee's English version specified (and privileged) men, even though the Hawaiian version was gender neutral.

The constitution of 1852 further clarified some of the responsibilities for the office of the kuhina nui, including authority in the event of the monarch's death or minority of the heir to the throne. While up until that point the kuhina nui had been high-ranking Kanaka women, at the time Keoni Ana (also known as John Kalaipaihala Young II) served in this capacity. He was the son of a high-ranking woman named Kaʻōʻanaʻeha and John Young, an English sailor who became a trusted advisor to Kamehameha I. Kamehameha III appointed Keoni Ana in 1845 because Victoria Kamāmalu, the designated successor of her mother Kīnaʻu, was still a minor. As noted in chapter 4, Keoni Ana and the king may have also had an *aikāne* relationship (a same-sex friendship that may include sex) in that period.[132] During the course of his life he served in the House of Nobles and Privy Council, as a Supreme Court justice, and as chamberlain of Kamehameha III's household. During the start of his role as kuhina nui, in June 1845, the Legislative Assembly passed several acts that organized the executive ministries and departments of the government, which also provided that the kuhina nui would serve jointly as minister of the interior.[133]

As Hawai'i became more integrated into the international community, governing required more expertise. In 1843 Kamehameha III began organizing a cabinet by first appointing a minister of foreign affairs. Other ministries followed, including Interior and Finance, whose jurisdiction effectively replaced most of the kuhina nui's responsibilities. This made the position not only redundant but an unnecessary check on the authority of the monarch. Here we see shifting gender in governance, perhaps necessitated because foreigners and settler leaders preferred to deal with men. As Silva explains:

> The reign of Kauikeaouli was the last in which women held political power publicly as members of the House of Nobles. The 1840 House of Nobles included five ali'i wahine, but in 1848 there were four, by 1855 it was down to two, and the final woman was appointed in 1855, the year following Kauikeaouli's death. The increasingly hegemonic European and American styles of governance and patriarchal social codes eroded the ancient Kanaka modes of governance that accorded ali'i nui places on the council based on their genealogy and talent, regardless of whether they were male or female.[134]

The next constitution, promulgated by Kamehameha V on August 20, 1864, entailed several changes. It abolished the office of the kuhina nui under Kamehameha V's leadership. The new constitution also consolidated the legislation into a single-house legislature, when it had been bicameral. Furthermore, it created property and literacy requirements for both legislative members and voters. Voter and candidacy details are spelled out in articles 61 and 62, and the English versions refer to male subjects of the kingdom.

> Article 61. No person shall be eligible for a Representative of the People, who is insane or an idiot; nor unless he be a male subject of the Kingdom, who shall have arrived at the full age of Twenty-One years—who shall know how to read and write—who shall understand accounts—and shall have been domiciled in the Kingdom for at least three years, the last of which shall be the year immediately preceding his election; and who shall own Real Estate, within the Kingdom, of a clear value, over and above all incumbrances, of at least Five Hundred Dollars; or who shall have an annual income of at least Two Hundred and Fifty Dollars; derived from any property, or some lawful employment.

> Article 62. Every male subject of the Kingdom, who shall have paid his taxes, who shall have attained the age of twenty years, and shall have been domiciled in the Kingdom for one year immediately preceding the election; and shall be possessed of Real Property in this Kingdom, to the value over and above all incumbrances of One Hundred and Fifty Dollars of a Lease-hold property on which the rent is Twenty-Five Dollars per year—or of an income of not less than Seventy-Five Dollars per year, derived from any property or some lawful employment, and shall know how to read and write, if born since the year 1840, and shall have caused his name to be entered on the list of voters of his District as may be provided by law, shall be entitled to one vote for the Representative or Representatives of that District. Provided, however, that no insane or idiotic person, nor any person who shall have been convicted of any infamous crime within this Kingdom, unless he shall have been pardoned by the King, and by the terms of such pardon have been restored to all the rights of a subject, shall be allowed to vote.[135]

As in the 1852 constitution, although the English version *says* "every male subject," the original Hawaiian language version says "O kēlā mea kēia mea o nā kānaka maoli," which means "all Hawaiian people" without reference to gender.[136] Evidence suggests, however, that the focus was specifically on men, even without any explicit reference to gender in the statute: the king at the time made it clear that he did not want universal suffrage even for men.

Silva offers some historical background on the fight over the 1864 constitution and Kapuāiwa's struggle that played out in the Hawaiian-language newspapers. After Alexander Liholiho (Kamehameha IV) died on November 30, 1863, Lota Kapuāiwa took the throne as Kamehameha V and ushered in an era of upheaval for the government.

> Kapuāiwa did not take the usual oath to uphold the constitution. He wanted to make several controversial changes, including instituting a property qualification both for voters and for representatives in the Hale ʻAhaʻōlelo Makaʻāinana (the lower legislative house); eliminating the office of Kuhina Nui, which had traditionally been held by an aliʻi wahine (woman) who co-signed all laws and proclamations with the Mōʻī; eliminating the ʻAha Kūkā Malū (Privy Council), a council of aliʻi nui advisers who might exert restraint on his executive powers; and changing the bicameral to a unicameral legislature.[137]

Here we see the adoption of new norms and mores, with white American standards becoming hegemonic. Since "respectable women" in Victorian society did not speak in public and certainly did not vote, perhaps it was not necessary explicitly to ban women. What is clear is that haole men who pushed for increased democracy used the process to bolster their own positions. These changes in governance effectively disenfranchised the Hawaiian people at large when the commoners are taken into account. As a result, society was reordered, with elite Kanaka men and haole men at the top, elite Kanaka women often subordinate to haole men, and then men and women Kanaka commoners at the bottom of the hierarchy as well as effectively landless and with the reciprocal ties between themselves and the chiefs substantially severed.

Sai's memo offers support for the inclusion of women in the vote but seems to disregard the mid-nineteenth-century exclusion of women as legislative representatives. There is no acknowledgment of (let alone reckoning with) the internal exclusions of the mid- to late- nineteenth century regarding the political subordination of women that was central to the Hawaiian bid for status as modern civilized subjects.

Sai's analysis can be seen as a serious attempt to provide a contemporary rereading of the constitutional law to permit Kanaka women's participation in constitutional governance today. If his argument holds, then it could be possible, from the perspective of interrogating Western gender norms, to support constitutional restoration and simultaneously recall and reimagine Kanaka women's roles in political leadership. In other words, under certain conditions, it could be politically useful to Kanaka women (at large) today to accept Sai's juridical reading. Tactically speaking, this approach may be what contemporary kingdom nationalists want to advocate because it is in the legal codes, as Sai says. If the independence project is also legalistic—abiding by the "letter of the law" rather than the spirit of it—then women cannot be excluded at any point. Yet in a historical context an even more complex story about (chiefly) Kanaka women's political leadership (and exclusion from democratic politics) exists. It tells of overlapping forms of imperialist forces that structure complicity, shared by Kanaka chiefs (women and men), in the process of acculturation to the imposition of Western law, social mores, and economic-political life. The constitutional adoption of a legal system that privileges male authority conforms to Western political and cultural norms (a factor sustained today even when reinterpreted by Sai), if the only way to recognize Kanaka women's political rights is to read them secondarily into the primary category "male" that appears as the norm of the document. Sai's reading of Hawaiian Kingdom case law allows for a porous form of inclusion in the twenty-first century within his political project of reserving space for the reassertion of the Hawaiian Kingdom government, as a way to mitigate against contemporary exclusions along gender lines.

Conclusion

Kanaka women occupied positions of authority and exerted power in social relations, as demonstrated by the key role that Ka'ahumanu played in adopting forms of marriage, family, and inheritance laws that conformed to Christianization. These acts took place in a broader context of social discord or dissolution (conversion to Christianity, the effects of epidemic disease) under adverse conditions. The laws that undergird dislodging women from politics—through marital regimes initiated to control their sexuality and leading to coverture and subsequent exclusion from suffrage—were established by high-ranking women in the name of the Hawaiian Kingdom. Hence to defend displacing women at large from independent Hawaiian politics is to uphold an effectively colonial legal order that does not conform to (premonarchical) traditional Indigenous modes of rule—the very ones that these two women chiefs, as well as male leaders, at the time gave up.

Perhaps the question is not only whether the constitution actually forbade Kanaka women from voting or participating in constitutional politics but also whether the adoption of gender mores had already led some plurality of Kanaka women to shift away from the political sphere by the mid-nineteenth century. In effect (whether there is positive evidence that a turn occurred or only negative evidence in the absence of evidence of women's political participation), this would also affirm the significance of Ka'ahumanu's and possibly other high-ranking women's decisions earlier in the nineteenth century to modify their own roles (by example) and, by dictate, other women's social roles to a more secondary or subordinate status in regard to their husbands as national leaders. Ka'ahumanu performed these acts while acting as kuhina nui, which suggests that she may have been adopting a cultural system that would eventually foretell or permit her disenfranchisement, but within the existing political system she could portend social transformation. Hence her acts and other early acts by women chiefs in the process of adopting/adapting to changing gender roles as part of a changing political world are complex. The process of democratization via haole encroachment entailed the disenfranchisement of Kanaka women categorically: women of rank were empowered to govern as chiefs and konohiki (land stewards) in the old system, while ordinary women were effective at the local level, as they were embedded in kin norms of reciprocity and undergirded by matrilocal patterns of dwelling and resource access (when they had access to land). Again, here we see the constraints on Kanaka women politically, economically, and socially— all with respect to their most important responsibilities in cultural terms.

FOUR. "SAVAGE" SEXUALITIES

Hawaii is already in great jeopardy. Instead of trusting in God and His provision, the Hawaii of today has embraced the materialistic American mindset and its hedonistic pop culture. Hawaii is also nearly totally dependent on imported goods (e.g. 95% of its food). Like Americans, Hawaii's people are deeply in debt, in abject slavery to the almighty dollar. And behind Hawaii's beautiful façade is a bristling military fortress. . . . Even worse, as a vassal of the United States, Hawaii has also come to reject God and His laws. Once an independent nation that upheld the laws of Jehovah God as the supreme law of the land, the STATE OF HAWAII became a key to legalizing practices that are abominable to God—such as abortion, sodomy and pornography. Hawaii is used as a "testing ground" for moral outrages depicted in terms like "sexual orientation," "gender identity," "same-sex marriage," "death with dignity," "hate crimes" and so on. The STATE OF HAWAII, like its mentor the United States, is foolishly and arrogantly in open hostility to God's laws. Persisting in this kind of defiant and rebellious behavior will only incur the consequences of God's righteous judgment.

This quotation is from the blog "A Biblical View of Hawaiian Sovereignty: A Challenge to Christians in Hawaii" by Leon Siu, a prominent kingdom nationalist.[1] Siu is one of the founders of Aloha Ke Akua Ministries, serves on the oversight committee for the World Christian Gathering on Indigenous Peoples, and heads Christian Voice of Hawaii (from 1988 to the present). He is also the editor of the *Hawaii Evangelical Voice*, a monthly newsletter distributed to over eight hundred ministers in Hawai'i. Siu is a longtime activist in the fight against both civil unions and same-sex marriage.[2] He heads the American Freedom Coalition and is one of the founders of the American Parents Association yet identifies as "a lawful citizen of the Hawaiian Kingdom and plays an active role in working toward the full restoration of that sovereign nation." As Siu puts it, he serves in the government of the Hawaiian Kingdom as its minister of foreign affairs: "In this capacity, it is his responsibility to reactivate Hawai'i's treaties and restore foreign relations with other nations of the world, including the United States."[3]

Siu's missive voices the politics that this book seeks to question regarding the paradoxes of Hawaiian sovereignty vis-à-vis the early–nineteenth-century colonial biopolitics of state regulation of sexuality and the implications of those contradictions today. That is, it reflects the idea that the legacy of the Hawaiian "achievement" of independent statehood and its relation to Indigenous practices—which Westerners viewed as "uncivilized"—needed to be abolished to secure recognition. My aim here is to move beyond the binary characteristic of debates regarding Indigenous tradition in light of a history of Christianization in order to challenge the dichotomy between the notion of Indigenous "savage" and that of "civilized" Christian.

Siu sketches a picture of the "before and after"—the earlier period when Hawai'i was independent as a God-abiding nation. Here the laws of Jehovah were considered the supreme law of the land, according to Kamehameha III's promulgation of the 1839 Declaration of Rights as well as the 1840 constitution. During the later period (from the U.S.-backed 1893 overthrow and 1898 unilateral annexation through the present time as the 50th U.S. state) Hawai'i has legalized "practices abominable to God": abortion, sodomy, and pornography. In short, Siu posits Hawai'i in the twenty-first century as the rejection of God exemplified, as evidenced not only in the form of materialism, hedonism, consumption, and dependence but also by its very loss of national governance.

Siu discusses Hawai'i as a "testing ground" but does not draw attention to the rampant military and GMO experimentation there (just two obvious examples of issues that he could have focused on). For Siu, Hawai'i is a laboratory for what he considers "moral outrages depicted in terms like 'sexual orientation,' 'gender identity,' 'same-sex marriage,' 'death with dignity,' 'hate crimes' and so on." He deems all of this to be "defiant and rebellious behavior" that serves to delay the restoration of the kingdom—evidence of the denial of God's sovereignty. Curiously, the terms are not analogous to each other. Nothing inherent in sexual orientation and gender identity could be argued to be "abominable to God" even by Siu's own purported beliefs. Heterosexuality is a sexual orientation, while identifying as a "man" or a "woman" is most often a straightforward (albeit cisgendered) claim to a gender identity. Here we are left to assume that he is pointing to these concepts as glosses for sexual and gender minorities. Yet these two concepts are lined up next to same-sex marriage, "death with dignity" (presumably a reference to euthanasia, consensual end-to-life via medical assistance), and "hate crimes" (presumably in relation to violence motivated by homophobia). In Siu's logic, the Hawaiian Kingdom is currently subject to the "consequences of God's righteous judgment," which is why its sovereignty has yet to be recognized again in the twenty-first century—Kanaka are lost sheep who simply need to find their way back to God in order to restore their nation.

This "thy kingdom come" stance invokes the notion of Christian redemption—the Kingdom of God with Christ as savior as related to the redemption of the Hawaiian Kingdom. This position also resembles a form of fundamentalism that currently pervades kingdom restoration activism in Hawai'i. Here I want to mark the play between the desire for the restoration of the kingdom that is central to the nationalist struggle and the way in which such play has morphed into a form of fundamentalism, believing merely that "thy Kingdom will come" (hence select leaders are respectively treated like the new messiah). An unmarked reliance on the Christian state in the kingdom's legal genealogy has profound cultural and other implications. My aim is not to reproduce the binaries (indigenous/citizen, savage/civilized, and heathen/Christian), however, but to engage them as enduring Western constructions.

Siu cites Kamehameha III's reliance on Christian law for his views on how to restore the Hawaiian Kingdom today. But what remains invisible in his account—like those of many kingdom nationalists who revere that monarch and his leadership—is the seemingly tortured history of the king's process of reform, given his own set of practices that were abhorrent to the missionaries and considered a violation of Christian law. Kauikeaouli (King Kamehameha III) had a sexually intimate relationship with a man named Kaomi, starting in 1832 and continuing intermittently until 1835. Kaomi had so much sway that Hawaiian chiefs endeavored to remove him from the inner circle of the monarch's court because he was politically influencing many of the king's decisions. In addition, Kauikeaouli was involved in a sexual relationship with his sister Nāhi'ena'ena, a union referred to in Hawaiian as a *pi'o* affiliation (known as incest in Western societies). The king also had known female lovers in extramarital affairs and produced children out of wedlock.

Here we see Siu's casting of a fallen nation in what he sees as the problems of "the Hawaii of today." He focuses on "hedonism" and "defiant and rebellious behavior"—the same words that missionaries used to describe Kamehameha III and his sister. Yet in 1827 and again in 1829 the king had issued proclamations called "No Ka Moe Kolohe" (regarding mischievous sleeping), translated in official government documents as "concerning illicit intercourse."[4] As discussed in chapter 3, the decree outlawed all sexual activity outside of Christian marital relations. The king laid down these kinds of moral laws but rarely followed them.

A range of sexual practices drew sustained attention and caused alarm among missionaries and eventually Hawaiian chiefs. These included close consanguineous matings in the service of producing genealogically high-ranking offspring among the chiefly class; same-sex sexual practices among men within both common and chiefly segments of society;[5] and women's sexual agency in general across differences in genealogical rank. Prior to Christianization, Indigenous practices were diverse and allowed for multiple sexual possibilities. From the historical research of Lilikalā Kame'eleihiwa, it is clear that bisexuality was normative, bisexual practices were common, and both polygamy and polyandry were also not exceptional. The aikāne was a same-sex intimate friendship that typically included sexual relations within the chiefly class and also among the maka'āinana.[6] The term *māhū*, defined in the twentieth century alternatively as "homosexuals" or "hermaphrodites" (intersexed subjects), has been reclaimed today by some transgender Kanaka Maoli.

Christianized chiefs and missionaries monitored those known to engage in these practices, which I ironically term "savage" sexualities, and targeted them with reform campaigns. They also crafted severe penalty regimes for those caught "backsliding" into "heathendom." Although seriously patrolled, this social formation itself seems perverse. What does it mean to institute a set of laws that banned "adultery" in a society that allowed both polygamy and polyandry along with bisexuality and had no requirement of "marriage" for sexual activity? I propose that any rigorous examination of sexuality in relation to colonial domination necessarily entails a focus on sovereignty and its sexual implications. As Foucault suggests, sexuality became a field of vital strategic importance in the West and its empires in the nineteenth century through the theory of degeneracy: sexuality was viewed as the source of individual diseases and the nucleus of immorality. In the early to mid-nineteenth-century Hawaiian context, Christianized chiefs and missionaries jointly pushed back against Indigenous sexual practices in the quest to modernize Kanaka Maoli and to transform what Westerners viewed as a "savage" society to one that was newly "civilized."

In this chapter I explore views of these so-called savage sexualities in the late eighteenth and early to mid-nineteenth century as well as within the terrain of contemporary nationalism. Responding in part to Siu's communiqué, I engage some of what he considers "moral outrages" and read them in relation to Kamehameha III's reign and the contemporary nationalist context. In the first section I present some explorer and missionary discourses about Hawaiian sodomy that suggest how commonplace it seemed to outsiders that chiefly men had sexual liaisons with other (often younger) men. In the second section I offer an account of the aikāne relationship between the king and his male companion Kaomi. In the third section I present the concept of piʻo unions and genealogical rank in relation to notions of incest and Christian resistance to the king's sexual relations with his sister Nāhiʻenaʻena. In the fourth section I examine contemporary debates about Hawaiian sexuality and gender as they are taken up within frameworks of decolonial reclamation. The fifth section discusses the category of māhū, which historically may have been reserved for intersexed subjects but in the contemporary period refers to those outside the male-female gender binary, including transgender individuals. The last section examines the 50th state's legalization of same-sex marriage and Christian opposition to it as well as the settler appropriation of Hawaiian same-sex sexual legacies in support of that form of state authorization.

I suggest that contemporary assertions of the enduring state power of the Hawaiian Kingdom have the potential to reproduce conditions of "recolonization." M. Jacqui Alexander has theorized this concept in her critical writings about Caribbean state nationalism. She argues that the identity and authority of colonialism relies on the racialization and sexualization of morality and that nationalist projects often reproduce these conditions in forms of recolonization. In keeping with my critical assessment of the two main competing political projects within the Hawaiian nationalist context—those who advocate for self-determination within U.S. federal policy on Indian tribes and those who are instead committed to the restoration of the Hawaiian Kingdom independent from the United States—I offer some analysis of the implications of these legacies for contemporary sovereignty debates in relation to state recognition and their respective problems. Hence I engage what Alexander calls "erotic autonomy as a politics of decolonization" to move beyond the duality of indigenous and Christian identity.[7]

With missionary assistance, Ka'ahumanu (who was co-ruling as kuhina nui) along with other Christianized chiefs declared a new social order that, among other things, would regulate Hawaiian sexual arrangements and practices. As Westerners cited precolonial sexual practices of Hawaiian "savagery" in myriad colonial discourses, this effort paradoxically helped protect kingdom sovereignty through a reorganization of Indigenous modes in a systematic reform that arguably served as a form of colonial biopolitics. Kamehameha III's tumultuous existence is perhaps emblematic of the Hawaiian Kingdom at the time; he struggled with transforming the Indigenous polity into a Western-recognized state while engaging in customary practices that he eventually rejected as he secured that status for the nation.

The missionaries' efforts to convert Hawaiian chiefs to Christianity served as a specific tool in the process by imposing a framework for gender and sexuality with particular consequences for anything deemed outside of a civilized form of heterosexually monogamous male dominance. The radical restructuring of Indigenous society (which included the privatization of land and transformation of women's legal status discussed in chapters 2 and 3) also bore down on a range of sexual practices. This was all central to the nineteenth-century Western civilizing process of colonial modernity, in which the bourgeois family was the model to be emulated.[8] In relation to securing recognition of independent statehood, conjugal norms imposed by white Americans included patriarchal nuclear households, colonial homophobia, and disregard for kinship practices that would bear high-ranking chiefly offspring. These new colonial biopolitical practices that missionaries foisted on Hawaiian society were in turn claimed by Kanaka elites as a form of social normalization that served to undercut these Indigenous epistemes and ontologies, the basis for ea (embodied indigenous sovereignty), to conform instead to a Western model. These forms of enclosure—of land, gender, and sexuality—were tied to notions of propriety entangled with concepts of (inheritable) property to constitute proprietary relations.

Western notions of sovereignty are premised on notions of possessive liberal individualism, which in turn require particular configurations of sexuality. Lisa Lowe has traced the rise of European modernity, which is inextricably linked to "the intimacies of four continents" in that the definition of modern humanism emerged out of global intimacies, as it is tied to enslaved and colonized labor that enabled the private family to be distinguished from the public realm of work, society, and politics. She theorizes bourgeois intimacy as a form of biopolitics produced by the public/private divide and controlled by racial governmentality as racialized ideas of family and reproduction became central to notions of humanism in the early nineteenth century. "For European subjects in the nineteenth century, this notion of intimacy in the private sphere became a defining property of the modern individual in civil society, and ideas of privacy in bourgeois domesticity were constituted as the individual's 'possession' to be politically protected, as 'the right to privacy.' Thus, defining intimacies as the relations of four continents critically frames the more restricted meaning of intimacy as the private property of the European and North American individual." This is the link between contracts of labor and marriage as symbols of full humanity, tied to notions of freedom. "The liberal promise that former slaves, natives, and migrant workers could enter voluntarily into contract was a dominant mode for the initiation of the 'unfree' into consensual social relations between 'free' human persons."[9] As discussed in the chapter 3, the marital contract became a key social force linked to the control of Hawaiian women's sexuality and of same-sex relations between men and to the banning of close consanguineous sexual intimacy and reproduction.

Here we must note the intentional restructuring of Indigenous kinship in the quest to solidify Hawaiian sovereignty. The linkages between sexuality and sovereignty cannot be overstated here. Combating polygamy and polyandry, same-sex sexuality, and close consanguineous mating formed an overarching framework for restructuring the Indigenous polity in order to fend off Western encroachment. Hence the paradox: to fight that imperialism, Hawaiian chiefs enacted forms of colonial biopolitics in order to secure sovereign recognition. The regulation of a range of Hawaiian sexual norms was critical to the nation-building project, all of which contributed to the new standard of heteromonogamy that became the basis for constituting Western modes of property. Christian missionaries on the island proclaimed themselves superior in modes of self-governance, especially in contrast to Kanaka Maoli, whom they saw as sinful sexual degenerates.

Historical Accounts of Same-Sex Sexuality

During James Cook's Third Voyage, members of the crew remarked on the young Hawaiian men called aikāne who appeared to serve male chiefs as sexual partners.[10] Robert Morris examined the journals of the Third Voyage for references to aikāne relationships and found a total of seven explicit and clear mentions of homosexual activity: two by James King (an officer in the Royal Navy), one by Charles Clerke (also an officer in the Royal Navy), and four by David Samwell (a naval surgeon). For example, in one account Samwell discussed Kalaniʻōpuʻu, the paramount chief of Hawaiʻi Island (grandfather to Keōpūolani, the mother of Kamehameha II and III):

> Another Sett of Servants of who he [Kalaniʻōpuʻu] has a great many are called Ikany [aikāne] and are of superior Rank to Erawe-rawe [*i lawelawe,* the ones who carry out duties]. Of this Class are Parea [Palea] and Cani-Coah [Kānekoa] and their business is to commit the Sin of Onan upon the old King. This, however strange it may appear, is fact, as we learnt from frequent Enquiries about this curious Custom, and it is an office that is esteemed honorable among them & they have frequently asked us on seeing a handsome youth fellow if he was not an Ikany [aikāne] to some of us. The Queen Kaneecapoo-rei [Kānekapōlei] was with him, who has several children by him notwithstanding the old Boy keeps such a number of Ikany's [aikāne], and they say he has many Concubines.[11]

Although Clerke may have interpreted Kānekapōlei as "wife" and the others as lovers, that would not be an accurate description in Hawaiian terms. Kalaniʻōpuʻu's female partners were simply his wāhine (women), and the men his aikāne. The "Sin of Onan" refers to the biblical account of Onan, who engaged in a sexual act for nonprocreational purposes. In Christian doctrine any sex that did not lead to procreation was deviant (even within marriage). Therefore homosexual activity as well as masturbation, bestiality, and nonconformity with the "missionary position" (face-to-face contact with male on top and female on her back) were viewed as "sins against nature." In another entry, Samwell noted that the high chief was engaged in "unnatural crime" with a number of "concubines, wives, and young fellows" and that he was "not anxious to conceal" this fact, which Samwell compared to the "depravity of Indians."[12]

Clerke also remarked that Kalaniʻōpuʻu "keeps many women and so many young men," who indulged him in "lusts and passions" and referred to these actions as "infernal practice": in other words, diabolical.[13] Yet, as Lee Wallace notes in her reading of this period, "the British were frequently dependent on the men involved with high chiefs to assist in their interactions with the rulers, and they recognized that their sexual role in no way diminished their political function."[14] This suggests that foreigners understood that these men involved with the male chiefs were often the key to gaining access and that they were influential in their own right.

The limited secondary scholarship on the writings of early explorers, missionaries, and nineteenth-century Kanaka historians suggests that aikāne relationships were prevalent (at least among male ali'i referred to in the literature). From Kalani'ōpu'u, who encountered Cook in 1778, and Kamehameha I (the first monarch), who had numerous male lovers, to Kamehameha III and beyond, many Kanaka elites had aikāne relations.[15]

The meanings ascribed to *aikāne* vary and sometimes compete—and the definitions have changed over time. The *Hawaiian Dictionary* by Mary Kawena Pukui, a Kanaka ethnographer renowned for her expertise in Hawaiian traditions, and Samuel H. Elbert defines it as "n. friend, friendly, to become a friend." As Leilani Basham explains, aikāne is not an identity; it is used to define a relationship between two people. Drawing from Pukui, she explains: "To clearly indicate the presence of sexual activity, it is designated as 'moe aikāne' an action, not a noun, and therefore not a label attached to a person as the word homosexual."[16] "Moe aikāne is a contraction of moe (sleep), ai (coitus), and kāne (man)." Aikāne indicated sexual intimacy when it was preceded by *moe* (to sleep), as in; *moe aikāne* "nvt, to commit sodomy; literally, friend mating."[17]

Pukui and Handy elaborate on the concept of aikāne: "This relationship can exist between man and man, or woman and women; but not between man and woman." They also assert that "the genuine aikāne was never homosexual." But this seems to contradict late–eighteenth-century and early–nineteenth-century accounts discussed above. Pukui and Handy further write: "A homosexual relationship is referred to as moe aikāne (moe, lie or sleep with). Such behavior is said to have been known amongst some idle and debauched ali'i, as it is found amongst similar unfortunates the world over. The vulgar and contemptuous term for male homosexuality was *upi laho* (laho, scrotum). The word *upi* described the cleaning of the squid or octopus in a bowl of water or salt to rid it of its slime. Homosexuality was looked upon with contempt by commoners and by the true *ali'i*."[18] In this context, Pukui and Elbert defined 'ūpī in relation to cleaning, since it can also mean to sponge or extract.[19] But the word can also mean to squirt or spray. So their note that when combined with *laho* it suggests washing off a slick substance from the scrotum seems metaphorically descriptive. It is unclear why this is necessarily a contemptuous reference, and handling the scrotum also could hasten ejaculation. Still, the implication in this late–twentieth-century account is that this was a despised practice engaged in by decadent elites.

With regard to sexual intimacy between women, in discussing social roles Pukui, E. W. Haertig, and Catherine Lee explain: "Only one class of women lived socially what amounted to men's lives. These were nā kāula wāhine, the women prophets." They note that these women were extremely rare and had all the privileges of male priests. "The sexual lives of these kāula is not, as far as we know, mentioned in any written accounts. There is no evidence that they were lesbians." With regard to precolonial Hawai'i they surmise: "Lesbian relationships and attitudes towards them may have varied by regions." One informant who spoke to Pukui for her study said that female homosexuality occurred when men were away fighting, while Pukui mentions that one newspaper comment referred to the women as *'ūpīlaho*, acting like men engaged in sodomy.[20]

It also seems important to recognize that Western understandings of sexuality to some degree affect discussions of Hawaiian sexuality as it is portrayed in Indigenous stories and histories, given the legacy of the Western political models as well as the complications of attempting to translate ideas and terms into English.[21] How do we bridge that conceptual gap between languages and worldviews (Western and Hawaiian but also between generations) when attempting to understand and articulate what our kūpuna were discussing or portraying in regard to gender and sexuality? The understanding of these concepts has evolved over time not only because language and culture are dynamic but also due to the introduction of new practices and misinterpretations that may gain a foothold.

The term *aikāne* is ambiguous because it describes a close relationship between people of the same gender (e.g., two men or two women) that may or may not include sexual intimacy. Silva explains that aikāne "meant a close companion of the same sex, with sexual relations implicit," but in "contemporary Hawaiian, aikāne now means 'friend' with no sexual implication."[22] John Charlot explains that the term has sexual implications, "used for a man who participated in an intense friendship with another man, a relationship that included sexual relations. The word was applied to lesbian friends as well. The word does not necessarily designate an exclusively homosexual person."[23] Kame'eleihiwa has suggested that the aikāne served as a "safe sex" measure of sorts: "In the Hawaiian world, pregnancy is only a danger if you're a high-ranking person sleeping with someone of low rank because the child could damage the rank of the high-ranking person."

As she explains: "A lot of same-sex lovers came into the court because there was a desire formed for their brother or sister, but [the ali'i] couldn't have them because that would interfere with the nī'aupi'o lineage if they bore children. Many male ali'i nui were bisexual, and the aikāne relationship offered a male certain pleasure without any threat to his lineage, unlike a liaison with a beautiful but low-ranking woman. Thus, the aikāne was chosen out of a sense of desire, not out of duty to one's lineage."[24] While Kame'eleihiwa acknowledges same-sex desire, she seems to advance an argument in which the aikāne relationship also has a practical function.

Brian Kuwada notes: "Aikāne appear most often in traditional Hawaiian stories, and are those who are in a very intimate relationship/friendship with someone of the same sex. Being an aikāne very often implied a sexual relationship as well, although it was based first and foremost on companionship, with the sex arising more out of that intimacy and closeness than being a requirement of the friendship."[25] Aikāne relationships are defined in multiple ways throughout time and include devoted friends as well as lovers. And, as ku'ualoha ho'omanawanui (she does not capitalize her name) suggests, "The sexual nature of aikāne relationships is difficult to pinpoint because of the clear Christian condemnation of homosexuality and bisexuality; in light of severe Christian condemnation, Kanaka Maoli quickly learned to suppress, deny, or reinterpret such practices." She notes the difficulty in ascertaining the sexual nature of aikāne relationships. "Despite reticence by some to acknowledge the sexual aspect of aikāne relationships, there is ample evidence to support it." As ho'omanawanui points out, "Relationships between female aikāne appear to be as commonplace and normal as do those between men."[26]

The epic cosmology "Hi'iakaikapoliopele" about Pele, the *akua wahine* (female deity) of the volcano, and her heroic youngest sister, Hi'iaka, also includes an aikāne relationship between Hi'iaka and Hōpoe (her female lover). Silva and ho'omanawanui have each analyzed the *mo'olelo* (story). Although *kāne* (man) is an integral part of the word *aikāne*, Silva notes that Hi'iaka's relationships with two young women, Hōpoe and Wahine'ōma'o, are described as aikāne in the story and are implicitly sexual and/or romantic. Although some mo'olelo were written and published earlier, the publication of the first "Moolelo no Hiiakaikapoliopele" was in the newspaper *Ka Hoku o ka Pakipika* (1861–1863 in serial form) and thus part of the Hawaiian people claiming the power of the press for themselves.[27] *Ka Hoku o ka Pakipika* was the first newspaper owned, written, and edited by Kanaka Maoli. According to Silva, it was also the first paper that was free of the colonizing censorship of the Calvinist missionaries, who had controlled the press until that time.[28] The moʻolelo of Hiʻiakaikapoliopele was a landmark event in the writing and publication of Kanaka literature because of the relatively complete nature of its narrative and the long *mele* (song or poetry) included, some of which reveres Pele.[29] "The use of words with these double, even triple, meanings demonstrates the composer's mastery of Hawaiian poetics. The last line uses the metaphor of sleeping grass to suggest that the two had slept together. The next section of verse emphasizes their romantic relationship: "He lei moe ipo, / Aloha mai ka ipo, / He ipo no- e" (A lover's lei, / Beloved is the sweetheart, / She is a lover). Silva contends that "since there was no need to restrict or regulate such activity, the categories heterosexual, homosexual, and bisexual were never created in the language." She further suggests: "In this and other Hawaiian moʻolelo, romantic love between people of the same sex is presented as a normal practice of everyday life rather than as an identity marker. In the stories, such love relationships are cherished by those engaged in them and are supported by others."[30]

Hoʻomanawanui explains: "Throughout the moʻolelo, women create and maintain different kinds of relationships; the power and significance of these female relationships exhibit camaraderie in many ways. Hiʻiaka's relationships with Hōpoe and Wahineʻōmaʻo are central to the moʻolelo (story). Hiʻiaka's relationship with both of them is described in all of the Hawaiian-language texts as aikāne." She further notes that in the moʻolelo sexual relations among aikāne are "embedded in kaona [hidden or submerged meaning], which heightens the intellectual and emotional enjoyment of the listening or reading audience" (evidence of the desire and intimacy of lovers is often described in song composed by one about the other). As hoʻomanawanui acknowledges, the ambiguity surrounding aikāne relationships "may be confounding or frustrating to some, but it was a hallmark of Hawaiian poetic expression that continues today, while the blatant exposure of something valuable is considered coarse."[31]

David Malo (1793–1853), a royal historian of the Hawaiian Kingdom writing in the mid-1840s, defined *aikāne* as a "male companion or confidant." He noted that among the (male) aliʻi, some slept with aikāne. Malo also suggests that "the sleeping of males together was widespread at the aliʻi's residence," where there were "no rules" with regard to this interest. Malo traces the origins of male homosexuality to the time of chief Līloa's rule:

1 Liloa, the son of Kiha, had the reputation of being very religious, along with being well-skilled in war. His reign was a long one. I have not gained much information about the affairs of his government.
2 Tradition reports the rumor that Liloa was addicted to the practice of sodomy (*moe-ai-kane*); but it did not become generally known during his lifetime, because he did it secretly.
3 During Liloa's reign, there was much speculation as to why he retained a certain man as a favorite. It was not apparent what that man did to recommend himself as a favorite (*punahele*) in the eyes of the king, and it caused great debate.
4 After the death of Liloa people put to this man the question, "Why were you such a great favorite of Liloa?" His answer was "He hana mai mai iau ma kuu uha."
5 When people heard this, they tried it themselves, and in this way the practice of sodomy became established and prevailed down to the time of Kamehameha I. Perhaps it is no longer practiced at the present time. As to that I can't say.[32]

Pukui, Haertig, and Lee translate "He hana ma'i mai ia'u ma ku'u ūhā " as "He uses me against my thigh."[33] Taken literally, that would suggest a reference to intercrural sex rather than anal sex.

Hawaiian historian Samuel Kamakau (1815–1876) commented on same-sex sexuality in a negative light. He had been enrolled as a student at Lahainaluna Seminary, a Protestant missionary school established in 1823 by the Reverend William Richards in 1833. Kamakau declared: "Homosexuality was an evil practice with which certain people in old days defiled themselves. It was not practiced by commoners but among the chiefs and lesser chiefs, even to the extent of putting away their wives."[34] It is important to point out that the writings in which this comment appeared reflect a Christian stance (and by this time Kamakau had long graduated from Lahainaluna and converted to Catholicism).[35] The distinction between chiefs and commoners in his narration may also have had to do with European and white American attitudes toward monarchies in the nineteenth century (that royal families were out of touch and backward compared to the middle class and ordinary people who were challenging their power).

In any case, missionaries at Lahainaluna struggled with young Hawaiian men engaged in same-sex activity. Lorrin Andrews (1795–1868), an early American missionary to Hawai'i and judge who also served as the first principal of the seminary, complained that the mature male students were engaged in "irregular sexual liaisons so widespread that it became useless even to dismiss individual men." He even noted that "one year the entire examinations had to be canceled because of 'fornicators' and 'adulterers.'"[36]

Kamakau also makes clear that there was no limit to the number of "wives" or "husbands" that a chief could have.[37] He also mentions aikāne relationships between female aliʻi. Kamakau discusses Kaʻahumanu's strategy of making beautiful women who were potential rivals her aikāne or *punahele* (favorite), including a woman named Hinupu who was also the "wife" of Hīnaʻi, a chief of Waimea.[38] Other than this reference, little seems to be documented about aikāne relationships between women, at least in the English-language sources. However, the ongoing work of Hawaiian-language scholars continues to bring to light histories that appear to be "hidden" but have merely remained inaccessible due to the legacy of the ban on the Hawaiian language as a medium of instruction throughout most of the twentieth century.[39]

"The Time of Kaomi"

Same-sex relationships were clearly not uncommon in Hawaiian society, but some accounts (including some by Kanaka writers) present them as the province of select debauched and self-indulgent male chiefs. Although Kauikeaouli reportedly had more than one sexually intimate relationship with a lower-ranking male,[40] here I would like to discuss the infamous Kaomi. Silva notes that he was a male lover of the king and therefore despised by the missionary establishment, especially since many "missionary-inspired laws were openly transgressed while Kaomi was an intimate of the king."[41] As Kamakau relates, Kaomi was Tahitian through his father and Hawaiian through his mother. He was originally a Protestant minister working with the circle of chiefs led by Kaʻahumanu. As the kuhina nui who was co-ruling the monarchy with Kamehameha III, Kaʻahumanu was forcefully pushing for Christian reform across the islands. While king, Kauikeaouli rebelled against the Christian ways that had been ushered in by his mother Keōpūolani, the highest-ranking person in the kingdom and one of the first Kanaka converts in Hawaiʻi,[42] Kaʻahumanu, and his half-sister Kīnaʻu (Kaʻahumanu's niece, who would become the next kuhina nui). They continued to uphold the new laws supported by the missionaries.[43]

Kamakau explains that gossip about the king and Kaomi was widespread even while Ka'ahumanu was still alive. She had tried to marry Kauikeaouli to a female chief, but he refused because he was already with Kaomi. When he began his relationship with the king in 1832, Kaomi left the ministry. He was said to be a charming man—a storyteller with a good sense of humor as well as a healer who could diagnose by touch. According to Kamakau,

> for these reasons he was admitted to intimacy with the king. When the king took up sinful ways he gave Kaomi the title of "joint king, joint ruler" (moi ku'i, aupuni ku'i), appointed chiefs, warriors, and guards to his service, and made his name honorable. Any chief, prominent citizen, member of the king's household, or any man at all who wanted land, clothing, money, or anything else that man might desire, applied to Kaomi. He had the power to give or lend for the government. Landless chiefs were enriched by Kaomi and landless men also received land through him.[44]

Here it seems that Kaomi served as an authority and that the people were aware of his position as joint ruler.

Kamakau asserts that when Ka'ahumanu died, "all Oahu turned to evil ways." "The king's love of pleasure grew, and evil ways that had been stamped out were revived. The natural impulses of the old days—prostitution, liquor drinking, the hula—came back. The liquor distilleries were again opened. Only in the district of Waialua was the distillation of liquor not allowed. All kinds of indulgence cropped up. People poured in from Hawaii, Maui, and Kauai, for on Oahu the marriage laws were not observed, but on the other islands the rulers were strict in their enforcement of Kau-i-ke-aouli's law." Here we see that on the island of O'ahu people could disregard the king's laws. At least for a time the Christian ban on adultery—and all other forms of sexual engagement outside of marriage—was not enforced. O'ahu had engaged in a continuing struggle over the Calvinist reforms for quite some time while Boki and Liliha ruled. They were the first chiefs to be baptized Roman Catholic and together were members of the delegation to England in 1824 (led by King Kamehameha II and Queen Kamāmalu). Ka'ahumanu influenced King Kamehameha III to ban the Roman Catholic Church from the islands. Given the religious division and different standards of Christian morality, Boki and Liliha were a constant political threat to Ka'ahumanu and her authority over Kauikeaouli. While Boki served as governor, he ran a mercantile and shipping business and established the Blonde Hotel, where he operated a liquor store. He also had become indebted to foreigners and attempted to cover his debts by traveling to Vanuatu (aka the New Hebrides) to harvest sandalwood. Before departing in 1829, he entrusted administration of Oʻahu to Liliha. When Boki and his entourage were lost at sea and pronounced dead, Liliha became governor of the island. Kaʻahumanu developed a fierce rivalry with her cousin Liliha, who was politically aligned with the anti-Christian segment of aliʻi nui.[45]

On April 1, 1831, Kaʻahumanu heard rumors of a planned rebellion, so she sent Hoapili to relieve Liliha of her position, replacing her with Kaʻahumanu's own brother, John Adams Kuakini, as de facto governor of Oʻahu. That period is described by Kamakau as a time of raw hedonism, excess filled with "sinful pleasures," "evil ways," and "things of darkness"—all steeped in rampant alcohol consumption. According to Kamakau, no one could persuade the king to change his ways; only his sister dared try, but he remained unconvinced.[46] Around this time the king began a relationship with Kaomi. As Marie Alohalani Brown explains, Kaʻahumanu "made ʻĪʻī companion of the Mōʻī's eating, sleeping, and waking, and for places where there was not a pastor to preach before the Mōʻī and his traveling companions, he took on that role." Brown further notes: "ʻĪʻī blamed Kaomi and his companions as a corrupting influence. Because of them, Kauikeaouli was no longer heeding his kahu. ʻĪʻī later wrote that because his efforts to help the Mōʻī were in vain, he left him to his own devices and allied himself with pious aliʻi such as Kekāuluohi and Kīnaʻu."[47] The Christian chiefs would blame Kaomi for many of the vices during this period. They had been baptized at Kawaiahaʻo church, which had been closely aligned with Kaʻahumanu while she ruled the kingdom (when Kauikeaouli was too young to take his position as monarch). Kaomi became the de facto kuhina nui instead of Kīnaʻu, who had been poised to serve in that capacity. The power of Kaomi's influence on Kauikeaouli seems rooted in their friendship and their intimacy, bonded through sex (which perhaps also circumvented competition by others).

The following year the king expressed interest in appointing Liliha as kuhina nui instead of Kīnaʻu, who was the choice of the Christian chiefs. On March 15, 1833, Kauikeaouli proclaimed himself Mōʻī at a public gathering of thousands in Honolulu, requesting that people be loyal to him. There he formally named Kīnaʻu the kuhina nui—and she in turn made speeches confirming his sovereignty, along with Hoapili and Kekāuluohi.[48] Yet the power base remained divided between the Calvinist chiefs and those who were not Christian (or were otherwise resistant to the reforms).

Sometime after he was confirmed, the king wanted to appoint Liliha as the kuhina nui. This put her at odds with her father, Hoapili, who insisted that Kīnaʻu remain the kuhina nui.[49] The king yielded but did not yet abandon practices that offended the Christian faction. Kauikeaouli went against Kīnaʻu and the other chiefs: he suspended the laws and reverted back to the old ways seen as heathen, including hula and games like *ʻulu maika* and *pūhenehene* (stone games sometimes accompanied by gambling), drinking, and various sexual activities.[50]

The king and his company soon made a circuit of the island. Some said that the chiefs were going to install Kīnaʻu as kuhina nui—then rumors spread that a fight would break out when king returned. While on their island journey, Kauikeaouli and Kaomi were teaching people to set up stills to produce their own alcohol. John Adams Kuakini also joined in the enjoyment with Kauikeaouli and Kaomi.[51] In the meantime chief Hoapili went around to different parts of the island along with ʻĪʻī, destroying the distilleries that held the alcohol. As Kamakau explained:

> Liquor distilling and drinking ceased in the city except when the king was present. Another important act of the chiefs was to restore wives and husbands to their legal spouses on other islands. Among these were some lesser chiefs and prominent citizens, but they were for the most part commoners. In the midst of wailing they were arrested by the chiefs and placed on ships bound for Kauai, Maui, and Hawaii. There was great excitement but it rapidly subsided, peace was restored, and as a result the whole nation turned to do right according to the word of God.

Here we see the quest to restore Christian order, temperance, and chastity. The Christian chiefs viewed Kaomi as a bad influence who was encouraging the king's self-indulgence. "The entire blame of his conduct was laid upon Kaomi."[52]

As he challenged the whole structure of Hawaiian society being ushered in, Kaomi held enough sway with the king that Hawaiian chiefs attempted to remove him from the inner circle of the monarch's court. Chief Kaikioʻewa, a *kahu* (guardian) to the king since he was an infant, along with Hoapili, even hatched a secret plan to kill Kaomi. Kaikioʻewa ordered a servant named Kaihuhanuna to tie Kaomi's hands behind his back and had a war club ready to murder him.[53] When Kīnaʻu protested, the king rushed in and fought with Kaikioʻewa to save Kaomi. According to Kameʻeleihiwa, the king took Kaomi home to protect him, but he died within the year.[54] Kaikioʻewa accused the monarch of abandoning his leadership responsibilities: "You are not the ruler over the kingdom if you keep indulging yourself in evil ways."[55] Here we see that the battle over Hawaiian sovereignty was at stake in the repression against "savage sexualities" and other activities deemed "uncivilized." And, as Kameʻeleihiwa suggests, Kauikeaouli's relationship with Kaomi "was indicative of a much more serious breach between his choice of traditional lifestyle and the new Christian kapu."[56]

I suggest that what is at stake in the history recounted here is the erasure not only of the king's various relationships that went against his own edicts but also of the ways in which the debates about these types of relationships took place at a contested crossroads of the future of the Hawaiian Kingdom and its standing as a nation that could gain international respectability.

"Wickedness in High Places"

After the promulgation of the "Kānāwai No Ka Moe Kolohe" (the 1827 and 1829 laws regarding mischievous sleeping) and during his relationship with Kaomi, Kauikeaouli also became involved in a sexual relationship with his sister Nāhiʻenaʻena intermittently for several years after 1834 (and possibly as early as 1833). This type of union between siblings is referred to as a piʻo affiliation in Hawaiian, a rank-preserving strategy among the highest chiefs to mate siblings.[57] Kamakau and Malo both explain these unions as the result of needing to produce a high-ranking heir, to keep the genealogical line that would perpetuate ascendancy.[58] Accounts of Kauikeaouli's relationship with Nāhiʻenaʻena note that they attempted to conceal the intimate nature of their connection because it was abhorrent to the missionaries as well as the Puritan-identified chiefs. What seems to emerge from the literature is that they worked to suppress their relationship for the good of the nation, as the Hawaiian Kingdom was in the midst of tumultuous transition and adaptation between the old customs and the new teachings.

Incest is often assumed to be a universal "taboo" (a gloss for "forbidden" in English), but exceptions include traditional Hawaiian society among others.[59] Perhaps ironically, what gets called incest was "taboo" in Hawaiian society in the deepest meaning of the term's origins found in the Polynesian term *kapu* (also known as *tapu*) before it made its way into the English lexicon through Cook's voyages—meaning that which is sacred and therefore restricted to those among the chiefly class. Moreover, the term "incest" is perhaps a misnomer in the Hawaiian context. The term, which has its origins in Middle English, dating back to the thirteenth century, comes from the Latin *incestus*, meaning sexual impurity (from *incestus* impure, from *in-* + *castus* "pure caste"). In the Hawaiian tradition mating between high-ranking people who were closely related—especially between siblings—was considered the exact opposite of impure. Missionary reflections on this Hawaiian practice, however, suggest that, besides being a sin, the practice involved risky biological effects of close consanguinity. They urged Hawaiian chiefs to halt these types of unions on these and other related grounds. Hence as a biopolitical effort the new laws against consanguineous sexual relations seem to have been a protective measure, shielding Kanaka Maoli while also working to make them more respectable as newly civilized Christians.[60] But these matings, while not commonplace, run deep.

The Kumulipo, a prominent Hawaiian genealogy of the universe, features a sibling mating at its origins. Wākea (Sky Father) and Papahānaumoku (Earth Mother, literally "she who births the islands") are primordial humans.[61] As Kame'eleihiwa asserts, they were half-siblings through the 'Ōpūkahonua lineage and mated to become parents of the islands as well as Ho'ohōkūkalani, their first offspring. The union between Wākea and Papahānaumoku was considered a *nī'aupi'o* mating (between siblings or half siblings, literally "bent coconut mid-rib," meaning of the same stalk), from which divine power is derived.[62] The terms for this kind of mating offer insights into how Kanaka Maoli at the time regarded lineage metaphors: pi'o means "arching," and a child born of such a union was a nī'aupi'o (coconut frond arched back upon itself).[63] William H. Davenport offers a contextual analysis of these patterns, which involved the legitimate unions of close relatives. He examined the social ranking system of pi'o marriages to see if they were pervasive but found that they were the prerogative of sacred chiefs. "The practice of inbreeding to the degree of brother-sister marriage was peculiar to ranking families in Hawai'i and limited to rare occasions of purposeful and conscious in-breeding for scions of supreme rank and in no way a general custom of the Hawaiian people."[64]

The speculations about the king and his sister have been vast and sensationalist. Elisha Loomis, who was part of the first missionary company sent by the American Board of Commissioners of Foreign Missions on the *Thaddeus* from Boston to the Hawaiian Islands, wrote in 1824 that they were already living "in a state of incest" when they were quite young. "It is well known here that the prince and princess for a considerable time past have lived in a state of incest. This would appear extraordinary in America, as the prince is but ten years of age and the princess less than 7 or 8. It should be remembered, however, that persons arrive at the age of puberty here much sooner than in a colder climate. Chastity is not a recommendation; the sexes associating without restraint almost from infancy."[65]

In addition to the obvious racial notions in his account (of Hawaiian children's sexuality as uncontrollable), this rendering is suspect. Kauikeaouli (born in either 1813 or 1814) would have been about six or seven years old when the missionaries arrived in 1820. So it is unclear what Loomis meant by the siblings having been involved before "for a considerable time" as prepubescent children when Nāhi'ena'ena would have been just four or five years old. Loomis seems to make no distinction between the period when the two were children (and may have engaged in sexual behavior) and the period when they matured to adulthood and chose to be with each other. Or perhaps he considered them always childlike, as if they did not know any better. Either way, here we see the characterization of Hawaiians enacting "savage sexualities" cast as beginning in infancy.

From other accounts it seems that Nāhi'ena'ena and Kamehameha III may have become intimate as early as 1833. The chiefs proposed in 1832 that Kamanele, the daughter of John Adams Kuakini (brother of Ka'ahumanu), would be the most suitable person in age, rank, and education for Kamehameha III to marry, but she died in 1834 before a wedding could take place. The young chief Keolaloa was to marry Nāhi'ena'ena in 1834 but died before any ceremony.[66]

The Lāhainā Church Record is full of notes by the Reverend William Richards about individuals being excommunicated for sexual and other transgressions against the religious codes of the time.[67] Having served as Nāhi'ena'ena's guardian and teacher after her mother's death, he described her struggle to remain a pious Christian. As early as October 1831 Richards wrote:

> The princess Nahienaena made a public acknowledgment of the crime of drunkenness. The acknowledgement was not written, but was more satisfactory than it would have been, had it been studied & written. The crime was committed on the 18th of Sept.; & from that time to this, a dark cloud has hung over the church of Lahaina, but has today been, in a degree, dispelled. During this period, the time of Mr. R has been entirely occupied in labouring with her; & in exerting to counteract the influence of her example on the people.[68]

The year 1834 was particularly eventful. In January Nāhi'ena'ena traveled from the island of Maui to O'ahu to visit Honolulu. Hoapili traveled with her, presumably to keep her under his watchful eye. Before departure, he conferred with Richards about a suitable husband for her. The two identified a potential Hawaiian man of appropriate rank (William Pitt Leleiohoku I), but that would come later. In the meantime, knowing that she was going away, Richards wrote to missionary Levi Chamberlain in Honolulu to request that he look after her while she was there. She stayed for a few months and wrote letters to Richards in January, February, and April. She presumably did not write in March because she was on an island tour with her brother and a large company of chiefs. Kauikeaouli was reportedly in a "debauched" state for much of the time, seen to be drinking excessively. Dr. Gerrit P. Judd (a physician and missionary who later became advisor to the king) eventually caught up with Nāhiʻenaʻena. After a ten-day stop at ʻEwa she left her brother and continued on a different journey with Judd and Hoapili. Hoapili addressed gatherings of Kanaka, urging them to give up liquor and to keep up with school to learn to write. Nāhiʻenaʻena spoke alongside him in some places to echo his message.[69] It is unclear from Kamakau what led her to change tack.

In mid-January (1834), Nāhiʻenaʻena abruptly returned to Lāhainā, Maui, with Hoapili. There she openly defied missionary teachings by smoking, playing cards, and drinking rum. She also reportedly interrupted church services. During this period Richards was absent from Lāhainā most of the time, being stationed at Wailuku (another part of Maui island) for six weeks. He wrote her several times to question her behavior, which he had heard about from others. She would reply, sometimes remorseful, at other times defiant. In March that same year she traveled to Hawaiʻi Island. Missionaries there reported that she complained about her lot and continued to drink, listen to Hawaiian chants, and "spend her nights in debauchery."[70]

Eventually Richards moved to excommunicate her from the church. Members of the congregation were to vote on May 23, but she rushed to Richards to ask for delay. He made that contingent on whether she would dismiss her "wicked companions," who were with her frequently. She refused, so the members of the church voted to excommunicate her on May 25 after Richards's letter was read publicly. She was said to be drinking on a ship when David Malo delivered the letter informing her of the expulsion. Sometime later, in early June, the king wanted his sister to move from Honolulu to join him at Pearl River, but she refused to go. The king attempted suicide by slashing his throat and attempting to drown himself but was rescued by a retainer. A week later he returned to Honolulu.[71]

In July of that same year Richards got confirmation of their worst fears that Kauikeaouli and Nāhiʻenaʻena had a sexual relationship. He noted that

John Papa ʻĪʻī (mentioned earlier), who was serving as a kahu (guardian) to Kauikeaouli, had come to tell him that Nāhiʻenaʻena "had fallen." In an entry on July 22, 1834, Richards wrote: "At 4 o'clock Ii arrived at my door from Oahu with the heart-rending intelligence of the fall of the princess. 'O tell it not in Gath, publish it not in the streets of Askelon.' How many tears have I shed on her account! but they are but the beginning of weeping. She is now living in incest with her brother, drinking, attending hulas, etc. This day I have spent in writing to her from the tomb of her mother."[72] Richards is referring to 2 Samuel 1:20, "Tell it not in Gath, publish it not in the streets of Askelon; lest the daughters of the Philistines rejoice, lest the daughters of the uncircumcised triumph." This suggests that he did not want word about the two being together to spread and that he would tend to the matter himself. Note that he mentions writing to Nāhiʻenaʻena "from the tomb of her mother." Keōpūolani made it clear on her deathbed right after being baptized that she wanted her surviving children, Nāhiʻenaʻena and Kauikeaouli, to live as Christians.

Nāhiʻenaʻena and Kauikeaouli wrote a letter to Kīnaʻu informing them of their union. The king sent a town crier through the streets to announce it. Missionary Levi Chamberlain also noted the relationship between Kauikeaouli and Nāhiʻenaʻena. Like Richards, in an entry also dated July 22, he wrote:

> A letter from Auhea to Kīnaʻu gave the distressing notice that the Princess has been guilty of Cohabiting with her brother. Last night at 3 o'clock the shameful & criminal act was done in the house of Paki. The King & his sister propose to go to Waianae to get as far away from their teacher as possible and to put him to all the trouble they are able to get to them. They do not consent that Auhea & Hoapili shall accompany them. This is indeed wickedness in high places. The Lord look upon it & overrule it for the good of his church in these islands. The Lord reigneth let the earth rejoice. He can lift up a standard when the enemy breaks in like a flood & overrule evil and bring the greatest good of it. May this be the case now.[73]

Richards continued to document the long struggle with Nāhiʻenaʻena over this issue. In an entry from August 7 (1834) he notes that he received a letter back from the princess but that it was "not satisfactory." The following year he wrote that on January 16, 1935, she arrived on the island of Maui while he was in the town of Wailuku. He wrote her a letter but "received no satisfactory answer." He then confronted her in writing again once back in Lāhainā: "If you are ready to forsake your sins, then write and let me know it, & we will meet each other at once." In response, as he put it: "She would not promise, but called at my house. I refused to see her until she would promise, which she refusing to do, I returned to Wailuku without meeting her." From there, Richards wrote a letter to the church that was publicly read and eventually returned there the next month. In an entry on February 5, 1835, he complained that a committee composed of Hoapili, Kalaikoa, and Malo was sent to "reclaim her" but that all efforts were in vain, so another letter of excommunication was drawn up to be read on the next Sabbath.[74] But the messengers pleaded that he not read the letter publicly and that she wanted to meet with him.

The same evening Nāhiʻenaʻena visited Richards at his house and promised reform. He wrote that she seemed "sincere" in promising to receive his instructions and "seek the right way," noting that "she continued to exhibit signs of sincerity until her visit to Hawaii in the month of April." He added: "She was then again guilty of intoxication & and commenced her games anew & spent her nights in debauchery."

> May 20th she again returned to Lahaina. I immediately called a church meeting & proposed to cut her off without further delay. In this I was not opposed. The vote finally passed on the evening of the 23rd & the letter was prepared. While the church were together. She was on board a foreign vessel engaged in drinking. She, however, came to my house as soon as she heard the vote of the church & again wished a delay; but still would not promise to dismiss her wicked companions. On Sabbath morning the letter of excision was publicly read & then carried by Malo & delivered to her. May the Lord have mercy on her soul.[75]

On September 1 that same year people assisting Kauikeaouli sent a ship for Nāhiʻenaʻena to travel to Honolulu because he was ill.[76] She reached Honolulu on September 5, accompanied by William Pitt Leleiōhoku I and the wife of Hoapili (known as Hoapili Wahine), Kalakua Kaheiheimālie. Nāhiʻenaʻena stayed in Honolulu for several months. By November rumors were spreading that she was pregnant by her brother.

Nāhiʻenaʻena had been betrothed to William Pitt Leleiōhoku I, the son of high chief William Pitt Kalanimoku (prime minister of the kingdom) and grandson of Kamehameha I. The chiefs had previously suggested him as a husband for Nāhiʻenaʻena, but the king intervened by advising that they hold off until Leleiōhoku attained more education.[77] They finally married on November 25, 1835, with Richards presiding.[78] Soon she was pregnant.

By January 1, 1836, Nāhiʻenaʻena was back on the island of Maui but moved to Wailuku instead of returning to Lāhainā. There the resident missionary complained to Richards about her being "mischievous" and "polluted." The Reverend Richard Armstrong, who came to the Hawaiian Islands with the fifth company of missionaries in 1832 and first worked on the island of Molokai before going to Maui, claims to have observed her for several months there and reported that she was caught in the state of madness and self-destruction. He noted a turnaround when she began attending church services but said that she was still miserable and that the changes seemed to be mostly for appearance's sake. She frequently asked to see Armstrong, but he refused each time.[79] His methods were similar to those of Richards: ostracize her as a way of bringing her back into the fold.

In late April 1836 the king sailed for the island of Maui, planning to bring Nāhiʻenaʻena back to Honolulu for the birth of her child. Hence some speculated that the child might have been his, but others recognized that it could have been her husband's. At that time she was approximately four months pregnant. Her baby would be next in line for the throne. The king stayed on Maui for three to four months. Hoapili and her guardian Kuakini watched from the side but could not interfere. They did eventually withdraw from attending to the king and Nāhiʻenaʻena. The two siblings eventually resumed the life that they had briefly shared together in 1834. By late August that same year, when the royal birth was expected, Kauikeaouli took Nāhiʻenaʻena back to Honolulu. Hoapili and Leleiōhoku sailed with them. Nāhiʻenaʻena was given a house built for her by Kīnaʻu, the kuhina nui at the time. Nāhiʻenaʻena's attendants were allowed to play cards, smoke, and so forth as she waited for her child in seclusion from the public. A newspaper announced on September 17 that her infant son had died only a few hours after being born. Kauikeaouli was said to have believed that the child was his.[80]

After her son's death Nāhiʻenaʻena became very ill through October and November. Chamberlain visited her and urged her to repent. In early November the high chiefs sent for Dr. Judd, who was back in Lāhainā. Nāhiʻenaʻena's condition had grown worse by December. On December 30, 1836, she died in the presence of her brother and her husband, with Kīnaʻu and other high chiefs by her side. There were two services, one held in Honolulu by Bingham. The second funeral was held in early April on Maui. Her brother made the necessary preparations and carried his sister to be buried next to their mother, Keōpūolani. Historians hold that her death had a sobering effect on her brother, who supposedly reconsidered the teachings of Christianity soon afterward. "He remembered the laws he had established for the welfare of his people, laws that he himself had broken." He supposedly waited to bury his sister until he had improved himself. He never joined the Christian church, but he married Kalama Hakaleleponi Kapakuhaili in a Christian ceremony performed by Bingham on February 14, 1837.[81] She was the hānai daughter of Miriam Kekāuluohi (the staunch Christian who became kuhina nui after Kīnaʻu died in 1839) and Charles Kanaʻina. Kalama was of lower chiefly genealogy as the daughter of Īʻahuʻula and Kona chief Nāihekukui, who had been in an aikāne relationship with Liholiho (Kamehameha II).

The king moved with his wife to Lāhainā, so he let Kīnaʻu rule in Honolulu—much to the dismay of the foreigners.[82] Although Kauikeaouli had periods in which he engaged in alcohol consumption and extramarital relationships, after 1837 he "allowed his Christian kahuna to teach him about Western laws and forms of land tenure." Kauikeaouli continued to live in Lāhainā for approximately eight years and was said to have remained there so long out of love for his sister.[83] He and his wife Kalama had two children, Prince Keaweawe'ulaokalani I and Prince Keaweaweʻulaokalani II, both of whom died while infants.[84] The king was said to have had an affair with Jane Lahilahi (daughter of his father's advisor, John Young, and also the sister of Keoni Ana, who reportedly also had an aikāne relationship with the king when he served as kuhina nui). Lahilahi had twin sons by the king. Kiwalaʻō was initially taken by his father to raise but died young. The other twin, Albert Kūnuiākea, survived and was later adopted by his father and Queen Kalama.

The stories of the king and his sister and his relationship with Kaomi offer two examples of deep and fraught contestation over what kind of nation the kingdom would become. This was a struggle over the future of Hawaiian sovereignty, forged in large part through the repression of Hawaiian sexuality in the face of Puritan teachings brought by Calvinist missionization. The chiefs were not aligned on these Christian reform campaigns: some segments of the Indigenous society were enacting these changes, while others unashamedly resisted them. The chiefs in support of them, however, especially the chiefly women who served in the capacity of kuhina nui, asserted their authority to drive the social field and consolidate their own power. In the two accounts we see different forms of coercion enacted by select elites who paradoxically took up a colonial approach in the form of eradicating Indigenous ways of being in the quest to reaffirm Hawaiian sovereignty. While Hawai'i supposedly was not a colony at the time and these actions took place under kingdom authority, we can see the broader context of coloniality at play. The contest over what it meant to be a civilized subject, a civilized society, and a competent, modern nation of people capable of self-governance rested on rejection, repression, and restraint of sexual practices deemed savage within a new Christian order that cannot be separated from colonial forces.

These complex legacies continue to play out in nationalist politics today. A new Christian evangelism is at work in the quest to suppress decolonial Indigenous resurgence projects of reclamation, often (again) in the name of protecting Hawaiian sovereignty.

"Beyond the Binary"

Jade Snow opens her article "Beyond the Binary: Portraits of Gender and Sexual Identities in the Hawaiian Community" in *Mana* by noting the controversies within Hawai'i's population at large over SB 1, the bill that legalized same-sex marriage under 50th state law in November 2013. Snow notes how the legislative proposal brought to the surface the ongoing contestation over "what is truly considered Hawaiian tradition when it comes to gender and sexuality." She identifies the split: "For some, devotion to the Christian faith accepted by revered ali'i was a means of honoring the wishes of their ancestors. For others, acknowledging the practices preceding missionary contact is true to Hawaiian tradition. When it comes to expression and identity, what does it mean to represent the culture of our 'āina hānau [birth land]?"[85] In an attempt to answer this question, which indeed is central to the article, Snow provides a portrait piece on select individuals and couples to document contemporary Kanaka thinking on gender and sexuality, with photography by Aaron Yoshino. Along with a focus on Kaumakaiwa Kanaka'ole and Hinaleimoana Kalu-Wong, both of whom discuss being māhū, the article also highlights the stories of well-known Hawaiian musician Keali'i Reichel and his longtime male partner, who had a wedding after the 50th state legalized same-sex marriage, and Kanaka scholar Valli Kalei Kanuha and her female partner, who adopted a baby girl as a lesbian couple.

This significant article, written for a popular audience, features a range of topics perennially up for debate in the Hawaiian nationalist movement and the broader community. The guiding question of what it means to represent Hawaiian culture when it comes to gender and sexual expression and identity is indeed one of the issues that this book explores with regard to the legacy of colonial biopolitics perpetuated by the Christian chiefs of the early nineteenth century. Snow notes that many male ali'i nui (high chiefs), including Kamehameha, Kalani'ōpu'u, Liholiho, and Kauikeaouli, had aikāne relationships in addition to multiple female partners. Also, in this article Kame'eleihiwa discusses her forthcoming book *Hawaiian Sexuality*, pointing out the Hawaiian ancestral emphasis on *le'a*—pleasure and fulfillment that kūpuna (elders or forebears) cherished, revered, and celebrated through the poetry of chants and song.

In contrast, Snow also includes an interview with executive pastor Kenneth Silva of New Hope Christian Fellowship, O'ahu—a church that meets at three locations on the island. Founded by Pastor Wayne Cordeiro in 1996, New Hope is a chartered church of the International Church of the Foursquare Gospel (an evangelical Pentecostal Christian denomination founded in 1923). In the article Silva alludes to restrictions based on his faith, explaining that his church follows the Bible and sees it as infallible. With that assumption—and an understanding that pre-Christian Hawaiians engaged in a range of sexual practices that his version of Christianity does not sanction—Silva relegates these practices to a past that Hawaiians have, or should have, moved beyond: "As a native Hawaiian, having roots that go back generations here, I don't think it's for me to judge. The mores and the values and all of the pressures of that time, we really aren't able to understand. If you really didn't know another way, if that's the society you lived and thrived in, then everything would appear to be acceptable because that's what society accepted at that time. But, for me, in today's world, knowing the different things that we do, my question is how shall we live now?"[86] Silva's statement implicitly speaks to a savage past, a society of people who did not know anything different or anything better. The subtext here is that "we know better now"—now that Hawaiians are civilized and Christianized (even if not all of them abide by New Hope's take on the scriptures). The proliferation of evangelical churches in Hawai'i during the last few decades has gone hand in hand with an overall right-wing political shift in the islands. It is noteworthy that the cover of this same issue of *Mana* features a stunning diptych photograph of Kaumakaiwa Kanaka'ole

FIGURE 4.1. The cover of *Mana*'s March 2014 issue. Photo from Pacific Basin Communications/Aaron Yoshinog

(with what appears to be masculine on the left and feminine on the right) with the headline "The Meaning of Māhū."

In contemporary Hawaiian vernacular, *māhū* is typically used to describe transgender women (and sometimes used to describe an effeminate man presumed to be gay) or those who are otherwise seen as gender liminal.[87] Given the paucity of research on the category of māhū it is unclear whether it is a sex or gender, but it may not make sense to think about the concept in these bounded terms. In any case, the category seems distinct from sexual orientation. Contemporary anthropology and gender studies make a distinction between sex and gender and theorize how sexuality is co-constituted by gender: all three are socially constructed (whereas sex was previously assumed to be a straightforward biological reality with two designations: male and female). Sexuality is frequently underpinned by gender, but they are not the same. Sexual desire is implicated through relations of power and by colonial exchange, which mutually transforms both the forms of sexual expression and their manifestation in practices of gender.[88] In the *Mana* article Kanakaʻole explains: "I want the concept of māhū to take itself out of the sexual context, exclusive of gender. Gender not as it applies to female and male as biological, but a natural spiritual definition of gender."[89] This seems to mean that māhū has been presumed to denote a person's sexuality. Kanakaʻole insists that rather than hitching māhū to gender conflated with one's sex it should be understood as being connected with something more transcendent.

Hinaleimoana Kalu-Wong also defines māhū as "an individual that straddles somewhere in the middle of the male and female binary. It does not define their sexual preference or gender expression, because gender roles, gender expressions and sexual relationships have all been severely influenced by the changing times. It is dynamic. It is like life."[90] Here the emphasis is on fluidity, liminality, and the potential of transformation rather than on static, fixed ways of being. Moreover, the link to relationships, and relationality more generally, is distinct from a focus on individual identity.[91] As Leilani Basham explains: "Ultimately, for Hawaiians, these kinds of relationships and activities are simply not defined and do not share the same boundaries as the equivalent terms and actions in English. In the Hawaiian context, both māhū identity and aikāne relationships are descriptive of a system in which there is some flexibility in one's gender and identity."[92]

Some have suggested that māhū is perhaps a "third gender." As noted earlier, in the *Hawaiian Dictionary* Pukui and Elbert defined it alternately as "homosexual or hermaphrodite."[93] Pukui, Haertig, and Lee define māhū as "those of the homosexual nature and practice, and the physical hermaphrodite." They continue: "A present-day, perhaps regional usage, also gives māhū the meaning of transvestite, an individual, not necessarily homosexual, who wears clothing of the opposite sex."[94] The term has also been used as a derogatory epithet, especially to belittle feminine māhū sexually, but it is unclear whether that signals a diminished social status within Hawaiʻi at large (as an occupied colonial site inundated with U.S. military bases, installations, and personnel among a steady stream of tourists) and/or within the Kanaka Maoli community more specifically.

Andrew Matzner notes that the word *māhū* itself is currently undergoing transformation.

> In old Hawai'i this term meant "hermaphrodite" and was also used to refer to both feminine men and masculine women. In present-day Hawaii locals use "māhū" to refer to male-to-female transgendered people, as well as effeminate and gender normative gay men. Over the years this word has taken on negative connotations, and today is often used as a slur. . . . However, the integrity of this word is slowly being revived by transgendered people of Hawaiian descent who, due to renewed interest in its cultural meaning, view the māhū of traditional Hawaiian society as role models. This groundswell can perhaps be traced back to the beginnings of the Hawaiian cultural renaissance, which gained momentum during the civil rights era of the 1970s. . . . However, it wasn't until the late 1990s that the māhū themselves began to organize for their rights within the larger context of the Hawaiian cultural reawakening.[95]

In other words, this is part of a broader Indigenous resurgence and claiming of difference, not merely a politics of recognition.[96] We can see this form of reclamation as a way to resist assimilation, whether by those who are hostile to same-sex sexuality and gender diversity or by non-Indigenous lesbian, gay, bisexual, transgender (LGBT) people who appropriate Kanaka cultural forms for their own ends, such as normalizing their own sexuality and gender in relation to the state.

In the 2001 documentary *Ke Kulana He Māhū: Remembering a Sense of Place*, directors Kathy Xian and Brent Anbe present a series of interviews and historical research to draw a relationship between LGBT struggles at large in Hawai'i and the struggles over Kanaka Maoli sovereignty in particular. The film examines how Western colonization and modernization gave rise to intolerance and homophobia in Hawai'i and documents the efforts being made by Kanaka Maoli to restore cultural practices in a way that asserts that both gays and transgender people in Hawaiian society held cherished roles. The filmmakers and many of the interviewees assert that Hawai'i's ancient traditions included "unconditional love, community solidarity and acceptance of the transgendered māhū," defined as "sacred healers in indigenous society." They define *māhū* as "both male and female." Furthermore, the filmmakers argue that Hawai'i's embrace of LGBT civil rights throughout the 1990s was anchored in the struggle against political and cultural imperialism. As they assert in the film description, "The spirit of aloha (love) lives on in the drag queens, social workers, educators, writers, activists, mothers and religious leaders working to reinstate Hawaii's traditions of tolerance and abundance for all."

Nonetheless, because the reclamation of "tradition" is always selective, the revitalization of identity can sometimes fall unevenly along gender and sexual lines (as discussed in chapter 3). Tengan documents how a number of Kanaka Maoli men have felt intensely disempowered by the legacies of colonization. This includes the tourist industry, which, besides occupying land, promotes a feminized image of Native Hawaiians marked by the pervasive figure of the dancing hula girl. Tengan focuses on a group of Native men on the island of Maui who responded by forming a group in the early 1990s called the Hale Mua (Men's House). As both a member of the Hale Mua and an ethnographer, Tengan analyzes how the group's members assert warrior masculinity through a range of Hawaiian and other Polynesian cultural practices to renew their identities to overcome the dislocations of a history of dispossession. Hale Mua rituals and practices connect to broader projects of cultural revitalization and Hawaiian nationalism. Yet strains in the group's efforts to reclaim Indigenous masculinity surface in debates over nineteenth-century historical source materials and during political and cultural gatherings held in spaces designated as tourist sites. And there are other tensions as well: men in the Hale Mua calling for the "remasculinization" of indigeneity as part of the Hawaiian sovereignty movement have to some degree contributed to the marginalization of māhū and condoning of homophobia.[97]

My point here is that the Hawaiian community is working out these complicated issues in ways that are in tension with Siu (whose missive opened this chapter) and his colleagues: there is a community effort to negotiate these cultural politics. The legal battle over same-sex marriage has long been a catalyst for debates about popular conceptions and appropriations of Hawaiian sexualities.

Same-Sex Marriage as Decolonization?

On September 9, 2013, then governor Neil Abercrombie announced that he would hold a special session on October 28 to consider a bill named the Hawaii Marriage Equality Act.[98] Tensions in the islands over the matter were heated. There was even threat of a citizens' filibuster to block it, even though it included a religious exemption to protect religious groups and clergy who do not want to solemnize or participate in same-sex weddings.[99] Despite the division splitting the population at large, the legislature passed the bill after meeting in special session.

Contemporary debates on the politics of same-sex sexuality in Hawai'i can be traced in part to the early 1990s, when the issue of sexual orientation in relation to nationalism emerged. This was arguably brought about by the first U.S. legal case for same-sex marriage. In the case of *Baehr v. Lewin* (852 P.2d 44, Haw. 1993; later *Baehr v. Miike*) the Hawai'i State Supreme Court ruled in 1993 that refusing to grant marriage licenses to same-sex couples was discriminatory under the state's equal rights amendment (on the basis of gender, not sexual orientation).[100] As such, the state was required to justify its position of opposing the marriages—to show that it had a "rational interest" in denying them this right.

In the midst of dispute a group of Kanaka Maoli formed an organization called Nā Mamo o Hawai'i. Founders identified as lesbian, gay, bisexual, transgender, and māhū (LGBTM). Nā Mamo's political work emerged at the interstices of two competing projects: the civil rights struggle for same-sex marriage and the sovereign rights struggle for the restoration of a Hawaiian nation.[101] Members of Nā Mamo drew from a range of Hawaiian histories while working to secure a place within the various competing nationalist groups. Even though a range of sexual arrangements and practices have a strong cultural genealogy, the reception of these sexual legacies has been uneven. The existence of same-sex sexual practices (for example) is undeniably Hawaiian, so leaders are hard pressed to cast homosexuality as a colonial import. Although activists by and large acknowledge that Hawaiian gender and sexual diversity is part of their recognized cultural tradition, however, that concession has not necessarily translated into explicit inclusion. Often the admission of same-sex sexual traditions was used as an alibi for nationalist exclusions in the name of political unity, casting the issue as "divisive."[102]

Nā Mamo pushed Kanaka Maoli leaders to consider all forms of decolonization. Their open reclamation of Indigenous practices with regard to sexual politics enabled a space for Hawaiians to consider a more complex view of history with regard to sexuality and intimate unions. In attempting to secure a visible place in Hawaiian nationalist politics, Nā Mamo highlighted genealogy as a central issue,[103] insisting that Hawaiian same-sex legacies inform contemporary identities and refusing to allow leaders to relegate these modes to "ancient times." For example, founder Ku'umeaaloha Gomes explained in a *Village Voice* article on the group in 1996 that King Kamehameha I had an aikāne named Kuakini, whom she identified as a high chief who later governed Hawai'i Island. In relation to this history, she told how the group got its name: before going into battle, King Kamehameha called his warriors *nā mamo,* meaning "favored descendants."[104] Gomes's invocation of royal naming practices worked to insinuate members of the group within a particular Hawaiian lineage. This is not an assertion of a transhistorical notion of sexual identities: within a Hawaiian ontological frame, genealogical precedence holds powerful sway in how the present is regarded, explained, and authorized.[105]

Notably, it was the Hawai'i case on same-sex marriage that led to the passage of the Defense of Marriage Act (DOMA) in 1996. Voters in Hawai'i passed an amendment to the state constitution in 1998 that allowed the state legislature to enact a ban on same-sex marriage: "The legislature shall have the power to reserve marriage to opposite-sex couples." That amendment led to the dismissal of the same-sex marriage lawsuit in 1999. Eventually, though, as several states followed Massachusetts in passing same-sex marriage laws, the Supreme Court of the United States eventually overturned DOMA on June 26, 2013. Subsequently, some states that had battled over the issues renewed efforts to pass new legislation supporting same-sex marriage, including Hawai'i, as Governor Abercrombie did just a few months later.

Just a week or so before the Hawai'i state legislature passed the same-sex marriage bill in November 2013, the *New York Times* published an opinion piece by editorial board member Lawrence Downes, who wrote:

> The victory, once it comes, will have a special resonance. This is the state whose Supreme Court in 1993 first opened the door to marriage equality by declaring marriage a basic civil right, setting off a reactionary scramble that led to the federal Defense of Marriage Act, a legal bulwark against gay couples that the United States Supreme Court has partly demolished.[106] . . . Passage would bring things full circle from the 1990s. But you could draw a circle much bigger than that. Start in the 1820s, when the first New England missionaries arrived on the islands, burning with a zeal to save heathen souls. Hawaii is one of our oldest live-and-let-live battlegrounds, where Western views of propriety and sexual morality grappled with a contrary point of view. Hawaii was a peaceable kingdom then, with relaxed attitudes toward sin and clothing. Missionaries saw drinking, dancing, tattoos, gambling and debauchery, and countered with hymns, bolts of crisp cotton and muslin—and monogamy. They worked fast. . . . Scholars

> have noted a deep Hawaiian tradition of tolerance and fluid sexual identity, of acceptance, toward gay people especially. Fast forward to 2013. Hawaii is still seen as the antithesis of uptight. . . . And politically, Hawaii is bluer than blue.. . . But . . . the issue is splitting the state evenly. . . . The debate has an upside-down feel to it. The people wearing the rainbow leis and invoking Hawaii's heritage and the "aloha spirit" are saying: Let's please get married, in the Western tradition. The conservatives' reply: No rites for you. Go have your wedding in California. There's fluid, and then there's topsy-turvy.[107]

Downes's account romanticizes old Hawaiʻi for its allowance for same-sex sexual practices and refers to Hawaii as having come "full circle"—not just since the same-sex marriage case that began in 1993 but also from the early nineteenth century, when Calvinist missionaries from New England arrived. In other words, he is suggesting that through a series of changes the islands have been led back to an original position or situation: same-sex sexual traditions restored.

But this is not about the return to same-sex sexual modalities in a decolonial sense. I suggest that the state legislature's passage of the same-sex marriage bill indicates a form of settler colonial continuity in Hawaiʻi that extends the introduction of male-female marriage and legal coverture for women in the early nineteenth century to the contemporary politics of assimilation and affirmation of settler colonial governance (and U.S. occupation) under the cover of LGBT inclusion in a multiracial liberal democracy. This is another version of the Hawaiian melting pot in the "land of aloha." Downes asserts at the end of his op-ed that "there's fluid, and then there's topsy-turvy." What is topsy-turvy is his notion of "coming full circle"—that same-sex marriage becomes the new symbol of "aloha." Far from Hawaiʻi coming full circle, same-sex marriage merely extends this tool of social control used by the government to regulate sexuality and family formation by establishing a favored form and rewarding it.[108] This form of state regulation links back to the colonial biopolitics in the context of Christian dominance in the early to mid-nineteenth century.

In the midst of the statewide battle over the issue, both proponents and opponents invoked Indigenous Hawaiian cultural models to their advantage, leading to contested discourses regarding Kanaka Maoli tradition and sexuality. On the one hand, non-Hawaiians like Downes appropriate concepts of Hawaiian culture (like aloha) to advance their own politics in support of same-sex marriage. On the other hand, non-Kanaka have mobilized

Hawaiian concepts in opposition from a right-wing Christian stance—such as ʻohana (which they use as a gloss for family in a hetero-nuclear sense rather than an extended, multigenerational family). In response to these perverted invocations of Hawaiian culture and in support of same-sex marriage, some Kanaka Maoli challenged their actions as a misappropriation and made important interventions.

One rich example is a network on Facebook that emerged at this time, "True Aloha," founded by allies of LGBTM Kanaka Maoli in fall 2013 while the state legislature debated the bill. True Aloha confronted the ways in which people distorted Hawaiian cultural concepts—such as ʻohana and aloha—for their own political ends in opposition to same-sex marriage.[109] As kuʻualoha hoʻomanawanui describes, the initiative developed in response to a paid television advertisement titled "Perpetuating Hawaiʻi's Covenant with God" at the time when discussion of SB 1 began at the legislature, which featured "OHA [Office of Hawaiian Affairs] Board Chairperson Collette Machado and at least one Hawaiian minister misrepresenting traditional Hawaiian values of aloha and ʻohana as Christian derived ones. In the spot, they claim 'aloha' for 'all people of Hawaiʻi,' but ask viewers to oppose SB 1, asserting that granting same sex marriage will 'affect our traditional sense of "ohana."' They state their position against same sex marriage is 'for the sake of the children,' and end with 'aloha ke akua' or God is love."[110]

Hoʻomanawanui explains that the misrepresentation of traditional Hawaiian values as rooted in Christianity was surprising to her and other Hawaiian educators and cultural practitioners and that these notions made their way into the testimonies of those who opposed SB 1 during the Senate Judiciary hearings. Some even claimed, counter to overwhelming historical evidence, that Captain Cook introduced same-sex relations and other gender and sexual variances. As hoʻomanawanui points out: "Cultural values such as aloha are so often misappropriated, particularly through capitalism and tourism, that it is easy to forget its true complexity of meaning: love, compassion, sympathy, mercy, kindness, charity, to recall with affection (hence its allusion to the more simplified greetings 'hello' and 'goodbye' which don't carry such emotional attachment)." Hence, in response to the TV commercial and other such distortions, "the 'True Aloha' movement began through social media with the intention of reclaiming the cultural root of aloha as reflective of all its meanings, applicable to everyone." The central purpose of the initiative was to remind everyone that "aloha does not discriminate." As hoʻomanawanui asserts, "Using the core value of aloha as a weapon against others is pure cultural hypocrisy." Instead, aloha "is an important cultural value inclusive of traditional Hawaiian practices of fluid sexuality, sexual identity, and relationship statuses."[111]

True Aloha highlighted (and drew on) decolonial forms of cultural recovery. This reclamation is enabled by Hawaiian language revitalization that empowers access to historical sources that illuminate the possibilities found within Indigenous customary practices revealing multiplicity in terms of gender and sexuality. True Aloha identified itself as being "inclusive of traditional Hawaiian values and practices of fluid sexuality, sexual identity, and relationship status such as: aikāne, māhū, punalua, po'olua, and hānai."[112] *Po'olua* (two heads) refers to a situation in which a child has two possible fathers; there was a way to accommodate contested fatherhood: along with the mother, both men would be responsible for caring for the child, who could also claim either genealogy or both. *Punalua* describes the relationship between first and secondary mates who are not family relations in cases where one man had two female partners or one woman had two male partners.[113] *Hānai* (to feed) is used to describe a form of adoption or other forms of foster parenting and often entails a child given to another relative besides the birth parents, such as grandparents, aunts, or uncles.[114] True Aloha offers a meaningful assertion of Hawaiian cultural concepts in order to challenge homophobia, gender binarism, and heterosexism rooted in colonialism while also advancing diverse models that together constitute the diversity of 'ohana.

True Aloha importantly confronted the distorted forms of cultural appropriation deployed by non-Kanaka along with impoverished and limited understandings by some Christian Kanaka opposing same-sex marriage. Clearly, these are very significant and laudable interventions offered by respected allies. But because "marriage equality" served as the primary frame of reference, these affirmations could easily be co-opted into state logics, in which marriage itself became the primary vehicle for the expression of aloha through assertions that the legalization of same-sex matrimony in Hawai'i is about the extension of that aloha. Same-sex marriage became the new symbol of "true aloha," which is problematic when put forth as the new return to the old, especially because it is not just premised on "till death do us part" monogamy but also bonded to coercive regulation by the settler colonial state in the context of U.S. occupation.[115] This is another version of state co-optation but with an added element: contestation over precolonial Hawaiian sexuality and gender norms in the service of same-sex marriage. This itself can be understood as a marker of settler colonial continuity, given that heterosexual marriage itself was a Christian imposition in the service of colonial biopolitics advanced by the kingdom government. What does it mean to deploy a precolonial Indigenous template for an institution that, in the Hawai'i context, is fundamentally colonial?

This book offers a critical assessment of the two main competing political projects within the Hawaiian nationalist context—one that advocates for self-determination within U.S. federal policy on Indian tribes and one that is instead committed to the recognition/restoration of the Hawaiian Kingdom independent from the United States. The implications of these legacies for contemporary sovereignty debates are related to the state push for a Native Hawaiian governing entity formed under U.S. federal policy, as the question of same-sex marriage will no doubt emerge again in the context of that entity's (limited) powers in relation to congressional plenary power.

The U.S. Supreme Court overturned DOMA in June 2013. But DOMA shows that Native nations were subject to federal power, not only referencing states (as is often represented in media and public discourse) but also including tribal nations and U.S. colonies. Section 2 ("Powers Reserved to the States") reads: "No State, territory, or possession of the United States, or Indian tribe, shall be required to give effect to any public act, record, or judicial proceeding of any other State, territory, possession, or tribe respecting a relationship between persons of the same sex that is treated as a marriage under the laws of such other State, territory, possession, or tribe, or a right or claim arising from such relationship."[116] While DOMA included tribes, it is unclear how, if at all, tribally recognized marriages (as just one example) will translate outside of their sovereign borders to states with marriage equality. The court's decision also does not extend to Indian reservations, because tribal nations are not subject to the Fourteenth Amendment.

As of 2015 only a dozen of the then 567 federally recognized tribal nations recognize same-sex marriage. The Little Traverse Bay Bands of Odawa Indians in Michigan, the Pokagon Band of Potawatomi Indians in Michigan, the Coquille Tribe of Oregon, the Suquamish Tribe of Washington, and the Santa Ysabel Tribe of California all allow same-sex marriage. Other tribes, however, have explicitly restricted same-sex marriage (all following the passage of DOMA), including the Navajo Nation, Cherokee Nation, Muscogee Nation, Chickasaw Nation, and Iowa Tribe.[117] Although Congress could pass a statute that affects Indian Country, Lindsay Robertson, director of the Center for the Study of American Indian Law and Policy, considers it highly unlikely, given the federal government's relatively hands-off support for tribal self-governance. However, he also notes that the U.S. Bill of Rights extends to tribal jurisdictions through the Indian Civil Rights Act of 1968. Thus claims made under that law have standing in tribal court, so citizens of the tribal nations that currently ban same-sex marriage could potentially use the Indian Civil Rights Act to challenge those laws.

Within the Navajo context, this issue has brought about deep debate about the nature of tradition. Joanne Barker has written about the battles over same-sex marriage in Navajo Nation (as well as Cherokee Nation). She documents how the tribal legislation bans and defenses of them affirm the discourses of U.S. nationalism, especially in their Christian and right-wing conservative forms. In these cases, the tribal nations' exercise of sovereignty and self-determination replicates the relations of domination and dispossession that resemble the U.S. treatment of Native Peoples.[118] Jennifer Nez Denetdale's work on the Diné Marriage Act of 2005 examines the conflation of American and Navajo nationalisms by scrutinizing the intersections of war, gender, and Navajo tradition and the ways in which the Diné have drawn upon tradition to support U.S. militarism. She offers an Indigenous feminist analysis to show how Native gender roles are significant to the construction of Native nations and how their histories have been shaped by histories of colonialism. Interrogating the ways in which Navajo causes and priorities have aligned with U.S. policies, she offers a decolonial approach to the recovery of traditional principles of governance to combat American patriotism as well as homophobia.

The question of tradition in regard to the legacy of U.S. colonial domination persists. In a National Public Radio interview Alray Nelson (Navajo) explains the barriers that he faces in terms of wanting to marry his male partner. Nelson, who was raised by traditional grandparents in the rural Navajo community of Beshbetoh, Arizona, explains:

> We both know now that if we leave the Navajo reservation that our relationship's validated off the reservation. But that's a big statement within itself too, is that in our own home community our relationship's not valid. So . . . we can, yes, remove ourselves from our community and go get married, like, say in a city, in San Francisco or in Albuquerque or let's say we go to a local border town, like Farmington or Gallup. But that's not our community. That's not where we're from. Our songs and those prayers that we were both raised with as traditional young people is located here. The ceremonies are conducted here.[119]

The report suggests they may challenge the Diné Marriage Act in tribal court.

As my critique of same-sex marriage suggests, even if a future Native Hawaiian governing entity—or a restored and recognized Hawaiian Kingdom, for that matter—offered same-sex marriage, these governmental forms of "inclusion" are a far cry from what Alexander has theorized as erotic autonomy as a politics of decolonization. As she suggests, the identity and authority of colonialism rely on the racialization and sexualization of morality. In turn, nationalist projects often reproduce these conditions of domination and enact forms of what she terms "recolonization." While a "new" Hawaiian nation (a federally recognized Native governing entity) or the "old" Hawaiian nation (the restored Hawaiian Kingdom) may affirm same-sex marriages, what I want to call into question here is the suggestion that any form of marriage sanctioned by the state moves Kanaka beyond the binary characteristic of debates regarding Indigenous tradition in light of a history of Christianization. To challenge the dichotomy in the notions of Indigenous "savage" and "civilized" Christians, it seems that the way to decolonize sexuality is not to make same-sex marriage "respectable" and part of the promotion of either homonormativity or homonationalism but to uncouple sexual relations from these forms of regulatory power and shift to a distinctly Kanaka form of ethical relationality. This refusal of recolonization, then, entails resisting assimilation efforts by LGBT activists who are in alignment with the state as well as by Christian evangelicals who insist that only they have the key to the kingdoms (of both Hawaiʻi and Jehovah).

Conclusion

In her work on the erotics of land, Kahikina de Silva offers a decolonial approach to Indigenous recovery that brings together sexual pleasure, Indigenous self-determination, and the restoration of wholeness for perceptions and treatment of our bodies and the ʻāina in a way that does not hinge on state regulation. She explicitly offers her work in the spirit of refusing "the logic of elimination of the native" (which, as Wolfe notes, undergirds settler colonialism):

> When the ultimate goal of colonization is to remove ʻōiwi from our land in order to access and suck dry the material and marketable resources our ancestors have maintained for generations, it follows that

> the stubborn, steadfast refusal to leave is essential to our continued existence as a lāhui. Once we leave, sell, or "settle" our land claims, we not only recast our ʻāina as commodities, but also open them and ourselves to continued injustice and colonization. However, the act of inhabiting our ʻāina, occupying our spaces, and making our presence as kānaka maoli known becomes increasingly difficult and painful as more and more of this land is absorbed by militarism, development, tourism, condemnation, and the like, all in the name of a "common good" that still eludes most of our people.

De Silva notes that it is imperative for Kanaka to continue to maintain a physical presence in the lands that are still accessible while also asserting a spiritual and cultural presence in those that are not. Part of this affirmation is "the development of a relationship *with* the land as well as the persistent presence of a responsible steward who ensures its ability to provide ʻaina . . . this is what creates the Hawaiian space."[120]

De Silva offers a reading of a *mele hoʻoipoipo* (love-making chant) composed for King Kalākaua in the mid 1800s called "Maikaʻi ka ʻŌiwi o Kaʻala." She notes that in this piece the land (in this case parts of the island of Oʻahu) is regarded as a lover and suggests that Kanaka understand their relationship with the ʻāina as "a decidedly intimate one." As de Silva explains, like a number of other love-making chants, this one relies heavily on place-names and ʻāina-based metaphors to both mask and reveal its hidden meaning of human intimacy and to help its audience achieve an appropriate degree of *leʻa* (pleasure). She further shows what is unique about this particular mele hoʻoipoipo: it assigns human body parts to features of the land. The ʻāina-Kanaka correlation continues as it recounts in subtle ways a sexual encounter in which "the lovers have been transformed by their meeting." Kanaka and ʻāina come together at the center of the island to celebrate and create life, returning to "inspire us to do the same."[121] De Silva advances a distinctly Kanaka Maoli form of "erotic autonomy as a politics of decolonization" (Alexander). This autonomy does not entail individuality but a form of relationality vis-à-vis land and sexuality that is not proprietary. Her offering takes us back to the concept of ea, the power and life force of interconnectedness among deities, ancestral forces, humans, and all elements of the natural world.

Returning to Siu's message at the beginning of this chapter, I want to reconsider the notion of Hawai'i as a testing ground in imagining a decolonial Kanaka erotic autonomy: a politics of sexuality that is grounded in rich Hawaiian lineages of possibility—consensual and sensual. Shifting away from modes of enclosure, and the property relations that those entail, is one route to the restoration of ea rooted in ethical practices of pleasure.

CONCLUSION. DECOLONIAL CHALLENGES TO THE LEGACIES OF OCCUPATION AND SETTLER COLONIALISM

Hawaiian elites in the early to late nineteenth century, faced with the conditions of imperial encroachment, fashioned their own national governance to protect Hawaiian sovereignty, but they did so in colonial biopolitical modes. These affected many aspects of daily life for the common Kanaka, including access to land, gender status, and sexual practices. Chapter 1 shows how the contestation between the two prevailing nationalist projects—one for federal recognition of a Native Hawaiian governing entity (NHGE) within U.S. domestic policy and the other for international recognition of an independent state—reveals the shortcomings of both. In light of a long legacy of colonial biopolitics under the kingdom, along with U.S. occupation and settler colonialism, neither federal law nor international law (as they both continue to subordinate Indigenous peoples) fully reckons with these historical injustices because they deal insufficiently with the particularities of the Hawaiian case. Chapter 2 demonstrates how Kamehameha III put a stake in the land to create a proprietor relationship between the ʻāina and the people as a means of bolstering political independence of the nation. That legacy is complicated with the contemporary property claims that are central to the Hawaiian Islands under U.S. occupation on the one hand and the question of federal recognition and U.S. ownership on the other—especially in relation to the Hawaiian Kingdom Government and Crown Lands. Acknowledging U.S. ownership of those lands is the only way an NHGE could in theory self-govern on them—but even then only if they were considered contiguous territory. Meanwhile kingdom nationalists relying on "perfect title" do not account for the history and continuance of massive land acquisition by foreigners and the ongoing structures of Kanaka dispossession as a result of land privatization. As chapter 3 shows, gendered property concepts undergird Christian marriage, while heterosexual Anglo-American models were central to the legal subordination of Hawaiian women. Coinciding with the subordination of land as a thing that could be owned, the civic status of women within a property model elevated men as husbands with authority over their wives and children, implicating what counts as family and contributing to the remaking of Hawaiian sovereignty. Chapter 4 examines the ramifications of marriage as an imposition from another angle in the commodification and cultural appropriation of contemporary understandings of precolonial same-sex sexual relations. Here the question of sexual norms is linked to property claims and state appropriation—back to a Christian Protestant ethos that subordinates, pathologizes, and criminalizes those outside the so-called norm. At the same time, the U.S. state subsidiary (Hawai'i as the 50th state) and settler populations appropriate specific genealogies of Kanaka sexuality for the project of same-sex marriage.

Colonialism often invites contradictions, so what about the paradoxes of Hawaiian sovereignty? By navigating the binaries wrought by these histories, the Hawaiian people can refuse recolonization by resisting the allure of state sovereignty models, as they are inextricably linked to the ongoing pulverization of Indigenous worldviews and lifeways. Even though chiefs often historically took up foreign ways as a protective measure in order to keep Westerners out of Hawaiian waters, lands, and lives, their efforts were implemented as a form of colonial biopolitics vis-à-vis new forms of state power exercised by the kingdom government. Today Kanaka Maoli live with the aftermath of those decisions while also still residing under U.S occupation and colonial domination. Given this fraught history, we must ask, what tropes and governmental practices are taken up and for what ends? What gets mobilized in the name of (or with the aim of) protecting Hawaiian sovereignty today? For those of us who are Kanaka Maoli, it seems that we must account for the history bequeathed to us by our ancestors—of all genealogical ranks—with regard for both the agency that they exercised and the structural limitations that they faced. This is a call for ongoing critical examination of the outgrowth of their choices as they led to the transformation of Hawaiians as a distinct people. The history of Christian conversion was wrought through a racist politics of colonial modernity that continues to shape the present.

Hawaiian leaders today, like elites of the nineteenth century, are perpetuating an internal war—a political war over what sovereignty should look like. Yet there is another paradox: while the historical recognition of the kingdom is what enables the enduring claim to restore independent statehood, that legal genealogy is perforated with a history of Indigenous disparagement and criminalization. Hence the move to independence for the nation required the commodification of land, the subordination of women, and the oppressive revision of sexual norms—the multifaceted juridical straitjacket that enabled Hawaiians to be seen as modern subjects in the first place. Kingdom nationalists have brought these contradictions into sharp relief, and this work is an effort to assess the implications. In their attempts to secure power, some continue to emulate Western monarchical power, and many are still captive to this move, which was effective for Hawaiian elites in the mid-nineteenth century. It may still be politically productive for the legal claims, but it flattens the contours of indigeneity in violent ways. Moreover, Kanaka Maoli are still subjects of colonization when mounting their claims in the terms of the colonizers.

The Hawaiian situation demands an approach that is not state-centered to explore recuperating a decolonial modality. But this involves a serious predicament: the U.S. government would be happy to see the independence movement relinquish its claims. In other words, while Hawaiians still have not cut off the head of the king (à la Foucault), it is clear that the United States is trying to behead the Hawaiian Kingdom. The outstanding national claim for independent statehood under international law contradicts preconceived notions of what is reasonable or possible. It too is paradoxical in that the argument for the restoration of Hawai'i's independence is based on acceptable premises and valid reasoning, while the conclusion is typically viewed as logically unacceptable. This claim seems absurd, but only because of U.S. global domination: it is a proposition that is grounded in the rule of law. Therefore I am not suggesting that Kanaka Maoli simply abandon the claim to independent statehood. The claim itself may not be viable or even desirable, but it is one tactic by which to wage battle against the U.S. hold on Hawai'i, especially since the government—if pressed by the world community—cannot substantiate its claim to the Hawaiian Islands, because the archipelago was never ceded through treaty or conquest. David Uahikeaikalei'ohu Maile argues that the DOI's Advance Notice of Proposed

Rule Making (ANPRM) and subsequent Notice for Proposed Rulemaking (NPRM)—through the public meetings discussed in the opening of this book—"are notices of settlement" by the U.S. government. Reconfiguring the biopolitics of settler colonialism in the context of Indigenous critiques of recognition, Maile further suggests that "the ANPRM and NPRM, animated by settler colonialism, attempt to settle Kanaka Maoli claims against the U.S. settler state and, simultaneously, settle Hawai'i." He further argues: "Recognition policies, like those offered to Kānaka, serve as a biopolitical instrument to manage Indigenous life under the logic of elimination."[1] And yet Kanaka Maoli refused the DOI's notices of settlement.

Regardless, most people would dismiss the independence claim as ridiculous because they consider the Hawaiian Kingdom retrograde at best and conquered at worst: who wants to reestablish a dead monarchy in the twenty-first century during the calls for global democracy? The political focus on the Hawaiian monarchy also seems retrograde to many because it is based on hereditary lineage to bolster leadership authority and the right to rule. Given these factors, among others, some consider the promise that Indigenous Hawaiians will secure domestic dependent status a really good deal, a "realistic compromise," and certainly "better than nothing." Yet the proposed tribal model for Hawaiians is a *federally driven* solution to the so-called Hawaiian problem—an attempt to extinguish the Hawaiian question as a moral, political, and legal one. Despite attempts by state officials to contain the outstanding Hawaiian sovereignty claim within U.S. federal policy, the claim to Hawaiian independence endures and is still playing out. Yet there is another paradox of Hawaiian sovereignty. Kanaka Maoli have an unextinguished claim, but it hinges on the very things that degraded the Indigenous polity in the early to late nineteenth century and now works to discount that social position today. It is also bitterly ironic that the formation of monarchy in the period of the Hawaiian Kingdom's establishment marked a modern achievement, yet claiming that political genealogy in the service of autonomy and self-determination is now regarded as backward.

In the present, as in the past, the kingdom nationalists want to protect the claim to elevated status of a nation-state—parity with the family of nations and states, not peoples. That historical recognition of kingdomhood is what allows descendants today to assert the enduring existence of the monarchy or push to restore it—a status that differs greatly from Indigenous political status as states currently limit it under international law. I argue that it is this political imposition on Indigenous peoples that is the problem, not indigeneity. The invocation of Native Americans along the lines of some of the dominant kingdom nationalist perspectives discussed herein seems to reveal complicated issues of projection—what counts as Indigenous and how some nationalists assert Hawaiian modernity in the face of what they perceive as an imposed primitivism. The disavowal of Indigenous status is a denial that entails a particular affective structure that includes abjectness and disgust at a supposed savagery. But the assertion of the kingdom's continuous existence is an empowering narrative, a resistance to U.S. domination—we are not American. The political struggle is steeped in visceral convictions. Hawaiian nationalist affect includes pride, anxiety, resentment, melancholy, anger, grief, and shame.

The concept of what is "Indigenous" Hawaiian now includes prestatist, statist, and antistatist sovereignty orientations, so my aim is not to discount any of these as less "authentic." Instead I suggest that one may be more conducive to Hawaiian flourishing and substantive self-determination. In other words, I am not suggesting that kingdom nationalists who are Christian-identified or those in support of federal recognition of an NHGE are "not really Indigenous" and/or too American to be authentic. What I am advancing here is a different ethical ground for decolonial Hawaiian futures that are based on nonproprietary relationships—those that are consensual and life affirming—reflected in select premonarchical Hawaiian practices. As I have documented, contemporary assertions of the enduring state power (in both articulations of an existing Hawaiian Kingdom or seeking a federally recognized NHGE) threaten to reproduce conditions for the recolonization (and reoccupation) of Kanaka Maoli land, gender, and sexuality. In response, I return to Alexander's theory of erotic autonomy as a politics of decolonization for remedying nationalist attempts at recolonization. She calls for an emancipatory praxis anchored "within a desire for decolonization, imagined simultaneously as political, economic, psychic, discursive, *and* sexual."[2]

Whether one asserts that Hawai'i/Kanaka Maoli underwent colonization prior to 1893 or not, Hawaiians must reckon with the dominance of coloniality. This entails an understanding of decolonization beyond its limited scope within international law or the easily available historical and political case studies of former colonies. It also means going beyond the narrow legal frame of occupation to account for the rampant destruction that U.S. militarism in Hawai'i has created, not only for the archipelago but also for a large part of the world. U.S. Pacific Command (USPACOM) in Honolulu has an area of command that includes thirty-six countries and over half the world's population.[3] Occupation is supposedly only a temporary situation, and the rights of the occupant are limited to the extent of that period.[4] Occupations typically end with the occupying power withdrawing from the occupied territory or being driven out of it. Also, the transfer of authority to a local government reestablishing the full and free exercise of sovereignty will usually end the state of occupation. Given the U.S. investment in Hawai'i for military purposes, it is clear that any struggle for Hawaiian sovereignty and self-determination must be linked to challenging U.S. global domination.

Although settler colonialism need not hinge on the existence or nonexistence of state entities, it is clear that the 50th state continues to expropriate the kingdom's national lands—'āina that it has no rightful claim to—even as Hawaiians challenge the legitimacy of the state. Illegality is not a barrier to power. Whether through the legislative branch or the executive branch, efforts by the U.S. government and its subsidiary to extinguish the outstanding claims to national sovereignty under international law threaten our lāhui. If a substantial proportion of the Hawaiian people go the domestic route, their participation in that process, even though regarded by many as a legal fiction, could be used as evidence of acquiescence. Hence many Kanaka are committed to kū'ē (resisting) this ongoing theft and all attempts by the 50th state and U.S. federal government to reduce Hawaiian political status further.

At the same time, this also means confronting the legacy of Hawaiian modernity. As Walter Mignolo argues in *The Darker Side of Western Modernity*, coloniality manifested throughout the world and determined the socioeconomic, racial, and epistemological value systems of contemporary society, commonly called "modern" society. This is precisely why coloniality does not just disappear with political and historical decolonization, the end of the period of territorial domination of lands when countries gain independence. Given this distinction, we can see that coloniality is part of the logic of Western civilization. This is where the concept of "decoloniality" is crucial. As Mignolo explains, the term "decoloniality" is used principally by emerging Latin American movements and "refers to analytic approaches and socioeconomic and political practices opposed to pillars of Western civilization: coloniality and modernity. This makes it both a political and epistemic (relating to knowledge and its validation) project."[5] It is the refusal of the assumption that Western European modes of thinking are in fact universal ones or that the Western ways are the best. Silvia Rivera Cusicanqui insists that a decolonial modality must be "radical and profound . . . political, economic, and, above all, mental."[6]

Rich examples of decolonial efforts in Hawai'i offer ethical projects centered on nonexploitative forms of sustainability and well-being for the lāhui, the Hawaiian people/nation, a definition not dependent on any state formation.[7] These are grounded in nonstatist forms of Indigenous Hawaiian sovereignty, what we might refer to today as ea, the power and life force of interconnectedness among deities, ancestral forces, humans and other animals, and all elements of the natural world. As noted earlier, ea is distinctly different from the Western concept of sovereignty. As Noelani Goodyear-Ka'ōpua points out from a Kanaka Maoli perspective: "In fact, one can use the same word to indicate life *and* sovereignty: *ea*. The two are crucial to one another."[8]

Kanaka Maoli need not rely on the U.S. state and its subsidiary or the resurrection of the Hawaiian Kingdom. Given the complex political realities that Kanaka Maoli face in the form of aggressive attacks on the Hawaiian nation and its lands, pursuing ea is critical. Increasingly, Kanaka are laboring to revive and strengthen Hawaiian cultural practices, including the work of lo'i restoration and kalo cultivation, ahupua'a and watershed replenishment, traditional voyaging, *kākau* (tattoo), *lā'au lapa'au* (traditional medicine), *lomi* (Hawaiian massage), *'ōlelo Hawai'i* (language), *hula* (reverence for specific people, deities, and natural elements), *mele* (song), *oli* (chant), *makahiki* and other spiritual ceremonies, and much more. All of this is part of the ongoing decolonial process, which refuses the "logic of the elimination of the Native." Such activities can also heal the internalized racism that self-degrades the "primitive." These forms of cultural renewal are central to fostering the continuous growth of ea, which does not need a state to survive and flourish. It is also important that we not allow the rebirth of Indigenous knowledge and practices to be used as a weapon in battles over Hawaiian "authenticity," commoditized for the market, or coopted by the state. International law still does not regard Indigenous peoples as fully human, given the enduring vestiges from the papal bulls and seemingly cemented by the Law of Nations, so it seems necessary to craft some mixture in order to appeal to the international arena while simultaneously responding with Indigenous revitalization, as many already are doing. As Alfred theorizes regarding Indigenous resurgence among Indigenous thinkers and select allies: "These people are dedicated to recasting Indigenous people in terms that are authentic and meaningful, to regenerating and organizing a radical political consciousness, to reoccupying land and gaining restitution, to protecting the natural environment, and to restoring the Nation-to-Nation relationship between Indigenous nations and

Settlers. This reframing of Indigeneity as Resurgence promotes the kind of action and provides the spiritual and ethical bases for a transformative movement that has the potential to liberate both Indigenous peoples and Settlers from colonialism."[9]

In the Hawaiian context persistent Indigenous practices that survive into (or are revived in) the twenty-first century can serve as modes of decolonization to undermine the legacy of reforms that affected the people's relationships to land as well as gender differences and open sexual norms. Decolonizing relations to land, gender, and sexuality are then crucial sites for the production of life for an ethical future and a substantiation of sovereignty through remaking indigeneity without the reliance on juridical regimes of power.

NOTES

PREFACE

1. Crawley 1929, 113–115.

2. Jankowiak et al. 2015.

3. Kamakau [1866–1871] 1991, 336.

4. Merry 2000 (245–246) recounts the impressions of Cheever (n.d.). She offers a rich and riveting account of the conversion of the Hawaiians in the nineteenth century with a focus on the manner in which Hawaiian and American lawyers and missionaries sought to make of Hawaiʻi a modern sovereign nation on the model of the "civilized world." That process necessitated the transformation of the Indigenous polity in relation to notions of the body, race, sexuality, gender, and citizenship. Merry also explains: "Other commentators noted that adulterers built most of the road system in Hawaiʻi during the mid-nineteenth century. A French visitor in Kailua in the 1830s found a twenty-five mile road almost finished 'thanks to the amorous propensities of the Hawaiians'" (246).

5. January 11, 1855, speech by Kamehameha IV quoted by Kuykendall (1938, 427), reprinted from *Polynesian*, January 13, 1855.

INTRODUCTION. *Contradictory Sovereignty*

1. U.S. Department of the Interior 2014, 25–28 (quotation); U.S. Department of the Interior 2015a; "DOI Hearing in Keaukaha, July 2, 2014—Mililani Trask" 2014.

2. U.S. Department of the Interior: Office of Native Hawaiian Relations 2014a. The meetings in Hawaiʻi were held from June 23 to July 8, 2014. In addition to the pub-

lic meetings held on the islands, five meetings were held in the continental United States, including one in Connecticut on August 6, 2014, at the Mohegan reservation. I took part in this meeting and offered testimony on my opposition to the proposed changes.

3. People from the DOI speaking to the panel were specifically asked to respond to five threshold questions, per the protocols for offering "Advanced Notice of Proposed Rulemaking": "1) Should the Secretary propose an administrative rule that would facilitate the reestablishment of a government-to-government relationship with the Native Hawaiian community?; 2) Should the Secretary assist the Native Hawaiian community in reorganizing its government, with which the United States could reestablish a government-to-government relationship?; 3) If so, what process should be established for drafting and ratifying a reorganized Native Hawaiian government's constitution or other governing document?; 4) Should the Secretary instead rely on the reorganization of a Native Hawaiian government through a process established by the Native Hawaiian community and facilitated by the State of Hawaii, to the extent such a process is consistent with Federal law?; and 5) If so, what conditions should the Secretary establish as prerequisites to Federal acknowledgment of a government-to-government relationship with the reorganized Native Hawaiian government" (U.S. Department of the Interior: Office of the Secretary 2014, 35297).

4. The number of tribes increased to 573 by January 2018 with the federal recognition of the Virginia tribes. Schilling 2018.

5. It is unclear what Trask means by "another true nation would emerge" under the right conditions: historically speaking, she has supported the nation-within-a-nation model similar to that of Indian tribes, which Ka Lāhui has exemplified since its inception. But her point seems to be that whatever model of governance is used should be forged through a process where the parties are on an equal footing.

6. This quotation and the following quotations are a composite of email threads from 2005.

7. Chang 2016, 245–246; see also Chang 2015.

8. Byrd 2011, 149.

9. The last version of the bill was S. 675, "The Native Hawaiian Government Reorganization Act of 2011," placed on Senate Legislative Calendar on February 12, 2012, under General Orders, Calendar No. 568: U.S. Congress 2011c. For the last report on this legislative effort, see U.S. Congress 2012.

10. Although the last version of the bill (S. 675) that passed the U.S. Senate Committee on Indian Affairs on December 12, 2012, did not include this allowance for the state, legislators vehemently opposed it after considering interventions from state actors, including Linda Lingle, then governor of Hawaiʻi. In the past this exact issue had been the sticking point whenever the proposal had been most hotly debated and the reason why it failed.

11. Kauanui 2005a, 2005b, 2008a, 2008b, 2011.

12. Keany 2009.

13. It should be noted that Abigail Kinoiki Kekaulike Kawānanakoa often is

referred to as a princess, given that she is the granddaughter of the late prince David Kawānanakoa, who was named an heir to the throne. However, by and large, she has not been part of the Hawaiian nationalist efforts to reassert kingdom sovereignty.

14. General Assembly Resolution 1514 (XV), December 14, 1960. For more information, see United Nations General Assembly 1960b.

15. United Nations General Assembly 2007.

16. Kauanui 2011.

17. Blaisdell 2005; Blaisdell and Mokuau 1994.

18. Wolfe 2006, 387–388.

19. Wolfe 1998, 393.

20. Kauanui 2011.

21. Kinzer 2006 is another case where an analysis of occupation is privileged at the expense of a critique of settler colonialism. He convincingly argues that the case of Hawaiʻi served as the model for subsequent U.S.-backed regime changes in the twentieth century by examining a dozen case studies of U.S.-backed toppling of foreign governments to gain access to natural resources. Kinzer points out that in Hawaiʻi the elite white minority worked in collaboration with the U.S. Navy, the White House, and Washington's local representative to remove Queen Liliʻuokalani from the throne in order to protect the continental U.S. sugar market. Although he argues that the Hawaiʻi case set the paradigm, Kinzer remains an apologist for Hawaiʻi's 50th (U.S.) statehood in 1959, claiming that there was no resistance because Native Hawaiians gained so much by being fully incorporated within the United States. He further suggests that Native Hawaiians are pleased with statehood and that the U.S. government's assumption of responsibility for the territories it seizes "can lead toward stability and happiness." Kinzer's account ignores settler colonialism while also entirely sidestepping the question of deoccupation (Kinzer 2006, 88).

22. Kauanui 2005b.

23. Kameʻeleihiwa 1992, 37.

24. Kamakau [1866–1871] 1991, 6–7.

25. Linnekin 1990, 94.

26. Kameʻeleihiwa 1992, 16.

27. Linnekin 1990, 76; Kameʻeleihiwa 1992, 26.

28. Handy and Pukui 1972, 202.

29. Osorio 2002, 10.

30. Beamer 2014, 15.

31. Beamer 2014, 19.

32. Beamer 2014, 48, 104 (quotations).

33. Merry 2000, 255.

34. Silva 2004, 32.

35. Merry 2000, 35.

36. Wilkes 1845, 22.

37. Kuykendall 1938, 190–199.

38. Merry 2000, 89.

39. See Beamer 2014.

40. Beamer 2014, 9.

41. Beamer 2014, 197.

42. Thanks to Ty P. Kāwika Tengan for making this point (personal communication, 2014).

43. Osorio 2003, 235.

44. Brown 2010, 132.

45. Osorio 2002.

46. Rifkin 2008, 43–45 (quotations on 44).

47. Mignolo 2011, 2.

48. Williams 2012 reexamines the history of the Western world through civilization's war on tribalism as a way of life. As he demonstrates, centuries of acts of violence and dispossession have been justified by citing civilization's opposition to these differences represented by the tribe.

49. Anghie 2005.

50. Silva 2004, 27.

51. Merry 2000, 230.

52. Osorio 2002.

53. Silva 2004, 37.

54. "About Leon Siu" 2011 (no longer available).

55. *Oxford English Dictionary* 2011, s.v. "paradox." An entry for this word was first included in *New English Dictionary* in 1904.

56. Scott 2004, 19–21 (quotations). Scott's work is speaking specifically to a postcolonial context, not a settler colonial one, to argue the need to reconceptualize the past in order to reimagine a more usable future. He describes how, prior to independence, anticolonialists narrated the transition from colonialism to postcolonialism as romance—a story of overcoming and vindication, of salvation and redemption. He contends that postcolonial scholarship assumes the same trajectory and that this imposes conceptual limitations. Scott suggests that tragedy may be a more useful narrative frame than romance. In tragedy, he proposes, the future does not appear as an uninterrupted movement forward but instead as a slow and sometimes reversible series of ups and downs. He reads *The Black Jacobins* for what it teaches about the paradoxes of colonial enlightenment (19–21).

57. Alfred 2013c.

58. The concept of Obligatory Passage Point (OPP) was developed by sociologist Michel Callon 1986.

59. Foucault 2003 argues that Prussian general and military theorist Carl von Clausewitz's formulation "War is the continuation of politics by other means" was originally an inversion from the original, to which Foucault insists that we revert (47–48).

60. See Neal 2004 for a critique of these assumptions.

61. Foucault 2003, 59–60. As Stoler 1995 puts it, "It is within the technologies of power nurtured in the 'society of normalization' that internal enemies will be constructed and that modern racism will be conceived" (65).

62. This is not the sovereign's right to take life or let live but its complement: the right to "make" live or "let" die. Foucault 2003, 241.

63. Foucault 1981. He further explains that this representation is "incongruous with the new methods of power whose operation is not ensured by right but by technique, not by law but by normalization, not by punishment but by control, methods that are employed on all levels and in forms that go beyond the state and its apparatus." He continues: "Hence the importance that the theory of power of right and violence, law and legality, freedom and will, and especially the state and sovereignty. . . . To conceive of power on the basis of these problems is to conceive of it in terms of a historical form that is characteristic of our societies: the juridical monarchy" (88–89).

64. Stoler 1995, 95.

65. Osorio 2002, 25.

66. Warrior 2008 identified these three main camps regarding the concept of sovereignty as the prevailing ones within the field. This is still the case.

67. Alfred 1999, 56–57.

68. Alfred 2006, 33.

69. Alfred 2005, 39–40.

70. Barker 2006, 19–21 (emphasis in original).

71. Moreton-Robinson 2008, 2.

72. King Kamehameha III said the words *Ua mau ke ea o ka ʻāina i ka pono* in a speech during a ceremony to mark his restoration. However, *ua* at the beginning of the motto marks it as a state that has come to be; the life of the land was perpetuated in righteousness. This translation seems fitting given that the Hawaii state government of the United States adopted the saying as its motto of the "50th state" in 1978.

73. The saying comes from the result of a conflict that began in February 1843 when Lord George Paulet on HMS *Carysfort* unilaterally established the provisional cession of the "Sandwich Islands." On July 26 Admiral Richard Darton Thomas sailed into Honolulu harbor on his flagship, HMS *Dublin*. He became the local representative of the British Commission (the government of the provisional cession) by outranking Paulet. His intention was to end the occupation, and on July 31 he handed the islands back to Kamehameha III, who named the place in downtown Honolulu where the ceremony was held in Thomas Square in his honor. In 1925 it was made into a park managed by the City and County of Honolulu. This is where (De)Occupy Honolulu set up camp in September 2011 when Occupy Wall Street took off.

74. Goodyear-Kaʻōpua, introductory essay in Goodyear-Kaʻōpua et al. 2014, 4.

75. Thanks to Mark Rifkin for urging me to clarify this point.

76. Osorio 2002, 7. And, as Kameʻeleihiwa 1992 asserts, "It is as if the Hawaiian stands firmly in the present, with his [*sic*] back to the future, and his eyes fixed upon the past, seeking historical answers for present-day dilemmas. Such an orientation is to the Hawaiian an eminently practical one, for the future is always unknown, whereas the past is rich in glory and knowledge" (22–23).

77. Kauanui 2008b; Handy and Pukui 1972, 197.

78. Foucault 1977.

79. Diaz and Kauanui 2001, 323.

80. Griggs 1992, 324–325. There have been ongoing, charged, and intense debates within cultural anthropology about the concept of the Indigenous. See Guenther et al. 2006.

81. Kauanui 2016.

82. Smith 2012, 33, 49, 61.

83. Barker 2011.

84. Rifkin 2011, 23.

85. Morgensen 2011b. O'Brien 2010 also contends with the question of settler modernity. She examines local histories in the early American period from Massachusetts, Connecticut, and Rhode Island to document how these narratives inculcated the myth of Indian extinction, a saga that has stubbornly remained in the American consciousness. She argues that local histories became a primary means by which European Americans asserted their own modernity while denying it to Indian peoples.

86. Morgensen 2011a.

87. McClintock 1995; Findlay 2000; Levine 2004; Barker 2011; Rifkin 2011. In addition to Merry 2000, for a stellar focus on the role of colonialism in targeting bodily practices, see Ballantyne and Burton 2005, who focus on "bodies as a means of accessing the colonial encounters in world history." They "emphasize the centrality of bodies—raced, sexed, classed, and ethnicized bodies—as sites through which imperial and colonial power was imagined and exercised" (4–6).

88. Burton 1999, 1.

89. Cited in Burton 1999, 4.

90. Matsuda 1988b, 135.

91. Shohat 2000, 136.

92. Foucault 1981, 88–89.

CHAPTER 1. *Contested Indigeneity*

1. "Akaka Bill and 'Native Sovereignty': What It Really Means to Hawaiians" 2010. Keppeler eventually worked for several years with Senator Akaka's staffers on the federal recognition effort, including his work in 2011 on the state senators on Senate Bill 1520, which created the Native Hawaiian Role Commission poised to form the NHGE. "Lawyer Promoted the Rights of Native Hawaiians" 2014, A22.

2. Other participants on the program included Mark Bennett, attorney general of the state of Hawai'i; Colleen Hanabusa, president of the Hawai'i State Senate; Robert Klein, former senior associate justice of the Hawai'i Supreme Court; Melody McKenzie, assistant professor of law and director of the Ka Huli Ao: Center for Excellence in Native Hawaiian Law, William S. Richardson School of Law, University of Hawai'i at Mānoa; Patricia M. Zell, J. D., an attorney who served for twenty-five years as staff director and chief counsel of the U.S. Senate Committee on Indian Affairs; and Steven Gunn, an attorney and law professor who specializes in the field of Native American law at Washington University Law School in Missouri. For more information, see the Office of Hawaiian Affairs (2009).

3. Wilkins and Stark 2011, 38.

4. U.S. Department of the Interior 2014a.

5. In the summer of 2014, when DOI officials held public meetings in Hawai'i on the Advanced Notice of Proposed Rule Making, another set of public meetings was held on the federal regulations for tribal acknowledgment. As a result, the regulations on federal acknowledgment were revised in 2015. See U.S. Department of the Interior: Indian Affairs 2015b.

6. Jessica Kershaw quoted in Blair 2015.

7. September 15, 2015, was the filing deadline for the "constitutional convention." Those who had not registered but wanted to vote in the elections had until October 15, 2015, to register. Blair 2015.

8. Crabbe 2014, 3.

9. Na Leo O Hawaii Access Center 2014.

10. Office of Hawaiian Affairs 2014.

11. Kuykendall 1938.

12. Oxford English Dictionary 2011, s.v. "Indigenous."

13. O'Brien 2010 documents the period between 1820 and 1880 to show how local historians and their readers embraced notions of racial purity rooted in the century's scientific racism and saw living Indians as "mixed" and therefore no longer truly Indian.

14. Mills 1997.

15. Nichols 2014. Carole Pateman (Pateman and Mills 2007) has also theorized what she terms the "settler contract." Extending Mill's theory to the logic of the original contract in the form of a settler contract, she argues that this is a specific form of the expropriation contract and refers to the dispossession of and rule over Indigenous inhabitants in the two New Worlds (the Southern and Northern New Worlds of the British Empire). Pateman asserts that to create a civil society colonizers had to assume *terra nullius* (an empty state of nature) and not simply dominate and govern; she suggests that the British usurped Indigenous peoples' authority in North America through this doctrine in two senses: (1) they claimed the lands as uncultivated wilderness and thus open to the "right of husbandry" because (2) they viewed inhabitants as having no recognizable form of sovereign government. The English government negotiated treaties with Indigenous Peoples in North America, however, so her point misses the mark. Nichols 2014 uses the term "settler contract," playing off Pateman, but offers modifications to her theory to propose a more qualified use, as settlers more often than not did recognize Indigenous title.

16. Nichols 2014, 101–102.

17. Bruyneel 2007, 3.

18. Kauanui 2013.

19. Kauanui 2005c.

20. For a critical analysis of the neoconservative forces on the island that organized against the legislation because they regarded it as a proposal for race-based government, see Kauanui 2008a.

21. U.S. Congress 1993.

22. Kauanui 2014.

23. This is the name of the chapter in which the distinctions are delineated. Wilkins and Stark 2011.

24. Section 2, clause 3, states: "Representatives and direct Taxes shall be apportioned among the several States ... excluding Indians not taxed"—meaning that Indians were not regarded as citizens. This section is referred to later in the Fourteenth Amendment, section 2, amending the apportionment of representatives to the U.S. House.

25. Deloria and Wilkins 2000.

26. The constitution distinguishes "Indian tribes" from "foreign nations." The U.S. government does not handle tribal nations through the U.S. Department of State; instead it deals with them through the Department of the Interior, which houses the Bureau of Indian Affairs along with the National Park Services, and the Office of Insular Affairs, which deals with the island colonies of the Pacific and Caribbean. The Indian Appropriation Act of March 3, 1871, ended recognition for any group of Indians in the United States recognized as an independent nation by the federal government. The act has two significant sections. First, it required that the federal government no longer interact with the various tribes through treaties but instead through statutes, stating in part that "no Indian nation or tribe within the territory of the United States shall be acknowledged or recognized as an independent nation." The act also made it a federal crime to commit murder, manslaughter, rape, assault with intent to kill, arson, burglary, and larceny within any territory of the United States. The 1886 ruling in *United States v. Kagama* affirmed the 1871 act by asserting that Congress has plenary power over all tribal nations within its claimed borders. The court offered this rationale: "The power of the general government over these remnants of a race once powerful ... is necessary to their protection as well as to the safety of those among whom they dwell." Therefore Congress directed that all Indians should be treated as individuals and legally designated "wards" of the federal government.

27. U.S. Department of the Interior: Indian Affairs 2013 (emphasis added). "Generally, tribal courts have *civil* jurisdiction over Indians and non-Indians who either reside or do business on federal Indian reservations. They also have *criminal* jurisdiction over violations of tribal laws committed by tribal members residing or doing business on the reservation" (emphasis in original).

28. At the time they were first introduced on May 7, 2009, they were identical. S. 1011 was given a hearing before the U.S. Senate Committee on Indian Affairs on August 6, 2009, and H.R. 2314 was given a hearing before the U.S. House Committee on Natural Resources on December 16, 2009: S. 1011 (111th): U.S. Congress 2009; H.R. 2314: U.S. Congress 2009–2010 (further quotations from these come from these same sources).

29. For more details, see Kauanui 2010.

30. For text of the bill, see U.S. Congress 2011a. For a legislative history of the bill, see State of Hawaii 2011.

31. http://hawaii.gov/gov/newsroom/in-the-news/governor-enacts-bill-to-

further-self-determination-for-native-hawaiians (accessed July 10, 2012; no longer available).

32. The political term "First Nation" itself is curious in this context, given that it is a term typically used to refer to the Indigenous Peoples of the Americas located in what is now Canada, except for the Arctic-situated Inuit and the Métis.

33. Other members of the Native Hawaiian Roll Commission named at the time were Na'alehu Anthony, chief executive director of 'Ōiwi TV and the founder of Palikū Documentary Films; Lei Kihoi, former staff attorney for Judge Walter Heen; Mahealani Pérez-Wendt, executive director of the Native Hawaiian Legal Corporation; and Robin Puanani Danner, president and chief executive officer of the Council for Native Hawaiian Advancement.

34. The commission is funded by the Office of Hawaiian Affairs and authorized to prepare and maintain a roll of qualified "Native Hawaiians" who meet specific criteria: each person must be at least eighteen years old, be able to trace ancestry back to 1778, show that he or she has maintained the Indigenous culture, and be willing to participate. "Kana'iolowalu Launches Online Registry for Native Hawaiians" 2012.

35. H.R. 1250, a House companion measure to S. 675, was introduced on the same day to the Committee on Natural Resources. No action has yet been taken on it. Before the 2011 proposals, at the start of the 111th Congress (January 3, 2009), three sets of proposals made their way to the table, all titled the Native Hawaiian Government Reorganization Act of 2009.

36. Section 5 "recognizes the Native Hawaiian right to reorganize under Section 16 of the Indian Reorganization Act; defines the membership of the Native Hawaiian people for the purposes of reorganization as those people appearing on the roll certified by the State of Hawaii Native Hawaiian Roll Commission authorized under Act 195; provides for the establishment of an Interim Governing Council, tasked with preparing the Constitution and by-Laws and submitting them for Secretarial approval; and requires the Interim Governing Council, with assistance from the Secretary, to conduct the election of officers of the Native Hawaiian governing entity, then terminates the Council." Section 6 "provides the following: the Native Hawaiian Governing Entity has the inherent powers and privileges of self-government of an Indian Tribe."

37. Kana'iolowalu: http://www.kanaiolowalu.org. The Office of Hawaiian Affairs web pages that were the source for the quotations in this paragraph are no longer available.

38. Na'i Aupuni 2015, 2016a, 2016b.

39. U.S. Department of the Interior 2016a, 2016b.

40. These assertions neglect to acknowledge that the kingdom government facilitated plantation pay scales and contracts. Moreover, there is an immense body of writing by and about Kanaka Maoli as a *lāhui* (people or nation) distinct from non-Native citizens. As Silva's and Osorio's respective works show, it is a salient discourse throughout Hawaiian history, at least from the 1820s.

41. There is one exception: the treaties of the "Five Civilized Tribes" (Cherokee,

Chickasaw, Choctaw, Muscogee, and Seminole) with the United States include provisions for freedmen and their descendants.

42. Byrd 2011, 150, 157–158.

43. Trask 1994, 68–87.

44. The 50th anniversary of U.S. statehood for Hawai'i in 2009 offered an opportunity for scholars to investigate the details of the vote issued by the colonial administration in the Hawaiian Islands at the time. Some of the issues that need research attention include the executive decisions that allowed both the U.S. military and other non-Hawaiian residents to vote (regardless of whether or not they were descendants of the Kanaka Maoli and non-Hawaiians residing in the islands prior to the unlawful U.S. annexation) and a careful study of the reports issued by the U.S. representative to the United Nations, who reported that Hawaiians had already exercised self-determination in the 1959 vote and therefore should be removed from the UN list of non-self-governing territories.

45. Human Sciences Research Council of South Africa 2009.

46. Roy 2001.

47. As Lâm 2000 notes, the U.S. government knew that these new guidelines were on their way to adoption and thus pushed statehood through a domestic process to escape them.

48. United Nations General Assembly 1960a.

49. In 1962 the General Assembly established a special committee, now known as the Special Committee of 24 on Decolonization, to examine the application of the declaration and to make recommendations on its implementation. United Nations 2016.

50. Barsh 1986, 373.

51. Griswold 1996, 101 (quotation), n. 14, 93.

52. Sai et al. 2013a. See also Hawaiian Kingdom Government 2013a.

53. Sai et al. 2014b.

54. For socioeconomic profiles of Native Hawaiians, see Blaisdell 2005 and Blaisdell and Mokuau 1994.

55. United Nations Department of Public Information 2005.

56. United Nations Department of Economic and Social Affairs: Division for Social Policy and Development 2009, 4.

57. United Nations Department of Public Information 2005.

58. United Nations Department of Public Information 2005.

59. Baker 2010 analyzes the theories of race and culture developed by American anthropologists during the late nineteenth century and early twentieth century. Ethnologists played a part in creating a racial politics of culture in which Indians had a culture worthy of preservation and exhibition, in contrast to African Americans, who in their view did not. He documents two early schools of anthropology in the United States. One was pioneered by Samuel Morton and Louis Agassiz, who focused on measuring brains and bodies to rank-order the races. The other was the late–eighteenth-century Americanist tradition, begun by Peter S. Du Ponceau and Albert Gallatin, who focused on Native American linguistics and philology,

emphasizing customs and behaviors. As Baker argues, many scholars believed the races were organized in an evolutionary hierarchy that began with savagery, moved through barbarism, and ended with Christian civilization. This was the hegemonic perspective within the field until the 1890s, when Franz Boas—a pioneer of modern American anthropology—began to demonstrate that racial groups were not organized in a grade and that cultures should be regarded within their own historical contexts.

60. United Nations General Assembly 1960a.

61. United Nations Department of Economic and Social Affairs: Division for Social Policy and Development 2009, 4 (emphasis added).

62. Newcomb 2008.

63. The WGIIP was informed by early organizations, such as the International Indian Treaty Council formed in 1977, which was the first organization of Indigenous Peoples to be reorganized as a nongovernmental Organization (NGO) with Consultative Status to the United Nations Economic and Social Council. Another example is the American Indian Law Alliance, founded in 1989, which also has such special consultative status.

64. United Nations General Assembly 2007, 1.

65. United Nations General Assembly 2007, 1 (the following quotations are also from this source).

66. Thanks to Andrea Carmen, executive director of the International Indian Treaty Council, who explained in an interview for my radio show *Indigenous Politics: From Native New England and Beyond* that article 46 can be interpreted for the benefit of Hawaiian independence from the United States. She also noted that the article became a catchall for states and that it was inserted after 2004 when prompted by countries in support of the declaration, including Mexico, Guatemala, Peru, and others. The Human Rights Council adopted it in 2006. The interview, which aired on January 13, 2009, is archived online: http://www.indigenouspolitics.org/audiofiles/2009/1-13%20International%20Indian%20Treaty.mp3. Tonya Gonnella Frichner, founder and president of the American Indian Law Alliance, was featured on another episode of the program, which includes a very comprehensive account of the activist history that led to the passage of the declaration as well as a critical analysis of the politics of careful negotiations that led to the compromises over these seemingly contradictory articles of the declaration: http://www.indigenouspolitics.org/audiofiles/2007/10-30%20International%20Law.mp3.

67. Lâm 1992.

68. Lâm 1992; Griswold 1996, 98.

69. For example, most Indigenous movements throughout North and South America continue to fight for an expansion of cultural, political, and territorial autonomy within the respective settler states that encompass them.

70. In the context of the United States, even if Indigenous Peoples have no vision of becoming nation-states, the most basic components for fuller autonomy would likely disrupt the territorial integrity of the settler state. For example, a major reordering of society in a way that would affect the existing state and the territory that

the U.S. government currently claims as its own would certainly occur if the U.S. government honored and abided by all of the treaties that it signed with Indigenous nations; returned most of the national parks to the Indigenous Peoples from whom they were taken; federally recognized all tribal nations and entities that seek this U.S. domestic model of acknowledgment (which includes over two hundred entities that have submitted their petitions and remain on the Bureau of Indian Affairs waiting list); and restored all previously terminated tribes with federal acknowledgment. None of these four examples need to be tied to the goal of Indigenous nations becoming nation-states, but the likelihood that the federal government would take this sort of action on any of these seems quite far-fetched at this particular time. Indeed, this contradiction is inherent in the U.S. nation-state and its very foundations: Indigenous dispossession.

71. The Indigenous Caucus at both the UN and the OAS had consistently taken the position that Indigenous Peoples are colonized and therefore fall under the decolonization model. The UN documents and international practices demonstrate that self-determination is a right available to all peoples. But there was widespread controversy over when a group of persons constitutes a "people" entitled to self-determination under international law. When the U.S. National Security Council took a position on Indigenous Peoples before the United Nations Commission on Human Rights and its Working Group on the Draft Declaration on Indigenous Rights, along with a similar OAS draft declaration, the council stated that the United States urged the use of the term "internal self-determination" for Indigenous Peoples. In other words, the U.S. position was that using the term was advisable only if it was defined to mean that the right to self-determination signified Indigenous Peoples' right to negotiate their respective political statuses within the framework of the existing nation-state. The debate over Indigenous Peoples' demand for the use of the term "peoples" was crucial to activist demands under international law. The U.S. government has continuously opposed the use of the plural term "peoples," which connotes peoplehood and attendant collective rights to full self-determination. However, this has the potential to change with the UN adoption of the Declaration on the Rights of Indigenous Peoples—especially if the declaration becomes a convention with the full force of international law.

72. It would also be useful to examine Hawaiian men's role in the U.S. military and how their socialization within that institution has contributed to sexism and violence in our communities by setting new cultural standards about what is appropriate for Hawaiian women in terms of the social roles that they can occupy. We need to consider the ways in which U.S. militarism perpetuates gendered violence against Hawaiian people and lands.

73. Kauai 2014 has suggested that the key to solving this problem is to repeal birthright citizenship, because the Hawaiian Kingdom had an 80:20 ratio of Kanaka to foreigners in the 1890s. He draws on the work of Ronen 2008, who examines six case studies (the Baltic states, Rhodesia, South Africa, Turkey and Cyprus, East Timor) with a history of introduction or implantation of large settler populations into the territory under dispute and traces the transition from an illegal regime to a lawful one

with regard to the question of settler expulsion and international human rights law constraints.

74. U.S. Pacific Command (USPACOM) 2017.

CHAPTER 2. *Properties of Land*

1. Silva 2008 (emphasis in original).

2. "Stop Selling Ceded Lands" 2015 (no longer available).

3. Thanks to Silva, who explained to me that Kānehoalani is mentioned as the father of Pele in Poepoe 1908 and in Emerson 1915. She also informed me that Konahuanui's name translates as "his big testicles" and that the area on the Koʻolau mountainside is Ulekola (erect penis). See Doug Herman's Nuʻuanu website for allusions to the story: Pacific Worlds & Associates 2015 .

4. Section 5(f) reads: "The lands granted to the State of Hawaii by subsection (b) of this section and public lands retained by the United States under subsections (c) and (d) and later conveyed to the State under subsection (e), together with the proceeds from the sale or other disposition of any such lands and the income therefrom, shall be held by said State as a public trust for the support of the public schools and other public educational institutions, for the betterment of the conditions of native Hawaiians, as defined in the Hawaiian Homes Commission Act, 1920, as amended, for the development of farm and home ownership on as widespread a basis as possible for the making of public improvements, and for the provision of lands for public use. Such lands, proceeds, and income shall be managed and disposed of for one or more of the foregoing purposes in such manner as the constitution and laws of said State may provide, and their use for any other object shall constitute a breach of trust for which suit may be brought by the United States" (Hawaii State Legislature, section 5(f) of the Hawaii Admission Act, https://www.capitol.hawaii.gov/hrscurrent/Vol01_Ch0001-0042F/04-ADM/ADM_0005.htm). Importantly, here "native Hawaiians" are defined statutorily as those who can prove that they meet a 50 percent blood quantum rule. For a critical account of this legislative definition of "native Hawaiian" through the Hawaiian Homes Commission Act, see Kauanui 2008b.

5. U.S. Congress 1898b.

6. U.S. Congress 1993.

7. Moon 2008; C. J. Moon, Nakayama Levinson, and J. J. Acoba; and Circuit Judge Chan, in place of Duffy, J. recused. See *Office of Hawaiian Affairs IV v. Housing and Community Development Corporation of Hawaii* HCDCH 2008.

8. *Office of Hawaiian Affairs IV v. Housing and Community Development Corporation of Hawaii* HCDCH 2008.

9. Investor Words 2015.

10. A preliminary statement is usually something in an introduction to a formal document that serves to explain its purpose.

11. U.S. Supreme Court 2008.

12. *Office of Hawaiian Affairs IV v. Housing and Community Development Corporation of Hawaii* HCDCH 2008.

13. For a thorough critical analysis of this case, see Kauanui 2014.

14. Kame'eleihiwa 1992, 15.

15. Kame'eleihiwa 1992, 297.

16. Yamamura 1949, 233–234; Linnekin 1990, 297.

17. Osorio 2002, 32, 11.

18. As Osorio 2002 notes, figures range from 93 percent to 95 percent depopulation by the end of the nineteenth century (9–10). See Stannard 1989.

19. Osorio 2002, 47.

20. Osorio 2002, 47.

21. Linnekin 1990, 198.

22. Osorio 2002, 44.

23. Linnekin 1990, 85. Linnekin has noted that "Hawaiian social organization does not neatly fit into established anthropological categories" (115). As Sahlins 1985 asserts: "Hawai'i is missing the segmentary polity of descent groups known to cognate Polynesian peoples: organization of the land as a pyramid of embedded lineages, with a corresponding hierarchy of ancestral cults, property rights, and chiefly titles, all based on genealogical priority within the group of common descent" (20). Ambilineality lends itself to fixed assets and territories, whereas bilateral Hawaiian kinship was not fixed in the same way, especially given the redistribution of lands under the mō'ī. Ambilineal descent groups, ramages, involve the formation of discrete and exclusive units (in contrast to bilateral systems), involving claims to group membership and status through only one parent, albeit with some choice.

24. Linnekin 1990, 94; Sahlins 1985, 19, 20.

25. Kame'eleihiwa 1992, 27.

26. Osorio 2002, 49.

27. Chinen 1958, 5.

28. Cited in Chinen 1958, 5, 7.

29. Osorio 2002, 25.

30. Osorio 2002, 25.

31. Hawaiian Kingdom constitution of 1840.

32. Chinen 1958, 7–8. Here he uses the term "form of ownership," but it is unclear whether by 1840 the concept of "ownership" was apt to describe the king's recognition that the maka'āinana had a place within this communal land that went deeper than their labor upon it for him.

33. See Lâm 1989 as well as Van Dyke 2008.

34. Beamer 2014, 142. Historically, allodial title distinguished ownership of land without feudal duties from ownership by feudal tenure with the tenurial rights of a landholder's overlord or sovereign. The concept of allodial title is typically used in reference to most independent state governments, whereas property ownership in common law jurisdictions is considered "fee simple" such as in the United States, where land is subject to eminent domain.

35. Beamer 2014, 129.

36. Van Dyke 2008, 30.

37. Hobbs 1935, 46.

38. Lâm 1989, 261.

39. Kame'eleihiwa 1992, 295; Lâm 1989, 262; Matsuda 1988b, 137; Chinen 1958, 31. Linnekin 1990 points to four statutes enacted in 1850 that in combination "made it impossible for commoners to subsist on the land without participating in the market economy, either through produce sales, cash cropping, or wage labor" (195). One was the Kuleana Act, which allowed commoners the right to be awarded their land in fee simple; the second was a law giving foreigners the right to own land in the kingdom; the third opened three more ports to foreign commerce on Hawai'i Island, which until that point had only been allowed in Lāhainā on Maui Island and Honolulu on O'ahu Island; and the fourth abolished payment of taxes in kind, requiring Hawaiians to pay land, labor, and poll taxes to the kingdom in cash. Linnekin 1990, 195–196. By the mid-1840s government taxes had to be paid in cash, which forced people in areas remote from foreign commercial activities to shift to port towns to earn the necessary money. These changes also led to the development of a different process of class formation. Ralston 1984 also explores the shift in commoner Kanaka Maoli lives, noting that between 1778 and 1854 the maka'āinana changed from being affluent subsistence farmers who were self-sufficient in terms of nearly all the essentials of life to being a class of unskilled and predominantly landless peasants who were dependent on their own labor to supply the food and increasing number of foreign goods required to sustain life.

40. Matsuda 1988b, 137.

41. Linnekin 1990, 201.

42. Osorio 2002, 53, 48.

43. Kame'eleihiwa 1992, 30–31.

44. Oliveira 2014, 44–45.

45. Osorio 2002, 55.

46. But, as Osorio 2002 notes, when the nobles in the Legislative Council introduced their "Act to Abolish the Disabilities of Aliens to Acquire and Convey Lands in Fee Simple Title" on July 9, 1850, they met opposition from the representatives.

47. Cachola 1995, 93.

48. Osorio 2002, 51.

49. Lâm 1989, 259; Chinen 1958, 20.

50. Chinen 1958, 21 (emphasis in original).

51. Matsuda 1988b, 137. Linnekin 1990 maintains that the land division accelerated migration to nascent urban centers in the islands and notes that "it is ironic that emigration was thus used as a justification for the individualization of title, for the land division was perhaps the single event most responsible for land abandonment" (198–199).

52. Until recently the assertion of broad dispossession and the figure of 1 percent prevailed in the literature. See Chinen 1958; Lâm 1989; Matsuda 1988b; Osorio 2002; Kame'eleihiwa 1992; Silva 2004.

53. Sai et al. 2013b argue that the real dispossession for the maka'āinana originated from the Bayonet Constitution forced on King Kalākaua in 1887, which institutionalized property qualifications for the enfranchisement of citizens.

54. Sai, personal communication, March 28, 2006.

55. Preza 2010.

56. Beamer 2014, 142: "In the most basic sense, the Māhele of 1848 created three separate land bases. The first was for 252 ali'i and konohiki, the second was for the government, and the third was for the mō'ī. All lands given to ali'i since the time of Kamehameha, but not in fee, reverted to Kauikeaouli, who then redistributed the lands in accordance with his own will—usually determined by the recipient's relationship to Kamehameha I." Beamer described the Māhele as "the last kālai'āina" because it granted ali'i fee title to their lands (143).

57. Beamer 2014, 142; Preza 2010, 3–4.

58. Beamer 2014, 142.

59. Beamer 2014, 144.

60. Beamer 2014, 151. Beamer even suggests that the process preserved Hawaiian place-names because of the ways in which the claims were filed, identifying land specifically in traditional terms.

61. Beamer 2014, 153.

62. Preza 2010 takes on previous scholarly work by Kame'eleihiwa 1992 to question the concern with an initial dispossession: "The problem is that it takes the approach of highlighting the loss of land rather than providing an explanation of the Māhele process. Kame'eleihiwa effectively shifted the argument from one of sovereignty to one of real property in the identification of the Māhele as the 'real loss' of sovereignty. This shift of focus from the loss of governance to a loss of land is identified as the 'misunderstanding'" (19).

63. Preza 2010, 1–2. Curiously, like Beamer, he refers to the scholarly research on Hawai'i that engages the analytic of colonialism as "colonial discourse" (e.g., "In the colonial discourse, it is well established that institutions of private property are considered to dispossess"), which is a misnomer since the term describes the discourse itself, not the subject of it.

64. Preza 2010, 3 (quotations), 6.

65. Preza 2010, 7, 16, 18.

66. Beamer 2014, 128–129.

67. Osorio 2002, 36, 68.

68. Perkins 2013, 47, 1, 47.

69. Perkins 2013, 44, 46–47.

70. Perkins 2013, 172–173 (emphasis in original), 203.

71. Sai, personal communication, March 28, 2006.

72. Lâm 1989, 244, 259; Chinen 1958, 20, 27–28.

73. Van Dyke 2008, 9–10.

74. As Stoler 1995 puts it, "it is within the technologies of power nurtured in the 'society of normalization' that internal enemies will be constructed and that modern racism will be conceived" (65).

75. Sai et al. 2013a.

76. Karp 2010. I should note that the author of this newspaper article contacted me as she was writing the story to ask if I could explain what an ahupua'a is without

mentioning that the piece would feature Rice. I responded to her questions in writing (hence my dismay at her twisted representation): "An *ahupuaʻa* is a traditional 'unit' of land with divisions from the uplands to the sea. Traditionally, each *ahupuaʻa* had a *konokihi* (land steward) serving the paramount chief (male or female) on each island. It was a very useful system because it ensured that resources would be shared among the people (such as food from the ocean going to those dwelling inland and foodstuffs grown in the mountains getting to those on the coast), as well as enabling tributary goods to be efficiently garnered for the chiefs. Today, many Kanaka Maoli (indigenous Hawaiians) are still familiar with the different *ahupuaʻa* on each island and where the boundary markers are for each in terms of geographical space and they are also part of indigenous mapping practices" (Kauanui email to Karp, personal communication, January 21, 2010).

77. Rice is neither "native Hawaiian," defined by the 50 percent blood quantum rule, nor "Native Hawaiian," a Kanaka Maoli person who does not meet that blood criterion. For a detailed historical account of the legal definition of each term, see Kauanui 2008b.

78. Although the majority opinion in *Rice v. Cayetano* in the end did not rule on the Fourteenth Amendment and thus did not affect the trust that the Office of Hawaiian Affairs is meant to manage, the ruling laid the essential groundwork for further assaults on Hawaiian lands and people through a rash of lawsuits throughout the 2000s. This is a crucial part of the story of the Akaka bill, as the OHA played a huge role in lobbying for support of the legislation by misconstruing the ruling in *Rice* to suggest the court ruled on the Fourteenth Amendment when it actually struck down racially exclusive voting *conducted by the state* on grounds of the Fifteenth Amendment. It did so as a way to try to make the case for securing a federally recognized NHGE that would be shielded from Fourteenth Amendment challenges by non-Natives, just as tribal nations are spared.

79. Nellist 1925.

80. Wolfe 2006, 388.

81. Vincent 2012. Ellison is worth an estimated $36 billion, according to *Forbes*, ranking him the third richest American.

82. Shimogawa 2016.

83. Shimogawa 2013.

84. Kerr 2013.

85. As Patrick Wolfe (1998, 2) argues: "Settler colonies were (are) premised on the elimination of native societies. The split tensing reflects a determinate feature of settler colonization. The colonizers come to stay—invasion is a structure not an event." Settler colonial policies push for the destruction of Indigenous societies and then impose assimilation programs for those who survive the process of systematic extermination and removal and become minorities in their own homeland.

86. The new Castle & Cooke was bought by Dole chief executive officer David H. Murdock, who remains the CEO of Castle & Cooke today.

87. Castle & Cooke 2015.

88. Runnette 2016.

89. Lyons 2013, 3, 7–8.

90. Lyons 2013, 9–10.

91. Notably, John Papa ʻĪʻī was appointed as *kahu* (guardian) for the aliʻi who attended. See Brown 2016.

92. Seven families who were eligible under succession laws stated in the 1840 Constitution of the Kingdom of Hawaii, who had converted to Christianity, and who were Kamehameha III's closest relatives constituted the school class.

93. According to Castle & Cooke 1951, Joseph Ballard Atherton had become a partner by 1865, and the company invested heavily in Hawaiʻi's sugar industry over the next few decades. Atherton became president after the deaths of Amos Starr Cooke in 1871 and Samuel Northrup Castle in 1894, when the company incorporated. After the death of Atherton, George Parmele Castle (1851–1932) became president. When he retired in 1916, Edward Davies Tenney became chairman. See Siddall 1917.

94. Mooallem 2014.

95. Lānaʻi Culture & Heritage Center 2017.

96. As Maly and Maly (2009) document, an important record from Kanaka Maoli residents of Lānaʻi was prepared in April 1845 and forwarded to the king. It listed "twelve issues and suggestions on the matter of the foreign role in the Hawaiian government, and sale of Hawaiian land to foreigners." The original document is housed in the Interior Department, Miscellaneous Files of the Hawaiʻi State Archives, but the Malys provide a full transcript of the petition (in both Hawaiian and English), along with photo images of the original record.

97. "Historic Summary," Lānaʻi Culture & Heritage Center 2017.

98. Mahalo to Laura E. Lyons for showing me the conveyances of land recorded in the Bureau of Conveyances. As part of a documentary study for Lānaʻi, Kepā and Onaona Maly undertook a review of all conveyances (Bureau of Conveyances—State of Hawaiʻi) from the island, which is recorded in the books (Liber) for the years between 1845 and 1961. Maly and Maly 2017.

99. Karp 2010.

100. Runnette 2016.

101. Williams 2005; Newcomb 2008.

102. Newcomb 2008. Moreover, he argues that this reliance violates the doctrine of separation of church and state.

103. U.S. Department of the Interior: Indian Affairs 2013 (emphasis added).

104. U.S. Department of the Interior: Indian Affairs 2013.

105. Cornell University Law School: Legal Information Institute 2005. This was the third case of the Oneida Indian Nation that reached the Supreme Court for litigation of its land rights claims. The earlier two cases were *Oneida Indian Nation of New York v. County of Oneida*, 414 U.S. 661 (1974) and *County of Oneida v. Oneida Indian Nation of New York State*, 470 U.S. 226 (1985).

106. Cornell University Law School, Legal Information Institute, Syllabus 2 (2005: https://www.law.cornell.edu/supct/html/03-855.ZS.html).

107. Bruyneel 2007 has an excellent reading of this same legal case. O'Brien 2010 documents a genealogy of this exclusion of Indians from concepts of modernity. She

examines over six hundred local histories in the early American period from Massachusetts, Connecticut, and Rhode Island and demonstrates how these narratives inculcated the myth of Indian extinction, a saga that has stubbornly remained in the American consciousness. O'Brien argues that local histories became a primary means by which European Americans asserted their own modernity while denying it to Indian peoples.

108. U.S. Supreme Court 2005.

109. "Small Businesses May Be Affected by New PLDC Rules" 2012; Moore 2012 (no longer available); Gutierrez 2012; Zoellick 2012; "Demands to Repeal Public Land Development Corporation Voiced at Public Hearing" 2012; Azambuja 2012: "Kaua'i is now the second county in Hawai'i to take an official stance against Act 55, after Big Island's county council passed a similar resolution Sept. 18."

110. The hearings were originally held to seek public input on the proposed adoption of three additions to Hawaii Administrative Rule (HAR) to establish operating procedures for the corporation, including the following: "Proposed adoption of a new Chapter 13-301, HAR, Practice and Procedure establishes operating procedures for the Corporation. It contains general provisions relating to the office location and hours, board meetings, and delegation of authority to the Executive Director; and sets forth procedures for proceedings before the board, contested case hearings, declaratory rulings, and petitions for amendment, adoption, or repeal of administrative rules; Proposed adoption of a new Chapter 13-302, HAR, Public Land Development Program sets forth a procedure for the Corporation to initiate, by itself or with qualified persons, or enter into cooperative agreements with qualified persons for the development or financing of projects that make optimal use of public land for the economic, environmental, and social benefit of the people of Hawaii; and Proposed adoption of a new Chapter 13–303, HAR, Project Facility Program establishes a procedure for undertaking and financing any project facility as part of a project. Project facilities include improvements, roads and streets, utility and service corridors, utility lines, water and irrigation systems, lighting systems, security systems, sanitary sewage systems, and other community facilities where applicable": http://hawaii.gov/dlnr./pldc/announcements/PLDC-agenda-120718.pdf (accessed January 1, 2014; no longer available). Notably, Kanaka Maoli who testified against the PLDC opposed it on the basis of the state having no claim to the land. Instead of appealing to the "public" land trust, Hawaiians pointed out that these are stolen lands that belong to another government, the Hawaiian Nation. The paradox here is that it took massive outcries in the name of the public to stop the PLDC; given the backlash against the Hawaiian nationalist movement, it is hard to imagine that the state would have repealed the PLDC if the majority of the protest had been based on the claim that these lands belong to the Hawaiian people.

111. Van Voorhis 2011.

112. AVA Konohiki Website Team 2013.

113. Peralto 2018.

114. Peralto 2018.

CHAPTER 3. *Gender, Marriage, and Coverture*

1. The Newlands Resolution annexing the Hawaiian Islands was approved by Congress on July 4, 1898, and signed on July 7 by President William McKinley. The formal ceremony marking the annexation was held at ʻIolani Palace on August 12, 1898.

2. The flag of the Hawaiian Kingdom was appropriated by the U.S. government as the flag of the 50th state. So the Hawaiʻi state flag and the American flag typically hang side-by-side in front of public buildings. On this day, however, the replacement of the stars and stripes with the Hawaiian flag was a clear nationalist assertion, even if temporary, by the Kanaka Maoli governor.

3. African, Asian, and Latin American nationalist movements, as well as some Pacific struggles, historically have generally emphasized the masculine struggle for liberation. Colonized women were relegated to "behind the scenes" labor, while men took the leadership positions, the credit, and the media attention. In many of those cases the women were fighting colonial power that was patriarchal while having to reckon with their own cultural forms of male domination. This also transpired in the U.S. context in the late twentieth century with the development of second-wave feminism among African American women in the Black Power movement and Mexican American women in the Chicano—or Brown Power—movement. See Blackwell 2011; Roth 2003; Mohanty et al. 1991.

4. Linnekin 1990, 228.

5. Trask 1993a, 21.

6. Tengan 2008 has pointed out that one of the Hale Mua members who is part of Noa's group was there at the time, and other members were visibly present as watchmen (64).

7. Besides being imposed by blunt force, the 1887 constitution was never ratified by the Hawaiian Legislative Assembly. The Honolulu Rifles militia group, whose members were Europeans and white Americans, was affiliated with the so-called Hawaiian League, a not-so-secret society of mostly white lawyers who were in favor of the U.S. annexation of Hawaiʻi and later became instrumental in the overthrow of the kingdom during Queen Liliuʻokalani's reign.

8. Ralston 1989a, 58.

9. Handy and Pukui 1972, 43.

10. Kameʻeleihiwa 1992, 37.

11. Silva 2003 and 2007.

12. With regard to "lesser chiefs" mentioned here, Kamakau [1866–1871] 1991 notes many degrees of chiefs within Hawaiian society and lists eleven different gradations (6–7).

13. Linnekin 1990, 238.

14. Kameʻeleihiwa 1992, 36; Linnekin 1990, 95.

15. Linnekin 1990, 110, 108–109.

16. Kameʻeleihiwa 1992, 46.

17. Linnekin 1990, 107–108.

18. Handy and Pukui 1972, 196–197.

19. Ralston 1989a, 54.

20. Kameʻeleihiwa 1992.

21. Handy and Pukui 1972, 56.

22. Basham 2004, 1–2.

23. Pukui and Elbert 1986, 26, 74, 34.

24. Emerson 1898.

25. Kamakau 1992 (from a 1931 translation of articles from a weekly paper, 1866–1871), 3, 25 (emphasis added). "The taking of many women as wives was a cause of trouble in old days. Women took too many husbands. This broke up the family and brought about quarreling and jealousy. Some women went off with whatever husband they pleased. Parents and friends assisted in this kind of thing so long as they could get a man or woman to take a wealthy person to mate. But one excellent thing there was in old days which is not so today, that was the guarding of the chastity and purity of the young women" (235). This is curious, because the concept of virginity and chastity was in place for high-ranking women to protect the rank of their first offspring, guarding her sexual activity to ensure that she reproduced with a high-ranking male, at least for her first child.

26. Grimshaw 1983, 499–500.

27. Ralston 1989a, 54; Malo [1898] 1951, 72; Handy and Pukui 1972, 109–110.

28. Pukui et al. 1972, 167.

29. Handy and Pukui 1972, 44.

30. Ralston 1989a, 52.

31. Ralston 1989a, 54; Pukui et al. 1972, 49–51; Handy and Pukui 1972, 90–91.

32. Ralston 1989a, 58.

33. Kameʻeleihiwa 1999. See also Osorio 2002, 114. Gething 1977 suggests that the position of kuhina nui was created for Kaʻahumanu at the death of Kamehameha and that the person holding the position would serve as regent while the new king was a minor and as co-ruler after he came of age (195; see also 197–198).

34. Kameʻeleihiwa 1999, 11. English translation from Kamakau [1866–1871] 1991; original text from *Ka Nūpepa Kūʻokoʻa*, September 21, 1867. See "Kuhina Nui Exhibit" 2006.

35. After Kaʻahumanu died in 1823, her niece Kamāmalu was set to be the next kuhina nui but died during travels to London, as did Kamehameha II on the same trip.

36. Kameʻeleihiwa 1999, 11.

37. Silverman 1987, 146.

38. Ralston 1989a, 61.

39. Grimshaw 1989a, 34.

40. Gething 1977, 195.

41. Ralston 1989a, 60–61.

42. Pukui et al. 1972, 110–111.

43. Malo [1898] 1951, 182–183.

44. Ralston 1989a, 46.

45. Grimshaw 1992, 166–167.

46. Cited in Ralston 1989a, 60.

47. Brown 2016, 75.

48. Silverman 1987, 75.

49. Brown 2016, 122.

50. Osorio 2002, 12. As Osorio also notes, this shows the power of Christian ritual even when it was new in Hawai'i: "The church became an institution promising life when death was everywhere, and the eventual conversion of Hawaiians by the thousands must be understood in the context of a time when their own religion, akua, and Ali'i could not prevent them from dying."

51. Grimshaw 1989b, 162. While polygyny is the counterpart to polyandry, Ralston (1988) notes that in common usage the term "polygamy" (the marriage practice of either sex having more than one spouse at the same time), while not specifically gendered, is typically used to describe a man with multiple wives (74). She discusses the assumptions that social anthropologists historically have made when looking at gender and sexual diversity, such as "a deep-seated, often unacknowledged belief that stable nuclear families are the ideal social unit" (Ralston 1988, 76). This legacy of representation led to a focus on needing to explain (and reform) the impermanence of husband-wife bonds and the instability of marriage in studies of past and present-day Polynesian societies, often at the expense of examining the central importance of the bonds between brother and sister.

52. Grimshaw 1989b, 41–42, 48.

53. Silverman 1987, 163–169, 93.

54. Osorio 2002, 11, 63.

55. Silverman 1987, 82–83.

56. Brown 2016, 62.

57. Kame'eleihiwa 1992, 157.

58. Brown 2016, 83.

59. Loomis 1937, 36 (1825).

60. Silverman 1987, 96 (quotation), 97, 91–92. As Silverman 1987 writes, "After the funeral [of Kaumuali'i] Kaahumanu became ill. The chiefs were sent for to be with her in her last days. Kapiolani, one of the younger women chiefs who had become a staunch Christian, said to Kaahumanu, 'You are the great chief, you are the old chief, you are frequently ill and perhaps you have come here to die, it becomes you therefore to exert your great influence while you live, in behalf of good things.' Kaahumanu acknowledged that she expected to die there in Lahaina [she was there to bury Kaumuali'i beside Keopuolani, the sacred queen of Kamehameha who had been baptized on her deathbed] and replied, 'I will do all the good I can before I die'" (91).

61. Silverman 1987, 102.

62. Silverman 1987, 97.

63. Brown 2016, 62, 66.

64. Merry 2000, 244–245.

65. Silverman 1987, 104–105.

66. Grimshaw 1989b, 32, 30 (quotations), 61.

67. Thigpen 2014. As Grimshaw (1989b) notes, "The most immediate, though

scarcely most pleasant, means by which the wives could please the chiefs was through their sewing skills" (34).

68. Ralston 1989a, 60–61.

69. Grimshaw 1983, 499.

70. Ralston 1989a, 60.

71. Grimshaw 1992, 156, 158. "By 1833, there were twenty thousand readers in the islands, most over the age of fifteen, and an equal proportion were male and female" (160).

72. Grimshaw 1992, 163. Ralston (1989a) traces this development to the 1850s, when commodification emerged as a dominant mode, in which a sale of services transpired. The underlying motivations changed, and this shift was further enabled by the open attitudes toward sexuality among Kanaka (58).

73. Grimshaw 1989b, 500 (quotation), 45.

74. Ralston 1989a, 57, 47–48, 58.

75. Grimshaw 1989b, 63, 62.

76. Merry 2000, 241 (quotation), 244–255.

77. Silverman 1987, 101, 103.

78. Silverman 1987, 103–104. For a full treatment of the Buckle affair, see Arista 2010.

79. Silverman 1987, 104.

80. Brown 2016, 64.

81. Silverman 1987, 106.

82. Bingham 1855, 284–285, 286 (emphasis in original).

83. Silverman 1987, 109; Brown 2016, 86–87.

84. Bingham 1855, 288–289 (see also 287).

85. Silverman 1987, 109–110, 114 (quotation).

86. Bingham 1855, 314–315.

87. Silverman 1987, 112.

88. Silverman 1987, 114–115.

89. Silverman 1987, 116–117.

90. Silverman 1987, 117–118.

91. Osorio 2002, 13 (quotation), 11.

92. Stoler 2006.

93. Gething 1977, 195–196, 202, 191 (quotation: these laws reached back to English colonial laws in the 1600s).

94. Grimshaw 1989b, 161–162.

95. Osorio 2002, 58.

96. Grimshaw 1989b, 171–172 (quotations), 168, 173. Yet Grimshaw gives one example of missionary abuse of Hawaiian children (45).

97. Merry 2000, 252, 256.

98. Grimshaw 1989b, 161.

99. Grimshaw 1989b, 170, 166, 162, 168.

100. Grimshaw 1989b, 166 (quotation), 167.

101. Grimshaw 1989b, 163–164.

102. "Letter from Mr. Andrews" 1836, 10.

103. Grimshaw 1989b, 160. Grimshaw does not identify the name of the woman who complained about this issue.

104. Grimshaw 1989b, 162.

105. Ralston 1898a, 61.

106. Grimshaw 1989b, 165.

107. Gething 1977, 188–190.

108. An early description of the theory explained that because Eve helped to seduce Adam, women "make no laws, they consent to none, they abrogate none." Furthermore, "All of them are understood either married or to be married and their desires are their husbands." Cited in Gething 1977, 191–192.

109. Gething 1977, 203 (quotation: she could regain her civil rights after separation if she was not guilty of adultery), 198, 192.

110. Ralston 1989a, 60; Grimshaw 1989b, 165 (quotation).

111. Kame'eleihiwa 1999.

112. Grimshaw 1989b, 166.

113. This terminology is still pervasive today in terms of Hawaiian Creole English, when referring to who exactly is "with" whom, even if not married.

114. Gething 1977, 205.

115. Gething 1977, 198.

116. Gething 1977, 198, 202.

117. Osorio 2002, 58.

118. Merry 2000, 252

119. Linnekin 1990.

120. James Campbell Company LLC 2016.

121. Osorio 2002, 57–59.

122. Linnekin 1990, 3, 239.

123. Linnekin 1990, 212, 226–227 (quotations on 227). This may account for the contemporary recognition of women's power in Kanaka Maoli communities and Hawaiian women's leadership in the nationalist struggle. Note that I problematize the suffix "ess" appended to word "chief," presumably used by Linnekin to make a feminine version of the noun "chief"; ali'i in the Hawaiian language is not gender specific.

124. Sai 1998.

125. Sai 1998.

126. Sai 1998 (emphasis in original).

127. Sai 1998 (emphasis in original).

128. Lydecker 1918, 12.

129. Lydecker 1918, 10–11, 12.

130. Osorio 2002, 85.

131. The information is found in an endnote to this part of the constitution. Kamehameha Schools 2015.

132. Kame'eleihiwa 1992.

133. Keoni Ana supported Kamehameha III and IV in their attempt to abolish the

office of the kuhina nui, even as he served in that capacity, because the authority challenged the king's prestige and power. But that would not happen until 1864.

134. Silva 2004, 43–44.

135. The Hoʻolina Project 2002; Kamehameha V 2003.

136. This discrepancy in the two languages with regard to gender is noted by the Hoʻolina project.

137. Silva 2017, 35. As Silva explains: "During the heated controversies that characterized the year of 1864, Henry Whitney's paper, *Ka Nupepa Kuokoa,* opposed all the changes that the new Mōʻī tried to effect, and especially, the ways that he implemented them. First, the Mōʻī called for an ʻAhahui ʻElele of aliʻi and makaʻāinana to come and discuss a new kumukānāwai (constitution) with him. Wini opposed this, as did many others, saying that there had recently been an election, and the elected representatives were the proper ones to deliberate with the Mōʻī. The Mōʻī instead held new elections for delegates and called a constitutional convention. All went well until the assembly had to decide on the property qualification for voters and Luna Makaʻāinana. Almost all the ʻElele (delegates) opposed any property qualification, while the Kuhina (cabinet ministers) and the Mōʻī stubbornly held out for it. The ʻElele represented the common working people and the Kuhina represented the landed and monied aliʻi and haole. No matter how low a property qualification was proposed (at one point it went down to $25), the ʻElele held firm. Finally, after several days, the Mōʻī adjourned the convention and announced the suspension of the existing kumukānāwai. He went into meetings with the Kuhina and drafted a new kumukānāwai without any input from the ʻElele" (Silva 2017, 35–36). She further notes: "These actions incensed Whitney, most of the missionary quarter, and many Kānaka Maoli, as well. *Nupepa Kuokoa* continuously ran editorials that were insulting to the Kuhina, and by extension, to the Mōʻī, although they did not print anything directly insulting to the Mōʻī. In an editorial the day before the election of the delegates, for example, *Kuokoa* asserted that there was a secret agenda for the constitutional changes, and that the government (by implication, the Kuhina) wanted the public to elect uninformed delegates so that the agenda could proceed without resistance" (Silva 2017, 36). *Kuokoa* also printed letters that were highly critical of these actions.

CHAPTER 4. *"Savage" Sexualities*

1. Siu 2015.

2. Siu 2008, 2009.

3. "About Leon Siu" 2011 (no longer available).

4. Kauikeaouli 1829.

5. I have yet to see any discussion treating this topic with regard to women during the period, which may simply reflect the era: homosexual practices among women were unfathomable to Euro-Americans. See Smith-Rosenberg 1975.

6. Aikāne relationships are defined in multiple ways throughout time and include being devoted friends as well as lovers. The term is ambiguous given that it describes

a close relationship between people of the same gender (e.g., two men or two women) that may or may not include sexual intimacy: hoʻomanawanui 2014, 135–142; Silva 2007; Charlot 1998.

7. Alexander 1997, 63.

8. Silva 2004; Merry 2000.

9. Lowe 2006, 204, 201–202 (citing Amy Dru Stanley), 2015, 29 (quotation).

10. Cook 1967.

11. Morris 1990, 28 (quotation), 30–31 (all bracketed notations are from Morris), citing Cook 1967, 1171–1172.

12. Onan, the second son of Judah, is discussed in Genesis 38. He was killed for being unwilling to father a child by his widowed sister-in-law, Tamar. After Onan's brother Er was slain by God, his father told him to fulfill his duty as a brother-in-law (the brother of a deceased man is obliged to marry his brother's widow) to Tamar by giving her offspring. Onan withdrew before climax and "spilled his seed on the ground," so God slew him. Freedman 2000.

13. Morris 1990, 35 (citing Clerke). Morris suggests that Clerke's language echoes that of William Blackstone, the solicitor general and legal scholar who wrote four volumes of *Commentaries on the Laws of England* that include "the infamous crime against nature, committed either with man or beast" as public wrongs. Morris notes that eighteenth-century European thought and jurisprudence regarding sex echoes 1 Corinthians 7:3–5a, in which Paul explains that sex between a husband and wife is a duty of "benevolence" and Romans 1:26, where he discusses the unnatural lust of men for men. Morris 1990, 34–35. It is not always clear what "sodomy" included or meant; sometimes individuals differentiated sexual acts as *per os* (by way of the mouth) or *per anum* (by way of the anus). Morris 1990, 36.

14. Wallace 2003, 45.

15. Kamehameha IV was also said to have had aikāne.

16. Pukui and Elbert 1986 s.v. "aikāne"; Basham 2004, 5.

17. Pukui et al. 1972, 109.

18. Handy and Pukui 1972, 73.

19. Pukui and Elbert 1968.

20. Pukui et al. 1972, 110–111.

21. Kameʻeleihiwa n.d. and Silva 2004 both note the difficulties of translation and interpreting Hawaiian concepts of those whose daily realities—whether historical, conceptual, linguistic, geographical, cultural, or social—were so different than today.

22. Silva 2007, 180.

23. Charlot 1998, 136; hoʻomanawanui 2014, 135–142.

24. Kameʻeleihiwa, cited in Snow 2014, 24.

25. Kuwada 2009. He continues: "What makes this word usage so interesting, and yet still mysterious, is that I have never come across an example of a Hawaiian story in which a human, or a demigod for that matter, took an object as an aikāne. Hawaiian stories often featured *kupua* (hero/demigod) who had aikāne, and some of these kupua could indeed change their shape, but I know of no stories in which they changed into manmade objects. J. W.'s usage implies either that the key is in some way

alive or that the translator has completely misunderstood the meaning of the word and has taken it to just mean 'friend,' as is common in today's usage" (28).

26. hoʻomanawanui 2014, 136, 139, 141.

27. Kapihenui cited in Silva 2007, 163.

28. Silva 2004.

29. Silva 2007, 161. See also hoʻomanawanui 2014.

30. Silva 2007, 168 (poem), 166.

31. hoʻomanawanui 2014, 138, 135–136.

32. Malo [1898] 1951, 256.

33. Pukui et al. 1972b, 109.

34. Kamakau [1866–1871] 1991, 234.

35. Silva, personal communication, 2015. He later served as a district judge in Wailuku, Maui, and was a legislator for the Hawaiian Kingdom; he represented the island Maui in the House of Representatives from 1851 to 1860 and the island of Oʻahu from 1870 to 1876.

36. Cited in Grimshaw 1989b, 175.

37. See also Kameʻeleihiwa 1992 for discussion of aliʻi having multiple relations with other aliʻi.

38. hoʻomanawanui 2014, 141; Kamakau [1866–1871] 1991, 314.

39. Silva 2004.

40. Weems 2011.

41. Silva 2004, 61. As Silva (personal communication, 2015) has conveyed to me directly, she infers a sexual aikāne relationship between Kauikeaouli and Kaomi based on her understanding on the tone of the missionary outrage and the use of the word *aikāne* to describe the relationship between them. "The word wasn't used that much for just friends or companions at that time and they thought that his influence over the Mōʻī was so great. . . . It could certainly be interpreted the other way, too." Although it is unconfirmed whether they were specifically sexually involved, she explains: "We do know for sure though that Kauikeaouli was a young man, originally raised in a Kanaka world that was changing to become more Christian as he grew up. Some of his mākua raised him to expect to have children with his sister and during that same period he openly flouted all the puritanical restrictions imposed by Kaʻahumanu. Nothing would have prevented him thinking he could take an aikāne as well."

42. Notably, several Kanaka Maoli had previously converted while in Connecticut at the Cornwall School for Heathen Youth before the ABCFM sent a mission to Hawaiʻi.

43. Kameʻeleihiwa 1992, 157.

44. Kamakau [1866–1871] 1991, 334, 335.

45. Kamakau [1866–1871] 1991, 335.

46. Kamakau [1866–1871] 1991, 336.

47. Brown 2016, 62, 72.

48. Kameʻeleihiwa 1992, 158.

49. Kamakau [1866–1871] 1991, 336–339.

50. Cachola 1995, 27; Kameʻeleihiwa 1992, 158.

51. Kameʻeleihiwa 1992, 157–158.

52. Kamakau [1866–1871] 1991, 340, 339.

53. Kamakau [1866–1871] 1991, 338.

54. Kameʻeleihiwa 1992, 160.

55. Kamakau [1866–1871] 1991, 338.

56. Kameʻeleihiwa 1992, 160.

57. Some popular accounts of brother-sister matings have been represented in mainstream publications. For example, a September 2010 article published in the *National Geographic* titled "The Risks and Rewards of Royal Incest" focused on the relationship between Kamehameha III and his sister, Princess Nāhiʻenaʻena. But the piece framed the union in a sensationalist way: "Royal incest . . . in Hawaii [was] an exclusive royal privilege. . . . Royal incest occurs mainly in societies where rulers have tremendous power and no peers, except the gods. Since gods marry each other, so should royals. . . . Incest also protects royal assets. Marrying family members ensures that a king will share riches, privilege, and power only with people already his relatives. . . . It can all seem mercenary." Dobbs 2010, 61. This sort of account seems to equate the genealogical alliances among chiefly Hawaiians with European monarchical wealth accumulation. Although the aliʻi nui accrued "riches" (they had feather work and other valued adornments), each piece was specially made and not easily transferred. In another example, with regard to land at this time (prior to privatization), they all had kuleana (responsibility and prerogative) over land districts that ensured they could get *waʻa* (voyaging vessels) made by makaʻāinana and kāhuna.

58. Kamakau 1992, 4–5, 21 (n. 3).

59. Ancient Egypt and Incan Peru are also known to have had close consanguine matings. See Davenport 1994.

60. For Lévi-Strauss the incest taboo was what allowed people to move from the state of nature to culture. In her comparative work on Jacques Lacan and Claude Lévi-Strauss, Camille Robcis (2013) examines Lévi-Strauss's work on the relationship between the familial and the social by focusing on what he terms "kinship and the structuralist social contract." She suggests reading Lévi-Strauss's writings on kinship as social contract theories, as treatises on the social bond and social integration. Robcis notes that the theory on kinship dwelled on "the political": for Lévi-Strauss, sexual difference gives society its foundation, unity, and basic coherence. For him this took the form of the incest prohibition. Robcis suggests that for Lacan this focus on sexual difference took the form of castration (155–156).

61. Silva 2003, 117–118.

62. Kameʻeleihiwa 1992, 23, 25. Valeri 1985 posits that they were first cousins (170). However, the same generation used the sibling terms of address, which may be the source of discrepancy between Valeri's reading and Kameʻeleihiwa's.

63. Handy and Pukui 1972, 108; Davenport 1994.

64. Davenport 1994, 63.

65. Loomis 1937, 16 (1824).

66. Kamakau 1992, 339.

67. After consultation with Marie Alohalani Brown, I believe that this source is by the Reverend William Richards. By noting the date of the entry one can narrow down which missionary was there at that time. William Richards was assigned to Lāhainā in 1823, and the records are marked "Lahaina, Maui, Church Records, 1823–1872."

68. Richards 1823–1872, 8–9.

69. Sinclair 1995, 138–139.

70. Sinclair 1995, 146–147, 151 (quotation).

71. Sinclair 1995, 151 (quotation), 141.

72. Richards 1823–1872, 13. The scanned journal jumps from page 9 to page 12, with pages 10 and 11 missing. Page 9 ends with an entry from 1832, while the year being written about on page 12 is unclear. However, on page 12 the top entry is from January 5, while the one at the bottom of that same page is an August entry that mentions something that took place in January 1835. Hence the entry about Nāhiʻenaʻena's "fall" is likely to be from 1834, because page 13 has an entry that is dated February 1835.

73. The same date is given for ʻĪʻī arriving from Oʻahu to Lāhainā to tell William Richards at the church there: *The Levi Chamberlain Journal* 1822–1849.

74. Richards 1823–1872, 13.

75. Richards 1823–1872, 14–15.

76. Sinclair 1995, 152.

77. Kameʻeleihiwa 1992, 161–162.

78. Kamakau [1866–1871] 1991. Richards had been an advisor to Kamehameha III since 1838 when he resigned from the mission.

79. Sinclair 1995, 153, 154.

80. Sinclair 1969.

81. Sinclair 1995, 160–161.

82. Kameʻeleihiwa 1992, 167.

83. Kamakau [1866–1871] 1991, 342.

84. Cachola 1995, 36.

85. Snow 2014, 22.

86. New Hope Christian Fellowship, http://www.enewhope.org (accessed July 1, 2015).

87. It is unclear whether the term *māhū* may or may not apply in the contemporary period to people raised female who transition to identify as men or to "masculine" women, which seems to show the limits of transhistoricizing a term that may have once referred to a person who today would probably be understood as biologically intersexed.

88. Manderson and Jolly 1997.

89. Snow 2014, 23.

90. Snow 2014, 84.

91. Hall and Kauanui 1994.

92. Basham 2004, 5.

93. Pukui and Elbert 1986, 220.

94. Pukui et al. 1972, 108.

95. Matzner 2001, 15.

96. Alfred 1999.

97. Tengan 2008, 159–161.

98. Prior to the bill's passage, same-sex couples in the state had been allowed to form civil unions since 2012 and to access recognition for "reciprocal beneficiary relationships" since 1997.

99. Ironically perhaps, the Hawai'i exemption was modeled after the one in Connecticut state law. As reported, each of the twelve states that have passed laws legalizing same-sex marriage also protects religious groups and clergy who do not want to solemnize or participate in same-sex weddings. "Some states that have passed legislation have gone even further. For example, gay marriage laws in Maryland and Connecticut include language allowing religiously affiliated groups that provide adoption, foster care and similar social services to refuse to serve same-sex couples, as long as they do not receive any state funds for the program in question. Furthermore, the gay marriage statutes in these two states, as well as in New Hampshire, Rhode Island and Vermont, allow religiously affiliated fraternal societies, such as the Knights of Columbus, to refuse to provide insurance or other services to members who are married to a same-sex partner." Masci 2013.

100. Here we can see how the U.S. federal government's plenary power functions over Native governing entities (federally recognized tribes) and island territories (the Commonwealth of the Northern Mariana Islands, Guam, American Samoa, the U.S. Virgin Islands, and Puerto Rico).

101. Goldberg-Hiller 2002 also discusses the Hawai'i debates over same-sex marriage in the 1990s, including a rich examination of the work of Nā Mamo along with the historical and rhetorical claims regarding "traditional marriage" in the Hawaiian context with regard to the notions of place, Indigenous sovereignty claims, tensions with Christian values, and implications for coalition politics (147–179). His study examines "the tensions between the deconstructive impulses of some sexual activists challenging state authority over sexuality and property, and the constructivist tendencies of the indigenous rights movement committed to nationalism and local control" (151–152).

102. Kauanui 2017.

103. Ragaza 1996.

104. Gomes quoted in Ragaza 1996, 12.

105. In his work on the politics of contemporary South Asian queer politics, Shah 1998 has written about how the search for an "indigenous tradition" and forms of "reclaiming the past" raises epistemological questions about what constitutes history. He warns against the presumption that sexuality is a definable and universal and transhistorical activity and flags this as a problem in "recovering the past" for those hoping to secure their identities as "timeless."

106. The Supreme Court overturned the Defense of Marriage Act on June 26, 2013, and (on the same day in a different ruling) upheld California's Proposition 8 that allows same-sex marriage.

107. Downes 2013.

108. Spade and Willse 2013.

109. According to ku'ualoha ho'omanawanui (personal correspondence, 2015), she co-administers True Aloha, which was started by Trisha Kēhaulani Watson Sproat. They launched the Facebook page to take a stand as heterosexual allies, "especially when the ignorant conservative Christian Kanaka started to try and re-define aloha in Christian-rooted ways."

110. ho'omanawanui 2013. The commercial is available online: https://www.youtube.com/watch?v=3yqMNtCgxZw (accessed July 1, 2015).

111. ho'omanawanui 2013.

112. True Aloha 2015.

113. Handy and Pukui 1972, 56.

114. Pukui et al. 1972, 167.

115. Today we see how same-sex marriage itself has overtaken broader queer political organizing, and Hawai'i is no exception. As Spade and Willse 2013 argue: "Same-sex marriage advocacy has accomplished an amazing feat—it has made being anti-homophobic synonymous with being pro-marriage. It has drowned out centuries of critical thinking and activism against the racialized, colonial, and patriarchal processes of state regulation of family and gender through marriage." It is important to highlight the importance of queer critique in challenging these state logics. I am inspired by the work of Against Equality, an online archive, publishing, and arts collective focused on critiquing mainstream gay and lesbian politics. As their mission statement says: "The collective is committed to dislodging the centrality of equality rhetoric and challenging the demand for inclusion in the institution of marriage, as well as the two other prongs of the 'holy trinity': the U.S. military, and the prison industrial complex via hate crimes legislation" (http://www.againstequality.org/, accessed July 1, 2015). I should add that the ways in which the U.S. military and the prison industrial complex pervade the everyday lives of Hawaiians need more scholarly and political attention.

116. Section 2, U.S. Congress 1996.

117. Burkes 2015.

118. Barker 2011.

119. Morales 2015.

120. De Silva 2012, 1, 2 (emphasis in original).

121. De Silva 2012, 3, 7.

CONCLUSION. *Decolonial Challenges*

1. Maile 2016, 3.

2. Alexander 2006, 100–101 (emphasis in original).

3. U.S. Pacific Command (USPACOM) 2017.

4. This is a key principle governing occupation, spelled out primarily in both the 1907 Hague Regulations (articles 42–56) and the Fourth Geneva Convention (GC IV, articles 27–34 and 47–78) as well as in customary international humanitarian law. International Committee of the Red Cross 2004.

5. Mignolo 2011, xxiv. Importantly, Silvia Rivera Cusicanqui (2012) has challenged

what she terms the North American academic appropriation of subaltern studies, including the work of Mignolo, citing how its (mis)use shifted "from any obligation to or dialogue with" the marginalized communities most affected by coloniality (98).

6. Writing in the Bolivian context, Rivera Cusicanqui 2012 advances a theory of Indigenous modernity as the simultaneous expression of the modern and the archaic, an assertion of Indigenous temporality. She maintains "there is no *post* or *pre* in this vision of history that is not linear or teleological but rather moves in cycles and spirals and sets out on a course without neglecting to return to the same point. The indigenous world does not conceive of history as linear; the past-future is contained in the present" (97).

7. There is an immense body of writing by and about Kanaka Maoli as a lāhui distinct from non-Native citizens. It is a salient discourse from the time the missionaries came to Hawaii through this period and arguably to the present. See Silva 2004 and Osorio 2002.

8. Goodyear-Kaʻōpua 2013, 6 (emphasis in original). Addressing the concept of "sovereign pedagogies," she theorizes the concept of ea.

9. Alfred 2013b.

GLOSSARY OF HAWAIIAN WORDS AND PHRASES

ʻAha Aliʻi	chiefly council
ahupuaʻa	land division usually extending from the uplands to the ocean
aliʻi	high chief
aloha	love, compassion, care
aloha ʻāina	love of the land
ʻaumākua	ancestral family gods
awaiāulu	to bind securely, fasten
ea	life, breath, sovereignty
hānai	to feed
haole	foreigner or white person
hoʻāo	to stay until daylight
hoʻokama	to make a child
kālaiʻāina	land carving
kalo	taro
Kanaka Maoli	Indigenous Hawaiian
kāne	man or men, male

kapu	sacred and therefore prohibited
kaukau ali'i	lesser chiefs
kāula	priest-prophets, sometimes women
keiki	children
kino lau	embodied manifestation of deities
konohiki	land stewards
kuhina nui	co-ruler
kuleana	to have responsibility or interest
kūpuna	grandparents and relatives of the grandparent generation
lāhui	people or nation
lo'i	irrigated terrace for taro
Māhele	to divide or portion, the privatized Hawaiian land distribution program instituted by Kamehameha III
maka'āinana	common person or common people
mākua	parents and relatives of the parent generation
mālama 'āina	care for the land
mō'ī	paramount chief
'ohana	intergenerational, extended family
po'olua	two heads, refers to two possible biological fathers
punalua	the relationship between first and secondary mates who are not family
wahine (pl. wāhine)	woman
wāhine kaua	battle women
wāhine koa	brave, bold, women

BIBLIOGRAPHY

"About Leon Siu." 2011. Accessed December 10, 2011 (no longer available). http://www.leonandmalia.com/Leonbio.html.

Agnew, John. *Globalization and Sovereignty*. Lanham: Roman and Littlefield, 2009.

"Akaka Bill and 'Native Sovereignty': What It Really Means to Hawaiians." 2010. *YouTube* video, 2:22, posted by Puukukui, January 18: http://www.youtube.com/watch?v=CF4Bzx3RmJ4.

Akaka, Daniel Kahikina. 2009. "'Akaka Bill' Native Hawaiian Government Reorganization Act Reintroduced in Senate and House." Press release, February 4.

Aldrich, Robert F. 2003. *Colonialism and Homosexuality*. London: Routledge.

Alexander, M. Jacqui. 1997. "Erotic Autonomy as Politics of Decolonization: An Anatomy of the Feminist and State Practice in the Bahamas Tourist Economy." In *Feminist Genealogies, Colonial Legacies, Democratic Futures*, ed. M. Jacqui Alexander and Chandra Talpade Mohanty, 63–100. New York: Routledge, 1997.

Alexander, M. Jacqui. 2006. *Pedagogies of Crossing: Meditations on Feminism, Sexual Politics, Memory, and the Sacred*. Durham, NC: Duke University Press.

Alfred, Taiaiake Gerald. 1999. *Peace, Power, Righteousness: An Indigenous Manifesto*. Don Mills, Ontario: Oxford University Press Canada.

Alfred, Taiaiake Gerald. 2005. *Wasáse: Indigenous Pathways of Action and Freedom*. Peterborough, ON: Broadview.

Alfred, Taiaiake Gerald. 2006. "Sovereignty." In *Sovereignty Matters: Locations of Contestation and Possibility in Indigenous Struggles for Self-Determination*, ed. Joanne Barker, 33–51. Lincoln: University of Nebraska Press, 2006.

Alfred, Taiaiake Gerald. 2013a. "Being and Becoming Indigenous: Resurgence against Contemporary Colonialism." Narrm Oration presented at the University of Melbourne, November 28. Accessed January 10, 2013 (no longer available). https://www.youtube.com/watch?v=VwJNy-B31PA.

Alfred, Taiaiake Gerald. 2013b."Being and Becoming Indigenous: Resurgence against Contemporary Colonialism." *Taiaiake,* December 13: https://www.youtube.com/watch?v=VwJNy-B3lPA.

Alfred, Taiaiake Gerald. 2013c. "Resurgence of Traditional Ways of Being." Public lecture, March 23, 2009, at the Heart Museum in Phoenix, presented by the Arizona State University Library Channel Classic Presentation. December 12. https://www.youtube.com/watch?v=3ABP5QhetYs.

Anaya, S. James. 2000. *Indigenous Peoples in International Law.* New York: Oxford University Press.

Andrews, Lorrin. 1836."Letter from Mr. Andrews, at Lahainaluna, December 2, 1836." *Missionary Herald, Containing the Proceedings of the American Board of Commissioners for Foreign Missions* 32 (October): 10.

Anghie, Antony. 2005. *Imperialism, Sovereignty and the Making of International Law.* Cambridge: Cambridge University Press.

Arista, Denise Noelani Manuela. 1998. "Davida Malo, Ke Kanaka O Ka Huliau David Malo, a Hawaiian of the Time of Change." MA thesis, University of Hawaiʻi.

Arista, Denise Noelani Manuela. 2010. "Histories of Unequal Measure: Euro-American Encounters with Hawaiian Governance and Law, 1793–1827." PhD diss., Brandeis University.

Asato, Laureen K. 1981, "Coverture, the Right to Contract, and the Status of Women in Hawaii: Pre-Contact to 1888." MA thesis, University of Hawaiʻi.

AVA Konohiki Website Team. 2013. "AVA Konohiki: Kamakakūokaʻāina, Ancestral Visions of ʻĀina." Accessed September 5, 2013. http://www.avakonohiki.org.

Azambuja, Léo. 2012. "Public Gives Standing Ovation on Resolution against Act 55." September 28. http://www.thegardenisland.com/2012/09/28/hawaii-news/public-gives-standing-ovation-on-resolution-against-act-55.

Baker, Lee D. 2010. *Anthropology and the Racial Politics of Culture.* Durham, NC: Duke University Press.

Ballantyne, Tony, and Antoinette Burton, eds. 2005. *Bodies in Contact: Rethinking Colonial Encounters in World History.* Durham, NC: Duke University Press.

Barker, Joanne. 2006. "Gender, Sovereignty, and the Discourse of Rights in Native Women's Activism." *Meridians* 7, no. 1: 127–161.

Barker, Joanne. 2008. "Gender, Sovereignty, Rights: Native Women's Activism against Social Inequality and Violence in Canada." *American Quarterly* 60, no. 2 (June): 259–266.

Barker, Joanne. 2011. *Native Acts: Law, Recognition and Cultural Authenticity.* Durham, NC: Duke University Press.

Barker, Joanne. 2015. "Indigenous Feminisms." In *Handbook on Indigenous People's Politics,* ed. José Antonio Lucero, Dale Turner, and Donna Lee Van Cott. New York: Oxford University Press. http://www.oxfordhandbooks.com/view/10.1093/oxfordhb/9780195386653.001.0001/oxfordhb-9780195386653.

Barker, Joanne. ed. 2006. *Sovereignty Matters: Locations of Contestation and Possibil-*

ity in Indigenous Struggles for Self-Determination. Lincoln: University of Nebraska Press.

Barnard, Alan. 2006. "Kalahari Revisionism, Vienna and the 'Indigenous Peoples' Debate." *Social Anthropology* 14, no. 1 (February): 1–16.

Barsh, R. L. 1986. "Indigenous Peoples: An Emerging Object of International Law." *American Journal of International Law* 80, no. 2 (April): 369–385.

Basham, Leilani. 2004. "Awaiaulu Ke Aloha: Hawaiian Sexuality, Gender and Marriage." Unpublished manuscript.

Beamer, Kamanamaikalani. 2014. *No Mākou Ka Mana: Liberating the Nation*. Honolulu: Kamehameha.

Bernstein, Mary, and Verta Taylor, eds. 2013. *The Marrying Kind? Debating Same-Sex Marriage within the Lesbian and Gay Movement*. Minneapolis: University of Minnesota Press.

Besnier Niko, and Kalissa Alexeyeff, eds. 2014. *Gender on the Edge: Transgender, Gay, and Other Pacific Islanders*. Honolulu: University of Hawai'i Press.

Bingham, Hiram A. M. 1855. *A Residence of Twenty-One Years in the Sandwich Islands or the Civil, Religious, and Political History of Those Islands: A Particular View of the Missionary Operations Connected with the Introduction and Progress of Christianity and Civilization among the Hawaiian People*. 3rd ed. Canandaigua, NY: H. D. Goodwin.

Blackwell, Maylei. 2011. *¡Chicana Power! Contested Histories of Feminism in the Chicano Movement*. Austin: University of Texas Press.

Blair, Chad. 2014. "US Interior to Propose Rule for Dealing with a Native Hawaiian Government." *Honolulu Civil Beat*, August 14. http://www.civilbeat.com/2015/08/us-interior-to-propose-rule-for-native-hawaiian-government/.

Blair, Chad. 2015. "Election Details Going Out to Native Hawaiian Roll Voters." *Honolulu Civil Beat*, July 31. http://www.civilbeat.com/2015/07/election-details-going-out-to-native-hawaiian-roll-voters/.

Blaisdell, Kekuni. 2005. "I hea nā Kanaka Maoli? Whither the Hawaiians?" *Hūlili* 2, no. 1: 9–20. Edited by Shawn Kana'iaupuni. Honolulu: Kamehameha.

Blaisdell, Kekuni, and Noreen Mokuau. 1994. "Kanaka Maoli, Indigenous Hawaiians." In *Hawai'i: Return to Nationhood*, ed. Ulla Hasager and Jonathan Friedman, 49–67. Document 75. Copenhagen: International Group for Indigenous Affairs.

Briggs, Laura. 2002. *Reproducing Empire: Race, Sex, Science, and U.S. Imperialism in Puerto Rico*. Berkeley: University of California Press.

Brown, James N., and Patricia M. Sant, eds. 1999. *Indigeneity: Construction and Re/Presentation*. Commack, NY: Nova Science.

Brown, Marie Alohalani. 2016. *Facing the Spears of Change: The Life and Legacy of John Papa'Ī'ī*. Honolulu: University of Hawai'i Press.

Brown, Wendy. 2010. *Walled States, Waning Sovereignty*. Cambridge: MIT Press.

Bruyneel, Kevin. 2007. *The Third Space of Sovereignty: The Postcolonial Politics of US-Indigenous Relations*. Minneapolis: University of Minnesota Press.

Burkes, Paula. 2015. "Same-Sex Marriage Rights May Not Extend to Indian Country Land." *Oklahoman*, April 13. http://newsok.com/article/5439817.

Burlin, Paul. 2006. *Imperial Maine and Hawai'i: Interpretive Essays in the History of Nineteenth-Century American Expansion.* Berkeley: University of California Press.

Burton, Antoinette, ed. 1999. *Gender, Sexuality and Colonial Modernities.* London: Routledge.

Byrd, Jodi, A. 2011. *The Transit of Empire: Indigenous Critiques of Colonialism.* Minneapolis: University of Minnesota Press.

Byrd, Jodi A., and Michael Rothburg. 2011. "Between Subalternity and Indigeneity: Critical Categories for Postcolonial Studies." *Interventions: International Journal of Postcolonial Studies* 13, no. 1 (February 23): 1–12.

Cachola, Jean Iwata. 1995. *Kamehameha III: Kauikeaouli.* Honolulu: Kamehameha Schools.

Callon, Michel. 1986. "Elements of a Sociology of Translation: Domestication of the Scallops and the Fishermen of St Brieuc Bay." In *Power, Action and Belief: A New Sociology of Knowledge?*, ed. John Law, 196–223. London: Routledge.

Castanha, Anthony. 1996. "A History of the Hawaiian Sovereignty Movement." In "The Hawaiian Sovereignty Movement: Roles of and Impacts on Non-Hawaiians." MA thesis, University of Hawai'i. http://www.hookele.com/non-hawaiians/chapter3.html#fn25.

Castle & Cooke. 1951. *The First 100 Years: A Report on the Operations of Castle & Cooke for the Years 1851–1951.* Honolulu: Castle & Cooke.

Castle & Cooke. 2015. "Castle & Cooke Hawaii." https://www.castlecookehawaii.com/Page/About-Home.

Chang, David A. 2015. "'We Will Be Comparable to the Indian Peoples': American Indians in Native Hawaiian Thought, 1832–1923." *American Quarterly* 67 (September): 859–886.

Chang, David A. 2016. *The World and All the Things upon It: Native Hawaiian Geographies of Exploration.* Minneapolis: University of Minnesota Press.

Charlot, John P. 1998. "Pele and Hi'iak'a: The Hawaiian-Language Newspaper Series." *Anthropos* 93: 55–75.

Chatterjee, Partha. 1993. *The Nation and Its Fragments: Colonial and Postcolonial Histories.* Princeton: Princeton University Press.

Chinen, Jon J. 1958. *The Great Mahele: Hawaii's Land Division of 1848.* Honolulu: University of Hawai'i Press.

Clifford, James. 1997. *Routes: Travel and Translation in the Late Twentieth Century.* Cambridge, MA: Harvard University Press.

Cook, James. 1967. *The Journals of Captain James Cook on His Voyages of Discovery.* Ed. J. C. Beaglehole. Vol. 3: *The Voyage of the Resolution and Discovery, 1776–1780.* Cambridge: Published by the Hakluyt Society at the University Press.

Cornell University Law School: Legal Information Institute. 2005. *City of Sherrill v. Oneida Indian Nation of New York,* (03-855) 544 U.S. 197 (2005) 337 F.3d 139, reversed and remanded. http://www.law.cornell.edu/supct/html/03-855.ZS.html.

Crabbe, Kamana'opono. 2014. "Re: Inquiry into the Legal Status of the Hawaiian

Kingdom as an Independent Sovereign State." Letter to the U.S. State Department, May 5. http://hawaiiankingdom.org/pdf/OHA_Ltr_to_US_State_Dept.pdf.
Crawley, Ernest. 1929. *Studies of Savages and Sex*. Edited by Theodore Besterman. London: Methuen, 1929.
Cumings, Bruce. 2009. *Dominion from Sea to Sea: Pacific Ascendancy and American Power*. New Haven: Yale University Press.
Davenport, William H. 1994. *Pi'o: An Enquiry into the Marriage of Brothers and Sisters and Other Close Relatives in Old Hawai'i*. Lanham, MD: University Press of America.
Deloria, Philip Joseph. 2003. "American Indians, American Studies, and the ASA." *American Quarterly* 55, no. 4 (December): 669–680.
Deloria, Vine, Jr., and David E. Wilkins. 2000. *Tribes, Treaties, and Constitutional Tribulations*. Austin: University of Texas Press.
"Demands to Repeal Public Land Development Corporation Voiced at Public Hearing." 2012. *Molokai News*, August 28. http://themolokainews.com/2012/08/28/demands-to-repeal-public-land-development-corporation-heard-at-public-hearing/?utm_source=supporter_message&utm_medium=email.
Denetdale, Jennifer Nez. 2009. "Securing Navajo National Boundaries: War, Patriotism, Tradition, and the Diné Marriage Act of 2005." *Wicazo Sa Review* 24, no. 2 (Fall): 131–148.
Denoon, Donald, ed. 1997. *The Cambridge History of Pacific Islanders*. Cambridge: Cambridge University Press.
de Silva, Kahikina. 2012. "Ka'ala, Molale i ka Mālie: The Staying Power of Love and Poetry." Presentation at the annual meeting of the Native American and Indigenous Studies Association, Mohegan Sun Resort, CT, June 4.
Diaz, Vicente M., and J. Kēhaulani Kauanui. 2001. "Native Pacific Cultural Studies on the Edge." *Contemporary Pacific* 13, no. 2 (Fall): 315–342.
Dibble, Sheldon. 1843. *History of the Sandwich Islands*. Lahainaluna: Press of the Mission Seminary.
Dobbs, David. 2010. "The Risks and Rewards of Royal Incest." *National Geographic* (September): 60–61.
"DOI Hearing in Keaukaha, July 2, 2014—Mililani Trask." 2014. *YouTube* video, 4:28, posted by Nanci Munroe, July 3: https://www.youtube.com/watch?v=O6wy4hv-Mf4.
Downes, Lawrence. 2013. "The Aloha Spirit, for Everyone." *New York Times*, November 3. http://www.nytimes.com/2013/11/03/opinion/sunday/the-aloha-spirit-for-everyone.html?ref=opinion&_r=3&&pagewanted=print.
Driskill, Qwo-Li, Chris Finley, Brian Joseph Gilley, and Scott Lauria Morgensen, eds. 2011. *Queer Indigenous Studies: Critical Interventions in Theory, Politics, and Literature*. Tucson: University of Arizona Press.
Elias, Norbert. 1978. *The Civilizing Process: The History of Manners*. Oxford: Basil Blackwell.
Emerson, Nathaniel Bright. 1898. "Regarding Ho-ao, Hawaiian Marriage." In *Fifth*

Annual Report of the Hawaiian Historical Society, 1897, 16–22. Honolulu: Hawaiian Historical Society.

Emerson, Nathaniel Bright. 1915. *Pele and Hiiaka: A Myth from Hawaii*. Honolulu: Honolulu Star-Bulletin.

"Equally Speaking: Malama LGBT, Part 1." 2012. Vimeo video, 27:48, posted by Equality Hawaii, March 5. https://vimeo.com/37986894.

Eveleth, Ephraim. 1831. *History of the Sandwich Islands: With an Account of the American Mission Established There in 1820, with a Supplement Embracing the History of the Wonderful Displays of God's Power in These Islands in 1837–1839*. Rev. ed. Philadelphia: American Sunday-School Union.

Falk, Richard, Balakhrishnan Rajagopal, and Jacqueline Stevens, eds. 2008. *International Law and the Third World: Reshaping Justice*. Abingdon, UK: Routledge-Cavendish.

Fanon, Frantz. "Concerning Violence" and "The Pitfalls of National Consciousness." 1961. In *The Wretched of the Earth*, 1–62, 97–144. New York: Grove.

Farmer, David John. 2005. *To Kill the King: Post-traditional Governance and Bureaucracy*. Armonk, NY: M. E. Sharpe.

Findlay, Eileen J. Suárez. 2000. *Imposing Decency: Politics of Sexuality and Race in Puerto Rico, 1870–1920*. Durham, NC: Duke University Press.

Fish Kashay, Jennifer. 2002. "'O That My Mouth Might Be Opened': Missionaries, Gender, and Language in Early 19th Century Hawai'i." *Hawaiian Journal of History* 36: 41–58.

Fish Kashay, Jennifer. 2007. "Agents of Imperialism: Missionaries and Merchants in Early Nineteenth Century Hawaii." *New England Quarterly* 80, no. 2: 280–298.

Fish Kashay, Jennifer. 2008. "From 'KAPUS' to Christianity: The Disestablishment of the Hawaiian Religions and Chiefly Appropriation of Calvinist Christianity." *Western Historical Quarterly* 39 (March): 17–39.

Foucault, Michel. 1977. "Nietzsche, Genealogy, History." In *Language, Counter-Memory Practice: Selected Essays and Interviews*, ed. by D. F. Bouchard. Ithaca: Cornell University Press.

Foucault, Michel. 1981. *The History of Sexuality, Volume 1: An Introduction*. Harmondsworth, UK: Penguin.

Foucault, Michel. 2003. *Society Must Be Defended: Lectures at the Collège de France, 1975–76*. Edited by Mauro Bertani and Alessandro Fontana. General editors François Ewald and Alessandro Fontana. Translated by David Macey. New York: Picador.

Foucault, Michel. 2004. *The Birth of Biopolitics: Lectures at the College de France, 1978–1979*. Edited by Michel Senellart. Translated by Graham Burchell. New York: Palgrave Macmillan.

Franklin, Cynthia, and Laura Lyons. 2004. "Remixing Hybridity: Globalization, Native Resistance, and Cultural Production in Hawai'i." *American Studies* 45, no. 3 (Fall): 49–80.

Frear, Walter F. 1894. "Evolution of the Hawaiian Judiciary." *Papers of the Hawaiian Historical Society*, no. 7: 1–25.

Freedman. David Noel. 2000. *Eerdmans Dictionary of the Bible*. Grand Rapids, MI: Wm. B. Eerdmans.

Freycinet, Louis Claude de Saulses de. 1978. *Hawaii in 1819: A Narrative Account*. Edited by Marion Kelly. Translated by Ella L. Wiswell. Honolulu: Bernice P. Bishop Museum.

Garroutte, Eva Marie. 2003. *Real Indians: Identity and the Survival of Native America*. Berkeley: University of California Press.

Gast, Ross H., and Agnes C. Conrad. 1973. *Don Francisco de Paula Marin*. Honolulu: University Press of Hawaii for the Hawaiian Historical Society.

Gething, Judith. 1977. "Christianity and Coverture: Impact on the Legal Status on Women in Hawaii, 1820–1920." *Hawaiian Journal of History* 11: 188–220.

Gilroy, Paul. 1987. *"There Ain't No Black in the Union Jack": The Cultural Politics of Race and Nation*. London: Hutchinson.

Goldberg-Hiller, Jonathan. 2002. *The Limits to Union: Same-Sex Marriage and the Politics of Civil Rights*. Ann Arbor: University of Michigan Press.

Goodyear-Ka'ōpua, Noelani. 2013. *The Seeds We Planted: Portraits of a Native Hawaiian Charter School*. Minneapolis: University of Minnesota Press.

Goodyear-Ka'ōpua, Noelani, Ikaika Hussey, and Erin Kahunawaika'ala Wright, eds. 2014. *A Nation Rising: Hawaiian Movements for Life, Land, and Sovereignty*. Durham, NC: Duke University Press.

Green, Karina Kahananui. 2002. "Colonialism's Daughters." In *Pacific Diaspora in the United States and across the Pacific*, ed. Paul R. Spickard, Joane L. Rondilla, and Debbie Hippolite Wright, 242–248. Honolulu: University of Hawai'i Press.

Griggs, Richard. 1992. "Background on the Term 'Fourth World.'" Center for World Indigenous Studies. Accessed June 3, 2014 (no longer available). http://cwis.org/GML/background/FourthWorld.

Grimshaw, Patricia. 1983. "'Christian Woman, Pious Wife, Faithful Mother, Devoted Missionary': Conflicts in Roles of American Missionary Women in Nineteenth Century Hawaii." *Feminist Studies* 9, no. 3: 489–521.

Grimshaw, Patricia. 1989a. "New England Missionary Wives, Hawaiian Women and 'The Cult of True Womanhood.'" In *Family and Gender in the Pacific: Domestic Contradictions and the Colonial Impact*, ed. Margaret Jolly and Martha Macintyre, 19–44. Cambridge: Cambridge University Press.

Grimshaw, Patricia. 1989b. *Paths of Duty: American Missionary Wives in Nineteenth-Century Hawaii*. Honolulu: University of Hawai'i Press.

Grimshaw, Patricia. 1992. "Response." *Pacific Studies* 15, no. 3: 156–170.

Griswold, Esther Ann. 1996. "State Hegemony Writ: International Law and Indigenous Rights." *Political and Legal Anthropology Review* 19, no. 1: 91–104.

Grube, Nick. 2012. "Does the Sale of a Hawaiian Island Matter?" *Civil Beat*, June 22. http://www.civilbeat.com/articles/2012/06/22/16135-does-the-sale-of-a-hawaiian-island-matter/.

Guenther, Mathias, Justin Kendrick, Adam Kuper, Evie Plaice, Trond Thuen, Patrick Wolfe, Werner Zips, and Alan Barnard. 2006. "The Concept of Indigeneity." *Social Anthropology* 14, no. 1 (February): 17–32.

Gutierrez, Ben. 2012. "Overflow Crowd Shows Up to Oppose New Law Allowing Private Development on Public Land." *Hawaii News Now,* August 30. http://www.hawaiinewsnow.com/story/19414195/overflow-crowd-shows-up-to-oppose-new-law-allowing private-development-onpublic%201and?autoStart=true&topVideo CatNo =default&clipId=7670126#.UD8-N3jB_jk.facebook.

Hall, Lisa Kahaleole Chang, and J. Kēhaulani Kauanui. 1994. "Same-Sex Sexuality in Pacific Literature." *Amerasia Journal* 20, no. 1: 75–81.

Hammer, Leonard M. 2007. *A Foucauldian Approach to International Law: Descriptive Thoughts for Normative Issues.* Burlington, VT: Ashgate.

Handy, E. S. Craighill, and Mary Kawena Pukui. 1972. *The Polynesian Family System in Ka'u, Hawai'i.* Rutland, VT: Charles E. Tuttle.

Hawaii 24/7. "Governor Enacts Bill to Further Self-Determination for Native Hawaiians." 2011. Media release. http://www.hawaii247.com/2011/07/07/governor-enacts-bill-to-further-self-determination-for-native-hawaiians/.

Hawaiian Kingdom Government. 2013a. "The Hawaiian Kingdom." Accessed June 15, 2013. http://www.hawaiiankingdom.org/.

Hawaiian Kingdom Government. 2013b. "International Treaties." http://www.hawaiiankingdom.org/treaties.shtml.

Hawaii Constitution. 1840. "Kingdom of Hawai'I Constitution of 1840." http://www.alohaquest.com/archive/constitution_1840.htm.

Hawaii State Supreme Court. 2008. *Office of Hawaiian Affairs IV v. Housing and Community Development Corporation of Hawaii HCDCH,* No. 25570. No. 94–4207-CV. Decided January 31. http://oaoa.hawaii.gov/jud/opinions/sct/2008/25570.htm.

Hobbs, Jean. 1935. *Hawaii: A Pageant of the Soil.* Stanford, CA: Stanford University Press.

Hodges, Sarah. 2008. *Contraception, Colonialism and Commerce: Birth Control in South India, 1920–1940.* Burlington, VT: Ashgate.

ho'omanawanui, kukualoha. 2013. "Living True Aloha." *Hawaii Independent,* October 30. http://hawaiiindependent.net/story/living-true-aloha.

ho'omanawanui, ku'ualoha. 2014. *Voices of Fire: Reweaving the Literary Lei of Pele and Hi'iaka.* Minneapolis: University of Minnesota Press.

Howland, Douglas, and Luise White, eds. 2009. *State of Sovereignty: Territories, Laws, Populations.* Bloomington: Indiana University Press.

Human Sciences Research Council of South Africa. 2009. "Occupation, Colonialism, Apartheid?: A Re-assessment of Israel's Practices in the Occupied Palestinian Territories under International Law." http://www.alhaq.org/attachments/article/236/Occupation_Colonialism_Apartheid-FullStudy.pdf.

Ikeda, Linda L. 2014. "Re-Visioning Family: Mahuwahine and Male-to-Female Transgender in Contemporary Hawai'i." *Oceania Newsletter* 74 (June): 135–161.

International Committee of the Red Cross. 2004. "Occupation and International Humanitarian Law: Questions and Answers." http://www.icrc.org/eng/resources/documents/misc/634kfc.htm.

Investor Words. 2015. "Perfect Title." Accessed July 20, 2015. http://www.investorwords.com/3664/perfect_title.html#ixzz11zb7LL35.

Ivison, Duncan, Paul Patton, and Will Sanders, eds. 2000. *Political Theory and the Rights of Indigenous Peoples*. Cambridge: Cambridge University Press.

Jacobson, Trudy, Charles Sampford, and Ramesh Thakur, eds. 2008. *Re-envisioning Sovereignty: The End of Westphalia?* Hampshire, UK: Ashgate.

James Campbell Company LLC. 2016. The Story of James Campbell." https://www.jamescampbell.com/about/the-story-of-james-campbell/.

Jankowiak, William R., Shelly L. Volsche, and Justin R. Garcia. 2015. "Is the Romantic-Sexual Kiss a Near Human Universal?" *American Anthropologist* 117, no. 3: 535–539.

Jordan, Mark D. 1997. *The Invention of Sodomy in Christian Theology*. Chicago: University of Chicago Press.

Judd, Bernice, Audrey B. Sexton, Barbara S. Wilcox, Elizabeth G. Alexander, and Albert F. Judd, eds. 1969. *Missionary Album: Sesquicentennial Edition, 1820–1970, Portraits and Biographical Sketches of the American Protestant Missionaries to the Hawaiian Islands*. Honolulu: Hawaiian Mission Children's Society.

Ka Haka ʻUla O Keʻelikōlani College of Hawaiian Language and Alu Like. 2017. "Nā Puke Wehewehe ʻŌlelo Hawaiʻi." Ulukau: Hawaiian Electronic Library. Accessed August 1, 2017. http://wehewehe.org.

Ka Lāhui Hawaiʻi. 1993. *The Sovereign Nation of Hawaiʻi: A Compilation of Materials for Education Workshops on Ka Lāhui Hawaiʻi*. Hilo: Ka Lāhui Hawaiʻi.

Kalani, Nanea, and Melissa Tanji. 2012. "Oracle Corp. CEO to Buy Lanai." *Maui News*, June 21. Accessed June 1, 2014 (no longer available). http://mauinews.com/page/content.detail/id/562213/Oracle-Corp-CEO-to-buy-Lanai.html?nav=10.

Kamakau, Samuel Manaiakalani. [1866–1871] 1991. *Ruling Chiefs of Hawaii*. Rev. ed. Honolulu: Kamehameha Schools.

Kamakau, Samuel Manaiakalani. 1992. *Ka Poʻe Kahiko: The People of Old*. Honolulu: Bishop Museum.

Kameʻeleihiwa, Lilikalā. 1992. *Native Land and Foreign Desires: Pehea Lā E Pono Ai? How Shall We Live in Harmony?* Honolulu: Bishop Museum.

Kameʻeleihiwa, Lilikalā. 1999. *Nā Wāhine Kapu: Divine Hawaiian Women*. Honolulu: ʻAi Pohaku.

Kameʻeleihiwa, LilIkalā. 2015. Presentation for Equality Hawaii. "Equally Speaking: Malama LGBT, Part 1," n.d. Accessed April 23, 2015. https://vimeo.com/37986894.

Kamehameha Schools. 2015. "Constitution and Laws of His Majesty Kamehameha III, King of the Hawaiian Islands." Ka Hoʻoilina: Puke Pai ʻŌlelo Hawaiʻi. http://hooilina.org/cgi-bin/journal?e=p-0journal-00-0-0-004-Document-0-1-1en-50-20-docoptions-search-issue-001-0110escapewin&a=p&p=frameset&cl=&d=HASH01ce5dd8c7981a7202feoffb.5.1.6.

Kamehameha V. 2003. "Ke Kumukānāwai o ka Makahiki 1864." *Ka Hoʻoilina: Journal of Hawaiian Language Sources*. http://hooilina.org/collect/journal/index/assoc/HASHe7d7.dir/5.pdf.

"Kanaʻiolowalu Launches Online Registry for Native Hawaiians." 2012. *Native Hawaiian Roll Commission Press Release*. http://www.oha.org/page/native-hawaiian-roll-commission.

Karp, Hannah. 2010. "Living in Old Hawaii: Henry Rice's 10,000-Acre Ranch Dates Back to the Monarchy." *Wall Street Journal*, January 22. http://www.wsj.com/articles/SB10001424052748704320104575015431045157378.

Kauai, Willy Daniel Kaipo. 2014. "The Color of Nationality: Continuities and Discontinuities of Citizenship in Hawai'i." PhD. diss., University of Hawai'i at Mānoa.

Kauanui, J. Kēhaulani. 2002. "The Politics of Blood and Sovereignty in Rice v. Cayetano." *Political and Legal Anthropology Review* 25, no. 1: 100–128.

Kauanui, J. Kēhaulani. 2003. "Why Here? Scholarly Locations for American Indian Studies." *American Quarterly* 55, no. 4 (December): 689–696.

Kauanui, J. Kēhaulani. 2005a. "Asian American Studies and the 'Pacific Question.'" In *Asian American Studies after Critical Mass*, ed. Kent Ono, 123–143. Malden, MA: Blackwell.

Kauanui, J. Kēhaulani. 2005b. "The Multiplicity of Hawaiian Sovereignty Claims and the Struggle for Meaningful Autonomy." *Comparative American Studies* 3, no. 3: 283–299.

Kauanui, J. Kēhaulani. 2005c. "Precarious Positions: Native Hawaiians and Federal Recognition." *Contemporary Pacific* 17, no. 1: 1–27.

Kauanui, J. Kēhaulani. 2007. Indigenous Peoples and International Law Podcast 19. Podcast audio. Indigenous Politics: From Native New England and Beyond. MP3, 55:07, October 30. http://www.indigenouspolitics.org/audiofiles/2007/10-30%20International%20Law.mp3.

Kauanui, J. Kēhaulani. 2008a. "Colonialism in Equality: Hawaiian Sovereignty and the Question of US Civil Rights." *South Atlantic Quarterly* 107, no. 4 (October): 635–650.

Kauanui, J. Kēhaulani. 2008b. *Hawaiian Blood: Colonialism and the Politics of Sovereignty and Indigeneity*. Durham, NC: Duke University Press.

Kauanui, J. Kēhaulani. 2009a. The International Indian Treaty Council Implementing the UN Declaration Podcast 46. Podcast audio. Indigenous Politics: From Native New England and Beyond. MP3, 53:19, January 13. http://www.indigenouspolitics.org/audiofiles/2009/1-13%20International%20Indian%20Treaty.mp3.

Kauanui, J. Kēhaulani. 2009b. "J. Kehaulani Kauanui 1." *YouTube* video, 9:24, posted by Imipono Projects, December 31. https://www.youtube.com/watch?v=SPAP8Gr0-os.

Kauanui, J. Kēhaulani. 2009c. "J. Kehaulani Kauanui 2." *YouTube* video, 9:26, posted by Imipono Projects, December 31. https://www.youtube.com/watch?v=U2WUJrZcrHw.

Kauanui, J. Kēhaulani. 2009d. "J. Kehaulani Kauanui 3." *YouTube* video, 8:37, posted by Imipono Projects, December 31. https://www.youtube.com/watch?v=5kmmjHABfh4.

Kauanui, J. Kēhaulani. 2010. "Understanding Both Versions of the Akaka Bill." *Indian Country Today*, January 15. http://indiancountrytodaymedianetwork.com/2010/01/15/kauanui-understanding-both-versions-akaka-bill-81799.

Kauanui, J. Kēhaulani. 2011. "Hawaiian Nationhood, Self-Determination, and International Law." In *Transforming the Tools of the Colonizer: Collaboration, Knowledge, and Language in Native Narratives*, ed. Florencia E. Mallon, 27–53. Durham, NC: Duke University Press.

Kauanui, J. Kēhaulani. 2013."Precarious Positions: Native Hawaiians and US Federal Recognition." In *Recognition, Sovereignty Struggles and Indigenous Rights in the United States: A Sourcebook*, ed. Amy Den Ouden and Jean M. O'Brien, 311–336. Chapel Hill: University of North Carolina Press.

Kauanui, J. Kēhaulani. 2014. "Resisting the Akaka Bill." In *A Nation Rising: Hawaiian Movements for Life, Land and Sovereignty*, ed. Noelani Goodyear-Ka'opua, Ikaika Hussey, and Erin Kahunawaika'ala Wright, 312–353. Durham, NC: Duke University Press.

Kauanui, J. Kēhaulani. 2016. "'A Structure, Not an Event': Settler Colonialism and Enduring Indigeneity." *Lateral* (Forum: Emergent Critical Analytics for Alternative Humanities) 5, no. 1 (Spring). http://csalateral.org/wp/issue/5-1/forum-alt-humanities-settler-colonialism-enduring-indigeneity-kauanui/#fnref-351-4.

Kauanui, J. Kēhaulani. 2017. "Indigenous Hawaiian Sexuality and the Politics of Nationalist Decolonization." In *Critically Sovereign: Indigenous Gender, Sexuality, and Feminist Studies*, ed. Joanne Barker, 45–68. Durham, NC: Duke University Press.

Kauikeaouli. 1829. "No Ka Moe Kolohe" (law enacted Oahu: September 21). Hawai'i State Archives, Honolulu, Hawai'i.

"Keanu Sai 1." 2009a. *YouTube* video, 8:19, posted by Imipono Projects, December 31. https://www.youtube.com/watch?v=voasu1wfUrY.

"Keanu Sai 2." 2009b. *YouTube* video, 9:19, posted by Imipono Projects, December 31. https://www.youtube.com/watch?v=XuhGUQcNsjo.

"Keanu Sai 3." 2009c. *YouTube* video, 5:55, posted by Imipono Projects, December 31. https://www.youtube.com/watch?v=68An_CM26VQ.

Keany, Michael. 2009. "Contenders to the Throne." *Honolulu Magazine*, November 2. http://www.honolulumagazine.com/Honolulu-Magazine/November-2009/Contenders-to-the-Throne/index.php?cparticle=4.

Kerr, Keoki. 2013. "Lanai Is Booming under Ellison; May Double in Population." *Hawaii News Now*, February 11. http://www.hawaiinewsnow.com/story/21129801/lanai-is-booming-under-ellison-may-double-in-population.

Kimport, Katrina. 2004. *Queering Marriage: Challenging Family Formation in the United States*. New Brunswick: Rutgers University Press.

Kinzer, Stephan. 2006. *Overthrow: America's Century of Regime Change from Hawaii to Iraq*. New York: Times Books, Henry Holt, 2006.

Knapman, Claudia. 1992. Review of *Paths of Duty: American Missionary Wives in Nineteenth Century Hawaii*, by Patricia Grimshaw. *Pacific Studies* 15, no. 3 (September): 135–169.

"KU'E 11–24–08 #8 Andre Perez.m4v: A Rally Demanding That Governor Lingle RESPECT NATIVE HAWAIIAN RIGHTS and WITHDRAW the Unnecessary Appeal of the Ceded Lands Case to the U.S. Supreme Court." 2008. *YouTube* video, 6:04, posted by Pono Kealoha, November 25. https://www.youtube.com/watch?v=tan5UPP_W4c.

"Kuhina Nui Exhibit." 2006. Hawaii State Archives. http://ags.hawaii.gov/archives/centennial-exhibit/.
Kuper, Adam. 2003. "The Return of the Native." *Current Anthropology* 44, no. 3 (June): 389–402.
Kuwada, Brian. 2009. "How Blue *Is* His Beard? An Examination of the 1862 Hawaiian-Language Translation of 'Bluebeard.'" *Marvels and Tales: Journal of Fairy-Tale Studies* 23, no. 1: 17–39.
Kuykendall, Ralph Simpson. 1938. *The Hawaiian Kingdom*. Vol. 1. Honolulu: University of Hawai'i Press.
Lâm, Maivân Clech. 1989. "The Kuleana Act Revisited: The Survival of Traditional Hawaiian Commoner Rights in Land." *Washington Law Review* 64 (April): 233–287.
Lâm, Maivân Clech. 1992. "Making Room for Peoples at the United Nations: Thoughts Provoked by Indigenous Claims to Self-Determination." *Cornell International Law Journal* 25, no. 3: 603–622.
Lâm, Maivân Clech. 2000. *At the Edge of the State: Indigenous Peoples and Self-Determination*. Ardsley, NY: Transnational.
Lāna'i Culture & Heritage Center. 2017. "A Timeline of Key Events in Lāna'i's History" and "Historic Summary." https://www.lanaichc.org/historic-summary.html.
"Lawyer Promoted the Rights of Native Hawaiians." 2014. *Honolulu Star Advertiser*, April 25, A22.
Lebra, Joyce Chapman. 1991. *Women's Voices in Hawaii*. Niwot: University Press of Colorado.
"Letter from Mr. Andrews, at Lahainaluna, December 2, 1836." 1836. *Missionary Herald, Containing the Proceedings of the American Board of Commissioners for Foreign Missions* 32 (October): 10.
The Levi Chamberlain Journal. 1822–1849. November 11, 1822–January 1, 1849. September 16, 1833—August 22, 1834. Vol. 18. Digitized collection of original documents housed at the Hawaiian Mission Children's Society Library, Honolulu.
Levine, Philippa. 2004. *Gender and Empire*. Oxford: Oxford University Press.
Liliuokalani, Queen of Hawaii. 1964. *Hawaii's Story by Hawaii's Queen*. Rutland, VT: Charles E. Tuttle.
Linnekin, Jocelyn. 1990. *Sacred Queens and Women of Consequence: Rank, Gender, and Colonialism in the Hawaiian Islands*. Ann Arbor: University of Michigan Press.
Lobel, Jules. 1988. *A Less Than Perfect Union: Alternative Perspectives on the U.S. Constitution*. New York: New York University Press.
Loomis, Elisha. 1937. "Hawaiian Mission Houses & Archives Digital Collection." Copy of the Journal of E. Loomis, May 17, 1824–January 27, 1825. Compiled by Dr. Wm. D. Westervelt assisted by Emil A. Berndt and Lili P. Berndy. Hawaiian Mission Children's Society Library, Honolulu.
Lowe, Lisa. 1996. *Immigrant Acts: On Asian American Cultural Politics*. Durham, NC: Duke University Press.

Lowe, Lisa. 2006. "The Intimacies of Four Continents." In *Haunted by Empire: Geographies of Intimacy in North American History*, ed. Ann Laura Stoler, 191–212. Durham, NC: Duke University Press.
Lowe, Lisa. 2015. *Intimacies of Four Continents*. Durham, NC: Duke University Press.
Lydecker, Robert C. 1918. *Roster Legislatures of Hawaii, 1841–1918: Constitutions of Monarchy and Republic Speeches of Sovereigns and President*. Honolulu: Hawaiian Gazette.
Lyons, Jeffrey K. 2004. "Memoirs of Henry Obookiah: A Rhetorical History." *Hawaiian Journal of History* 38: 35–57.
Lyons, Laura E. 2013."Island of Debts: Lānaʻi and the New Feudalism." Paper presented at the annual meeting of the American Studies Association, November 21–24.
Maile, David Uahikeaikaleiʻohu. 2016. "Notices of Settlement: US Federal Recognition and Kanaka Maoli Politics of ʻAʻole." Paper presentation at the annual meeting of the American Studies Association, November 17–20, Denver, Colorado.
"Maivan Clech Lam 1." 2009a. *YouTube* video, 9:50, posted by Imipono Projects, December 31. https://www.youtube.com/watch?v=-H5P9IVQ22g.
"Maivan Clech Lam 2." 2009b. *YouTube* video, 8:08, posted by Imipono Projects, December 31. https://www.youtube.com/watch?v=rSR2Eso5lxQ.
"Maivan Clech Lam 3." 2009c. *YouTube* video, 10:18, posted by Imipono Projects, December 31. https://www.youtube.com/watch?v=muNXwORYd70.
Malo, David. [1898] 1951. *Hawaiian Antiquities (Moolelo Hawaii)*. 2nd ed. Honolulu: Bishop Museum.
Malo, David. 1997. *Ka Moʻolelo Hawaiʻi (Hawaiian Traditions)*. Translated by Malcolm Naea Chun. Honolulu: First People's Productions.
Maly, Kepā, and Onaona Maly. 2009. "A History of Royal Patent Land Grants on the Island of Lānaʻi." Lānaʻi Culture & Heritage Center. https://nebula.wsimg.com/c5b199e5239bec568c4e317d2669e30f?AccessKeyId=28B6B9B521ECBFB5989C&disposition=0&alloworigin=1.
Maly, Kepā, and Onaona Maly. 2017. "Lānaʻi Conveyances: Records of Land Title and Genealogical Descent: (1860–1961)." https://www.lanaichc.org/land-title.html.
Manderson, Lenore, and Margaret Jolly. 1997. *Sites of Desire, Economies of Pleasure: Sexualities in Asia and the Pacific*. Chicago: University of Chicago Press.
Masci, David. 2013. "States That Allow Same-Sex Marriage Also Provide Protections for Religious Groups and Clergy Who Oppose It." Pew Research Center, November 20. http://www.pewresearch.org/fact-tank/2013/11/20/states-that-allow-same-sex-marriage-also-provide-protections-for-religious-groups-and-clergy-who-oppose-it/.
Matsuda, Mari J. 1988a. "Law and Culture in the District Court of Honolulu 1844–1845: A Case Study of the Rise of Legal Consciousness." *American Journal of Legal History* 32: 16–41.
Matsuda, Mari J. 1988b. "Native Custom and Official Law in Hawaii." *Law and Anthropology: Internationales Jahrbuch für Rechtsanthropologie* 3: 135–147.

Matzner, Andrew, ed. 2001. *'O Au No Keia: Voices from Hawai'i's Mahu and Transgendered Communities*. Bloomington, IN: Xlibris Self-Publishing and Print on Demand.

McClintock, Anne. 1995. *Imperial Leather: Race, Gender, and Sexuality in the Colonial Contest*. New York: Routledge.

Merry, Sally Engle. 2000. *Colonizing Hawai'i: The Cultural Power of Law*. Princeton: Princeton University Press.

Mignolo, Walter D. 2011. *The Darker Side of Western Modernity: Global Futures, Decolonial Options*. Durham, NC: Duke University Press.

Miller, Charles William. 2006. "The Voyage of the Parthian: Life and Religion Aboard a 19th-Century Ship Bound for Hawai'i." *Hawaiian Journal of History* 40: 27–46.

Miller, Susan. 1994a. "Between Nations." *Island Lifestyle* (January): 22–28.

Miller, Susan. 1994b. "Native Gays Help Leaders Redefine Hawaiian Nation." *Island Lifestyle* (February): 6–10.

Mills, Charles W. 1997. *The Racial Contract*. Ithaca, NY: Cornell University Press.

Mohanty, Chandra Talpade, Ann Russo, and Lourdes Torres, eds. 1991. *Third World Women and the Politics of Feminism*. Bloomington: Indiana University Press.

Mooallem, Jon. 2014. "Larry Ellison Bought an Island in Hawaii. Now What?" *New York Times*. September 23. https://www.nytimes.com/2014/09/28/magazine/larry-ellison-island-hawaii.html?_r=0.

Moon, C. J., for the Court. 2008. "Appeal from the First Notice regarding Reopening of Appeal No. 25570 and Order to Transmit Trail Records to the Hawaii Supreme Court." Appeal from the First Circuit Court (Civ. No. 94-4207), January 31. http://oaoa.hawaii.gov/jud/opinions/sct/2009/25570ord.htm.

Moore, Wanda. 2012. "Public Land Development Corporation Sparks Outrage on Maui." Accessed September 1, 2012 (no longer available). http://news.akakutv.org/video/public-land-development-corporation-sparks-outrage-on-maui.

Morales, Laurel. 2015. "Same-Sex Marriage Isn't Law of the Land from Sea to Shining Sea." National Public Radio, August 5, 2015, radio broadcast, 3:54. http://www.npr.org/2015/08/05/429597127/same-sex-marriage-isnt-law-of-the-land-from-sea-to-shining-seap.

Moreton-Robinson, Aileen, ed. 2008. *Sovereign Subjects: Indigenous Sovereignty Matters*. Australia: Allen and Unwin.

Morgan, Jennifer. 2004. *Laboring Women: Reproduction and Gender in New World Slavery*. Philadelphia: University of Pennsylvania Press.

Morgan, Lewis H. [1877] 1998. *Ancient Society: Researches in the Lines of Human Progress from Savagery through Barbarism to Civilization*. Vol. 3. London: Routledge/Thoemmes.

Morgensen, Scott Lauria. 2011a. "The Biopolitics of Settler Colonialism, Right Here, Right Now." *Settler Colonial Studies* 1, no. 1: 52–76.

Morgensen, Scott Lauria. 2011b. *Spaces between Us: Queer Settler Colonialism and Indigenous Decolonization*. Minneapolis: University of Minnesota Press.

Morris, Robert J. 1990. "Aikāne: Accounts of Hawaiian Same-sex Relationships in the

Journals of Captain Cook's Third Voyage (1776–80)." *Journal of Homosexuality* 19, no. 4: 21–54.
Morris, Robert J. 1996. "Configuring the Bo(u)nds of Marriage: The Implications of Hawaiian Culture & Values for the Debate about Homogamy." *Yale Journal of Law & the Humanities* 8: 105–159.
Na'i Aupuni, 2015. "Na'i Aupuni Releases List of 152 Participants to February 'Aha.'" News Release, December 23. http://www.naiaupuni.org/docs/RevisedNewsRelease-NaiAupuniReleasesListOf152Participants-122315.pdf.
Na'i Aupuni, 2016a. "Na'i Aupuni Announces Participant Total for February 'Aha Is 154." News Release, January 6. http://www.naiaupuni.org/docs/NewsRelease-NaiAupuniAnnouncesParticipantTotalForAhaIs154-010616.pdf.
Na'i Aupuni, 2016b. "Na'i Aupuni Decides Not to Pursue Ratification Vote." News Release, March 16. http://www.naiaupuni.org/docs/NewsRelease-NaiAupuniDecidesNoRatificationVote-031616.pdf.
Na Leo O Hawaii Access Center. 2014. "Meetings on Native Hawaiian Recognition." 'Ōlelo Community Media (each numbered, with the number at the end of the URL varying accordingly [1, 2, etc.]). Accessed December 20, 2014. https://archive.org/details/DOI_Meetings_on_Native_Hawaiian_Recognition_1.
Nally, David. 2008. "That Coming Storm: The Irish Poor Law, Colonial Biopolitics, and the Great Famine." *Annals of the Association of American Geographers* 98, no. 3 (September): 714–741.
Neal, Andrew W. 2004. "Cutting Off the King's Head: Foucault's *Society Must Be Defended* and the Problem of Sovereignty." *Alternatives: Global, Local, Political* 29: 373–398.
Nellist, George F., ed. 1925. "Statewide County HI Archives Biographies: Rice, Harold Waterhouse, November 10, 1883." In *The Story of Hawaii and Its Builders*. Honolulu: Honolulu Star Bulletin, Territory of Hawaii. http://files.usgwarchives.net/hi/statewide/bios/rice495bs.txt.
Newcomb, Steven T. 2008. *Pagans in the Promised Land: Decoding the Doctrine of Christian Discovery*. Golden, CO: Fulcrum.
"New Hope Oahu Homepage." 2015. *New Hope O'ahu*: http://www.newhope.org/.
Nichols, Robert. 2014. "Contract and Usurpation: Enfranchisement and Racial Governance in Settler-Colonial Contexts." In *Theorizing Native Studies*, ed. Audra Simpson and Andrea Smith, 99–121. Durham, NC: University of Duke Press.
O'Brien, Jean M. 2010. *Firsting and Lasting: Writing Indians Out of Existence in New England*. Minneapolis: University of Minnesota Press.
Office of Hawaiian Affairs. 2009. "Akaka Bill & 'Native Sovereignty': What It Really Means to Hawaiians." Press release. Accessed March 14, 2015 (no longer available). http://www.oha.org/pdf/100114_AkakaTV_Release.pdf.
Office of Hawaiian Affairs. 2014. "Comments of the Office of Hawaiian Affairs in Support of Action to Reestablish a Government-to-Government Relationship with the Native Hawaiian Government." July 15. https://docgo.net/philosophy-of-money.html?utm_source=140715-oha-comments-doi-anprm-july-15-2014-final-1.

Office of Hawaiian Affairs. 2015. "Home Page." OHA. Accessed January 1, 2015. http://www.oha.org/.

Office of Hawaiian Affairs IV v. Housing and Community Development Corporation of Hawaii HCDCH. 2008. No. 25570. Decided January 31. http://caselaw.findlaw.com/hi-supreme-court/1329148.html.

Oliveira, Katrina-Ann R. Kapāʻanaokalāokeola Nākoa. 2014. *Ancestral Places: Understanding Kanaka Geographies*. Corvallis: Oregon State University Press.

Osorio, Jonathan Kay Kamakawiwoʻole. 2002. *Dismembering Lāhui: A History of the Hawaiian Nation to 1887*. Honolulu: University of Hawaiʻi Press.

Osorio, Jonathan Kay Kamakawiwoʻole. 2003. "Kūʻē and Kūokoʻa: History, Law, and Other Faiths." In *Law and Empire in the Pacific, Fiji and Hawaii*, ed. Sally Engle Merry and Donald Brennis, 213–238. Santa Fe: SAR.

Osorio, Jonathan Kay Kamakawiwoʻole, ed. 2014. *I Ulu I Ka ʻĀina: Land*. Honolulu: University of Hawaiʻi Press.

Oxford English Dictionary. 2011. 2nd ed. 20 vols. Oxford: Oxford University.

Pacific Worlds & Associates. 2015. "Legendary Setting." Nuʻuanu: Oʻahu Hawaiian Islands, Pacific Worlds. Accessed October 15, 2015. http://www.pacificworlds.com/nuuanu/arrival/setting.cfm.

Pahuja, Sundhya. 2011. *Decolonising International Law: Development, Economic Growth and the Politics of Universality*. Cambridge: Cambridge University Press.

Pateman, Carole, and Charles Mills. 2007. *Contract and Domination*. Cambridge: Polity.

Peralto, Noʻeau. 2018. "Mālama ʻĀina Koholālele: Recalling the Roots of Our Resurgence." In *Everyday Acts of Resurgence: People, Places, Practices*, ed. Jeff Corntassel, Taiaiake Alfred, Noelani Goodyear-Kaʻōpua, Noenoe K. Silva, and Hokulani Aikau, 63–66. Olympia: Intercontinental Cry.

Perkins, Mark ʻUmi. 2013. "Kuleana: A Genealogy of Native Tenant Rights." PhD diss. in political science, University of Hawaiʻi at Mānoa, May. https://search.proquest.com/docview/1430295574.

"Perpetuating Hawaiʻi's Covenant with God." 2013. *YouTube* video, 0:30, posted by KodomoNoTameNi, October 25. https://www.youtube.com/watch?v=3yqMNtCgxZw.

Pierce, Henry E. 1869. *In the Matter of the Legitimacy of Henry E. Pierce, a Native of the Hawaiian or Sandwich Islands (Testimony, Argument, and Text of Laws)*. Honolulu: n.p.

Pierson, Ruth Roach, Nupur Chaudhuri, and Beth McAuley, eds. 1998. *Nation, Empire, Colony: Historicizing Gender and Race*. Bloomington: Indiana University Press.

Plane, Ann Marie. 2000. *Colonial Intimacies: Indian Marriage in Early New England*. Ithaca, NY: Cornell University Press.

Poepoe, Joseph M. 1908. "Ka Moolelo Kaao o Hiiaka-i-ka-Poli-o-Pele." *Kuokoa Home Rula*, January 10. http://www2.hawaii.edu/~kroddy/moolelo/Hiiakaikapoliopele_poepoe/mokuna1.htm.

Preza, Donovan C. 2010. "The Empirical Writes Back: Re-Examining Hawaiian

Dispossession Resulting from the Mahele of 1848." MA thesis in geography, University of Hawai'i, May. http://library.wcc.hawaii.edu/ld.php?content_id=1244009.

Pukui, Mary Kawena, and Samuel H. Elbert, eds. 1986. *Hawaiian Dictionary*. Rev. ed. Honolulu: University of Hawai'i Press.

Pukui, Mary Kawena, E. W. Haertig, and Catherine Lee. 1972. *Nana I Ke Kumu*. Vol. 2. Honolulu: Hui Hanai, an Auxiliary of the Queen Liliuokalani Children's Center.

Ragaza, Angelo. 1996. "Sovereignty and Sexuality in Hawaii: Aikane Nation." *Village Voice*, July 2, 12–13.

Rajagopal, Balakrishnan. 2003. *International Law from Below: Development, Social Movements and Third World Resistance*. Cambridge: Cambridge University Press.

Ralston, Caroline. 1984. "Hawaii 1778–1855: Some Aspects of Maka'ainana Response to Rapid Cultural Change." *Journal of Pacific History* 19, no. 1: 21–40.

Ralston, Caroline. 1988. "'Polyandry,' 'Pollution,' 'Prostitution': The Problems of Eurocentrism and Androcentrism in Polynesian Studies." In *Crossing Boundaries: Feminists and the Critique of Knowledges*, ed. Barbara Caine, Elizabeth Grosz, and Marie de Lepervanche, 71–81. Sydney, Australia: Allen and Unwin.

Ralston, Caroline. 1989a. "Changes in the Lives of Ordinary Women in Early Post-Contact Hawaii." In *Family and Gender in the Pacific: Domestic Contradictions and the Colonial Impact*, ed. Margaret Jolly and Martha Macintyre, 45–65. Cambridge: Cambridge University Press.

Ralston, Caroline. 1989b. "The Mahu of Hawai'i." *Feminist Studies* 15, no. 2: 312–326.

Reeves-Ellington, Kathryn Kish Sklar, and Connie A Shemo, eds. 2010. *Competing Kingdoms: Women, Mission, Nation and the American Protestant Empire, 1812–1960*. Durham, NC: Duke University Press.

Richards, Rev. William. 1823–1872. "Lahaina, Maui, Church Records, 1823–1872" (scanned copy). Box 16, Church Records 1823–1945. Hawaiian Evangelical Association Archive, Hawaiian Mission Children's Society Library, Honolulu.

Richardson, Valerie. 2010. "Obama Adopts U.N. Manifesto on Rights of Indigenous Peoples." *Washington Times*, December 16. http://www.washingtontimes.com/news/2010/dec/16/obama-adopts-un-manifesto-on-rights-of-indigenous-/?page=all.

Rifkin, Mark. 2008. "Debt and the Transnationalization of Hawaii." *American Quarterly* 60, no. 1 (March): 43–66.

Rifkin, Mark. 2011. *When Did Indians Become Straight? Kinship, the History of Sexuality, and Native Sovereignty*. Oxford: Oxford University Press.

Rivera Cusicanqui, Silvia. 2012. "*Ch'ixinakax utxiwa*: A Reflection on the Practices and Discourses of Decolonization." *South Atlantic Quarterly* 111, no. 1: 95–109.

Robcis, Camille. 2013. *The Laws of Kinship: Anthropology, Psychoanalysis, and the Family in France*. Ithaca, NY: Cornell University Press.

Ronen, Yael. 2008. *Status of Settlers Implanted by Illegal Regimes under International Law*. Hebrew University International Law Research Paper No. 11-08. Jerusalem: Hebrew University.

Roth, Benita. 2003. *Separate Roads to Feminism: Black, Chicana, and White Feminist Movements in America's Second Wave.* Cambridge: Cambridge University Press.

Roy, Audrey Jane. 2001. "Sovereignty and Decolonization: Realizing Indigenous Self-Determination at the United Nations and in Canada." MA thesis, University of Victoria. http://citeseerx.ist.psu.edu/viewdoc/download?doi=10.1.1.473.1475&rep=rep1&type=pdf.

Runnette, Charles. 2016. "Larry Ellison's Private Eden Is Open for Business." *Bloomberg,* April 13. https://www.bloomberg.com/news/features/2016-04-13/four-seasons-manele-bay-lanai-hawaii.

Sahlins, Marshall. 1985. *Islands of History.* Chicago: University of Chicago Press.

Sai, David Keanu. 1998. "Memorandum to Subjects of the Kingdom, From: Office of the Regent, Re: Suffrage of Female Subjects." *Hawaiian Kingdom,* March 12. http://www.hawaiiankingdom.org/info-suffrage.shtml.

Sai, David Keanu, et al. 2013a. "Government Re-Established." *Hawaiian Kingdom,* August 21. http://www.hawaiiankingdom.org/govt-reestablished.shtml.

Sai, David Keanu, et al. 2013b. *Ua Mau Ke Ea Sovereignty Endures: An Overview of the Political and Legal History of the Hawaiian Islands.* 2nd ed. Honolulu: Pū'ā Foundation.

Sai, David Keanu, et al. 2014a. "The Hawaiian Kingdom Government." *Hawaiian Kingdom.* http://www.hawaiiankingdom.org.

Sai, David Keanu, et al. 2014b. "Why the Hawaiian Kingdom, as an Independent State, Continues to Exist." Hawaiian Kingdom blog, March 1. http://hawaiiankingdom.org/blog/why-the-hawaiian-kingdom-as-an-independent-state-continues-to-exist/.

Sanborn, Curt. 1993. "Homosexuality in Hawai'i of Old." *Honolulu Weekly,* May 12.

Sankaran, Krishna. 2009. *Globalization and Postcolonialism: Hegemony and Resistance in the Twenty-First Century.* Lanham, MD: Rowman and Littlefield.

Schilling, Vincent, "Now There`s 573! 6 VA Tribes Get Federal Recognition as President Signs Bill," *Indian Country Today,* January 30, 2018, https://newsmaven.io/indiancountrytoday/news/now-there-s-573-6-va-tribes-get-federal-recognition-as-president-signs-bill-Hw-X2bNHo02AyivBTsXg3w/.

Schmitt, Robert C., and Rose C. Strombel. 1966. "Marriage and Divorce in Hawaii before 1870." *Hawaii Historical Review* 2 (January): 267–271.

Scott, David. 2004. *Conscripts of Modernity: The Tragedy of Colonial Enlightenment.* Durham, NC: Duke University Press.

Scott, James C. 1998. *Seeing Like a State: How Certain Schemes to Improve the Human Condition Have Failed.* New Haven: Yale University Press.

Scott, James C., John Tehranian, and Jeremy Mathias. 2002. "The Production of Legal Identities Proper to States: The Case of the Permanent Family Surname." *Comparative Studies in Society and History* 44, no. 1 (January): 4–44.

Shah, Nayan. 1998. "Sexuality, Identity, and the Uses of History." In *Q & A: Queer in Asia America,* ed. David Eng and Alice Horn, 141–156. Philadelphia: Temple University Press.

Shimogawa, Duane. 2013. "Larry Ellison Plans to Build Huge Tennis Academy on Lanai." *Pacific Business News*, June 21. http://www.bizjournals.com/pacific/news/2013/06/21/larry-ellison-plans-to-build-tennis.html.

Shimogawa, Duane. 2016. "PBN Confirms Amount Billionaire Larry Ellison Paid for Hawaiian Island of Lanai." *Pacific Business News*, January 7. https://www.bizjournals.com/pacific/blog/2016/01/pbn-confirms-amount-billionaire-larry-ellison-paid.html.

Shohat, Ella. 2000. "Notes on the 'Post-Colonial.'" In *The Pre-Occupation of Post-Colonial Studies*, ed. Fawzia Afzal-Khan and Kalpana Rahita Seshadr, 126–139. Durham, NC: Duke University Press.

Siddall, John William, ed. 1917. *Men of Hawaii; A Biographical Reference Library, Complete and Authentic, of the Men of Note and Substantial Achievement in the Hawaiian Islands*. Vol. 1. Honolulu: Honolulu Star Bulletin, Territory of Hawaii.

Silva, Noenoe K. 1997. "Kūʻē! Hawaiian Women's Resistance to the Annexation." *Social Process in Hawaii* 38: 2–15.

Silva, Noenoe K. 2003. "Talking Back to Law and Empire: Hula in Hawaiian-Language Literature in 1861." In *Law and Empire in the Pacific: Fiji and Hawaiʻi*, ed. Sally Engle Merry and Donald Brenneis, 101–122. Santa Fe: SAR Press.

Silva, Noenoe K. 2004. *Aloha Betrayed: Native Hawaiian Resistance to American Colonialism*. Durham, NC: Duke University Press.

Silva, Noenoe K. 2007. "Pele, Hiʻiaka, and Haumea: Women and Power in Two Hawaiian Moʻolelo." In "Women Writing Oceania," ed. Caroline Sinavaiana and J. Kēhaulani Kauanui. Special issue of *Pacific Studies* 30, nos. 1/2 (March/June): 159–181.

Silva, Noenoe K. 2008. "Kupuʻāina Coalition: A Rally Demanding That Governor Lingle RESPECT NATIVE HAWAIIAN RIGHTS and WITHDRAW the Unnecessary Appeal of the Ceded Lands Case to the U.S. Supreme Court." *YouTube* video, 7:44, posted by Pono Kealoha, November 25. https://www.youtube.com/watch?v=eYoolVxUYjM.

Silva, Noenoe K. 2017. *The Power of the Steel-tipped Pen: Reconstructing Native Hawaiian Intellectual History*. Durham, NC: Duke University Press.

Silverman, Jane L. 1982. "Imposition of a Western Judicial System in the Hawaiian Monarchy." *Hawaiian Journal of History* 16: 48–64.

Silverman, Jane L. 1987. *Kaahumanu: Molder of Change*. Honolulu: Friends of the Judiciary Center of Hawaii.

Sinclair, Marjorie. 1969. "Princess Nahienaena." *Hawaiian Journal of History* 3: 3–30.

Sinclair, Marjorie. 1995. *Nāhiʻenaʻena: A Life Ensnared*. Honolulu: Mutual.

Siu, Leon. 2008. "10th Anniversary of Hawaii's Traditional Marriage Vote." *Christian Voice Hawaii* (blog), December 12. http://cvhawaii.org/Christian_Voice/Christian_Voice_Hawaii/Entries/2008/12/12_10th_Anniversary_of_Hawaiis_Traditional_Marriage_Vote.html.

Siu, Leon. 2009. "Rally Planned to Protest Proposed Hawaii Civil Union Bill." *Hawaii Reporter*, February 22. http://www.hawaiireporter.com/story.aspx?5d68a571–63ba-4d94–8419—13c95b6a71a5.

Siu, Leon. 2015. "A Biblical View of Hawaiian Sovereignty: A Challenge to Christians in Hawaii." *What Really Happened.* Accessed July 10, 2015. http://whatreally happened.com/WRHARTICLES/HAWAII/leonsiu/Biblical%20View%20Text .htm.

Skwiot, Christine. 2011. "Migration and the Politics of Sovereignty, Settlement, and Belonging in Hawaii." In *Connecting Seas and Connected Ocean Rims: Indian, Atlantic, and Pacific Oceans from the 1830s to the 1930s,* ed. Donna R. Gabaccia and Dirk Hoerder, 440–464. Leiden: Brill.

"Small Businesses May Be Affected by New PLDC Rules." 2012. *Maui Now,* August 21. http://mauinow.com/2012/08/21/small-businesses-may-be-affected-by-new-pdlc-rules/.

Smith, Linda Tuhiwai. 2012. *Decolonizing Methodologies: Research and Indigenous Peoples.* 2nd ed. London: Zed.

Smith-Rosenberg, Carroll. 1975. "The Female World of Love and Ritual: Relations between Women in Nineteenth-Century America." *Signs* 1, no. 1 (Fall): 1–29.

Snow, Jade. 2014. "Beyond the Binary: Portraits of Gender and Sexual Identities in the Hawaiian Community." *Mana: A Journal of Hawai'i* (March): 22–29.

Spade, Dean, and Craig Willse. 2013. "Marriage Will Never Set Us Free." *Organizing Upgrade,* September 6. http://www.organizingupgrade.com/index.php/modules-menu/beyond-capitalism/item/1002-marriage-will-never-set-us-free.

Spaulding, Thomas Marshall. 1923. *The Crown Lands of Hawaii.* Honolulu: University of Hawai'i.

Stannard, David. 1989. *Before the Horror: The Population of Hawaii on the Eve of Western Contact.* Honolulu: University of Hawai'i Press.

State of Hawaii. 2011. S.B. 1520. "A Bill for an Act." Act 195. "First Nation Government Bill." July 7, 2011. https://legiscan.com/HI/text/SB1520/id/180990/Hawaii-2011-SB1520-Amended.html.

Stauffer, Robert H. 2004. *Kahana: How the Land Was Lost.* Honolulu: University of Hawai'i Press.

Stewart, Charles Samuel. 1839. *A Residence in the Sandwich Islands.* 5th ed. Edited by William Ellis. Boston: Weeks, Jordan.

Stoler, Ann Laura. 1995. *Race and the Education of Desire: Foucault's History of Sexuality and the Colonial Order of Things.* Durham, NC: Duke University Press.

Stoler, Ann Laura. 2006. *Haunted by Empire: Geographies of Intimacy in North American History.* Durham, NC: Duke University Press.

"Stop Selling Ceded Lands." 2015. Accessed July 1, 2015 (no longer available). http://stopsellingcededlands.com/.

Supreme Court of Hawaii. *Baehr v. Lewin.* 852 P.2d 44, Haw (1993).

Tengan, Ty P. Kāwika. 2008. *Native Men Remade: Gender and Nation in Contemporary Hawai'i.* Durham, NC: Duke University Press.

Thigpen, Jennifer. 2014. *Island Queens and Mission Wives: How Gender and Empire Remade Hawai'i's Pacific World.* Chapel Hill: University of North Carolina Press.

Thomas, Nicholas. 2010. *Islanders: The Pacific in the Age of Empire.* New Haven: Yale University Press.

Thurston, Lorrin A., ed. 1904. *The Fundamental Law of Hawaii*. Honolulu: Hawaiian Gazette.

Tracy, Joseph. 1842. *History of the American Board of Commissioners for Foreign Missions: Compiled Chiefly from the Published and Unpublished Documents of the Board*. 2nd ed. New York: M. W. Dodd.

Trask, Haunani-Kay. 1993a. *From a Native Daughter: Colonialism and Sovereignty in Hawai'i*. Honolulu: University of Hawai'i Press.

Trask, Haunani-Kay. 1993b. "Women's *Mana* and Hawaiian Sovereignty." In *From a Native Daughter: Colonialism and Sovereignty in Hawai'i*, 111–129. Monroe, ME: Common Courage.

Trask, Mililani. 1994. "The Politics of Oppression." In *Hawai'i Return to Nationhood, IWGIA—Document 75*, ed. Ulla Hasager and Jonathan Friedman, 68–87. Copenhagen: IWGIA.

True Aloha. 2015. Facebook page: "About True Aloha." Accessed January 30, 2015. https://www.facebook.com/truealoha/info?tab=page_info.

Trudy, Jacobsen, Charles Sampford, and Ramesh Thankur, eds. 2008. *Re-Envisioning Sovereignty: The End of Westphalia?* Farnham, UK: Ashgate.

United Nations. 2016. "The United Nations and Decolonization." Accessed June 1, 2016. http://www.un.org/en/decolonization/specialcommittee.shtml.

United Nations Department of Economic and Social Affairs: Division for Social Policy and Development. 2004. "The Concept of Indigenous Peoples." Background paper prepared by the Secretariat of the Permanent Forum on Indigenous Issues for Workshop on Data Collection and Disaggregation for Indigenous Peoples. PFII/2004/WS.1/3, New York, January 19–21.

United Nations Department of Economic and Social Affairs: Division for Social Policy and Development. 2009. *State of the World's Indigenous Peoples*. Secretariat of the Permanent Forum on Indigenous Issues. New York: United Nations.

United Nations Department of Public Information. 2005. "Indigenous Peoples, Indigenous Voices: Fact Sheet." Secretariat of the Permanent Forum on Indigenous Issues: http://www.un.org/esa/socdev/unpfii/documents/5session_fact sheet1.pdf.

United Nations General Assembly. 1960a. Resolution 1514. "Declaration on the Granting of Independence to Colonial Countries." December 14. http://www.un.org/en/decolonization/declaration.shtml.

United Nations General Assembly. 1960b. "The United Nations and Decolonization." http://www.un.org/en/decolonization/index.shtml.

United Nations General Assembly. 2007. Resolution 61/295. "United Nations Declaration on the Rights of Indigenous Peoples." September. http://www.un.org/esa/socdev/unpfii/documents/DRIPS_en.pdf.

United Nations: Office of the High Commissioner of Human Rights. 2001. "Indigenous Peoples: The Question of Definition." September 13. http://www.un.org/esa/socdev/unpfii/documents/DRIPS_en.pdf.

United Nations Permanent Forum on Indigenous Issues. 2005. "Who Are Indigenous

Peoples? Factsheet." http://www.un.org/esa/socdev/unpfii/documents/5session_factsheet1.pdf.
United Nations Permanent Forum on Indigenous Issues. 2013. "Homepage: Indigenous Peoples." Accessed July 12, 2013. https://www.un.org/development/desa/indigenouspeoples/unpfii-sessions-2.html.
U.S. Congress. 1871. "The Indian Appropriation Act of March 3, 1871." 25 U.S.C. § 71 (2009). Accessed June 15, 2016 (no longer available). http://www.gpo.gov/fdsys/pkg/USCODE-2009-title25/html/USCODE-2009-title25-chap3-subchapI sec71.html.
U.S. Congress. 1898a. "Joint Resolution to Provide for Annexing the Hawaiian Islands to the United States." H.R. No. 259, 55th Cong., 2nd sess., July 7. http://www.ourdocuments.gov/doc.php?flash=true&doc=54.
U.S. Congress. 1898b."Newlands Resolution to Provide for Annexing the Hawaiian Islands to the United States," Resolution No. 55, 2nd Session, 55th Congress, July 7; 30 Sta. at L. 750; 2 Supp. R. S. 895. https://www.ourdocuments.gov/doc.php?flash=false&doc=54.
U.S. Congress. 1900. "The Act of Congress Organizing Hawaii into a Territory: An Act to Provide a Government for the Territory of Hawaii," also known as the "Organic Act." Pub. L. No. 56–331. 31 Stat. 141. April 30. http://moses.law.umn.edu/darrow/documents/Organic_Act.pdf.
U.S. Congress. 1993. S.J. Resolution 19. "Public Law 103–150," known as the "Apology Resolution." Nov. 23. http://www.gpo.gov/fdsys/pkg/STATUTE-107/pdf/STATUTE-107-Pg1510.pdf.
U.S. Congress. 1996. The Defense of Marriage Act (DOMA) Pub.L. 104–199, 110 Stat. 2419.
U.S. Congress. 2009. Sen. Daniel K. Akaka, Chairman, Select Committee on Indian Affairs. "Native Hawaiian Government Reorganization Act of 2009." S. Doc. No. 112–162. May 7. https://www.govtrack.us/congress/bills/111/s1011/text.
U.S. Congress. 2009–2010. H.R.2314 . "Native Hawaiian Government Reorganization Act of 2010." https://www.congress.gov/bill/111th-congress/house-bill/2314/text.
U.S. Congress. 2010. Sen. Byron Dorgan, Chairman, Select Committee on Indian Affairs. "To Express the Policy of the United States Regarding the United States Relationship with Native Hawaiians and to Provide a Process for the Recognition by the United States of the Native Hawaiian Governing Entity." S. Doc. No. 111–162. March 11. https://www.congress.gov/congressional-report/111th-congress/senate-report/162/1.
U.S. Congress. 2011a."A Bill for an Act Relating to Government." S.B. 1520, S.D. 2., H.D. 3, C.D. 1. http://www.capitol.hawaii.gov/session2011/bills/SB1520_CD1_.pdf.
U.S. Congress. 2011b. Rep. Mazie K. Hirono. "Native Hawaiian Government Reorganization Act of 2011." S. 675, H.R. No. 1250. March 30. https://www.congress.gov/bill/112th-congress/house-bill/1250/text.
U.S. Congress 2011c. S. 675, "The Native Hawaiian Government Reorganization Act

of 2011," placed on Senate Legislative Calendar on February 12, 2012, under General Orders, Calendar No. 568. https://www.congress.gov/bill/112th-congress/senate-bill/675.
U.S. Congress. 2012. Sen. Daniel K. Akaka, Chairman, Select Committee on Indian Affairs. "Native Hawaiian Government Reorganization Act of 2011." S. Doc. No. 112–251. 112th Congress (2011–2012), December 17. https://www.congress.gov/112/crpt/srpt251/CRPT-112srpt251.pdf.
U.S. Congress. 2015. Rep. Adam Smith. "Accountability in Immigration Detention Act of 2015." H.R. 2314. May 13. https://www.congress.gov/bill/114th-congress/house-bill/2314/text.
U.S. Department of Hawaiian Homelands. 1921. "Hawaiian Homes Commission Act." July 9. https://dhhl.hawaii.gov/wp-content/uploads/2011/06/HHCA_1921.pdf.
U.S. Department of the Interior. 2014. "Public Meeting regarding whether the Federal Government Should Reestablish a Government-to-Government Relationship with the Native Hawaiian Community," Public Meeting: Keaukaha Elementary School, 240 Desha Avenue, Keaukaha, Hawai'i 96720, July 2, 2014, 6:00 p.m., Moderator: Dawn Ching. Recorded and Transcribed by Elsie Terada, RPR, CSR 437, Ralph Rosenberg Court Reporters, 25–28. https://www.doi.gov/hawaiian/reorg.
U.S. Department of the Interior. 2015a. "Advance Notice of Proposed Rulemaking." Office of Native Hawaiian Relations. https://www.doi.gov/hawaiian/reorg.
U.S. Department of the Interior. 2016a. "Interior Department Finalizes Pathway to Reestablish a Formal Government-to-Government Relationship with the Native Hawaiian Community." Press release, September 23. https://www.doi.gov/pressreleases/interior-department-finalizes-pathway-reestablish-formal-government-government.
U.S. Department of the Interior. 2016b. "Procedures for Reestablishing a Formal Government-to-Government Relationship with the Native Hawaiian Community: Final Rule." https://www.doi.gov/hawaiian/procedures-reestablishing-formal-government-government-relationship-native-hawaiian.
U.S. Department of the Interior: Indian Affairs. 2013. "Frequently Asked Questions." The United States Bureau of Indian Affairs. Accessed December 20, 2015. http://www.bia.gov/FAQs/.
U.S. Department of the Interior: Indian Affairs. 2015a. "Revisions to Regulations on Federal Acknowledgement of Indian Tribes (25 CFR 83 or "Part 83")." United States Bureau of Indian Affairs, June 29. https://www.bia.gov/WhoWeAre/AS-IA/ORM/83revise/index.htm.
U.S. Department of the Interior: Indian Affairs. 2015b. "Who We Are." The United States Bureau of Indian Affairs. Accessed July 8, 2015 (no longer available). https://www.bia.gov/WhoWeAre/.
U.S. Department of the Interior: Office of Native Hawaiian Relations. 2014a. "Interior Considers Procedures for Reestablishing a Formal Government-to-Government Relationship with the Native Hawaiian Community." Press release,

Washington, DC, June 18. https://www.doi.gov/hawaiian/procedures-reestablishing-formal-government-government-relationship-native-hawaiian.
U.S. Department of the Interior: Office of Native Hawaiian Relations. 2014b. "Public Meeting regarding Whether the Federal Government Should Establish a Government-to-Government Relationship with the Native Hawaiian Community." Public meeting, Keaukaha, Hawai'i, July 2.
U.S. Department of the Interior: Office of the Secretary. 2014. 43 CFR Part 50, [145D0102DM DS61400000 DLSN00000.000000 DX.61401] RIN 1090–AB05, "Procedures for Reestablishing a Government-to-Government Relationship with the Native Hawaiian Community." *Federal Register* 79, no. 119, Friday, June 20, 2014, 35297. https://www.gpo.gov/fdsys/pkg/FR-2014-06-20/pdf/2014-14430.pdf.
U.S. Pacific Command (USPACOM). 2011. "Headquarters, United States Pacific Command." USPACOM. Accessed January 4, 2011. http://www.pacom.mil/About-USPACOM.aspx.
U.S. Pacific Command (USPACOM). 2017. "Area of Responsibility." Accessed July 29, 2017. http://www.pacom.mil/AboutUSPACOM/USPACOMAreaofResponsibility.aspx.
U.S. Senate. Committee on Indian Affairs. 2009. "Hearing on Native Hawaiian Reorganization Act." S. Hrg. 111–283. Washington, D.C., August 9. https://www.gpo.gov/fdsys/pkg/CHRG-111shrg54811/pdf/CHRG-111shrg54811.pdf.
U.S. Supreme Court. 1886. *United States v. Kagama*. 118 U.S. 375 (1886). https://supreme.justia.com/cases/federal/us/118/375/.
U.S. Supreme Court. 1974. *Oneida Indian Nation of New York v. County of Oneida*. 414 U.S. 661 (1974). https://supreme.justia.com/cases/federal/us/414/661/case.html.
U.S. Supreme Court. 1985. *County of Oneida v. Oneida Indian Nation of New York State*. 470 U.S. 226 (1985). http://www.ncai.org/attachments/LegalBriefing_gEwBoR-WkSnevhLYlzKuUEDwLuiaCJqJUGaaYrpWmeHDjUYrfKRY_Oneida.pdf.
U.S. Supreme Court. 2000. *Rice v. Cayetano*. 528 U.S. 495 (2000). https://supreme.justia.com/cases/federal/us/528/495/.
U.S. Supreme Court. 2005. *City of Sherrill v. Oneida Indian Nation of N.Y.* 544 U.S. 197 (2005). http://www.law.cornell.edu/supct/html/03–855.ZS.html.
U.S. Supreme Court. 2008. Syllabus: *Hawaii et al. vs. Office of Hawaiian Affairs et al.* http://www.supremecourt.gov/opinions/08pdf/07-1372.pdf.
U.S. Supreme Court. 2009. *Hawaii et al. v. Office of Hawaiian Affairs et al.* 556 U.S. (2009). http://www.supremecourt.gov/opinions/08pdf/07-1372.pdf.
Valeri, Valerio. 1985. *Kingship and Sacrifice*. Chicago: University of Chicago Press.
Vancouver, George. 1801. *A Voyage of Discovery to the North Pacific Ocean and Round the World*. Vol. 3. London: J. Stockdale.
Van Dyke, Jon M. 2008. *Who Owns the Crown Lands of Hawai'i?* Honolulu: University of Hawai'i.
Van Voorhis, Vanessa. 2011. "Seeds 101: Syngenta Hawai'i LLC." *Garden Island*,

March 19. http:///www.thegardenisland.com/2011/03/19/business/seeds-101-syngenta-hawaii-llc.
Vergès, Françoise. 1999. *Monsters and Revolutionaries: Colonial Family Romance and Métissage*. Durham, NC: Duke University Press.
Vincent, Roger. 2012. "Oracle Founder Larry Ellison Buying Hawaiian Island of Lanai." *Los Angeles Times*, June 22. http://articles.latimes.com/2012/jun/22/business/la-fi-ellison-buying-lanai-20120622.
Wagner, Sandra E. 1985. "Mission and Motivation: The Theology of Early American Mission in Hawaii." *Hawaiian Journal of History* 19: 62–70.
Wagner-Wright, Sandra. 1990. *The Structure of the Missionary Call to the Sandwich Islands, 1790–1830: Sojourners among Strangers*. San Francisco: Mellen Research University Press.
Wallace, Lee. 2003. *Sexual Encounters: Pacific Texts, Modern Sexualities*. Ithaca, NY: Cornell University Press.
Warrior, Robert Allen. 2003. "A Room of One's Own at the ASA: An Indigenous Provocation." *American Quarterly* 55, no. 4 (December): 681–687.
Warrior, Robert Allen. 2008. "Organizing Native American and Indigenous Studies." *PMLA* 123, no. 5 (October): 1683–1691.
Weems, Mickey. 2011. "Aikāne." *Qualia Folk . . . Dedicated to LGBT Scholarship* (December 8). Accessed September 13, 2015 (no longer available). http://www.qualiafolk.com/2011/12/08/aikane/.
Wilkes, Charles. 1845. *Narrative of the United States Exploring Expedition, during the Years 1838, 1839, 1840, 1841, 1842*. Philadelphia: Lea and Blanchard.
Wilkins, David E. 2002. *American Indian Politics and the American Political System*. Lanham, MD: Rowman and Littlefield.
Wilkins, David E., and Heidi Kiiwetinepinesiik Stark. 2011. *American Indian Politics and the American Political System*. 3rd ed. Lanham, MD: Rowman and Littlefield.
Williams, Robert A., Jr. 2005. *Like a Loaded Weapon: The Rehnquist Court, Indian Rights, and the Legal History of Racism in America*. Minneapolis: University of Minnesota.
Williams, Robert A., Jr. 2012. *Savage Anxieties: The Invention of Western Civilization*. New York: Palgrave Macmillan.
Wolfe, Patrick. 1998. *Settler Colonialism and the Transformation of Anthropology: The Politics and Poetics of an Ethnographic Event*. London: Continuum International.
Wolfe, Patrick. 2006. "Settler Colonialism and the Elimination of the Native." *Journal of Genocide Research* 8, no. 4 (December): 387–409.
Wolfe, Patrick. 2008. "Structure and Event: Settler Colonialism and the Question of Genocide." In *Empire, Colony, Genocide: Conquest, Occupation, and Subaltern Resistance in World History*, ed. A. Dirk Moses, 102–132. Oxford: Berghahn.
Wynter, Sylvia. 2003. "Unsettling the Coloniality of Being/Power/Truth/Freedom: Towards the Human, after Man, Its Overrepresentation—An Argument." *CR: The New Centennial Review* 3, no. 3 (Fall): 257–337.
Yamamura, Douglas Shigeharu. 1949. "A Study of Some of the Factors Contributing to the Status of Contemporary Hawaiians." PhD diss., University of Washington.

Yamashiro, Aiko, and Noelani Goodyear-Ka'ōpua, eds. 2014. *The Value of Hawai'i 2, Ancestral Roots, Oceanic Visions*. Honolulu: University of Hawai'i.
Yaukey, John. 2010. "Clock Ticking on Akaka Bill." *Honolulu Advertiser*, January 19. http://www.angelfire.com/big09a/AkakaHist11Jan2010.html.
Xian, Kathy, and Brent Anbe. 2001. *Ke Kulana He Māhū: Remembering a Sense of Place*. Documentary film.
Zoellick, Sarah. 2012. "Angry Crowd Opposes Public Land Agency." *Star Advertiser*, August 30. https://www.highbeam.com/doc/1P3-2748746811.html.

INDEX

NOTE: Page numbers followed by *f* indicate a figure.